THE FUTURE OF
STATE-OWNED
FINANCIAL INSTITUTIONS

THE WORLD BANK GROUP

THE INTERNATIONAL MONETARY FUND

THE BROOKINGS INSTITUTION

This book is based on the sixth annual financial markets and development conference held April 26–27, 2004, in Washington, D.C. The conference was jointly sponsored by the World Bank Group, the International Monetary Fund, and the Brookings Institution.

The previous volumes in this series are available from the Brookings Institution Press:

Financial Markets and Development: The Crisis in Emerging Markets (1999)

Managing Financial and Corporate Distress: Lessons from Asia (2000)

*Open Doors: Foreign Participation in Financial Systems
  in Developing Countries* (2001)

*Financial Sector Governance: The Roles of the Public
  and Private Sectors* (2002)

The Future of Domestic Capital Markets in Development Countries (2003)

GERARD CAPRIO
JONATHAN L. FIECHTER
ROBERT E. LITAN
MICHAEL POMERLEANO
Editors

THE FUTURE OF STATE-OWNED FINANCIAL INSTITUTIONS

BROOKINGS INSTITUTION PRESS
Washington, D.C.

Copyright © 2004
THE BROOKINGS INSTITUTION
1775 Massachusetts Avenue, N.W., Washington, D.C. 20036
www.brookings.edu

Library of Congress Cataloging-in-Publication data
The future of state-owned financial institutions / Gerard Caprio . . . [et al.], editors.
    p.   cm.
Conference proceedings.
Summary: "Focuses on the rationale and performance of state-owned financial institutions in emerging markets, as well as on possible government policies for either privatizing or managing them"—Provided by publisher.
Includes bibliographical references and index.
ISBN 0-8157-1335-5 (pbk. : alk. paper)
    1. Banks and banking—Government ownership.   2. Financial institutions—Government ownership.
    3. Privatization.   I. Caprio, Gerard.   II. Title.
HG1725.F88 2005
332.1—dc22   2004027181

9 8 7 6 5 4 3 2 1

The paper used in this publication meets minimum requirements of the American National Standard for Information Sciences—Permanence of Paper for Printed Library Materials: ANSI Z39.48-1992.

Typeset in Adobe Garamond

Composition by Lynn Rivenbark
Macon, Georgia

Printed by Victor Graphics
Baltimore, Maryland

Contents

Preface

M ARKET CAPITALISM MAY be spreading around the globe, but there remain pockets of heavy state involvement—and state ownership of enterprises in particular—throughout the world. This volume focuses on state ownership of financial institutions, especially banks, and examines a series of issues:

—How extensive is such state ownership, and what are the recent trends in this regard?

—What have been the announced (and implicit) objectives of state ownership of financial institutions?

—How have these institutions performed relative to those objectives? Has the performance varied by country?

Most of the authors who address these issues, in one fashion or another, conclude that the optimal course is to privatize most, if not all, state-owned financial institutions. On the whole, their records do not justify the subsidies that governments necessarily have had to provide them, or the distortions in the capital markets that their presence creates.

Several of the authors recognize, however, that governments may face political constraints that prevent privatization. Accordingly, certain authors address "second-best" options, including tighter supervision and limits on their activities.

This book is the sixth in a series of volumes on finance in emerging markets that have grown out of conferences sponsored by the World Bank, the International Monetary Fund (in some years), and the Brookings Institution. Many individuals contributed to the success of the conference and to the production of this volume, and we thank them for their diligence and hard work. Colleen Mascenik at the World Bank was the conference organizer. Shannon Leahy at Brookings provided additional organizational assistance. Diane Hammond and Elizabeth Forsyth edited the manuscript.

Funds for the conference and proceedings volume were generously supplied by the World Bank, the International Monetary Fund, and the Brookings Institution.

GERARD CAPRIO
World Bank

JONATHAN L. FIECHTER
International Monetary Fund

ROBERT E. LITAN
Brookings Institution

MICHAEL POMERLEANO
World Bank

THE FUTURE OF STATE-OWNED FINANCIAL INSTITUTIONS

GERARD CAPRIO
JONATHAN L. FIECHTER
ROBERT E. LITAN
MICHAEL POMERLEANO

1

Introduction

IT WAS ONLY a short time ago that it was fashionable for some to speak of "the end of history"—or the conversion of most of the world's economies to various forms of democratic capitalism. The tragic events of September 11, 2001, and the terrorism leading up to and following the Iraq war clearly demonstrate that democracy has not yet taken root in much of the world. Meanwhile, on the economic front—even outside former planned economies (such as China)—neither has capitalism completed its triumph. The state, it turns out, still is alive and well in owning a key sector—finance—in the economies of many countries.

This volume focuses on the rationale and performance of these state-owned financial institutions as well as on policies that governments may wish to take to privatize them (the ideal outcome, for reasons developed in the chapters that follow) or to manage them (the more likely outcome in most countries). The issue is important in light of growing evidence from the official development institutions and private economists around the world documenting the linkage between more rapid (and stable) economic growth, on the one hand, and sound financial systems, on the other.

The chapters in this book stem from papers presented and discussed at the Sixth Annual Conference on Finance in Emerging Markets held at the World Bank in late April 2004 and cosponsored by the World Bank, the International Monetary Fund, and the Brookings Institution. The opinions expressed in the chapters in this volume are those of the chapters' authors. In this introduction, we highlight the key themes of those chapters.

How Much State Ownership, and Why?

Despite numerous privatizations over the past decade, publicly owned banks and other state-owned financial institutions still serve the majority of individuals in developing countries (see the chapters by James Hanson and by George Clarke, Robert Cull, and Mary Shirley). State-owned financial enterprises are less prevalent in developed economies, with very few exceptions, such as Germany and, to a lesser extent, the United States, with its large government-sponsored entities supporting residential home ownership that have what is perceived to be implicit government backing (see the chapter by David Marston and Aditya Narain). Public ownership of these financial institutions (and others) has been rationalized on several grounds:

—To counter the power of strong private sector banks or to promote the development of home-grown banks in the early stages of an economy's history, the so-called infant industry rationale. Both arguments helped justify the formation of the First and Second National Banks of the United States in the early 1800s, for example.

—To ensure that economic growth is consistent with national objectives. This is a clear rationale for socialist economies, but even in private economies there is a view that governments have better knowledge of socially beneficial investment opportunities than private banks.

—To ensure that underserved groups or sectors, such as agriculture and small businesses, receive credit.

—To respond to financial crises, which have hit developed and developing countries alike. In some of these cases, government ownership is temporary, but in some cases it lasts for significant periods.

Among government officials around the world there is support for some government ownership of financial institutions based on one or more of these rationales. Economists generally, however, are skeptical of these rationales, except for the last.

Performance of State-Owned Banks

With rare exceptions, public sector banks have performed poorly by conventional financial measures, such as returns on equity or assets, the extent of nonperforming loans, and expense levels (see the chapter by Hanson). In principle, these banks may fare better when account is taken of their broader social missions (for example, to finance roads, sewers, and the like), wherein the benefits to the entire economy may exceed those to the specific borrower. But in practice these banks tend to extend much if not most of their credit to large borrowers, in which case one would not think that social returns would be larger than private gains.

Public sector banks often provide subsidized lending and directed credit to special industries or enterprises identified by the government. They also can burden their governments with large contingent liabilities arising from explicit guarantees or the implicit assumption that some of these banks are "too big to fail." In China, for example, nonperforming loans of major financial institutions at year-end 2003 stood at RMB 2,440 billion, equivalent to about 18 percent of the loans of these institutions and 21 percent of gross domestic product (see the chapter by Nicholas Lardy). Furthermore, as much as 90 percent of these loans might be regarded as a government contingent liability. Public sector banks have also demonstrated a poor collection record with their borrowers, especially in bad economic times, and thus tend simply to roll over their loans.

These patterns help account for the negative relationship between economic growth and state ownership of banks found by various researchers (see the chapter by Hanson). They also help explain why independent rating agencies such as Moody's find that, relative to their private counterparts, state-owned banks tend to be less well capitalized, to be less profitable, and to have thinner core earnings—and thus typically to have explicit or implicit guarantees to depositors regarding the safety of their funds. For all these reasons, a number of authors urge governments that own financial institutions to be more transparent in their financial results, in the amounts of explicit (and implicit) subsidies that governments extend to them, and in the government's contingent liabilities to them (see the chapters by Hanson, by Marston and Narain, and by Manal Fouad and colleagues).

Several types of costs arise from public sector banks, including directed lending, subsidies, and fiscal (macroeconomic) costs. For example, the two main public sector banks in Uruguay—Banco de la Republica Oriental del Uruguay (BROU), the former central bank, and Banco Hipotecario del Uruguay (BHU)—lend at subsidized rates and therefore cater mainly to poor credit risks in the agriculture sector and (to a lesser extent) in other sectors in crisis. The cost of BROU's and BHU's interest rate policy can be measured in the lower profitability of these banks compared to their private sector competitors: Although the after-tax return on equity for private banks averaged 12 percent in 1995–2000, it averaged only 5 percent for BROU and –1 percent for BHU. At the macroeconomic level, the quasi-fiscal activities in Uruguay may have cost between 0.8 and 1.2 percent of gross domestic product on average in the period 1996–2002 (see the chapter by Fouad and others).

A fiscal analysis of this type also should take into account the tendency of governments to overtax through provisioning rules that understate the true extent of loan losses and that lead to erosion in real bank capital. As a result, the fiscal burden imposed by state-owned financial institutions may be much higher than some of the contributors to this volume calculate.

Country Experiences with State-Owned Financial Institutions

China is perhaps the best-known example of a country with dominant public sector banking. Most of its banks are owned by the central, provincial, or local governments, and nonperforming loans to other state-owned enterprises loom large in its economy. The outlook for the Chinese banking sector is mixed (see the chapter by Lardy). On the one hand, the official returns on assets of China's state banks dropped precipitously during the 1980s and 1990s, while nonperforming loans grew rapidly during the mid-1990s, reaching 25 percent of total bank loans by 1997. On the other hand, Chinese officials in recent years have recognized the importance of dealing with the banks' problems. They therefore have reduced the government's involvement in the banks' allocation of credit and have created four asset management companies to deal with the nonperforming loans. The results so far are impressive: Nonperforming loans have declined significantly (largely because many were transferred to the asset management companies), while the banks appear to be more efficient. Yet the outlook remains guarded: Lending by Chinese state-owned banks soared in 2003 and early 2004 and was initially resistant to attempts to check the expansion, which raises the risks of higher nonperforming loans in the future.

The experiences of state-owned banks in other countries are also mixed. A relatively positive picture emerges from the portrait of the largest such institution in South Africa (see the chapter by Lewis Musasike and colleagues). Indonesia had well-known problems with its state-owned banks and connected lending among its private banks before the Asian financial crisis of 1997–98. Since then, the state-owned banks have been recapitalized by the government (their bad debts taken over by a separate agency), and prospects for them may now be somewhat brighter (see the chapter by Pak Rudjito and Hendrawan Tranggana). Two economists from the World Bank, however, paint a somewhat darker view; although recorded profitability may have improved, large uncertainties remain about the magnitude and ultimate cost of the banks' nonperforming loans (see the chapter by P. S. Srinivas and Djauhari Sitorus). Pakistan's government-owned banks (especially its agricultural development bank), meanwhile, have had the more common experience with such institutions: high nonperforming loans, overstaffing and other inefficiencies, and poor customer service (see the chapter by Ishrat Husain). Through much of the 1990s, however, Pakistan has been privatizing its banks while beefing up the prudential regulation of privately owned banks—so far, with good results.

Outside of China, government ownership of banks is highest in India (accounting for about 75 percent of all banking assets). India has used state ownership to allocate resources to both the public and private sectors and to help provide credit to the mass of low-income individuals and businesses not served by privately owned institutions (see the chapter by Urjit Patel). There is now clear evidence that government ownership and involvement in the banking sector has become excessive, not only costing taxpayers money (through bailouts) but also increasingly giving preference to government securities instead of to loans to their intended borrowers. As long as this situation continues, India's economic growth rate—which has surged in recent years with the opening up of the economy to foreign investment and the growth of a vibrant information technology sector—will remain lower than it could be with more private sector allocation of credit.

Privatization: The Ideal Course

From strictly an economic point of view, the optimal policy for governments that own financial institutions—given the poor performance record of these institutions throughout the world—is to privatize them. This course not only can save governments money (by eliminating subsidies) but also can improve the performance of their economies (by ensuring that credit is channeled through the market rather than through government officials). The banks themselves are also likely to be more efficiently run.

There are various routes to privatization, however, each with advantages and risks. A privatized bank appears to do best when sold to a single strategic investor, but this course carries with it obvious political risks—the impression that the government has "sold out," especially when the buyer is foreign. Excluding foreigners can prove costly, however. In Mexico's first round of bank privatizations in the early 1990s, for example, the banks subsequently expanded too rapidly (behind the wall of protection from foreign competition) and later had to be renationalized. Other countries (notably in Eastern Europe) have had similar problems, underscoring the importance of a sound regulatory framework for privately owned banks. Furthermore, when foreigners are not allowed to bid, governments are likely to reap less revenue when they do privatize and to lose the advantage of the banking skills that foreign institutions can bring to economies whose financial sectors lack them (see the chapter by Clarke, Cull, and Shirley).

In whatever way that privatization is accomplished, it should not be done partially. If the government still holds a portion of the stock, especially if it holds a majority of the stock, the bank still tends to perform poorly by conventional financial measures (see Clarke, Cull, and Shirley).

Another way to privatize banks is to sell them, in part or in whole, to employees through stock ownership plans. So far, twenty countries have used this technique, though the tendency is for these plans to own only a minority interest and for other private investors to own the rest; or, in some cases, the state might even retain some ownership (see the chapter by David Binns and Ronald Gilbert). Stock ownership plans predictably tend to be most successful when subsequent control is vested in a single strategic investor, which provides capital and expertise. Some experts believe that the plans should complement a strategic privatization scheme and not be considered in isolation. Many feel that foreign strategic investment provides the surest method of privatization, by offering independence from vested interests and an infusion of outside expertise.

Yet another route to privatization is by offering shares to the public through an initial public offering. Not surprisingly, developed economies that sold off their state-owned financial enterprises first used this technique; it has been used since the early 1990s by a number of developing countries. So far, thirty-three of the eighty countries outside the Organization for Economic Cooperation and Development (OECD) have privatized 156 state-owned banks. Initial public offerings account for 44 percent of all emerging country bank privatizations (see the chapter by Fred Huibers).

There are side advantages to privatizing through initial public offerings. For one thing, these offerings can help develop local stock markets (since the privatized institutions become some of the largest enterprises on these exchanges). This effect is not automatic, however, and the cornering of the market in privatization vouchers marks some of these efforts. More developed stock exchanges, in turn, facilitate access to capital by other types of domestic enterprise and thereby can improve overall economic growth. Although in principle governments may also realize more revenue by selling shares to many investors than to a single strategic investor—especially if the initial public offerings are carried out when market valuations are high—empirical studies find that governments tend to underprice their share offerings in order to entice citizens to participate in shareholding. But even this outcome has a potentially significant benefit: By stimulating wider ownership of the privatized enterprises among many investors, initial public offerings effectively inhibit the ability of governments to later renationalize the enterprises.

Governments are likely to damage confidence in privatizations led by initial public offerings, however, if they retain an ownership interest in the "privatized" institutions and continue to direct their lending toward favored borrowers. Such behavior not only perpetuates practices antithetical to general economic growth but also, by damaging the earnings prospects of the institutions, clearly can harm the investors who have purchased their shares. Also, if the public offerings can be (and have been) carried out in a way that limits information available to investors, then investors are likely to overpay when they do buy shares. Shareholders face even greater problems when the institutions whose shares they purchase subsequently are not effectively supervised (a subject discussed next), as happened in the first bank privatization in Mexico (see the chapter by Huibers).

Experiences in Pakistan and Uganda

Ishrat Husain and Louis Kasekende (in their chapters on Pakistan and Uganda, respectively) share perspectives on the comprehensive privatization programs and the strategic vision of policymakers in these countries. Hussain suggests that Pakistan's experience demonstrates the benefits of privatization for both the banking sector and the economy, but he warns that privatization must be handled carefully and that the legal framework is critical to success. The central bank and the state-owned banks must be independent, the assets of state-owned banks must be easily disposed of, and fit and proper criteria for privatization must be strictly applied. Both experts note that tough measures must be taken before attempted privatization (such as cutting down on excess staff and overbranching), which arouse countervailing political pressure. At the same time, Kasekende warns that preprivatization "beautification" should not be overdone, as it may be unduly costly and bring little long-term benefit.

Both of these experts also agree that selecting the right buyer was a critical decision in their countries. Kasekende emphasizes the importance of conducting a comprehensive market survey of viable sale options, of a thorough investigation of the investor's market reputation and not just capital strength, and also of understanding the investor's future intentions to strengthen capital and management of a bank. Husain highlights the valuable role of international bank managers and professional specialists and recommends that governments actively seek their involvement during privatization. Both suggest that governments need to deal swiftly and decisively with nonperforming loans and to reverse the weak repayment ethic among borrowers from state banks. This works best when fitted into a broader privatization program for state-owned enterprises and when efforts are made to deepen capital markets as alternative sources of financing for large enterprises. With a strong and stable financial system as the objective, both authors agree, revenue considerations should be secondary in planning the privatization.

Managing State-Owned Financial Institutions

Where they exist, state-owned banks still have powerful constituencies: their borrowers, their managers, and of course, many officials in government who still see the institutions as an "off-the-books" way to allocate capital toward uses believed to enhance economic growth (despite overwhelming evidence to the contrary presented here and elsewhere in the literature). For this reason, as a practical political matter, various authors in this volume—even those skeptical of state ownership—believe that many if not most state-owned banks will continue to exist.

Under these circumstances, are there "second-best" options that governments can pursue either to minimize losses associated with state ownership or, in the best of worlds, to achieve some positive results? Unfortunately, the record so far has not been encouraging; by and large, efforts to replace poor managers, write off bad loans and replace them with supposedly safer government debt, reduce staff and expenses, merge troubled institutions, and improve information technology have not been successful (see Hanson's chapter). This does not mean that these steps should not be tried when divestiture is not possible, but the rare instances of success must be acknowledged.

At the very least, the institutions can and should be effectively supervised, just as if they were privately owned. This, unfortunately, is not currently the case in most parts of the world, and it must change. State-owned financial institutions not only pose systemic risks to their economies but also threaten governments with potentially significant liabilities and thus the need for a rise in taxes or a reduction in other government spending—or both—to make up for such financial shortfalls (see the chapter by Jonathan Fiechter and Paul Kupiec). Unfortunately, the inherent conflict of interest in both owning and supervising banks is difficult to resolve.

Oversight is not likely to be effective, however, unless the overseers are independent and their missions well defined. Other codes of conduct are also relevant, including: careful limits on the activities of (and thus the risks posed by) the institutions; rules governing minimum capital (and adherence to those rules); supervision of the institutions' internal controls and other means for limiting risks and expenses; and annual, honest reports by the supervisors of what they have found. The World Bank and the International Monetary Fund can help countries implement these basic steps, perhaps beginning by organizing regular meetings of supervisors of state-owned financial institutions to exchange views and best practices (see the chapter by Fiechter and Kupiec).

Other Alternatives

When a state-owned financial institution cannot be either sold or successfully reformed, there are still three other options: The institution can be closed, it can be converted into a government agency, or it can be converted into a "narrow" bank (a depository holding only government securities as assets). A few governments, mostly in Eastern Europe, have closed banks, and the banking systems in these countries survive and even prosper without the troubled banks. Conversion into a government agency makes the bank an official arm of the government and therefore makes its activities more transparent, though this conversion may complicate efforts to collect loans (as in China). Narrow banks have been supported by a number of economists in other contexts (including by one of the authors of this introduction) but are not well suited for entire banking systems, especially in developing countries, where there are few if any alternative providers of credit.

Conclusion

State-owned financial institutions are likely here to stay in many countries, for political rather than economic reasons. (Interestingly, as this is being written, Egyptian authorities are showing signs of moving to reduce the roughly 65 percent state ownership in their banking system by allowing at least one of the three large state banks to be sold.) Nonetheless, even when politically motivated, governments that own financial institutions would serve their citizens better if they made the financial commitments to those institutions more transparent, managed them more soundly, and restricted their activities to a few sectors in which the social returns from extending credit are likely to exceed the private returns.

PART I

Overview of State Ownership in the Financial Sector

JAMES A. HANSON

2

The Transformation of State-Owned Banks

STATE-OWNED BANKS often have high nonperforming assets and high costs and make only a limited contribution to development. Improving their performance is important because they still dominate banking for the majority of people in developing countries, despite the rash of bank privatizations in the 1990s. In 2002 these banks held 60 percent or more of bank assets in Algeria, Bangladesh, China, Egypt, Ethiopia, India, Indonesia, Iran, and Vietnam (table 2-1).[1] In Latin America, privatizations have reduced the role of state-owned banks, but they remain important in Argentina, Brazil, Ecuador, and Uruguay. In the transition countries, the role of state-owned banks also has declined since 1992 because of the entry of private banks and the privatization or closure of

The author is grateful to Jerry Caprio, Michael Fuchs, Ruth Neyens, Michael Pomerleano, Elisabeth Sherwood, and Ahmet Soylemezoglu for comments.

1. Two databases exist on public sector banks around the world. Barth, Caprio, and Levine (2001a, 2001b, updated in 2004) refer to the share of government ownership in all commercial banks in 150 countries, as reported by the country's central bank. La Porta, López-de-Silanes, and Shleifer (2000, 2002) study the share of government ownership (direct and indirect) in the ten largest commercial and development banks in ninety-two countries in 1970, 1985, and 1995. The data of La Porta, López-de-Silanes, and Shleifer tend to show a higher percentage of public sector ownership, as might be expected. In addition to these two sources, Sherif, Borish, and Gross (2003) report data in transition countries. Since 2002, major privatizations include the remaining renationalized banks in Mexico, most of the banks taken over after the crisis in Indonesia, and two of the three state-owned banks that remained in Pakistan.

Table 2-1. *State Ownership of Banks, Selected Developing Countries, 2000–02*
Percent of bank assets

Less than 10 percent			
Armenia	Estonia	Kyrgyz Republic	Paraguay
Aruba	Gambia, The	Latvia	Peru
Bolivia	Georgia	Lebanon	Samoa
Botswana	Guatemala	Liechtenstein	Seychelles
Cayman Islands	Honduras	Macedonia	South Africa
Croatia	Hungary	Malaysia	Tajikistan
Cyprus	Jordan	Mauritius	Tonga
El Salvador	Kazakhstan	Moldova	Venezuela
10 to 24 percent			
Bulgaria	Czech Republic	Nigeria	St. Kitts and Nevis
Cambodia	Guyana	Panama	Trinidad and Tobago
Chile	Jamaica	Philippines	Ukraine
Colombia	Kenya	Poland	Vanuatu
Côte d'Ivoire	Nepal	Solomon Islands	Zambia
25 to 59 percent			
Argentina	Indonesia	Morocco	Sri Lanka
Bosnia and Herzegovina	Korea, Republic of	Romania	Tanzania
Brazil	Lesotho	Russian Federation	Thailand
Costa Rica	Lithuania	Rwanda	Tunisia
Ecuador	Malawi	Slovak Republic	Turkey
Ghana	Mexico	Slovenia	
60 to 100 percent			
Afghanistan	Belarus	India	Turkmenistan
Albania	Bhutan	Indonesia	Uruguay
Algeria	China	Iran	Uzbekistan
Azerbaijan	Egypt	Maldives	Vietnam
Bangladesh	Ethiopia		

Source: Barth, Caprio, and Levine (2001b); Sherif, Borish, and Gross (2003); and World Bank estimates.

state-owned banks. Nonetheless, state-owned banks remain important in Russia and some other transition countries.[2] In Africa, the picture is also mixed.

Improving the performance of state-owned banks involves understanding the rationale for them and how the hopes for their performance compare with actual

2. Sherif, Borish, and Gross (2003).

outcomes. To improve performance also requires an analysis of the interactions between the owner (the government), the bankers, and the clients to see how these interactions can be improved. Numerous attempts have been made to improve these banks, without much success, but there are some lessons to be learned for improving their performance by making their incentives, managerial accountability, and governance more like those of private banks. Privatizing a state-owned bank is a major transformation, but many issues need attention if privatization is to succeed, particularly in unfavorable institutional environments. Some other options also exist for transforming these banks when neither reform nor privatization seems feasible; these include closing the bank or turning it into either an agency or a narrow bank.

Rationales for State-Owned Banks

Various overlapping political and economic rationales have been advanced for state-owned banks. One rationale is political: to counter the substantial economic and political power of large private banks. Although private banks are chartered and regulated by the government, officials may nonetheless consider them to be abusing their power. As U.S. President Andrew Jackson said in the speech accompanying his 1832 veto of the rechartering of the (private) Second Bank of the United States, "It is to be regretted that the rich and powerful too often bend the acts of government to their selfish purposes."[3] More recently, as part of decolonization newly independent African nations often nationalized banks based in the former colonial power. One of the many reasons for India's 1969 bank nationalization was to reduce the power of economic conglomerates and concentrated lending. In justifying Mexico's 1982 bank nationalization, President José López-Portillo blamed the banks (and the "dollar exporters") for the peso's devaluation. Thus to reduce the economic and political power of private banks, government often creates state banks or nationalizes private sector banks rather than attempt to create competition among private banks.

Second, the state-led approach to economic development that was prevalent for many years naturally involved government control of such important institutions as banks. Lenin, just before the October 17 revolution in Russia, said, "Without big banks, socialism would be impossible. The big banks are the 'state apparatus' which we need to bring about socialism and which we take ready-made

---

3. Remini (1967, p. 83). The Second Bank of the United States was a private sector bank that had a monopoly in carrying out government financial activities. Remini (1967) discusses the political issues.

from capitalism."[4] Communist regimes in China, Cuba, and Eastern Europe nationalized banks after World War II.[5]

A more moderate, post–World War II version of this rationale was that government ownership of firms in "strategic sectors" or "commanding heights" was critical to development and that these firms need assured, low-cost funding by government banks. Thus countries that adopted socialist or planned economic regimes nationalized private banks or set up state-owned banks.[6] For example, India's 1969 nationalization of fourteen major banks was legally justified by the "need to control the commanding heights of the economy and to meet progressively the needs of development of the economy in conformity with national policy objectives."[7] The continued large role of state-owned banks in many countries reflects the overhang of these models of development.[8]

A third, oft-cited, and related economic rationale for state-owned banks is the need to allocate credit to underserved groups, such as long-term industrial credit and loans for agriculture, small businesses, housing, and export finance. This rationale was not necessarily part of the state-directed approach to development but was a response to perceived failures in financial markets and demands from the public. The response involved both the redirection of nationalized banks and the creation of new state-owned banks. In many countries, state-owned development banks were set up to mediate between foreign lenders and users of long-term credit (often public sector enterprises) or small- and medium-size borrowers.[9] Housing banks often were also set up.

For example, in India another rationale for nationalization of commercial banks was the lack of credit for agriculture and the importance of rural moneylenders. In addition, agricultural credit was an important need signaled in India's Fourth Plan (1969), particularly with the newly begun green revolution increasing demand for credit to finance commercial inputs. Small firms were also considered neglected by

4. Quoted in La Porta, López-de-Silanes, and Shleifer (2002, p. 266).

5. La Porta, López-de-Silanes, and Shleifer (2002) find a statistical tendency for more public sector control of banking in communist and former communist countries.

6. Gerschenkron (1962) was among the first to provide academic support for the view that public sector banks were needed to provide funds for large-scale industrialization and long-term credit.

7. Preamble of the Banking Companies [Acquisition and Transfer of Undertakings] Act of 1969.

8. See Sherif, Borish, and Gross (2003), for a discussion of how the transition countries in Eastern Europe and the Commonwealth of Independent States dealt with banks after 1991.

9. The World Bank made over 350 loans to more than 140 development finance institutions from the 1950s to 1984. The development financial institutions intermediated these and other funds by acting as second-tier lenders through banks, as first-tier direct lenders, or as both (for example, Banco Nacional de Desenvolvimento Econômico e Social in Brazil). The World Bank's lending initially focused on private development financial institutions. Later, lending through public sector development financial institutions came to dominate the program.

India's formal credit system. Some thought that farmers and small-scale business-men would use the credit more productively than traditional borrowers. Finally, a major goal was to mobilize deposits in order to finance development, and public sector banks were urged to expand the number of their branches.[10] These issues became even more important in the 1971 Abolish Poverty campaign of Prime Minister Indira Gandhi.[11] In Africa, concerns about foreign banks that focused on traditional export lending and neglected new industries and nonexport agriculture were one of the rationales for bank nationalizations. In Latin America concerns about long-term and agricultural credits led to the setting up of development banks and agricultural banks. In the transition countries, after 1992 the mono-bank structure often devolved into sectoral banks.[12]

Thus the third rationale argues that state-owned banks were needed to correct perceived market failures, which would be remedied by public sector bank loans (rather than treasury grants). Public sector banks were a substitute for priority sec-tor lending by private banks or were intended to ensure the implementation of priority sector lending and the extension of branch networks. In other words, they were intended to change the allocation of credit within a market system. In addition, their funding benefited from the political and economic power of the state: They typically were able to raise money at lower rates than private banks because of the implicit state guarantee, and they often received low-cost, directed credit. Yet the lack of credit to underserved sectors that they were intended to

10. In India between 1969 and 1979, the number of public sector commercial bank offices nearly tripled, rising from about 7,200 to 22,400; in addition, regional rural banks were created in the 1970s, and they had 2,400 offices by the end of the decade. The growth of public sector bank offices continued in the 1980s, albeit more slowly. By 1992 there were about 44,000 commercial bank offices and 14,700 regional rural bank offices. Burgess and Pande (2004) find an association between the expansion of bank offices in the social banking era and the reduction of poverty and the expansion of nonagricultural output.

11. India had long had public sector development banks for long-term credits and had created other second-tier, public sector institutions to provide banks with credit for agriculture and small-scale industry, but in the late 1960s the approach was extended to the commercial banks directly. Social control of the pri-vate commercial banks was tried before nationalization through a National Credit Council modeled on France's Bank Nationalization Act of 1945. The Indian Council first met in 1968 and set credit targets for the banks. However, the targets represented only a modest reallocation of credit and the government was concerned about the banks' condition and the permanence of their former management (Sen and Vaidya 1997; Tandon 1989). In 1969 the fourteen largest private banks were nationalized; this, together with the existing public sector State Bank of India, raised the public sector banks' share of deposits to 86 percent. Although pressures continued to extend more credit to the underserved sectors, only in March 1979 were specific priority-sector requirements set (40 percent of loans, of which 18 percent was for agriculture and 10 percent was for the "weaker sectors"). In 1980 six more commercial banks were nationalized, and the public sector commercial banks' share of bank assets rose to 92 percent. In addition, India's public sector development banks were relatively large.

12. Sherif, Borish, and Gross (2003).

address was not simply a market failure. It also reflected the public sector's pre-emption of a growing fraction of bank credit as well as the difficulty of mobilizing deposits and allocating credit in an environment of repressed interest rates and uncertain legal, political, and economic conditions.[13]

Fourth, public sector control of banks often arises from government takeovers of weak banks in the aftermath of crises. For example, the nationalization of Indian banks in 1969 may also have reflected concerns regarding the frequent bankruptcies of the private banks. Numerous banks were taken over in the 1980s.[14] During the 1990s, crises and failed privatizations led to nationalizations or renationalizations, at least temporarily, of banks in countries as diverse as the Czech Republic, Hungary, Indonesia, Mexico, and Uganda.

The Performance of State-Owned Banks

In general state-owned banks have performed poorly in developing countries, although there are some exceptions. Among the exceptions are Singapore and Mauritius, where the State Bank of Mauritius is recognized as one of the best commercial banks in the country.[15] The approach of Bank Rakyat Indonesia (BRI) to small-scale credits is recognized as one of the best in the world.[16] More than 90 percent of BRI's small loans continued to perform during the Asian crisis, although BRI's corporate lending was always weak and suffered large defaults, similar to those of the other Indonesian state-owned banks.

13. La Porta, López-Silanes, and Schleifer (2002) find a correlation between public sector banks and countries that they characterize as having less investor protection, less developed financial markets, and more interventionist governments than common law countries. As is well known, high-inflation countries tend to have lower ratios of deposits to GDP, and high inflation makes long-term lending difficult.

14. Sheng (1996, pp. 21–23).

15. The State Bank of Mauritius is owned by a number of public sector entities, not the government directly.

16. See, for example, Yaron, Benjamin, and Piprek (1997); Robinson (2001, 2002). BRI currently has about 2.9 million small-scale loans that carry market-based interest rates covering the cost of funds and expenses. About 30 percent of its loans are under Rp 2 million (about $200). BRI has an enviable record of loan recovery on small credits that it maintained during the 1997–98 crisis. Its good record of recovery probably reflects its close supervision of loans and its incentives to staff and operational units for good loan performance, within the context of decentralized authority. BRI also has a good training program. It has some 27 million deposit accounts. However, BRI's performance on small scale-lending has not always been good. In the 1970s, under the BIMAS program, it provided subsidized credit to small borrowers, in this case to support the green revolution. As in India, this activity helped to spread the green revolution, but the credits often went to wealthier farmers, were often linked to packages of inputs that were not suited to the borrowers' needs, and often were not repaid. BRI's current success reflects its shift in 1984 to the approach described above, made possible by the general financial liberalization in 1983. See, for example, Cole and Slade (1996); Robinson (2002).

Unfortunately, the performance of most state-owned banks has been weak, particularly in the area of nonperforming loans.[17] For example, in China recent official estimates suggest nonperforming loans of more than 20 percent in the four state-owned commercial banks; estimates of private analysts are higher. In Brazil the estimated cost of recapitalizing the state (provincial) banks included some $20 billion for the Bank of the State of São Paulo (Banespa) before it was privatized in 2001. In addition, in 2002 the Brazilian finance ministry estimated that the recapitalization of the federal banks, when completed, might cost more than $50 billion, mostly to recapitalize the Federal Mortgage Bank (Caixa Economica Federal). In Africa and the transition countries, numerous costly restructurings of state-owned banks have occurred, often more than once for the same bank.[18] The 1980s also witnessed massive nonperforming loans in public sector banks.[19] These problems are not limited to developing countries; the European Commission has estimated the cost of cleaning up France's Credit Lyonnaise at more than $20 billion.

In countries in which public and private sector banks coexist, public sector banks typically have much higher ratios of nonperforming loans to total loans. For example, in Bangladesh nonperforming loans in state-owned banks constituted more than 40 percent of loans recently, about three times the rate in private banks.[20] In India in 2000 the ratio of gross nonperforming loans to total loans in public sector banks (14 percent) was about 25 percent higher than in the "old" private banks, which had a similar clientele.[21] In Latin America, Argentina's provincial banks reported nonperforming loan ratios in 1991 of over 50 percent, more than five times those in the largest private banks.[22] In Kenya, banks under the state's influence account for about two-thirds of nonperforming loans but only 28 percent of total loans. In Indonesia before the East Asian crisis, the ratio of nonperforming loans to credit in state-owned banks was three to four times the ratio in large, local private banks and about 20 percent higher than in small private banks.[23] Of the estimated cost of the crisis in the Indonesian banking system (liquidity credits to banks and replacement of bad loans by government bonds),

17. National figures on banks' nonperforming loans should be taken as indicators, not as definitive figures, given the significant differences in bank regulation and supervision across countries and the fact that in crises nonperforming loans usually are much larger than previously reported figures.

18. For some African examples, see box 2-1; for Eastern Europe, see Sherif, Borish, and Gross (2003); Tang, Zoli, and Klytchnikova (2000); Zoli (2001).

19. See Sheng (1996, pp. 21–24).

20. These figures include special (development) banks, which have by far the highest ratios of nonperforming loans.

21. Hanson (2003).

22. World Bank (2001, p. 132).

23. World Bank (1997).

nearly 55 percent was due to the state-owned banks, although they accounted for less than 45 percent of total bank assets before the crisis.[24]

State-owned banks also tend to be less efficient, in terms of spreads and costs, than private banks. La Porta, López-de-Silanes, and Shleifer show a positive relation (statistically significant) between spreads and overhead costs and the proportion of government ownership in a banking system.[25] Barth, Caprio, and Levine also show a positive correlation, although the statistical significance is lower.[26] State-owned banks may have higher spreads because they have higher costs, including the costs of provisioning their higher nonperforming loans, as is the case in India.[27] The lack of competition from private banks may reflect either a strategy to be profitable and noncompetitive or their limited ability to compete because of government regulations protecting state banks, such as regulations regarding branching or placement of treasury deposits.

The performance of state-owned banks may also be rated in terms of their service to underserved clients, but one must distinguish between rhetoric and reality. First, many state banks tend to lend mainly to the public sector, which was often a rationale for their founding. The converse is that they often lend less to the private sector. For example, in Argentina provincial banks largely lent to state governments. In Ghana the state-owned banks' main lending was to the government. In India, the banking sector, which is dominated by public sector banks, has typically lent nearly 40 percent of its deposits to the government and public sector enterprises.[28] Barth, Caprio, and Levine show a strong negative statistical relationship between state-owned bank assets and private sector credit.[29]

Second, state-owned banks are associated with a concentration of credit to larger borrowers. La Porta, López-de-Silanes, and Shleifer find that the larger the share of state banks in 1970, the greater the subsequent share of bank lending to the largest twenty firms.[30] Various studies document the links between state agricultural banks and large agricultural borrowers.[31] A well-known example is Costa

24. See Enoch and others (2001) for data on liquidity credits by banks and Indonesian finance ministry data for figures on recapitalization bonds by bank. For purposes of comparison, the data on liquidity credits are converted into dollars by monthly exchange rates, and the bonds are converted into dollars at the exchange rate at the end of 1999, around the time of their issue.

25. La Porta, López-de-Silanes, and Shleifer (2002).

26. Barth, Caprio, and Levine (2001a).

27. Hanson (2003).

28. Hanson (2003).

29. Barth, Caprio, and Levine (2001b).

30. La Porta, López-de-Silanes and Shleifer (2002).

31. See, for example, Adams and Vogel (1986); Adams, Graham, and Von Pischke (1984); Von Pischke, Adams, and Donald (1983); Yaron, Benjamin, and Piprek (1997).

Rica in the mid-1970s. The state-owned Banco Nacional's interest rate subsidy on agricultural credit was equal to about 4 percent of gross domestic product (GDP) and 20 percent of agricultural value added; about 80 percent of this credit went to 10 percent of the borrowers. The average subsidy on these loans alone would have put each recipient in the upper 10 percent of the income distribution.[32]

The negative cross-country correlations between state-owned banks and GDP growth are not surprising, given the generally poor performance of public sector banks. As noted, Barth, Caprio, and Levine show a strong negative statistical relationship between state-owned bank assets and private sector credit, a key factor in growth.[33] La Porta, López-de-Silanes, and Shleifer find a negative correlation between the share of government ownership of banks in 1970 and per capita GDP growth from 1965 to 1995, controlling for other variables correlated with growth.[34] The negative correlation is particularly strong for low-income countries. The negative correlation between state-owned banks and growth remains even after taking into account distortions such as inflation, the importance of state-owned enterprises, and an index of government intervention. La Porta, López-de-Silanes, and Shleifer also find a correlation between the size of public sector banking in 1970 and slower productivity growth over the 1965–90 period.[35]

Explanations for Poor Performance

Why has the performance of public sector banks been poor and associated with slow development? One obvious explanation is the difference in credit allocation between these banks and private sector banks, which is the rationale for state-owned banks. This difference means that unless private banks really do not recognize the loans with the best return-risk characteristics, public sector banks will do worse than private banks. In fact, the results of credit allocation by public sector banks seem worse, not better, than those of private banks. In particular, their nonperforming loans are generally higher, and their profits are lower. Higher nonperforming loans mean that the use of the state-owned banks' credit is not sufficiently productive to service the loan and that alternative uses of the credit would be productive. Alternatively, the recipient of the loan might use a credit for private profit in a way that does not raise measured output and then choose not to repay the loan.[36] In this case the other

32. World Bank (1989).
33. Barth, Caprio, and Levine (2001b).
34. La Porta, López-de-Silanes, and Shleifer (2002).
35. La Porta, López-de-Silanes, and Shleifer (2002).
36. For example, measured output would not grow if credits were used for capital flight, which could yield good private returns.

clients of the lending institution or the taxpayers provide the borrower, in effect, with a subsidy. The borrower benefits from the loan, but other investors must bear higher taxes and higher credit costs. Thus either the productivity of the credits of public sector banks is worse than that of private banks or the recipients of their credits receive a subsidy that must be covered by taxes or higher loan costs to other borrowers.

Thus lower efficiency in public sector bank loans and higher nonperforming loans at the bank level translate into bank crises and less growth at the macroeconomic level. Moreover, in most countries there appears to be no offsetting distributional benefit from any improvement in access to credit or from credit subsidies as a result of lending by these banks.

According to La Porta, López-de-Silanes, and Shleifer, the evidence is "consistent with the political view of government ownership of firms, including banks, according to which ownership politicizes the resource allocation process and reduces efficiency."[37] For example, in India and Indonesia, even small credit allocations have been directed by government at some points in time.[38] In this view, public sector banks, like other public sector enterprises, are instruments to transfer wealth to supporters and, through bribes, to politicians and bureaucrats.[39] No doubt part of the poor performance of public sector banks across countries reflects these issues.

Yet even the best-intentioned governments, aiming, for example, to use these banks to improve the provision of credit to underserved sectors, face at least five severe problems inherent in such banks. These problems hinder even the best-motivated efforts to improve the performance of state banks.

First, state-owned banks suffer from multiple objectives. This makes it difficult to set up appropriate incentives and enforce accountability. Private banks face the difficult task of balancing return and risk. But state banks face the extra problem of additional objectives, such as the desire to serve the underserved, to develop particular geographic areas or sectors of the economy, and to meet sporadic demands from the government to help resolve financial problems. How can the government set up incentives for the manager to meet these diverse objectives? How can the government judge how well the manager meets these objectives? Obviously, trade-offs are necessary between the objective of prudent, profitable banking and, say, the provision of access to farmers or small- and medium-size

37. La Porta, López-de-Silanes, and Shleifer (2002, p. 290).
38. In India during the late 1980s, parliamentarians organized loan *melas* (fairs) at which banks simply gave loans to farmers on their signature. In Indonesia during the 1970s and early 1980s, BRI was often directed to provide credits to particular farmers or groups of farmers by the minister of agriculture.
39. Shleifer (1998).

industries. But these trade-offs usually are hard to specify, especially in advance. The typical result is that managers are not held accountable as long as they meet the sporadic requests of government and major problems do not emerge. In this environment, public sector bank managers—who typically are poorly paid—tend to avoid risks, ignore problems, and focus on careers in public service.

Moreover, one of the objectives of state-owned banks often becomes providing and ensuring employment in the banks themselves and increasing staff welfare. These banks typically are overstaffed compared with private banks. Overstaffing is often greater at lower staff levels. One study in India estimates that the ratio of management employees (officers) to assets is five times higher in public sector banks than in foreign banks, while the ratio of total employees to assets is seven times higher.[40] While salaries are usually low for management, at the lower levels they are often high relative to similarly qualified workers. The result is that wage costs in state banks are often fairly high as a percentage of margins. In addition, state banks often offer their employees low-interest loans.[41]

Second, information is lacking with which the owner—the state—could judge performance and hold management accountable. Information on banks is always obscure to outsiders: The risk and return on assets may change very quickly, as may funding costs on market borrowings. All banks face difficulties in providing transparent, up-to-date information, particularly in developing economies. However, the problems of state-owned banks are usually much worse. These banks tend to lack good information systems because operations are too widespread, national communications are weak, and information technology equipment and personnel are lacking.

The information problem of state-owned banks is, however, political as well as technical. The state often requests a public sector bank to make ad hoc interventions outside the bank's stated objectives—for example, to benefit well-connected supporters or to correct problems that have arisen. The government typically wants as little public information as possible about such interventions. Hence it has only limited incentives to demand regular, up-to-date, transparent information on what a public sector bank is doing. The bank's management also has little incentive to provide good information on which it can be judged. Thus it is to the advantage of both the government and the banks' management to limit information on what the bank is doing and how well it does it. The result, unfortunately, is poor information on performance and large undiscovered problems (which tend to appear suddenly in a crisis).

40. Sarkar (1999).
41. See Hanson (2001), for India.

This information problem and the conflicts of interest facing the government limit the supervision of state-owned banks. Information for supervisors, which is a political as well as a technical problem, is lacking. If the banks' managers themselves lack information, then supervisors have even less information. Lacking information, supervisors are unable to provide a strong, separate channel for evaluating the condition of the banks. In addition, supervisors often lack the legal powers to supervise state banks, particularly development banks.

Moreover, the government faces a conflict of interest between its role as owner of the bank—which may seek regulatory forbearance—and as the defender of the taxpayers' interests. The government, lacking funds to recapitalize state-owned banks, may apply pressure for easy supervision or encourage regulatory forbearance, such as easing the norms of income recognition, provisioning, and restructuring. Supervisors may face laws preventing them from supervising the state banks, or they may use a different procedure for them, particularly in the case of public sector development banks. Of course, supervisors in developing countries tend to have little independence from the finance ministry, which is the owner of the banks. But even if supervisors were independent, they would lack the political power to withdraw the license of a weak state bank.

The market also demands little or no information about public sector banks. Their deposits carry an implicit government guarantee. Thus depositors in and lenders to these banks expect to be fully repaid, irrespective of the banks' activities, except when government solvency collapses.

Third, state-owned banks face a political difficulty in lending at market rates and in collecting loans and executing collateral. This is true not only in dealings with the politically powerful but also in dealings with poor, underserved clients. Lending rates would have to be well above prime rates to cover the risks of default on long-term loans in an unstable macroeconomic environment or on loans to underserved clients who face high risks and about whom little is known. But such rates typically are politically impossible. As a result, state banks set lending rates well below what the market would charge. Rates also tend to be adjusted slowly to inflation. As a result, in high-inflation environments the capital of public sector banks is quickly eroded. This may explain many of the problems experienced by state development banks in the inflationary Latin American countries.[42] In low-inflation environments, an important issue in poor performance is nonper-

---

42. Some Latin American countries used indexing to limit the problem of keeping interest rates in line with inflation. However, when relative prices changed sharply, indexed loan contracts encountered problems, as did loan contracts that were not indexed.

forming loans. Here too, state banks face political problems. The ability to collect is limited either because the borrowers have strong political connections or because the government does not want to be viewed as antipoor because it executes the collateral of small borrowers that are in arrears.

Fourth, state-owned banks often face a culture of nonpayment. Borrowers may consider the loan a transfer by the government, which does not require payment, a problem related to the third issue. If a noticeable number of borrowers either decide not to pay or cannot pay, then borrowers in general may decide that loan repayment is foolish and would put them at a competitive disadvantage. At this point, a general default may arise. Execution of collateral would reduce the culture of nonpayment over time. However, even if state banks were politically willing to execute collateral, they would find it difficult because of the weak legal framework in most countries.

Fifth, corruption and capture by unintended beneficiaries are problems that come on top of the problems facing well-meaning governments. Bank loans at less-than-market rates are highly desirable, even more desirable if pressure for repayment is low. Such loans must be allocated by something other than market forces and bank interest rates. Borrowers may use political pressure and bribery to get them. At the same time, the bankers, who receive civil service salaries, may seek bribes as a way of dividing the "rents" on the loans; the bribe is often added into the loan.[43] As a result, credits notionally designated for small borrowers often go to large firms or large farmers.

Transforming State-Owned Banks

The poor performance of state-owned banks typically leads to their bankruptcy, followed by attempts at "reform." The reform usually begins with announcements that the banks will be made as good as the best banks. The typical reform package involves

—New management

—The writing off or removal of bad loans and their replacement with government debt or equity or by government takeover of an equal amount of the bank's debt[44]

---

43. See World Bank (1997, box 5.13), for an example from Indonesia.

44. The bad loans that are removed may be placed in an asset management company or a treasury agency that collects debts. Tang, Zoli, and Klytchnikova (2000) discuss the approaches that were used in transition countries. Enoch, García, and Sundarajan (1999) provide a general discussion with country examples.

—Efforts to reduce costs by reducing staff and branch offices, particularly overseas, and in some cases by pursuing mergers

—Better information technology and risk-management methodology.

These reform packages typically fail. First, the reforms are often too small and involve regulatory forbearance.[45] In addition, they leave a substantial amount of bad debts on the books without a new approach to collecting them. One study finds a need for multiple recapitalizations in almost 25 percent of the cases of restructuring.[46] Box 2-1 discusses the repeated attempts at reform in three African countries. Moreover, the write-offs and the easy treatment of bad debtors may encourage further defaults.

Second and more important, the reforms do not address the fundamental problems of state-owned banks: their multiple objectives, the government's own ad hoc interventions in them, the lack of information on their performance, the lack of accountability because of multiple objectives and the desire to obscure what the banks actually do, and the difficulties in charging enough and collecting on loans, let alone any problems associated with corruption.

To put it another way, substantial bad loans will almost certainly recur unless the basic character of the state-owned bank changes along the following lines:

—Eliminate government interference in their lending.

—Improve incentives for their management and staff to lend and collect well.

—Install a good information system and use it to hold bank officers accountable.

—Improve staff quality.

—Cover costs of lending to high-risk clients with loan rates.

—Eliminate the culture of nonpayment by the borrowers through the enforcement of contracts.

Unless such changes are made in restructured banks, the fundamentals of their business continue undisturbed, and new bad loans may increase rapidly. In addition to the lack of operational change, bad loans tend to increase for two reasons: There is often political pressure to begin lending again (because the bank crisis may be associated with the need for a stabilization program that constrains other expansionary measures); and a public sector bank can raise deposits for lending because the implicit government guarantee limits market discipline. As a result, reformed state-owned banks often return to losses in a few years, as seen in Africa and the transition countries.[47]

45. For example, governments sometimes give recapitalized state-owned banks nontradable, low-return assets or tax credits as capital. Such assets do not generate a market rate of return for the bank.

46. Klingebiel and Honohan (2002).

47. Sherif, Borish, and Gross (2003); Tang, Zoli, and Klytchinikova (2000); Zoli (2001).

The few cases in which restructuring has been successful support the importance of the changes described above.[48] Specifically,

—The government should define a simple objective—usually privatization over a short time horizon—and give management the power to reject requests not related to that objective. In other words, the government needs to avoid further interventions, except for failure to achieve the objective. If privatization is the objective, but timing is vague, then restructured banks tend to revert to their earlier status.

—The new management should be chosen for its capacity to manage, although this alone is not sufficient for good results. All of the successful cases drew managers from reputable international banks: a bank itself, a twinning arrangement with an international bank, or citizens who had worked in such banks. In some cases, the management (or twinning bank) was given an incentive for good performance based on the results of the privatization (for example, in Poland).

—Information systems should be put in place to allow the new management to monitor performance frequently, with a short time lag, and to allow the finance ministry and the central bank to evaluate progress toward the objective. If lending is aimed at targeted groups, then the information systems should also make clear the success in reaching these beneficiaries and the full costs of doing so, including interest rate subsidies and rates of nonperforming loans.

—Staff capacity typically should be upgraded.

—New lending usually should be constrained, especially large loans, in order to limit new nonperforming loans.

Bad loans typically are removed from the restructured banks and are replaced by government recapitalization bonds (although in the case of Poland they were left in the banks to be resolved by the new management before privatization).[49]

In India, where public sector banks continue to dominate, bank managers were given the objective of reducing their nonperforming loans after the small recapitalizations of 1994 and 1995 about 2 percent of GDP. Generally the banks achieved that goal through a combination of more careful lending, higher provisions than other banks (out of higher margins), larger purchases of new government debt than other banks, and debt restructurings that were encouraged by regulatory changes and falling interest rates.[50] Nonetheless, the state-owned banks

---

48. Some relatively successful reforms include Korea's Seoul Bank (Kang 2003), Poland (Kawalec and Kluza 2003), Pakistan (Husain 2004; Soomro 2003); and AgBank in Mongolia and NBC in Tanzania (Dressen, Dyer, and Northrip 2002). In all these cases, the banks were either privatized or transformed into a narrow savings bank that focused on deposits and payments.

49. Kawalec and Kluza (2003). Placing bad loans in an asset management company is likely to be expensive unless it has a strong incentive to collect and the legal framework is strong (see Klingebiel 2000).

50. Hanson (2003).

Box 2-1. *The Rise, Reprieve, and Fall of State Banks in Africa in the 1980s and 1990s*[1]

"Where the same strong interests that derailed earlier reforms still dominate a country's politics, outcomes from bank privatization will tend to be disappointing. . . . Most African countries opted to create at least one large state bank after independence to support indigenous industries and state ventures and to make banking services available for the broad population, including those in rural areas. In many countries, these big state banks still dominate the banking sector and, after decades of politicized management and soft budget constraints, have been difficult to restructure or privatize. The disappointing results from restructuring and the problems in privatization can be seen from three African countries that attempted banking reform programs during the 1990s: Ghana, Tanzania, and Uganda.

Ghana

Ghana started economic reforms in the early 1980s after a politically unstable period of heavy state involvement in the economy. The state owned three commercial banks, three development banks, and the Cooperative Bank. There were also two foreign banks and a merchant bank.

All the state-owned banks were restructured and recapitalized under the financial reforms that started in 1987, with bad loans removed to an AMC [asset management company]. Management was improved through extensive technical assistance.

Both before and after restructuring, the primary function of the Ghanaian banks has been funding the deficit of central government and public enterprises (this averaged 73 percent of domestic credit in the 1990s). The very high treasury bill yields received by the banks helped offset the continued loan losses from other lending.

Bank privatization has been a stop-and-go process, being held up, for example, by disagreement between the privatization agency's values on the price and external estimates of those values. With the program years behind schedule, the government decided to sell some shares in two state commercial banks domestically even before finding a strategic investor. This made it difficult subsequently to reduce the price to attract a strategic investor. Eventually, in late 1996, the government dropped its requirement that the strategic buyer should be a bank and managed to sell the Social Security Bank to a consortium of foreign investment funds. By 1998 this newly privatized bank had about 13 percent of total banking system assets.

The largest bank, Ghana Commercial Bank (GCB), continued to have problems even after the restructuring of the late 1980s. With the failure of a planned sale in 1996 to a Malaysian manufacturing firm, it remains government controlled, with just 41 percent held by Ghanaians after the initial public offering. In preparation for privatization in the mid-1990s, it was found that there were serious reconciliation problems in the accounts and shortcomings in management, and some of the loss-making branches had never been closed. In 1997 the entire senior management of GCB had to be removed in the wake of a check fraud scandal.

Tanzania

. . . Twelve banks had been nationalized in 1967 and merged into a dominant commercial bank, National Bank of Commerce (NBC), which had a virtual monopoly for twenty-five years. The only other financial institutions were a small state cooperative bank and a few specialized state banks for housing.

By the mid-1980s the NBC was insolvent, illiquid, and losing money at an alarming rate. Restructuring moved a significant portion of the NPLs [nonperforming loans] out of the bank, closed some loss-making branches, and retrenched staff, but operating costs as a percentage of assets doubled and spreads became negative in 1992. The bank was recapitalized in 1992, but as the losses continued to mount, restructuring intensified with an "action plan" in 1994 that changed the board of directors, curtailed lending, and laid off further staff. However, the salaries of the remaining staff were doubled by the new board of directors, thus offsetting the reductions in costs. The benefits from removing bad loans to the AMC were short-lived. By 1994, 77 percent of the remaining loans were nonperforming.

In 1995 another attempt to restructure failed. The bank was split in November 1997 into two banks and a holding company. The holding company took the nonbanking assets—for example, staff housing and the training center. The business bank—named NBC-1997—took all lending and 45 percent of the deposits, and a service bank took the remainder of the deposits. [This bank,] the National Microfinance Bank, was to provide basic depository services to the general population and took the small deposits but no lending. The decision to set up a microfinance bank that would keep the rural branch network may have softened some of the political opposition to the privatization of the business bank. The separation proved difficult. Poor financial and operational controls led to the need for significant provisions on unreconciled balances, and there was a significant delay in producing financial statements after the split.

NBC-1997 was sold in late 1999 to the Amalgamated Banks of South Africa Group (ABSA), with International Finance Corporation participation. The microfinance bank . . . [could not be sold. With the support of aid donors, an international development firm was contracted to manage and restructure the bank. The bank focused] on the provision of payments and savings services [and some microcredits] in its ninety-five branches [and is doing relatively well; see Dresser, Dyer, and Northrip (2002)].

(continued)

Box 2-1. *The Rise, Reprieve, and Fall of State Banks in Africa in the 1980s and 1990s*[1] *(Continued)*

Uganda

By the early 1990s . . . the government had stakes in all nine commercial banks and owned the largest two: Uganda Commercial Bank (UCB), with about 50 percent of the market, and the Cooperative Bank. As of late 1991 about one-third of the loans of the commercial bank were nonperforming, and the negative net worth of the bank was estimated at $24 million.

Timid restructuring efforts started. Loss-making branches were converted into agencies rather than being closed. The AMC that was to take bad loans was not created until 1996, and even then there was a significant lag in transferring bad loans. There was a performance agreement in 1994 between the Ministry of Finance and the bank's board of directors, but the strategy pursued was to try to reduce the proportion of NPLs by growing the loan portfolio. Bank supervisors did not monitor compliance. Every improvement in profitability was temporary, and losses continued to mount. By mid-1996 the financial position had deteriorated so that its negative net worth tripled from earlier estimates.

While the government's intention was that the restructuring would culminate in privatization, the management of the UCB was actively opposed to sale. Eventually, after three years of unsuccessful attempts to restructure the bank, it was agreed that a reputable merchant bank be selected to implement the sale, giving the buyer greater freedom to define which assets and branches were to be purchased. Again there was a lag, and the merchant bank was finally hired in February 1996. At its request, top management was finally changed in July 1996. Losses were mounting throughout the delay, and the UCB was losing market share. Audited financial statements for 1997 showed another fall in interest income, wiping out the core profits advertised to investors six months earlier. With few expressions of interest, a sales agreement was signed in late 1997 with a Malaysian industrial and real estate company. By December 1998, however, the deal had unraveled amid allegations of corruption."

1. From World Bank, *Finance for Growth: Policy Choices in a Volatile World* (Oxford University Press, 2001), box 3.3.

continued to suffer a number of problems: Nonperforming loans before provisioning remained about 10 percent of loans, margins and costs remained high (despite savings on wage costs from a self-financed voluntary retirement scheme in 2000–01), profits on lending were too low to maintain the ratio of capital to un-risk-weighted assets, and some of the banks remained undercapitalized for many years.[51] There was no consolidation among public sector banks—even those that experienced problems and required multiple capital injections—and information technology was weak.[52] Some private banks, including some of the nine licensed in 1994, also experienced problems, as India's information and legal frameworks for lending remained weak. A new, large private bank, ICICI—created recently through the merger of ICICI Bank and an old private bank and then the reverse merger of ICICI Development Bank into that bank—may put public sector banks under increased competitive pressure.

Privatization of State-Owned Banks

If government seeks to make public sector banks as good as private banks through restructuring, then the obvious question is, Why not simply privatize, rather than just restructure, them?[53] Presumably one answer is that the government wishes to retain control over the credit allocation instrument, in order to reward favored groups, and to keep the implicit taxes and transfers provided by the public sector banks off the government budget. As with other state enterprises, this suggests that politicians may apply a sort of cost-benefit calculus to privatization, privatizing when the cost of continued state ownership exceeds the benefit of the ability to reward favored clients, provide employment, and so forth.[54] This calculus must be adjusted to take into account the political support for the privatization of state-owned enterprises in the transition countries.

Assessing the political calculus for privatization is more complex for banks than for state-owned enterprises, but the analysis seems to hold. The most detailed studies relate to Argentina; they find that provincially owned banks tended to become privatized when the banks' easy access to the central bank ended, gains from seigniorage declined with falling inflation, and runs on the banks developed in 1995, when the "tequila crisis" reached Argentina.[55] Moreover, across provinces badly performing banks were more likely to be privatized, while large overstaffed banks in provinces with high unemployment and large public employment were

---

51. Hanson (2003).

52. Verma (2000).

53. This section focuses on privatization of public sector banks; it does not deal with the reprivatization of banks that were taken over by the government during a crisis, except for the cases of Mexico and Seoul Bank.

54. World Bank (1995).

55. Clarke and Cull (1999, 2002).

less likely to be privatized.[56] There is also some tentative support for the importance of falling seigniorage and the other factors in privatizations in Brazil and across countries.[57] In Eastern Europe the cost of serial recapitalizations also played a role.[58] In Mexico the government sought to obtain large revenues from the sale of banks to help finance the government and adjusted the terms of the sale to improve banks' revenues.[59]

Shifts in national ideology appear to be another factor in privatization across countries. Certainly ideology played an important role in the large privatizations of banks in the transition countries (table 2-2). The shift to a more market-based model of development also contributed to the privatization of banks in Latin America. In contrast, less commitment to a market-based system and the continued strength of the postcolonial elites appear to have slowed privatizations in some African countries.

Despite the shift in ideology, governments in the transition countries tended to privatize their banks later than many of their other privatizations. The relative slowness of bank privatization may reflect not just the desire of governments to retain the instrument of public sector banks—indeed, they typically retained a large interest—but also macroeconomic issues and the costliness of the initial recapitalization that would have been required to privatize the banks.

Among the larger countries in Eastern Europe, substantial bank privatization before 1995 took place only in the Czech Republic (three of the four state-owned banks were included in the voucher program). Privatization was much more limited in Hungary (one bank was partially privatized) and in Poland (two banks were partially privatized); and in all three cases the government retained a significant share of ownership in the partially privatized banks (25–30 percent). In the Czech case, the banks were privatized through vouchers that were traded in the stock market, with the government retaining a 30 percent share. The Czech banks, dominated by government and owners of other voucher-privatized companies, made loans to increasingly overindebted companies that eventually went into default, requiring another bank recapitalization. A similar problem occurred in Allied Bank in Pakistan, where the privatization of Allied Bank to its staff was eventually followed by the purchase of a controlling interest by one of the bank's major loan defaulters, and the central bank had to replace the chairman and change three members of the board.[60]

---

56. On average, employment fell by more than a third in the privatized banks (Clarke and Cull 2002).

57. For Brazil, see Beck, Crivelli, and Summerhill (2003); for a cross-country perspective, see Boehmer, Nash, and Netter (2003).

58. See Bokros (2003).

59. Haber and Kantor (2003).

60. Husain (2004).

Table 2-2. *Assets of State-Owned Banks as Share of Total Bank Assets,
Transition Economies, 1993–2000*
Percent

Country	1993	1996 or 1997	2000
Albania	n.a.	93.7	64.8
Armenia	n.a.	3.2	2.6
Azerbaijan	n.a.	77.6	60.4
Belarus	n.a.	54.1	66.0
Bosnia and Herzegovina	n.a.	n.a.	55.4
Bulgaria	n.a.	82.2	19.8
Croatia	n.a.	36.2	5.7
Czech Republic	20.6	16.6	28.2
Estonia	25.7	6.6	0
Georgia	72.7	0	0
Hungary	74.4	16.3	8.6
Kazakhstan	4.6	28.4	1.9
Kyrgyz Republic	77.3	5.0	7.1
Latvia	24.0	6.9	2.9
Lithuania	53.6	54.0	38.9
Macedonia[a]	n.a.	0	1.1
Moldova	n.a.	0.3	9.8
Poland	86.2	69.8	24.0
Romania	n.a.	80.9	50.0
Russian Federation	n.a.	37.0	41.9
Slovak Republic	n.a.	54.2	49.1
Slovenia	n.a.	40.7	42.2
Tajikistan	n.a.	5.3	6.8
Turkmenistan	n.a.	64.1	n.a.
Ukraine	n.a.	n.a.	11.9
Uzbekistan	n.a.	75.5	77.5
Yugoslavia	n.a.	92.0	90.0
Unweighted regional averages[b]			
Central and Eastern Europe	n.a.	53.0	36.7
Baltics	n.a.	22.5	13.9
Commonwealth of Independent States	n.a.	31.9	26.0

Source: Sherif, Borish, and Gross (2003); Tang, Zoli, and Klytchnikova (2000); EBRD (1999).
n.a. Not available.
a. Former Yugoslav Republic.
b. Countries without data are excluded from regional averages.

Finally, other factors in bank privatizations seem to have been national governance and opportunities for new markets, which increased the demand for bank ownership from well-known foreign banks. In the transition countries, once the possibility of access to the European Union opened up, there was a large inflow of foreign banks. For example, in Bulgaria foreign banks rose from one of forty banks in 1994 to twenty-five of thirty-five banks in 2000; in the Czech Republic foreign banks rose from thirteen of fifty-five banks in 1994 to sixteen of forty in 2000; in Hungary they rose from seventeen of forty-three banks in 1994 to thirty of thirty-eight in 2000; and in Poland they rose from eleven of eighty-two banks in 1994 to forty-seven of seventy-four in 2000.[61] In Latin America, the rapid purchase of Mexico's banks by well-known international bankers in the second round of privatization probably reflected the likelihood of better governance and less government intervention, as signaled by the North American Free Trade Agreement (NAFTA). Concerns about relatively weak regulatory and legal environments limited the interest of well-known international banks in Africa and much of Southeast Asia. However, South African banks played an increasing role in the southern part of Africa at the end of the 1990s.

Privatization, if done well, appears to yield significant gains. Again, the most detailed study is of provincial banks in Argentina.[62] Estimates suggest that the present value of the cost, over time, of continuing to recapitalize provincial banks at the usual rate would have been two to four times greater than the net cost of privatizing (taking the bad debts out of the bank, recapitalizing it, and then privatizing it for what was typically obtained for bank assets); the estimated median savings were equal to about one-third of provincial government expenditures.[63] Once privatized, the banks' nonperforming loans dropped substantially, and their credit allocation resembled that of the other private banks more than the provincial banks that were not privatized.

Privatized banks also appear to be more efficient than state-owned banks when the bank is privatized to a strategic investor, particularly a well-known foreign investor, while privatizations through the stock market, particularly when the government retains a significant share, do not seem to improve performance significantly and may even require further injections of capital.[64] These conclusions

---

61. Sherif, Borish, and Gross (2003).

62. Clarke and Cull (1999).

63. The range reflects differences in assumptions regarding the discount rate, rates of recapitalization, and sale proceeds.

64. See the studies presented at the World Bank conference on bank privatization, November 20–21, 2003 (www.worldbank.org/research/projects/bank_privatization_conference.htm [June 30, 2004]). Many of these studies measure performance in terms of the degree to which banks deviate from an econometrically estimated efficiency frontier; in addition, standard indicators of performance are explored.

appear to be supported by a comparison of privatizations in the Czech Republic (three banks in the first round), in Poland (two banks in the first round), in the second rounds in these same countries, in Argentina, in Brazil (in a comparison between privatized and restructured banks), in Nigeria, in Pakistan (Allied Bank), and in a nine-country sample.[65] The partially privatized banks tended to have higher loan-loss provisions and higher labor costs than comparators. Reflecting these problems, the equity shares of the partially privatized banks tended to do worse than the market index in a nine-country sample and in India. This evidence also suggests that partial privatizations may generate revenue but rarely improve bank performance.

Partial privatizations may even be a problem if the intent is eventually to sell the bank to a strategic investor. The initial sale may later make it difficult to adjust the sale price to a strategic investor, as occurred in Ghana. Minority shareholders may even be able to block the deal legally.

Full privatization to a well-known, international bank acting as a strategic investor seems to have yielded better results than cases in which foreign participation was limited. This difference may be a major factor accounting for the improved results in the second round of privatizations in the Czech Republic and Poland and the good results so far in some other privatizations in Eastern Europe.[66] The reprivatizations in Mexico also produced much better results than the initial sales, which were limited to nationals.[67] Well-known international banks bring modern banking and risk management techniques. They also provide some counterbalance to the dominant political elite in small countries. Of course, even such banks may run into problems in environments of weak governance, weak information, and weak legal systems. However, such banks usually resolve their problems without government support, since the costs of failure to do so would be higher, in terms of their international reputation, than the costs of resolution.[68] In contrast, privatization to foreign investors without a reputation to protect can often lead to

65. As noted, the Czech government retained 30 percent of the shares in the first-round privatizations through vouchers, and recapitalization was needed before the banks could be resold (Bonin, Hasan, and Wachtel 2003; Kawalec and Kluza 2003). In Poland's first round of privatization, where the state retained 30 percent of the shares, employees were sold 20 percent on preferential terms, and the rest was divided into small and large investor lots; performance improved somewhat, but much less than in the second round (Bonin, Hasan, and Wachtel 2003). For Argentina, see Clarke and Cull (1999); for Brazil, see Beck, Crivelli, and Summerhill (2003); for Nigeria, see Beck, Cull, and Jerome (2003); for Pakistan, see Husain (2004); and for the nine-country sample, see Ochere (2003).

66. Bonin, Hasan, and Wachtel (2003).

67. Haber (2003); Haber and Kantor (2003).

68. For example, in the recent Uruguay banking crisis, the fully owned foreign banks were excluded from central bank liquidity support.

problems—foreign investors may be harder to supervise than national investors, may pull out if local conditions deteriorate, and may create problems if their home country businesses run into trouble.

Although bank privatization generates benefits, doing it well is not easy. Delays and resistance occur because of pressure from beneficiaries of the current arrangements—clients, management, and staff—as well as nationalist politics. Governments and ministers may face legal or political difficulties in selling a bank for less than the substantial amount put into it for restructuring, as occurred in Ecuador and Ghana. The valuation problem is significant, since after restructuring much of the bank's assets may be government debt. Government debt in external markets may well sell at a large discount, and a buyer wanting to take country risk could simply buy that debt rather than invest capital in a bank, with all the problems of dealing with bad loans that have not been removed from the books and with a politically active staff accustomed to working in a public enterprise.

Above all, privatization is costly when the buyers prove to be unsound. The worst case is the well-known first round of privatization in Mexico in 1991–92.[69] Foreign buyers were excluded, and the buyers paid excessively for what appeared to be a protected market and access to non-arm's-length lending, even in any credit crunch. The banks expanded credit rapidly, not only to the industrial financial conglomerates to which they belonged but also to homeowner mortgages.[70] The quality of capital in the privatized banks has also been called into question, as it was alleged that the buyers bought the banks largely with borrowed funds. The rising loans increasingly proved uncollectible; the reported ratio of nonperforming loans to total loans more than doubled between 1991 and 1993, reaching nearly 20 percent of loans.[71] As the crisis deepened, related lending nearly doubled; its terms were much easier and the defaults much higher than those of unrelated borrowers.[72] The Mexican government was forced to renationalize the bankrupt banks; it cleaned up their balance sheets at an estimated cost of more than $70 billion (nearly 20 percent of GDP) and reprivatized them, beginning in 1998, to international banks.

69. See Haber and Kantor (2003); Haber (2003); La Porta, López-de-Silanes, and Zamarripa (2003).

70. A fifth of all large loans went to insiders, according to La Porta, López-de-Silanes, and Zamarripa (2003). Also see the description of the interventions in Banco Unión and Banco Cremi in Preston and Dillon (2004).

71. These figures follow international practice and include both the past-due interest (all that was officially reported as nonperforming before 1997) and the rolled-over principal of loans with past-due interest. See Haber and Kantor (2003) for the data.

72. La Porta, López-de-Silanes, and Zamarripa (2003).

Such problems have developed in other privatizations as well. The first rounds of partial privatizations in the Czech Republic, Poland, and Hungary led to problems, though not as big as the first round of recapitalizations; avoiding such costs probably contributed to the countries' including foreign investors in the later rounds. In Africa privatizations often went to nationals or foreign investors without an international reputation to protect, which created problems later.[73]

In sum, bank privatization has large benefits, and moving toward it fairly rapidly is desirable, but privatization done poorly can be costly. A desirable approach would probably entail improving the informational, regulatory, and supervisory environment, while setting a well-defined, short timetable for privatization. Improvements in the informational environment would include frequent publication of data on banks, use of internationally audited accounts, and a system for publicizing the recipients of loans from the state-owned banks and the subsidies on them. Subjecting state-owned banks to regulation and supervision similar to that for private sector banks would provide the government with an independent source of information regarding their condition. In addition, regulatory and supervisory standards should be improved to ensure that reasonable capital and income recognition and provisioning standards are maintained, credit exposures to individuals or particular industrial groups are limited, and strong and prompt corrective action is in place—issues that are very important after privatization to reduce the chance of looting. The Argentine results suggest that this approach is desirable: Its regulatory and supervisory system on the eve of privatization was one of the best in the developing world.[74] It may be desirable to hire international managers, but this should not occur much before privatization, as it is difficult for state officials to supervise the managers or to maintain incentives for a long time.

Recapitalization is probably necessary before privatization. The new owners typically want a relatively clean balance sheet and do not want to sort out the problems of the previous managers.[75] This is particularly true if the nonperforming borrowers are state-owned enterprises, from which collection may be politically

---

73. Mozes (2003).

74. Minimum capital was 11.5 percent with risk weights based on market and credit risk, liquidity requirements were 20 percent, nine of the top ten banks were well-known foreign banks, and information on the banks was readily available (World Bank 1998). The later problems in the banking system reflected the macroeconomic problem of an overly indebted government, the freezing of deposits, the judicially enforced unfreezing of some deposits, and the asymmetric conversion of deposits and loans when the convertibility board was abolished, problems that even the best regulated and supervised banks could not withstand.

75. It is probably desirable to limit any "insurance" contracts against bad loans that are discovered. While failure to provide insurance will limit the sale price, the experience with such contracts has proved costly in some cases, notably the sale of the Long-Term Credit Bank (now Shinsei Bank) in Japan.

difficult. Recapitalization should probably not be done substantially before the privatization, lest the government decide that privatization is not necessary. The traditional approach to recapitalization has been to split the bank into a "good" bank, with deposit liabilities, performing loans, and government recapitalization bonds, and a "bad" bank, which receives the bad loans and focuses on asset recovery—the so-called Spanish model, used in the crisis in Spain in the early 1980s. However, in Poland some success was achieved by keeping some nonperforming loans in the banks and relying on bank managers—who knew their clients best, who could invoke relationships to improve debt service, and who received incentives for their performance—to reduce the nonperforming loans before privatization.[76]

The actual privatization should be done to bidders who have passed a "fit and proper" test, and foreign buyers should be allowed to participate. In Eastern Europe it was relatively easy to find good buyers once it appeared that the European Union would be expanded. However, recent attempts to sell banks in other parts of the world have not attracted well-known international banks.[77] When buyers are national banks or less well-known international banks, they may be undercapitalized (as in the first Mexican privatization) and subject to various pressures. Good regulation and supervision of the privatized banks and good information about them are extremely important to limit new losses.

Alternatives to Restructuring and Privatization

Three broad approaches have been used to deal with state-owned banks when neither restructuring nor privatization seems appropriate: closure and liquidation, conversion to a government agency, or conversion to a savings bank holding only government debt as assets (a narrow bank).

Closure of state-owned banks has been used in many countries, for example, Yugoslavia, Romania (Bancorex), Ukraine (Ukraina), Brazil (some provincial banks), and Benin, which closed all its public sector banks, briefly leaving the country without onshore banking services.[78] In addition numerous development finance institutions have been closed around the world.[79] Closure has been done

---

76. Kawalec and Kluza (2003).

77. For example, in Indonesia, the reprivatizations of banks that were taken over during the crisis received bids from only one well-known international bank.

78. No provincial bank in Argentina was closed, because the central government used its Fondo Fiduciario to encourage privatization. Access to the Fondo (fund) meant that the provinces got loans to cover their residual obligations after they split their banks into "good" and "bad" banks.

79. The membership of the Latin American Association of Financial Institutions for Economic Development declined from 171 in 1988 to 73 in 2003. The decline reflects the closure of many development financial institutions during the 1990s, for example, in Argentina and Peru.

when the lending culture of the bank seemed beyond repair and it was recognized that restructuring would simply lead to more bad loans—a degree of realism that unfortunately was missing in many restructurings.

The key point to remember with regard to closure is that banking is essential; a particular bank is not.[80] The bank to be closed should be thought of as a service provider, and consideration should be given to alternate ways to provide these services—deposit taking, payments, loans—an approach that unfortunately is complicated by the demands of a public sector bank's employees. Regarding deposits and payments, closure is easiest in the case of development finance institutions, which often do not provide these services because their main source of finance is borrowing offshore or directed credit from domestic banks. For such institutions, the government can simply assume these liabilities, write off uncollectible loans, and place the remaining debts into asset recovery institutions and the courts. For commercial or savings banks, the issue is more complex. Closure of state-owned commercial banks, savings banks, or agricultural banks means that depositors must be paid off or transferred to another bank along with some performing assets or recapitalization bonds. Thus in the case of a transfer, other banks provide deposit and payment services to former depositors. One major concern with the closure of such state banks has been that rural depositors may have no good alternatives for protecting their savings and making and receiving payments and remittances from migrant family members. In Africa, for example, foreign banks seem to have discouraged small deposits in some cases. However, branches of the closed bank can be sold or transferred to other intermediaries, including nonbank financial institutions, microfinance institutions, or narrow banks. Improvement in the payments systems can allow such institutions or post office banks to handle remittances and other payments.

Another concern in closure is that the former small borrowers from the bank may find it difficult to get credit. However, these fears are often exaggerated. Elimination of state-owned banks that lend but do not collect can open the way for other institutions to engage in small lending, particularly if information on borrowers and the legal framework are improved (box 2-2).

A second approach is to replace a state-owned bank or state-owned bank offices with an agency of the federal or state government for reasons of transparency, as Mexico did by closing BanRural and setting up the Financiera Rural. Such an agency can disburse funds but not take deposits. Transparency comes because private deposits are not used to make what, in effect, are fiscal allocations, with "the bill"—the contingent liability of the government—only coming later,

80. Andrews and Josefsson (2003).

Box 2-2. *Replacing Small Borrowers' Bad Credit with Good Credit, without State-Owned Banks*

A standard criticism of closing or privatizing public sector banks is that it reduces the access of small borrowers to credit. It is often argued that closure will eliminate small borrowers and that foreign banks will serve only the best clients.

In fact, closure or privatization may not affect small-scale lending much and may even lead to its increase. The rhetoric of small borrowers being served by state-owned banks is often untrue, unfortunately. Various studies suggest that large borrowers often get a substantial part of state-owned bank loans, especially in rural areas, even from banks supposedly dedicated to small borrowers.[1] Attempts to subsidize small borrowing often encourage diversion of credits from small borrowers to politically connected borrowers.

Bad credit also drives out good credit. State-owned banks often channel loans at below-market rates to small borrowers and neglect collection, destroying the demand for *sustainable* rural and small and medium enterprise finance and eliminating any interest in such lending by profit-making intermediaries. Some evidence suggests that micro-credit lenders and private and foreign banks are reasonable suppliers of credit to small borrowers when the role of state-owned banks and subsidized credits is reduced. In Bangladesh, small-scale credit is offered not through state-owned banks but largely through Grameen-type operations. In India, credit to small and medium enterprises has grown much faster among foreign banks than among state-owned banks. In Argentina, Chile, and Peru, foreign banks do at least as well as local banks in providing small-scale credit.[2] The role of foreign banks may reflect their technology for managing small-scale credit; in the United States, for example, the cost of making a small-scale loan has fallen below $15. Finally, private banks specializing in small-scale credit have expanded rapidly after the decline of state-owned banks, for example, in Ecuador (Cred-iFe) and Peru (MiBanco). Thus removing state-owned banks' credit from the market will create demand for sustainable small-scale lending and allow its providers to expand.

The sustainable expansion of credit access can be supported by improved information on borrowers and better creditors' rights. Better information on borrowers not only

when "loans" are not repaid. In the agency approach, the payments to recipients are treated as public expenditures and reviewed annually as part of the budget process. The review depends on the quality of the budget process. The agency could, of course, make loans, not expenditures. However, an agency may have even less ability to collect its loans than a public sector bank, as Cull and Xu suggest was the case in China.[81] Since no deposits are taken by an agency, there is less disruption of deposit taking by private banks and more possibility of market dis-

81. Cull and Xu (2000).

cuts the costs of lending but also provides an incentive for borrowers to repay in order to maintain an intangible asset—their credit rating. Attempts to improve information on borrowers are growing in many developing countries. For example, twenty-three developing countries—mostly transition countries—have established public credit bureaus since 1994. In many other countries public and private credit bureaus are being improved. The legal and judicial framework, particularly with regard to the definition and execution of collateral and bankruptcy, also is important to credit access. Again, a viable threat to execute collateral, which state-owned banks often cannot do politically even in the presence of a good legal and judicial framework, provides an incentive for prompt debt service.

Finally, sustainable institutions for small-scale lending need to follow a few key principles:

—Collect on loans.

—Charge enough to cover costs.

—Encourage staff to reduce costs.

—Select borrowers well and collect loans.

—Provide deposit services, thereby reducing dependence on donors.

—Provide transparent information on accounts, clientele, and any subsidies.[3]

Institutions that follow these principles will contribute to sustainable access to credit; institutions that do not will tend to attract nontarget borrowers and reduce the development of sustainable access to credit. Although some state institutions have followed these principles—notably Bank Rakyat Indonesia's Unit Desa program and Thailand's Bank for Agriculture and Agricultural Cooperatives—private institutions are likely to be more successful in their application than public institutions.[4]

1. See, for example, Adams, Graham, and Von Pischke (1984); Adams and Vogel (1986); Von Pischke, Adams, and Donald (1983); Yaron, Benjamin, and Piprek (1997).

2. Clarke and others (2004).

3. Yaron, Benjamin, and Piprek (1997).

4. Robinson (2001, 2002); Yaron, Benjamin, and Piprek (1997).

cipline for the other banks. Some other provision may need to be made to provide deposit and payments services.

A third approach is to replace a state-owned bank with a narrow savings bank, holding only government debt as assets. This approach avoids the main problem of public sector banks: future nonperforming loans. It may be especially applicable when the "good" bank that is left after the usual restructuring approach has a large share of public sector debt and only a limited amount of loans. For example, in Indonesia in 2000—an extreme case—the state-owned banks had less than 20 percent of their assets in loans (net of provisions) and nearly 70 percent in recapitalization bonds, cash and reserves, and central bank securities; the largest (accounting for half of the state-owned banks' assets) had only 10 percent of its assets in loans (net of provisions) and about 75 percent in recapitalization bonds, cash and reserves, and central bank securities. A number of banks in transition countries also have relatively low ratios of loans to assets.[82] In effect, such banks are already nearly narrow banks. One or more could easily be converted into narrow banks by the sale or transfer of the small volume of good loans to another bank along with an equal amount of deposits; this would leave the remaining deposits and the recapitalization bonds in a narrow bank.

Narrow banks have a long intellectual history and are favored by many distinguished economists because they provide safer payment services and deposits to the public.[83] Thus the conversion of a state-owned bank into a narrow savings bank would reduce concerns that small depositors, particularly in rural areas, would lose banking and payments services—two of the three functions of banks. The narrow banks would, however, not lend to private or public enterprises, the banking function that public sector banks have done poorly.

Narrow banks have a number of advantages in addition to satisfying the need for deposit and payments services. Compared to standard, fractional-reserve banks, they are less subject to bank runs and protect the payments system.[84] Narrow banks have minimal credit risk, except in the case of sovereign default.[85] Other

---

82. Sherif, Borish, and Gross (2003).

83. Bossone (2001) provides a good review of the history of the idea. During the great depression of the 1930s in the United States, the well-known economists Henry Simons, Lloyd Mints, and Frank Knight from the University of Chicago and Irving Fisher from Yale University all argued for 100 percent reserves on demand deposits to avoid bank panics and monetary fluctuations. Milton Friedman resurrected the "Chicago Plan" in his *Program for Monetary Stability* (Friedman 1959). More recently, concerns about the impact of rapid financial innovation and the costs of banking crises have led to reconsideration of narrow banking, in, for example, Bossone (2001); Phillips (1995); Tobin (1985); and World Bank (2001).

84. Deposit runs on state-owned banks have been less frequent than on private banks and are likely to be even less likely in the case of narrow banks. A narrow bank can meet a deposit outflow by simply selling government debt or using it as loan collateral, meaning that it can get funds more easily, and at less potential cost to the authorities, than a commercial bank trying to meet a deposit outflow through a similar use of private loans. Monetary fluctuations are reduced by narrow banks, because switches into or out of currency in a narrow bank leave total currency plus deposits unchanged in the economy. In contrast, in a fractional reserve bank, switches into or out of currency tend to lead to larger changes in deposits. Regarding the payments system, narrow bank proponents typically assume that all banks will carry out their payments through narrow banks, thereby protecting the payments system. However, the increasing use of collateralized real-time gross settlement payments systems reduces the risks associated with allowing other banks to participate in the payments system.

85. In such circumstances, credit risk is also likely to rise on loans to private parties, and a narrow bank would probably suffer lower losses than a commercial bank. Exactly how such a government default would affect depositors remains an open question. The effective default on government bonds as a result of infla-

risks can be reduced by limiting their assets to government debt that is short term or has floating rates and by not allowing them to trade government debt.[86] Consequently, the deposits of narrow banks do not need guarantees or deposit insurance; they are guaranteed by assets. Thus narrow banking could also be a way of reducing the blanket guarantee of deposits that many countries have put in place during crises. Supervision of narrow banks is easy—simply by checking that the investment policy is followed and that deposits equal government bond holdings. Supervision is especially easy if the government debt market is computerized and dematerialized (with ownership by book entry), which is the international trend. Finally, narrow banks that arise during crises probably will have plenty of assets to buy in the future, since crisis countries often have large volumes of recapitalization bonds, which are likely to grow over time because of interest costs.

In practice, few narrow banks exist except postal savings banks. The best-known example is the Japanese Postal Savings Bank. This and other postal savings banks suggest that demand for narrow banks exists and that commercial banks, which could offer better returns on deposits because of the higher rates of return on assets, will not compete away all the demand for narrow bank deposits, particularly in rural areas. Postal banks and narrow banks could also benefit from better information technology, to improve the handling not only of accounts but also of remittances. One long-term issue is that public sector savings banks have often become victims of their own success: The large volume of deposits they mobilize have sometimes generated funds for financing not only central government deficits but also state and local government infrastructure projects, which have had low rates of return and encountered difficulties in repayment. To reduce the inflows, deposit rates could be lowered, but this has proved difficult to do because of the political power of depositors. Such problems are a long way off in countries in which there has been a major bank recapitalization and much of the banking system's assets already consist of public sector debt.

Few failed public sector banks have been converted into narrow banks, probably because the government usually wants to restart state-owned bank lending.

---

tion has been a more common risk than an announced default. Issuing indexed or floating-rate bonds to narrow banks would reduce this risk.

86. Limiting the portfolio of narrow banks to short-term government bonds or floating-rate government debt would reduce term transformation risk substantially. However, even if a narrow bank holds long-term, fixed-interest government bonds, it represents less risk to the authorities than the portfolio of private sector loans of a normal commercial bank. The purchase or takeover of government debt at face value by the authorities, if necessary, liquidates an equivalent amount of government debt (at face value), while the purchase or takeover of private credit entails commercial risk.

In some recent cases, failed public sector banks have been turned into quasi-narrow banks that also offer a small volume of microcredits. Two examples of this approach, which seem to be doing well, are Mongolia's AgBank and Tanzania's National Microfinance Bank, which was the rural portion of the National Bank of Commerce.[87] In both cases, the governments were concerned about the political ramifications of closing a failed state-owned bank that had provided substantial banking services to much of the population but attracted little interest from buyers. In both cases, with the support of donors, an external agency was hired to manage the bank with a contract that protected the bank from political interference. In both cases, the rural branch network proved to be an asset, and improved technology allowed easier access to deposits. New loans were kept small—in the case of the National Microfinance Bank, the average size was less than $400, or about 1.5 times the national income. The volume of loans grew sharply, but arrears were minimal. In both cases, the government continues to search for a private buyer. This approach represents another possible solution to the problem of maintaining access to banking services when a rural state-owned bank fails. Critical to turning a failed state-owned bank into a microcredit institution is whether this institution continues to collect or whether it reverts to past high levels of nonperforming loans if a new wave of populism develops.

Conclusions

State-owned banks continue to dominate banking for the majority of people in developing countries, despite the substantial privatizations that have occurred in Latin America, the transition countries, and to a lesser degree, Africa. State banks have performed poorly in terms of nonperforming loans and costs. Cross-country evidence suggests that countries with a large state bank presence have slower financial and economic development, other things being equal.

This poor performance reflects the multiple objectives facing state-owned banks, government intervention in credit decisions and collection, lack of incentives for sound information and sound lending, and the public's culture of nonpayment with respect to public sector banks, not to speak of corruption. Serial restructurings typically have not worked because of the failure to address these problems. In the few restructurings that have succeeded, even partially, governments have set well-defined objectives that could be monitored (typically privatization within a short time); hired managers with excellent reputations and paid

---

87. Dressen, Dyer, and Northrip (2002).

them reasonably well by international standards; improved the banks' information framework for monitoring the objectives; and avoided interventions or requests unrelated to the preset objectives.

Bank privatizations have been a response to the high costs of the public sector bank approach and the shift in ideology to a more market-based approach, particularly in Latin America and the transition countries. Bank privatization has proved difficult in many cases, however, particularly when foreign banks were excluded from the bidding and politically well-connected domestic groups took advantage of the privatizations to gain access to banks for non-arm's-length loans to related companies. Despite these difficulties, privatization has yielded substantial benefits when done well, especially in sales to well-known international banks that provided better risk management and were willing to cover any problems. Concerns that such privatizations will reduce credit to small borrowers may be overstated; in Latin America, for example, such banks have done reasonably well in terms of lending to small borrowers. Moreover, with the bad credit of public sector banks no longer driving out good credit, countries have seen sustainable increases in access to credit by a variety of institutions.

National governance seems important in attracting well-known international banks to bid in the sale of public sector banks. Transition countries were able to sell many of their state-owned banks to international banks, which sought a foothold in countries that would join the European Union; the attraction of Mexico's banks was increased by NAFTA. Some Latin American and African countries have also benefited from the desire of international banks to expand. However, in many areas, concerns about state intervention and legal systems have discouraged purchasers from buying public sector banks.

Preparations for privatization, or even restructuring, would benefit from strengthening the regulatory and supervisory framework, the information framework that can support market discipline, and the general legal framework. These elements are important in limiting risks if privatizations cannot be made to well-known international banks. They will also help in expanding access to credit. When public sector banks have proved costly but privatizations have proved difficult, countries have tried alternatives such as closing state-owned banks with a long history of failures, replacing state-owned banks with agencies of the government that disburse funds but do not take deposits and are subject to budget discipline, and replacing state banks with variants of narrow banks that provide deposit and payments services to underserved areas but limit assets to government recapitalization bonds and microcredits. Better technology can help to reduce costs and provide better service in narrow institutions.

References

Adams, Dale, Douglas Graham, and J. D. Von Pischke, eds. 1984. *Undermining Rural Development with Cheap Credit.* Boulder, Colo.: Westview Press.

Adams, Dale, and Robert Vogel. 1986. "Rural Financial Markets in Developing Countries: Recent Controversies and Lessons." *World Development* 14, no. 4: 477–87.

Andrews, Michael, and Mats Josefsson. 2003. "What Happens after Supervisory Intervention? Considering Bank Closure Options." Working Paper WP/03/17. Washington: International Monetary Fund.

Barth, James, Gerard Caprio, and Ross Levine. 2001a. "Banking Systems around the Globe: Do Regulation and Ownership Affect Performance and Stability?" In *Prudential Supervision: What Works and What Doesn't,* edited by Frederic Mishkin, pp. 31–96. University of Chicago Press.

———. 2001b. *The Regulation and Supervision of Banks around the World: A New Data Base.* Policy Research Paper 2588. Washington: World Bank.

Beck, Thorsten, Juan Miguel Crivelli, and William Summerhill. 2003. "State Bank Transformation in Brazil: Choices and Consequences." Paper presented at the World Bank conference on bank privatization, Washington, November 20–21 (www.worldbank.org/research/projects/bank_privatization_conference.htm [June 30, 2004]).

Beck, Thorsten, Robert Cull, and Afeikhena Jerome. 2003. "Bank Privatization and Performance: Empirical Evidence from Nigeria." Paper presented at the World Bank conference on bank privatization, Washington, November 20–21 (www.worldbank.org/research/projects/bank_privatization_conference.htm [June 30, 2004]).

Boehmer, Ekkehart, Robert Nash, and Jeffry Netter. 2003. "Bank Privatization in Developed and Developing Countries: Cross-Sectional Evidence on the Impact of Economic and Political Factors." Paper presented at the World Bank conference on bank privatization, Washington, November 20–21 (www.worldbank.org/research/projects/bank_privatization_conference.htm [June 30, 2004]).

Bokros, Lajos. 2003. "Transforming Public Sector Banks in Central and Eastern Europe." Paper presented at the World Bank conference on transforming public sector banks, Washington, April 9–10 (www.worldbank.org/wbi/banking/bankingsystems/psbanks/ [June 30, 2004]).

Bonin, John P., Iftekhar Hasan, and Paul Wachtel. 2003. "Privatization Matters: Bank Performance in Transition Countries." Paper presented at the World Bank conference on bank privatization, Washington, November 20–21 (www.worldbank.org/research/projects/bank_privatization_conference.htm [June 30, 2004]).

Bossone, Biagio. 2001. "Should Banks Be Narrowed?" Working Paper WP/01/159. Washington: International Monetary Fund.

Burgess, Robin, and Rohini Pande. 2004. *Do Rural Banks Matter? Evidence from the Indian Social Banking Experiment.* CEPR Discussion Paper 4211. London: London School of Economics, Centre for Economic Policy Studies.

Clarke, George, and Robert Cull. 1999. "Why Privatize? The Case of Argentina's Public Provincial Banks." *World Development* 27 (May): 865–86.

———. 2002. "Political and Economic Determinants of the Likelihood of Privatizing Argentine Banks." *Journal of Law and Economics* 45 (April): 165–99.

Clarke, George, and others. 2004. "Bank Lending to Small Businesses in Latin America: Does Bank Origin Matter?" Forthcoming in *Journal of Money, Credit, and Banking.*

Cole, David, and Betty Slade. 1996. *Building a Modern Financial System.* Cambridge University Press.

Cull, Robert, and Lixin Colin Xu. 2000. "Bureaucrats, State Banks, and the Efficiency of Credit Allocation: The Experience of Chinese State-Owned Enterprises." *Journal of Comparative Economics* 28 (March): 1–31.

Dressen, Robert, Jay Dyer, and Zan Northrip. 2002. "Turning around State-Owned Banks in Underserved Markets." *Small Enterprise Development* 13 (4): 58–67.

EBRD (European Bank for Reconstruction and Development). 1999. *Transition Report.* London.

Enoch, Charles, and others. 2001. "Indonesia: Anatomy of a Banking Crisis: Two Years of Living Dangerously." IMF Working Paper WP/01/52. Washington: International Monetary Fund.

Enoch, Charles, Gillian García, and V. Sundarajan. 1999. "Recapitalizing Banks with Public Sector Funds." IMF Working Paper WP/99/139. Washington: International Monetary Fund.

Friedman, Milton. 1959. *A Program for Monetary Stability.* Fordham University Press.

Gerschenkron, Alexander. 1962. *Economic Backwardness in Historical Perspective: A Book of Essays.* Harvard University Press.

Haber, Stephen. 2003. "The Mexican Banking System, 1982–2003." Paper presented at the World Bank conference on transforming public sector banks, Washington, April 9–10 (www.worldbank.org/wbi/banking/bankingsystems/psbanks/ [June 30, 2004]).

Haber, Stephen, and Shawn Kantor. 2003. "Getting Privatization Wrong: The Mexican Banking System, 1991–2003." Paper presented at the World Bank conference on bank privatization, Washington, November 20–21 (www.worldbank.org/research/projects/bank_privatization_conference.htm [June 30, 2004]).

Hanson, James. 2001. "India and Indonesia, Contrasting Approaches to Repression and Liberalization." In *Financial Liberalization: How Far, How Fast?* edited by Gerard Caprio, Patrick Honohan, and Joseph Stiglitz, pp. 233–64. Cambridge University Press.

———. 2003. "Indian Banking: Market Liberalization and the Pressures for Institutional and Market Framework Reform." In *Reforming India's External, Financial, and Fiscal Policies,* edited by Anne Krueger and Sajjid Chinoy, pp. 97–126. Stanford University Press.

Husain, Ishrat. 2004. "Policy Considerations before Bank Privatization: Country Experience." Paper presented at the World Bank conference on the role of state-owned financial institutions—policy and practice (www.worldbank.org/wbi/banking/finsecpolicy/stateowned2004/agenda.html [July 8, 2004]).

Kang, Chungwon. 2003. "From the Front Lines at Seoul Bank: Restructuring and Reprivatization." IMF Working Paper 03/325. Washington: International Monetary Fund.

Kawalec, Stephan, and Krzysztof Kluza. 2003. "Two Models of Systemic Bank Restructuring." Paper presented at the World Bank conference on transforming public sector banks, Washington, April 9–10 (www.worldbank.org/wbi/banking/bankingsystems/psbanks/pdf/Kawalec.ppt [July 8, 2004]).

Klingebiel, Daniela. 2000. *The Use of Asset Management Companies in the Resolution of Banking Crises: Cross-Country Experience.* Policy Research Paper 2284. Washington: World Bank.

Klingebiel, Daniela, and Patrick Honohan. 2002. "Controlling the Fiscal Costs of Banking Crises." Discussion Paper 428. Washington: World Bank.

La Porta, Rafael, Florencio López-de-Silanes, and Andrei Shleifer. 2000. "Government Own-ership of Banks." NBER Working Paper 7620. Cambridge, Mass.: National Bureau of Eco-nomic Research.

———. 2002. "Government Ownership of Banks." *Journal of Finance* 57 (February): 265–301.

La Porta, Rafael, Florencio López-de-Silanes, and Guillermo Zamarripa. 2003. "Related Lend-ing." *Quarterly Journal of Economics* 118 (February): 231–68.

Mozes, Dan. 2003. "Commercial Banks: Privatization Lessons from Sub-Saharan African Countries." Paper presented at the World Bank conference on transforming public sector banks, Washington, April 9–10 (www.worldbank.org/wbi/banking/bankingsystems/psbanks/ [July 8, 2004]).

Ochere, Isaac. 2003. "Do Privatized Banks in Middle- and Low-Income Countries Perform Better than Rival Banks? An Intra-Industry Analysis of Privatization." Paper presented at the World Bank conference on bank privatization, Washington, November 20–21 (www.worldbank.org/research/projects/bank_privatization_conference.htm [June 30, 2004]).

Phillips, Ronnie J. 1995. *Narrow Banking Reconsidered: The Functional Approach to Financial Reform.* Policy Brief 17. Annandale-on-Hudson: Bard College, Jerome Levy Economics Institute.

Preston, Julia, and Samuel Dillon. 2004. *Opening Mexico.* New York: Farrar, Straus, and Giroux.

Remini, Robert V. 1967. *Andrew Jackson and the Bank War.* New York: Norton.

Robinson, Marguerite. 2001. *The Microfinance Revolution.* Vol. 1: *Sustainable Finance for the Poor.* Washington: World Bank.

———. 2002. *The Microfinance Revolution.* Vol. 2: *Lessons from Indonesia.* Washington: World Bank.

Sarkar, Jayati. 1999. "India's Banking Sector: Current Status, Emerging Challenges, and Policy Imperatives in a Globalized Environment." In *India: A Financial System for the Twenty-First Century*, edited by James Hanson and Sanjay Kathuria, pp. 71–131. Oxford University Press.

Sen, Kunal, and Rajendra Vaidya. 1997. *The Process of Financial Liberalization in India.* Oxford: University Press.

Sheng, Andrew. 1996. "Banking Fragility in the 1980s: An Overview." In *Bank Restructuring: Lessons from the 1980s,* edited by Andrew Sheng, pp. 5–24. Washington: World Bank.

Sherif, Khaled, Michael Borish, and Alexandra Gross. 2003. *State-Owned Banks in the Transi-tion: Origins, Evolution, and Policy Response.* Washington: World Bank.

Shleifer, Andrei. 1998. "State versus Private Ownership." *Journal of Economic Perspectives* 12 (Fall): 133–50.

Soomro, Zubyr. 2003. "Driving Change: The Restructuring of United Bank Limited." Paper presented to the World Bank conference on transforming public sector banks, Washington, April 9–10 (www.worldbank.org/wbi/banking/bankingsystems/psbanks/ [June 30, 2004]).

Tandon, Prakash. 1989. *Banking Century: A Short History of Banking in India and the Pioneer: Punjab National Bank.* India: Penguin Press.

Tang, Helena, Edda Zoli, and Irina Klytchnikova. 2000. *Banking Crises in Transition Eco-nomies: Fiscal Costs and Related Issues.* Policy Research Paper 2484. Washington: World Bank.

Tobin, James. 1985. "Financial Innovation and Deregulation in Perspective." *Bank of Japan Monetary and Economic Studies* 3, no. 2: 19–29.

Verma, Shri M. S. 2000. *Report of the Working Group on Restructuring and Strengthening Weak Public Sector Banks.* Mumbai: Reserve Bank of India.

Von Pischke, J., D. Adams, and G. Donald, eds. 1983. *Rural Financial Markets in Developing Countries.* Johns Hopkins Press for the World Bank.

World Bank. 1989. *World Development Report 1989: Financial Systems and Development.* Washington.

———. 1995. *Bureaucrats in Business.* New York: Oxford University Press for the World Bank.

———. 1997. *Indonesia: Sustaining High Growth with Equity.* 16433 IND. Washington.

———. 1998. *Argentina Financial System Review.* 17864-ARG. Washington.

———. 2001. *Finance for Growth: Policy Choices in a Volatile World.* Oxford University Press for the World Bank.

Yaron, Jacob, McDonald P. Benjamin, and Gerda L. Piprek. 1997. *Rural Finance: Issues, Design, and Best Practices.* Environmentally and Socially Sustainable Development Studies and Monographs series 14. Washington: World Bank.

Zoli, Edda. 2001. "Cost and Effectiveness of Banking Sector Restructuring in Transition Economies." IMF Working Paper 01/157. Washington: International Monetary Fund.

DAVID MARSTON
ADITYA NARAIN

3

Observations from an International Monetary Fund Survey

T HE STATE HAS a major presence in the financial sector of many countries around the world. This is particularly visible in banking, where despite several privatization initiatives over the last decade, public sector banks are still estimated to account for a significant portion of total banking sector assets.[1]

State intervention, however, is not confined to ownership in banking but also extends, albeit in a lesser degree, to insurance and contractual savings schemes. Further, though state intervention is often more prominent in the developing world, it can also play an important role in the developed world, taking a variety of different forms from direct presence, such as banking in Germany, to indirect presence, such as government-sponsored enterprises in the United States (box 3-1).

In the course of their country work, the staff of the International Monetary Fund (IMF) regularly faces issues of how state-owned financial institutions should be dealt with, given the overwhelming perception of these institutions as being inefficient and a fiscal drag. The resulting "wisdom" is that privatization is the route to efficiency and more effective supervision. Notwithstanding, and even after the spate of privatizations in the 1970s, state-owned financial institutions continue to play significant roles in financial stability—from being a catalyst to a crisis in Turkey to being a stabilizing force in Russia.

---

1. See, for example, data on the "percentage of bank assets government owned" for the 107 countries tabulated in Barth, Caprio, and Levine (2001).

Box 3-1. *State Intervention in the Financial Sector in the United States*

In the United States the intervention of the state in the financial sector takes the form of direct loans and guarantees as well as government-sponsored private enterprises. The range of intervention and the public perception of these programs is summarized in this extract from the U.S. budget document for fiscal year 2003:

> Federal credit programs offer direct loans and loan guarantees for a wide range of activities, primarily housing, education, business and rural development, and exports. At the end of 2001 there were $242 billion in Federal direct loans outstanding and $1,084 billion in loan guarantees. Through its insurance programs, the Federal Government insures bank, thrift, and credit union deposits up to $100,000, guarantees private defined-benefit pensions, and insures against other risks such as natural disasters.
>
> The Federal Government also enhances credit availability for targeted sectors indirectly through Government-sponsored enterprises (GSEs)—privately owned companies and cooperatives that operate under Federal charters. GSEs provide direct loans and increase liquidity by guaranteeing and securitizing loans. Some GSEs have become major players in the financial market. In 2001 the face value of GSE lending totaled $3.1 trillion. In return for serving social purposes, GSEs enjoy some privileges, which include eligibility of their securities to collateralize public deposits and be held in unlimited amounts by most banks and thrifts, exemption of their securities from SEC registration, exemption of their earnings from State and local income taxation, and ability to borrow from Treasury, at Treasury's discretion, in amounts ranging up to $4 billion. These privileges leave many people with the impression that their securities are risk-free. GSEs, however, are not part of the Federal Government, and their securities are not federally guaranteed. By law the GSEs' securities carry a disclaimer of any U.S. obligation.[1]

The reasons given for state intervention are information opaqueness (for example, about start-up businesses and farmers), externalities (the fact that people may invest less

Over and above privatization, a quick survey of news headlines over a few months' time (October 2003 to March 2004) reveals a spectrum of issues with regard to state-owned financial institutions: the recapitalization of banks using central bank reserves (China), government-sponsored housing enterprises and concerns over their supervisory framework (United States), the buyback of the equity of state-owned banks and the merger of development bands with state-owned banks (India), proposed mergers of development banks (Jamaica, Thailand, Taiwan, Indonesia, and Iran), and the threatened lowering of ratings of state-owned banks (Germany).

than socially optimal amounts in activities that generate positive externalities and over-invest in those that generate negative externalities), resource constraints (of the private sector, for example, in deposit insurance), and imperfect competition (because of barriers to entry, economies of scale, and foreign intervention). In the U.S. context, the main rationale for the federal role is to "provide credit and insurance that private markets would not provide."

A host of government departments and programs and government-sponsored enterprises are involved in the administration of these programs and their oversight—the Department of Housing and Urban Development; the Department of Veterans Affairs; Fannie Mae, Freddie Mac, and the Federal Home Loan Bank system; the Department of Education and Sallie Mae; the Small Business Administration, Farmer Mac, and the Farm Credit Administration; the Departments of Agriculture, Defense, State, and Treasury, and the Agency for International Development; the Overseas Private Investment Corporation and the Export-Import Bank; the Federal Deposit Insurance Corporation; the Pension Benefit Guarantee Corporation; the Federal Emergency Management Agency; and the Risk Management Agency. The scope and content of these programs is substantial, so much so that the Budget Document of fiscal year 1998 mentions that "the Federal government continues to be the largest financial institution in the United States."

Concern has been expressed about the exponential growth in the contingent liabilities of some government-sponsored enterprises, especially in the housing finance and pension segments, and calls for capping these have been reported in the press. At the same time, there is also discussion on the strengthening of the supervisory arrangements for some of these agencies, following accounting irregularities in one of the largest of these enterprises.

1. U.S. Office of Management and Budget (2003, p. 177).

While information failures, externalities, economic disequilibrium, failure of competition, incomplete markets, institution building, and the need to redistribute resources according to the social agenda (serving the underserved) are often the rationale for intervention by the state, its detractors remain unconvinced.[2]

2. U.S. Office of Management and Budget (2003) (www.whitehouse.gov/omb/budget/fy2003). Budget documents contain an informative account of the rationale for state intervention in the financial sector. See, for instance, chapter 8 of the 1998 budget document ("Analytical Perspectives"). For a discussion on the adverse effects of state ownership, see International Monetary Fund (1998, chapter 3) and Carmichael (2002).

They see state ownership as creating market distortions, thwarting competitive forces, limiting supervisory effectiveness, clouding the budgetary process, leading to frequent recapitalization, and increasing the scope for patronage and corruption (serving the undeserved). In any case, the state can always intervene directly through the budget process to address market failures instead of seeking ownership of financial institutions and then lending through them.

Many reasons have been offered as to why the state chooses to "own" a financial institution—for instance, private sector institutions may not have developed, or the state may want to directly control the outcomes (that is, to make a political statement).[3] While many institutions have been created specifically for the purpose of lending to priority regions or activities or of offering subsidized insurance to vulnerable target groups, there have also been waves of nationalization of private sector institutions, particularly in the decolonization phases, when the attempt may have been in part to reduce the economic concentration of power. Although there has been a gradual return of ownership to the private sector, particularly in Europe and Latin America, the state will continue to be a dominant player in the financial sector for some time to come.

The IMF Survey

Against this background, in October 2003 the IMF conducted a survey of the structures, relationships, and incentives that affect the performance, supervision, and governance of state-owned financial institutions.[4] The research agenda did not address the issue of ownership but rather recognized these institutions as a fact of the financial landscape. It sought to answer the following questions: Do these institutions have a competitive advantage over the private sector in terms of funding? Are they subject to less effective supervision? Are their governance policies intrinsically weak? Staff experience has been that oversight arrangements vary markedly among institutions, and the research agenda therefore aimed at developing good practice guidance on oversight, which would better inform the work of the IMF.

The survey sought responses from a large group of member countries on all state-owned financial institutions, whether commercial and specialized development banks and nonbanks, insurance companies, or contractual savings and investment schemes, such as mutual, investment, provident, and pension funds. Keeping in mind that the influence of ownership could be exercised by the state, even in the absence of a majority stake, *state owned* was defined as "any share-

---

3. See chapter by Manal Fouad and others, this volume, for a discussion of the rationale for state ownership of banks.
4. See appendix to this chapter for the format of the survey.

holding arrangement by which the state (central, state, local, or other elected body) or any entity of the state has a controlling ownership interest or a minority that allows the state to exercise management control." Information was sought from national authorities on the following broad areas: types of institution and activity, ownership structures, policy goals, funding arrangements, supervision and oversight, and governance arrangements.

Of the twenty-five countries that responded, three countries reported no state-owned institutions.[5] The remaining twenty-two countries reported 678 institutions in all three broad segments—banking, insurance, and securities and investments—though commercial banking was by far the most significant.

In the following discussion, some of the results of the survey are presented. However, there are some very important caveats to be kept in mind while interpreting these results. First, the sample is actually by default based on those countries that responded to the survey in time, and hence these results should not be taken to be representative of the universe. For instance, of the 680 reported institutions, one developed country reported 520 banking institutions owned by the local and state governments, which would tend to give a skewed picture of such institutions in the developed world. As data for these were presented on an aggregate basis, these institutions have not been taken into account even though they represent many of the responses.

Second, in some cases the responses are incomplete, that is, the authorities contacted reported only on the institutions supervised by them or under their regulatory influence. As the contact agencies in most cases were the central banks and bank supervisors, the number of institutions, especially nonbanks, may have been underreported. In addition, several other factors likely inhibited or delayed the authorities' responses. The first is possible apprehensions that the survey results might be used to promote the privatization agenda of the international financial institutions, since this has often been an important component of the advice of the IMF and the World Bank. A second reason is simply that no single agency has all of the information, and it would require a coordinated effort among many agencies to obtain this information.

The Landscape of State-Owned Financial Institutions

State-owned financial institutions were found to be prevalent in many areas of financial activity, although commercial banking was dominant (and the most

5. Australia, Bahrain, Bolivia, Brazil, Bulgaria, Chile, China, Costa Rica, Cyprus, Denmark, Egypt, Germany, Greece, Guyana, Kenya, Latvia, Macau SAR, Mauritius, Netherlands, New Zealand, Portugal, Singapore, Spain, Russia, and Turkey.

Table 3-1. *State-Owned Financial Institutions in Responding Countries,*
IMF Survey

Institution	Advanced economies		Emerging or developing economies		Total	
	Insti-tutions	Countries	Insti-tutions	Countries	Insti-tutions	Countries
Commercial banks	19[a]	5	56[b]	11	75	16
Development banks	4	4	9	5	13	9
Commercial-cum-development banks	1	1	9	3	10	4
Postal banks	1	1	2	2	3	3
Nonbank finance companies	0	0	2	2	2	3
Development financial institutions	1	1	6	2	7	3
Leasing companies	0	0	2	1	2	1
Mutual guarantee companies	21	1	0	0	21	1
Insurance companies	3	2	2[c]	2	5	3
Asset management companies or funds	0	0	10	3	10	3
Mutual funds	0	0	2	1	2	1
Pension or provident funds	0	0	3	2	3	2
Investment companies or funds	0	0	4	1	4	1
Health insurance funds	0	0	1	1	1	1
Total	50[d]	. . .	108	. . .	158	. . .

a. Includes one bank providing both banking and insurance services and one bank providing banking, insurance, and asset management services.

b. Includes four banks providing banking and asset management services and one bank providing banking, insurance, and securities services.

c. Includes one reinsurance company.

d. Excludes 520 savings banks owned by state and local governments reported by one country for which aggregated data were reported.

discussed). Further, these institutions are features in both the developed and developing countries in the sample, although in the former, their presence was only in the banking and insurance sectors (table 3-1). Among banking institutions, some were reported as banks, others as development banks, and in five countries, as institutions engaged in both commercial and development banking.

The assets of the institutions varied from insignificant to 159 percent of gross domestic product (GDP). Among the different types of institution, banks tended to have the most assets as a percentage of GDP (with one bank reported as having assets of 47 percent of GDP). The largest reported development bank had assets equal to 13 percent of GDP; the insurance company had assets equal to 2.9 percent; the development financial institution, 2.3 percent; and the pension fund, 18 percent. (The size of the assets under the management of asset management companies was not given.)

Of the responses in which institution-level data were provided, about half were fully owned by the state (40 percent by the central government and less than 10 percent by state or local government). Another 20 percent were majority owned by the central government (with the stake ranging from 50 percent to 99 percent) and 20 percent majority owned by the state government. In the remaining 10 percent, the government held a minority stake but held control over management.

Only nine institutions in three countries were reported to be nationalized private sector institutions. All others were set up in the public sector with specific objectives. In the case of banks, these objectives ranged from benefiting a particular region, trade, or activity (small- and medium-size enterprises, artisans, and tradesmen) to a focus on agriculture, trade, encouragement of thrift, housing, and even collection of judicial deposits. In the case of development banks the objectives ranged from general economic development to development of infrastructure, middle- and low-income housing, and international trade. The development financial institutions had been set up for the support of specific sectors such as industry, agriculture, housing, and tourism. Insurance companies included general insurance, reinsurance, and export credit insurance. Mutual guarantee companies specialized in providing financial guarantees to their participant partners and focused on specific regions or sectors of activity. (The government reinsures the majority of transactions under public policy programs.) Investment funds were mainly linked to social safety nets such as health insurance and retirement, while the nature of business of the asset management funds or companies was not specified.

Below is a sampling of the objectives of the institutions, as laid out in the authorizing or acquiring law.

—Commercial banks: To support the economic development of the country; to take money from juridical and natural persons and to allocate them; to establish conditions for the implementation of the regional economic and social programs; to direct lending to the priority industries and the population; to order the financial and economic relations between enterprises, establishments, organizations, financial institutions, state bodies, financial flows, and the region's budget; to ensure timely receipt of tax payments; to undertake mortgage lending and issue of mortgage bonds; to participate in the realization of national investment policy in priority sectors of the economy; to earn profits; to receive and grant loans on behalf and by order of the government; to create a system of financing and lending to producers of the agroindustrial sector; to liven the work of the administration on capital markets; to make operations with budget accounts of the district and local authorities; to develop progressive forms of the external economic links to widen the export potential; to ensure the equilibrium of the balance of payments and increase the efficiency of public production; to support artisans, tradesmen, and small and medium enterprises; to stimulate public savings; and to collect and manage deposits imposed by the law or by the courts.

—Postal banks: To grant loans to the public sector; to encourage savings by households; to protect small depositors; and to support the government housing policies by granting subsidized housing loans.

—Development banks: To promote the state's economy by ensuring credit to all economic sectors; to promote productive activities in the region; to specialize in medium- to long-term operations; to provide fixed and working capital; to offer guarantees and direct technical assistance for the preparation and capacitation of personnel specializing in the execution of projects aiming at the social and economic development of the state; to further financing according to state commission; to make loans to the public sector; to support the country's development policies by extending loans to joint stock companies; to channel savings in the country and abroad toward development-oriented investments; to contribute to the improvement of the capital markets; to support infrastructure investments and other investments of the municipalities; to favor the development of the national economic activities; to serve as the financial arm of the development policy of the state; to provide exclusive management of consignations; to support of government's housing policies by granting residence loans to government employees; to provide asset management services to other public entities; and to provide second-floor operations to private financial entities.

—Development financial institutions: To develop small- and medium-size enterprises countrywide; to provide agricultural credit to farmers; to finance tourism; to provide loans and grants of public moneys for the construction of dwellings; and to grant loans for housing purposes, with priority given to persons of middle or low income.

—Insurance companies: To act as an insurer in respect to the assets and prospective liabilities of the state and statutory corporations; to transact workers' compensation insurance; to administer a motor accident compensation scheme; to carry out functions in relation to the management and control of moneys and other assets of the state and statutory corporations; and to create a local reinsurance capacity.

—Export credit agencies: To improve exports, diversification of exported goods and services, causing exportation to enter into new markets; to provide exporters and overseas contractors with support for increasing the competitiveness and security in international markets; and to support and encourage overseas investments and production and sale of export-oriented capital goods.

—Health fund: To support the development of an efficient and equitable health care system by providing affordable, accessible health insurance.

—Asset management companies: To mobilize investment and to make operations on the securities market.

The multitude of objectives assigned to just one state-owned financial institution is shown in box 3-2.

Issues of Competition and Financial Relations

Among the many reasons that state-owned financial institutions are seen to thwart competition is that they are perceived to have a funding advantage over the private sector on account of their access to the deep pockets of their owner, often through concealed subsidies and transfers that can bail them out of trouble. This often implicit and sometimes explicit guarantee allows them to access funding at cheaper rates. Governments recognize this contingent liability, but this is not often reflected in their budgetary estimates. Besides, particularly in the case of banks, they are often the preferred bankers for the state, receiving both deposits and government business. Though the survey does not address these issues primarily, the responses provide an insight into some of these issues and are discussed in this section.

While commercial banks, as well as commercial-cum-development banks, rely mainly on retail deposits as their main funding sources, 90 percent of development banks have no retail deposits. Two development banks, however, report around 40 percent exposure to retail deposits, clouding the distinction between development banks and commercial banks and presenting a situation in which the rationale for the regulation for both could be the same. In addition, one reinsurance company, one investment company, and three development financial institutions also report high (more than 70 percent) retail deposits. Development banks rely more than these others on wholesale deposits and long-term borrowings from the treasury and central bank as their major funding source. In addition, direct government grants are reported as funding sources for commercial banks (two countries), for commercial and development banks (two countries), for guarantee companies (one country), and for other institutions (two countries). Far more important and widespread is the reliance on government deposits,

Box 3-2. *Public Policy Expectations and State-Owned Financial Institutions*

When state-owned financial institutions are seen as instruments to implement the state's economic and development policies, they can be entrusted with a variety of objectives. Such public policy expectations can be challenging for the management of these institutions. The objectives of a leading state-owned financial institution in one major emerging economy extracted from one response to the International Monetary Fund's survey question on policy objectives in authorizing-acquiring law is shown here (see appendix to this chapter for the survey questions):

> To help the federal government in carrying out its credit policy and aims by taking deposits of any kind; offering banking services; managing the federal lotteries; acting as pawnbroker; offering services on behalf of the federal government provided those services are of the nature of a financial institution or provided other services under agreements with other entities or companies; operating in the financial and capital markets; operating as an underwriter, broker, or dealer in the stock market, securities market, or any other capital market; operating as an issuer and manager of credit cards; operating in the foreign exchange market; operating as an insurance dealer, stocks dealer, and in the leasing market; offering services related to the incentive of culture and tourism; managing the federal government's housing and sanitation programs; managing the Government Severance Indemnity Fund for Employees; managing the funds of programs on behalf of the federal government; granting loans and financing of [a] social nature; operating in the financial and capital markets on behalf of the federal government; operating as a custody agent; and offering services of consultancy and management of economic activities, public policies, welfare, and other subjects related to its activities.

> The spectrum of objectives incorporates, other than the traditional banking, insurance, and securities, more exotic areas such as pawn broking, lottery management, sanitation, culture, and tourism. Considering that state-owned financial institutions can also suffer from mission creep in that more objectives can be added to their mandate to meet specific situations, they may often face situations in which they are guided by conflicting objectives. In this context, devising better methods to measure their performance to more accurately reflect their goals can be as challenging as managing and supervising their multifaceted operations.

which are reported by banks and development banks in nine countries but which are more significant in development banks (up to 65 percent of the total) than in commercial banks (up to 3 percent of the total).

In a few cases, the state provides explicit guarantees for the liabilities of these institutions. While one country offers full coverage for all deposits of the state-owned banks, another country covers retail deposits in full for four of the nine-teen state-owned banks it reports and for medium-term notes, marketable bonds, and commercial paper issued by two other banks; while two countries offer this coverage for the deposits held before the takeover of acquired banks. In the case of development banks, two countries explicitly guarantee retail and wholesale deposits as well as bond and other borrowings of development banks, while one country each covers the retail deposits of its postal bank, commercial-cum-development bank, and development financial institution.

Policy lending is an important feature, though in what could be a conflict of interests, bank supervisors are at times used for monitoring policy targets. Sixty-one institutions (including thirteen institutions operating as commercial banks) report receiving annual or periodic policy targets from the government. These tar-gets are monitored regularly, with periods varying from one week to one year and by different bodies—the concerned ministry (ministry of property, development, industry, foreign trade, foreign affairs, science and technology, and any other min-istry that allocated the resources for the institution); the board of directors, the Securities and Exchange Commission, the audit court, and in several cases (eigh-teen institutions in five countries), bank supervisors or the central bank. Again, in many cases, the performance is monitored jointly by more than one agency.

Transfers to the institutions from the state are often off the budget and non-transparent. Nine institutions report receiving annual or periodic funds from the government, all of them itemized in the government budget. Another forty-one institutions (in eleven countries) report receiving government funds only under "infrequent special conditions"; of these, thirteen (in five countries) report that the funds are not itemized in the government budget.

State-owned financial institutions are also used for raising finances for the gov-ernment. Of the thirty-four institutions reporting government bonds as an area of activity, twenty have an exposure less that 10 percent of assets, nine between 10 and 50 percent, and five (three banks and two postal banks) greater than 50 percent. In addition, of the thirty-six institutions reporting average net prof-its transferred to the government, nearly half report a transference of more than one-third.

Though the majority of the institutions were intended to be run on a for-profit basis, with the rest to be run on a zero-cost basis, nearly one-third of all institutions for which individual data are available report a loss in at least one of the three previous years. Capital injections are fairly widespread and not infre-quent and take many forms, such as subscriptions of shares, reinvestment of div-idends receivable, issue of shares in lieu of dividends, fiscal appropriation, issues of special government bonds, transfers from the concerned ministry, grants, assumption of debts (banks), and assumption of losses (insurance). Of seventy-one for-profit institutions, eighteen report losses in one or more of the three previous years and forty-one report capital injections. Of eleven zero-cost institutions, six report losses and ten report capital injections.

As many as sixty-three institutions report capital injections since inception (thirty-two banks, nine development banks, eight commercial-cum-development banks, one postal bank, four development financial institutions, three insurance and guarantee companies, three asset management companies, and one export credit agency. In forty-two cases the most recent injection took place in the period 2000–03, while in thirty-seven cases there had been more than one capital injection in the past, including in nineteen banks, one postal bank, five development banks, eight commercial-cum-development banks, two asset management companies, two development financial institutions, and two insurance companies.

It could be argued that because the state has a history of bailing out its financial institutions in times of distress and because many of these institutions are used to effect policy lending or investment, institution managers are encouraged to engage in riskier lending and investing behavior—which could be reflected in a higher level of nonperforming loans. When this behavior is combined with the desire of the state to minimize the reported cost of operating these institutions to meet its own budgetary needs, lower provisioning for nonperforming loans could be the result. According to the survey data,
     —Twenty-seven of the institutions have 0–5 percent nonperforming loans.
     —Twenty-one have 5–10 percent.
     —Twelve have 10–20 percent.
     —Eight have 20–50 percent.
     —Three have over 50 percent.
Of more interest is the level of provisioning coverage:
     —Seven of the institutions have 0–5 percent coverage.
     —Twelve have 5–10 percent.
     —Eight have 10–20 percent.
     —Nine have 20–50 percent.
     —Thirty-nine have over 50 percent.
No solid conclusions should be drawn from the data above (except that managing credit risk remains challenging for state-owned financial institutions) in the absence of comparative private sector data and given that there may be a difference in classification, provisioning, and taxation regimes. However, one-third of state-owned financial institutions report nonperforming loans higher than 10 percent, while a similar proportion also show that their provisioning covers less than half of these loans.

Issues in Supervision and Governance

Most state-owned financial institutions are subject to some form of minimum prudential standards. The exception to this are two postal banks, three development
banks, the two mutual funds, the two pension funds, and the four investment
companies. While the standards are prescribed under the relevant banking laws for
state-owned banks, for one postal bank it was the state corporations act and for
development banks it varied among the law incorporating the institution, legislative decrees, the companies act, special resolutions or regulations of the central
bank, the central bank act, or the banking law or its amendments. For insurance
companies, it was mainly the insurance act; for guarantee companies, it was a special act; for development financial institutions it was a state corporations act; and
for the nonbank company, it was the central bank law combined with federal law.

The responses suggest that in many countries the approaches to supervision or
regulation applicable to commercial banks are being carried over to development
banks and development financial institutions and that in most cases the supervision of these entities was entrusted to the banking supervisor. For instance, most
development banks—like their commercial banking counterparts—are subject
to risk-weighted capital requirements. However, practices are not as uniform in
other aspects; for instance, even though many development banks are subject to
some form of borrower exposure limit, this limit is not always linked to the
entity's equity. In some cases, the limit is an absolute amount; in some cases, it is
determined by budgetary laws or internal resolutions or estimates. On the other
hand, mutual guarantee companies are subject to regulation identical to banks
and are also supervised by the bank supervisor, as are three development financial
institutions.

The plethora of agencies involved in the oversight of state-owned financial
institutions could lead to conflicting interests and coordination issues. For banks,
compliance with regulations is most often supervised by the banking supervisor.
In addition, in many cases, performance targets are also monitored by the supervisor, a situation that could create a conflict of interest. In one of the two countries reporting the biggest sector, the authorities for monitoring compliance with
the standards are, in addition to the bank supervisory agency, the ministry of
finance, national auditors, and the foreign exchange administration. In the other
country, compliance is monitored by the supervisory agency and by the state government (for banks) and the ministry of finance with the ministries of economy
and labor (for the development bank). In another case, compliance with the standards for the development bank is monitored by the banking supervisor at the
request of the ministry of finance, although the final responsibility lies with the

ministry. For the one postal bank, the relevant agencies are the ministry of finance and the office of the president. For some nonbanks, compliance is monitored by the administrative ministry (the ministries of finance or economy or the concerned ministry for development financial institutions, such as tourism and agriculture). For insurance companies, the supervisor is the insurance supervisory agency, except in two cases, in which it is the treasury in one case and a combination of a private auditor, the economy ministry, and a parliamentary tribunal in the other.

Regulatory forbearance is more likely to be implicit rather than explicit. Exemption from banking law is specifically provided only in a few cases, involving development banks and postal banks. Further, supervisory standards could differ between state-owned enterprises and their private sector counterparts. Although in most cases in which institutions are subject to prudential standards, they are reported to be subject to the same standards as their counterparts in the private sector; some countries report that different standards are applied to state-owned financial institutions. This ranges from banks, including development banks (one country), postal savings banks (one country), commercial-cum-development banks (one country), funds under public sector management (two countries), insurance agencies (one country), and development financial institutions (one country). Other responses are nuanced, with a country with major state-owned financial institution presence indicating that "while the supervisory principles were the same, the standards may differ among different types of institutions."

Even in cases in which development banks are subject to supervision by the supervisory agency, one supervisor states that the supervisors could "only draw the attention of the bank to the developments concerned and try and find a solution in consultation with the Ministry of Finance, which could take corrective action," while another states that they would "take minor action while leaving stronger action to the Ministry of Finance." Of course, in the case of postal banks and those development banks and development financial institutions that are not subject to supervision, no corrective action is available to the supervisors. On the issue of whether the supervisor has to consult with the government before taking corrective action, one country states that this is so in case of "severe punishment" measures; two others report that this is necessary for their banks; another for the supervised postal bank; and in one case for a commercial-cum-development bank.

On-site inspections are a regular feature at the banks and insurance companies. Only one bank reports no on-site supervision (supervisors rely on off-site surveillance for all banks in that country). In addition, one development bank that is otherwise supervised reports that it is not inspected on site, although all other development banks and development financial institutions are inspected regularly by their supervisors. While regular audits by external auditors are required in all cases, in several nonbank institutions this is performed by an arm of the state, most often the comptroller and auditor general (one postal bank, one commercial-cum-development bank, five development financial institutions, two insurance companies, and all the funds). In addition, in one country fiscal authorities audit all asset management companies, while in another the audit office of the banking association audits its numerous state-owned savings banks. The way external auditors are chosen varies across countries and institutions: sometimes the appointing authority is the annual general meeting of the shareholders, sometimes it is the owner; sometimes selection is by open competition, by public bidding, by the audit committee of the supervisory board from a list approved by the central bank, or by the bank supervisor. In the case of asset management companies in one country, the results are not disclosed, although authorities agree in principle that the results should be disclosed at the right time. The report of independent auditors is not disclosed in many cases, although the opinion on the annual accounts is presented without the report's being disclosed.

Overall, the responses suggest that governance practices leave room for improvement. Twenty-seven institutions (including thirteen banks, four development banks, and three commercial-cum-development banks) do not have any form of nongovernmental representation on their boards. With a few exceptions, most of these are fully owned by the state. However, twenty-one fully owned institutions do have nongovernmental representation on the board.

A variety of responses were received for the appointing authority for senior management, among them the general assembly of the shareholders, the board of directors, the supervisory board, the advisory board, the office of the president, the prime minister, the governor, the ministry of finance, the concerned ministry; or royal decree. While in the case of commercial banks, the supervisor is almost always consulted before the appointment of proposed senior managers, this is not often the case (as reported for the eleven development banks, the general insurance company, and the guarantee companies). Again, the appointment of chief executives is not often for a fixed term (as reported for eleven banks, seven development banks, one development commercial bank, two development financial institutions, three insurance companies, and three funds). A few other institutions report that their chief executive is appointed for a one-year renewable term. For one institution the chief executive serves by rotation from the board of directors for a one-year term. For one postal bank, the chief executive is the ex-officio finance secretary.

In the discussion on the incentive systems that thwart the professionalization of public institutions, and hence their performance, is the issue of how the employees and management of these institutions are treated—like civil servants for their pay and terms of employment; or like their better paid, but less secure, private sector counterparts? The responses indicate that most employees of banks are not paid like civil servants but instead have separate compensation agreements determined by the government or the board of directors or through collective bargaining; or they have contracts as private sector workers. Employees of twelve development and postal banks are, however, compensated like government employees, even though their management is compensated more competitively.

Conclusions

While no conclusive observations are being drawn from the limited and idiosyncratic sample given here, the variety of institutions and practices do suggest that there are several issues in the supervision and governance of state-owned financial institutions that need to be specifically addressed. In particular, these pertain to the unlevel playing field that state ownership may create; the conflict of interests that may arise out of the many roles that the supervisors are at times expected to play (for instance the monitoring of policy lending targets and the appointment of bank managers); the overlap between the jurisdiction of the supervisors and the controlling ministries; the difficulties that supervisors may have in subjecting these institutions to standards or corrective action similar to those of their peers in the private sector; and the lack of good governance practices and structures.

Should there, for instance, be a subset of supervisory standards that apply to banks and other institutions in the public sector? Ideally, one would expect the standards applicable to the industry to be applied to all participants, but it is recognized that certain features of state ownership need to be kept in mind. In the case of commercial banks, the Basel Core Principles (the standards for bank supervision) obliquely refer to their application to these institutions in an appendix, which states that, "in principle, all banks should be subject to the same operational and supervisory standards regardless of their ownership; however, the unique nature of government-owned commercial banks should be recognized." They go on to emphasize that these banks should be required to "operate to the same high level of professional skill and discipline as required of privately owned commercial banks" and that supervisors should "apply their methods in the same manner to (these) institutions as they do to all other commercial banks."[6]

6. Basel Committee on Banking Supervision (1997, pp. 2, 43). The Basel Core Principles comprise twenty-five basic principles that serve as a basic reference for supervisory and other public authorities internationally and that need to be in place for a supervisory system to be effective. The principles relate to pre-

Yet the issue faced by supervisors in such an environment is the extent to which they take into account the support of the government (which can keep technically insolvent institutions open), so the corrective action regime and the exit policy resolution regime for these institutions would be different—as would licensing conditions.

The issues are more marked for development banks and financial institutions, the supervision of which may derive more from a fiscal imperative rather than from a depositor protection viewpoint. This picture becomes a bit clouded when we focus on development banks (with large retail deposits), commercial banks (with small retail deposits), and nonbanks (with large retail deposits). In addition, when an institution operates both as a development bank and as a commercial bank, managing the risks may be especially challenging. Developing a regulatory paradigm for both deposit-taking nonbanks and non-deposit-taking development banks and for development financial institutions and other nonbank credit institutions would the be the next step in the process. At the same time, this paradigm should also provide for the supervision of refinancing second-tier institutions and not just those involved in direct finance. Here too the Basel Core Principles offer a suggestion to supervisory authorities, albeit through a footnote—that these principles are capable of application to nonbank financial institutions that provide financial services similar to those of banks.

A similar approach would have to be crafted for the insurance companies (which are subject either to different standards or to treasury or administrative ministry) and for mutual and other funds (which are outside the supervisory scope of the usual supervisors). As long as supervision of these various nonbank entities is within the jurisdiction of the controlling ministries, their supervisors will suffer from both resource and independence issues. One approach would be to bring them under an umbrella supervisor for state-owned financial institutions. Another approach would be to integrate their supervision with the supervisor for the sector to which they correspond but with a subset or expanded set of standards applicable to them.

Finally, the governance structures of these institutions would have to be addressed in an environment in which the state is the main stakeholder—as the owner, lender, borrower, shareholder, and sometimes depositor—and in which

---

conditions for effective banking supervision, licensing and structure, prudential regulations and requirements, methods of ongoing banking supervision, information requirements, formal powers of supervisors, and cross-border banking. The principles have been developed by the Basel Committee on Banking Supervision, a committee of banking supervisory authorities established by the central bank governors of the Group of Ten countries in 1975. It usually meets at the Bank for International Settlements in Basel, where its permanent secretariat is located.

the supervisor and the auditor are also controlled by the state. Thus many recommendations made in other contexts regarding public sector governance remain important.[7] "The ultimate challenge . . . is to define a set of manageable public sector governance practices that constrain the role of the public sector to its legitimate roles and that do so in such a way that mitigates the inefficiencies and conflicts that might still arise while minimizing the temptation for corruption."[8]

Appendix: International Monetary Fund, 2003 Survey of State-Owned Financial Institutions

BB General Information

1. Name
2. Central government shareholding (as percentage of total)
3. State and local governments total shareholdings (as percentage of total)
4. Ratio of assets to gross domestic product (GDP)
5. Does this institution operate as
   —A commercial bank?
   —A postal savings bank?
   —A development bank?
   —An international trade bank?
   —A mutual fund?
   —An insurance company?
   —An asset management or reconstruction company fund?
   —Other financial institution?

Sources of Funding as a Percentage of Total Assets

1. Retail deposits
2. Deposits explicitly guaranteed by the government
3. Wholesale deposits including syndicated loans
4. Wholesale deposits or loans explicitly guaranteed by the government
5. Domestic marketable bonds, medium-term notes, or commercial paper
6. International bonds, medium-term notes, or commercial paper
7. Marketable bonds, medium-term notes, or commercial paper explicitly guaranteed by the government
8. Insurance or guarantee fees
9. Direct government grants
10. Long-term borrowing from the treasury or central bank
11. Government deposits
12. Other

Recent Performance and Operating Statistics

1. Return on assets prior year
2. Average return on assets over prior three years

---

7. See Litan, Pomerleano, and Sundararajan (2002).
8. Carmichael (2002, 134–35).

3. Profit or loss history over prior three years
4. Ratio of nonperforming assets to total assets
5. Ratio of provisions for nonperforming assets to nonperforming assets
6. Average percentage of net profits transferred to government

Business and Policy Objectives

1. Originally established as public sector enterprise
2. Originally private, subsequently acquired by government
3. Law or decree authorizing institution
4. State institutional policy objective in authorizing or acquiring law
5. Institution intended to be run at a profit, at zero cost to the government enterprise, or on a subsidized basis
6. Percentage of institution's assets or activities devoted to
   —Agriculture
   —Housing
   —Industrial projects
   —Specialized lending to small and medium enterprises
   —Microfinance institutions
   —Import and export
   —Other specialized finance
   —Commercial lending to corporations
   —Government bonds

Relationship with Government

1. Legal minimum state ownership required by law
2. Receives annual or periodic government funds
3. Receives annual or periodic policy target goals
4. Performance regularly monitored relative to policy targets
5. Agencies, ministries, or organizations that do the monitoring
6. Funds itemized in government budgets
7. Process by which funds are allocated
8. Receives government funds only under infrequent special conditions
   —Method of accomplishing capital injections
   —Most recent capital injection date and amount
   —Other prior capital injection dates and amounts

Supervision Prudential Standards

1. Minimum prudential standards
2. Minimum capital standard (regulatory basis and level)
3. Maximum loan-to-value forms
4. Maximum indebtedness measure
5. Foreign exchange exposure limits
6. Market risk limits
7. Maximum total lending limits
8. Single- or group-related borrower limits with any exceptions
9. Limits on the use of derivatives

10. Maximum internal risk manage-
    ment guidelines
11. Rules for recognition of nonper-
    forming assets
12. Rules for minimum provisions
    required for nonperforming assets

Authorizing Legislation and Prudential Oversight

1. What laws or decrees authorize
   prudential standards?
2. Are privately owned institutions
   of similar character subject to the
   same standards?
3. What supervisors or ministries
   monitor compliance with these
   standards?
4. How is the supervisory agency
   funded?
5. How is the head of the supervisory agency appointed and for
   what term?
6. In what circumstances can the
   head be removed and by whom?
7. What is the range of corrective
   actions available to the supervisor?
8. Is the supervisor required to consult with the government before
   initiating corrective action?
9. Is any exemption in compliance
   available to these institutions?
10. Is the supervisor consulted on the
    fitness and propriety of proposed
    senior managers?

11. What powers does the supervisor
    have to require changes in invest-
    ment or operating policies?
12. Does the supervisor have the
    power to recommend changes in
    investments or operating policies?

Auditing and Examination Policies

1. Are regular inspections or exami-
   nations conducted by the
   supervisor?
2. Are regular audits required?
3. Who performs the audits?
4. How are the auditors selected?
5. Are the audit results publicly
   disclosed?
6. If so, how?

Governance Policies

1. Does the board include nongovernmental representatives?
2. How is the institution's chief
   executive appointed?
3. Does the executive serve for a
   fixed term?
4. Under what conditions can the
   chief executive be removed?
5. Are employees compensated as
   regular government employees?
6. How are managers compensated?

References

Basel Committee on Banking Supervision. 1997. *Core Principles of Effective Banking Supervision.* Basel: Bank for International Settlements.

Barth, James R., Gerald Caprio, and Ross Levine. 2001. "The Regulation and Supervision of Banks around the World—A New Database." Washington: World Bank.

Carmichael, Jeffery. 2002. "Public Sector Governance and the Finance Sector." In *Financial Sector Governance: The Roles of the Public and Private Sectors,* edited by Robert E. Litan, Michael Pomerleano, and V. Sundararajan, pp. 134–35. Brookings.

International Monetary Fund. 1998. "Toward a Framework for Financial Stability." Washington.

Litan, Robert E., Michael Pomerleano, and V. Sundararajan, eds. 2002. *Financial Sector Governance: The Roles of the Public and Private Sectors.* Brookings.

U.S. Office of Management and Budget. 2003. *Analytical Perspectives: Budget of the United States Government, Fiscal Year 2003.*

PART **II**

Fiscal Implications

MANAL FOUAD
RICHARD HEMMING
DAVIDE LOMBARDO
WOJCIECH MALISZEWSKI

4

Fiscal Transparency and State-Owned Banks

INSUFFICIENT ATTENTION HAS been paid to the activities of public financial institutions in discussions of fiscal transparency, although the benefits of fiscal transparency are widely recognized. These benefits are highlighted in the International Monetary Fund's *Manual on Fiscal Transparency*, which opens by referring to "a clear consensus that good governance is of central importance to achieving macroeconomic stability and high-quality growth, and that fiscal transparency is a key aspect of good governance."[1] An important requirement of fiscal transparency is the provision of information to the legislature and the public about all fiscal activities, no matter where in the public sector they are undertaken. In this connection, the focus has been primarily on transparency in government operations, following Kopits and Craig.[2] However, when fiscal activities are undertaken outside government, these should also be disclosed, and this includes fiscal activities associated with the operations of public financial institutions.[3]

The focus of this chapter is on the fiscal transparency issues raised by a subset of public financial institutions, namely state-owned banks. (The central bank and various nonbank institutions are touched upon only in passing.) The chapter

1. International Monetary Fund (2001a, p. 1).
2. Kopits and Craig (1998).
3. The term *public financial institutions,* which is used in the 2001 *Manual on Fiscal Transparency,* corresponds to what in terms of the institutional coverage of the *System of National Accounts* (1993) are referred to as *financial public corporations.*

describes the role of these banks, discusses the fiscal aspects of their operations, and addresses relevant disclosure practices and requirements. Case studies of Mozambique, Romania, Turkey, and Uruguay are provided in the appendix.

The Role of State-Owned Banks

State-owned banks are either fully or partially owned by the government, and the functions they perform are usually different from those performed by their private counterparts.[4] In developing countries, before the emergence of state-owned banks, formal financing systems were dominated by foreign banks that mainly catered to the financing needs of foreign-owned trading, mining, and other companies. Governments in many of these countries, instead of undertaking deep-seated structural reforms to widen the availability of and access to credit (by modernizing legal systems, enforcing contracts, clarifying property rights, improving bank regulation, and so on), which would have taken time to produce results, resorted to direct intervention in credit allocation by banks that they owned. Thus private banks were nationalized, and new state-owned banks were created as sources of credit, often at low cost, for activities that private banks refused to finance because they were either too risky or not profitable. Infrastructure projects are a case in point. These projects have large financing requirements, especially for a single borrower, they often involve significant and highly specialized risks that cannot be easily diversified, and they are usually justified by reference to their social rather than their financial returns, making them unprofitable.

During much of the post–World War II period, developing countries and transition economies relied on state-owned banks to provide financial support to sectors that were seen to be engines of growth and development, again on the assumption that private banks would fail to do this.[5] Industry, agriculture, and exporting have been the main beneficiaries of preferential credit, because these sectors tend to be regarded by governments as too important politically and economically to be left to the market. Governments pursue a range of objectives through intervention. In the case of industry, the aim is to promote investment and rapid industrialization; in the case of agriculture, it is to bridge the gap between sowing and the sale of agricultural produce, to rapidly introduce new seed varieties and technologies, and to otherwise increase agricultural output; and with export credit programs, the aim is to bridge the period between production

---

4. The following description draws on World Bank (1989) and Leviatan (1993).

5. Special financing institutions date from the nineteenth century, when they appeared in Europe to promote long-term finance and industrial growth.

and payment and to compensate exporters for industrial and trade policies that could be biased against them. As indicated in the appendix, both Mozambique and Romania set up specialized state-owned banks to undertake lending in support of these key sectors and activities. Nonfinancial public enterprises also benefit from preferential credit provided by state-owned banks. The fact that the government can mobilize savings in rural areas, where it is uneconomical for private banks to locate, provides further justification for state-owned banks.

While responding to market failure may provide legitimate justification for state-owned banks, it is interesting to ask why government intervention takes the form of owning banks rather than undertaking the activities of these banks directly. There are three main reasons for conducting public policies through state-owned banks.[6] First, for political reasons, it may be necessary to produce a budget that can be easily approved politically and that will be viewed favorably by domestic and foreign lenders. It may also be important to avoid explicit commitments to sectors that can upset political and other vested interests. Second, state-owned banks can raise funds at a lower cost than the government. Third, these banks may respond to institutional requirements set by foreign lenders (for example, the World Bank) with a preference for lending to state-owned banks because it involves fewer administrative bottlenecks and less red tape.

While these banks are defined by reference to government ownership, the key concept is control—that is, the extent of government influence over the activities that banks undertake. It is not ruled out that private banks could be made to provide preferential credit or that state-owned banks could engage in lending on a largely commercial basis. The next sections focus on the fiscal activities of state-owned banks, but the discussion is relevant to all banks that undertake such activities.

Government Intervention through State-Owned Banks

It is useful to distinguish three forms of government intervention through state-owned banks: directed credit, subsidized lending, and guarantees.

—Directed credit: The government can require its own banks to lend to specific borrowers with low credit ratings (farmers, public enterprises) or to undertake risky activities (infrastructure investment). These poorly secured loans are a reason for the high level of nonperforming loans often found on the balance sheets of these banks. In addition, the government can impose credit ceilings on its own banks, which prevent them from taking advantage of profitable lending opportunities.

6. See Leviatan (1993) for further discussion.

—Subsidized lending: State-owned banks can be required to lend at below market interest rates without compensation from the government. However, the costs involved in terms of forgone income may be offset in other ways. These include a requirement that government agencies maintain deposits at these banks, earning correspondingly low interest; access to preferential rediscounting facilities at the central bank; low-cost loans from international institutions; and cross-subsidization, by charging above-market interest rates to other captive borrowers, especially given the quasi-monopoly status granted to state-owned banks, say for mortgage or foreign currency transactions.

—Guarantees: The government can provide guarantees to state-owned banks, either by explicitly guaranteeing loans that they make or by providing an implicit guarantee through the presumption that it stands behind borrowers—or behind the banks themselves when they get into financial difficulties.[7] These banks can also guarantee loans provided by a third party (such as an external lender), although the government may have to provide an explicit or implicit counterguarantee to bolster such guarantees.

Whatever the form of government intervention, the governance structure of state-owned banks—and in particular a failure by the government to maintain an arm's-length relationship with bank management—plays a key role in determining the extent to which intervention has its—intended or unintended—effects. (Governance issues are not discussed in this chapter.)

Quasi-Fiscal Activities and Contingent Liabilities

Directed credit and subsidized lending are quasi-fiscal activities. These are essentially fiscal activities undertaken outside the government, the effects of which can be replicated using instruments (notably taxes and subsidies) traditionally available to the government. Directed credit and subsidized lending are quasi-fiscal activities because of the implicit subsidies associated with them if borrowers are not creditworthy (implying that the loan is really a transfer) or if the interest rate charged is below the market rate.

Mackenzie and Stella as well as others identify a number of problems resulting from government-controlled lending operations.[8]

—These operations can have a macroeconomic impact on the economy if they create losses or if the diminished profits are large enough to be an indirect source of monetary expansion and inflation.

7. These types of guarantees can also be provided to private bank loans.
8. Mackenzie and Stella (1996).

—By being nontransparent, these operations contribute to an underestimate of the true size of the government in terms of the taxes and subsidies they imply in the economy.

—These operations can distort resource allocation by channeling credit to less efficient uses or unproductive sectors and enterprises.

—Because they are outside the conventional measure of deficit, these operations are less subject to scrutiny and more difficult to control and monitor.

—Because of these operations, funds are diverted to other uses. Credit often fails to reach its intended beneficiaries, as lenders misclassify loans to comply with central bank or government directives. Larger and more influential borrowers benefit, with adverse distributional consequences.

—These operations crowd out nonpriority, less well-connected borrowers.

Guarantees can also be regarded as quasi-fiscal activities, because once risk is removed by the guarantee the lender is willing to charge a lower interest rate. However, although the two are closely linked, it is usual to distinguish between quasi-fiscal activities and guarantees. In particular, quasi-fiscal activities pose fiscal risks that lead to financial difficulties, as profits are reduced and loan delinquency increases (which can cause guarantees to kick in). Guarantees can also pose fiscal risks in their own right, in that they are contingent liabilities of the government that can turn into real liabilities and thus compromise debt sustainability.

Bank Restructuring

Once a state-owned bank gets into financial difficulty or becomes insolvent, it may need to be recapitalized, restructured, or liquidated. Any of these would create either direct costs to the budget or indirect costs if the central bank bears the restructuring costs (and is not consolidated with the government). However, the latter would give rise to another quasi-fiscal activity and further contingent liabilities. It is therefore typically the government's role to assist state-owned banks it deems worth saving and to liquidate others. There are a number of ways for governments to assist financially distressed state-owned banks, including recapitalization (through direct capital injection, issuing securities, or assuming the bank's liabilities), or lending, which in the case of an insolvent bank amounts to a transfer.[9] As debt-creating operations, government bailouts have an impact on debt sustainability, aggregate demand, and the macroeconomic environment, in much the same way as any other transfer. (This is illustrated by the discussion of

9. For a more detailed discussion, including on indirect methods of intervention, see Daniel (1997).

Turkey in the appendix.) Significant fiscal adjustment may then be needed to restore sustainability and credibility (which was also the case in Turkey).

Reporting Government Transactions with State-Owned Banks

The standard way to examine the links between the government and state-owned banks is by recording their routine cash interactions and the government's bank support operations. State-owned banks would thus be considered to be like any other entity outside of government. An appropriate framework for reporting transactions between the government and state-owned banks is the 2001 *Government Finance Statistics Manual,* a fiscal reporting framework that formally integrates stocks and flows, stresses accrual-based reporting, and incorporates a government balance sheet.[10] More specifically, it links the government's net worth at the beginning and end of a year by reference to flows recorded in a statement of government operations and a statement of other economic flows. Government operations cover revenue and expense transactions (the latter are the accrual-based equivalent of current spending and include consumption of fixed capital—that is, depreciation), transactions in nonfinancial assets, and transactions in financial assets and liabilities. Other economic flows cover valuation and volume changes that affect net worth but are not related to transactions. The 2001 manual's guidelines also incorporate a statement on the sources and uses of cash, in recognition of the importance of cash flows from a macroeconomic point of view. It defines two main fiscal indicators: the net operating balance, which excludes transactions in nonfinancial assets and in financial assets and liabilities, and net lending and borrowing, which includes transactions in nonfinancial assets.

Within the framework of the 2001 manual's guidelines, routine flows between the government and state-owned banks are recorded in the operating statement. Thus dividends paid by these banks to the government are recorded as revenue, subsidies given to them by the government are recorded as an expense, and loans to these banks and equity injections by the government are recorded as the acquisition of a financial asset, while subsequent loan interest and amortization paid to the government are recorded as revenue and a reduction in financial assets, respectively. These transactions are also recorded in cash-based fiscal accounts, in particular using the 1986 *Manual on Government Finance Statistics.*[11] In both cases, they are reflected in fiscal indicators, namely net lending and borrowing and overall balance, respectively. In addition, loans to state-owned banks and equity injec-

10. International Monetary Fund (2001c).
11. International Monetary Fund (1986).

tions by the government, as well as amortization, are recorded on the government balance sheet.

Government support to insolvent state-owned banks is also recorded. When this support takes the form of loans or equity, the recording is as above. Recapitalization through a transfer of government securities (not involving an exchange of assets) is recorded as the incurrence of a liability and as a liability on the government balance sheet, while carrying costs—that is, interest payments by the government and redemption costs of maturing bonds—are recorded as an expense and a reduction in liabilities, respectively. The full costs of bank recapitalization are thus reflected in net lending and borrowing. For cash-based fiscal accounts, only the carrying costs are recorded, and it is for this reason that an "augmented" fiscal balance is proposed by Daniel and Saal as a means of capturing the full costs of recapitalization in a predominantly cash-based fiscal indicator.[12] Government support for weak or insolvent state-owned banks can also involve other debt operations; these can be handled more easily using the 2001 manual than using cash-based fiscal accounts. These items include debt assumption, debt forgiveness, debt restructuring and rescheduling, debt write-offs and write-downs, and debt-for-equity swaps.

Called government guarantees comprise two possibilities: Either the government assumes the liabilities concerned and there is no financial claim on the original borrower, or the government lends to the borrower on the assumption that the borrower will repay at a later time. In the first case, the government records the full cost of called guarantees as an expense and the assumption of a loan as a liability. In the second case, the government has a claim on the borrower, which is recorded as the acquisition of a financial asset. When the loan is repaid, interest is recorded as revenue and amortization as a financial transaction.

Reporting Quasi-Fiscal Activities and Contingent Liabilities

While the reporting of government transactions with state-owned banks may be fairly comprehensive, especially under the guidelines of the 2001 manual, these transactions are not a good estimate of the risk the government will take in bailing out these banks; the costs involved (including called guarantees) are recorded only after the event. Any attempt to reflect this risk in a forward-looking manner in the fiscal accounts means reporting those operations that are a potential source of risk. In this connection, the focus is on disclosure requirements for quasi-fiscal activities and contingent liabilities.

12. Daniel and Saal (1997).

The disclosure of the fiscal risks posed by state-owned bank operations is not straightforward. As noted, quasi-fiscal activities are sources of fiscal risk in that they can lead to financial difficulties, while guarantees can also be a source of fiscal risk in their own right, independent of these activities. It is therefore important to report such activities and contingent liabilities with a view to providing information about fiscal risks and as a basis for controlling them.

The International Monetary Fund's *Code of Good Practices on Fiscal Transparency* requires that "statements describing the nature and fiscal significance of central government contingent liabilities and tax expenditures, and of quasi-fiscal activities, should be part of the budget documentation" and that "the public sector balance should be reported when nongovernment public sector agencies undertake significant quasi-fiscal activities."[13] The Organization for Economic Cooperation and Development only says that contingent liabilities should be disclosed in the budget.[14] The International Monetary Fund's 2001 *Government Finance Statistics Manual* provides for contingent liabilities to be reported as a memorandum item to the balance sheet.[15]

Quasi-Fiscal Activities

If directed credit and subsidized lending are not reported as part of the budget process, government fiscal activity will be understated. The *Manual on Fiscal Transparency* states that "it is important to identify, where possible to quantify, and report information on quasi-fiscal activities."[16] The *Code of Good Practices on Fiscal Transparency* limits its requirement to the provision of information on the policy purpose, duration, and intended beneficiaries.[17] To this end, independent audits of state-owned banks should be available publicly, and their annual reports should disclose the loans made to any government-owned agency, nonmarket loans, and information on nonperforming loans.[18] However, the quantification of quasi-fiscal activities is difficult and contentious. Therefore, a pragmatic approach is often devised whereby an attempt to estimate the cost involved is made depending on the general financial magnitude of these activities (if they are suspected to account for large financial losses) and whether they are deemed to create a major distortion.

13. International Monetary Fund (2001b), paragraphs 2.1.3 and 3.2.4 (www.imf.org/external/np/fad/trans/code.htm).

14. Organization for Economic Cooperation and Development (2000).

15. International Monetary Fund (2001c).

16. International Monetary Fund (2001a, p. 28).

17. International Monetary Fund (2001b) (www.imf.org/external/np/fad/trans/code.htm).

18. An external audit of two state-owned banks in Uruguay in 2000 resulted in a significant downward revision of their estimated capital of about 5 percent of GDP.

When this is the case, one approach—applicable to subsidized lending rather than directed credit—is to identify the subsidy component of a loan and treat it as an expenditure item. Accounting for implicit subsidies is complicated, however. For one thing, future costs need to be converted into current cash equivalents when the loan is committed.[19] Further, the subsidy component of the loan should be separated from the market value so that these can be treated as expenditure and financing, respectively. In practice, however, it is difficult to identify the required components, particularly in developing countries, or to identify a meaningful interest rate for basing the grant element. The discussion of Uruguay in the appendix shows that accounting for quasi-fiscal activities in the budget can significantly increase the size of the deficit—and thus its measured macroeconomic impact. This illustrates the importance both of quantification when quasi-fiscal activities are significant and of technically sound estimates of quasi-fiscal activities.

The *Manual on Fiscal Transparency* proposes that statements on quasi-fiscal activities should be compiled by the ministry responsible for the state budget on the basis of information provided by the institution conducting these activities. In the absence of a precise calculation of their fiscal cost, the manual advocates that statements on such activities should include information to allow an assessment of the potential fiscal significance of each activity—such as the interest rate on subsidized lending.

Contingent Liabilities

If lending carries an explicit government guarantee, or if the government stands behind lenders or borrowers, a contingent liability arises, which could lead to a large direct fiscal cost. Moreover, continuous and extensive lending to unprofitable enterprises or sectors adds to the costs to lending institutions, which can lead to bank failure and the need for government bailouts. Such bailouts may be quite costly to the budget and the economy in general. While there may be no immediate recorded costs to the government, such operations increase the true size of the deficit in the short term, and in the longer term the fiscal costs may be substantial. Claessens and Klingebiel report fiscal costs of banking crises that reach into the range of 40–60 percent of gross domestic product (GDP) (in Chile, 1981–83; in Indonesia, since 1997; and in Argentina, 1980–82).[20] Moreover, even lower levels of government support can be a source of severe problems in debt sustainability; this was the case in Turkey, where such costs were 15 percent of GDP in 2001.

19. U.S. Congressional Budget Office (1989).
20. Claessens and Klingebiel (2001).

This being the case, bank restructuring costs provide a mechanism for turning a banking crisis into a fiscal crisis. There is also a moral hazard problem, in that borrowers may be more likely to default on their payments in light of a government guarantee, and lenders may have little incentive to collect loan payments, particularly if they are weak institutions with a poor track record in recovering loans.

As noted, the *Code of Good Practices on Fiscal Transparency* requires statements as part of the budget documentation that describe the nature and significance of all contingent liabilities. Good disclosure practice is to publish detailed information on guarantees covering the public policy purpose of each guarantee or guarantee program, the total amount of the guarantee classified by sectors and duration, the intended beneficiaries, and the likelihood of being called. Information should also be provided on past called guarantees. Best practice would be to compute the expected value of the increase in government liabilities due to called guarantees. Only a few countries do this.

To be fully effective, these transparency requirements have to placed in a broader framework for managing guarantees and other contingent liabilities, and for controlling fiscal risks. To this end, Schick proposes a framework with the following elements:

—An independent assessment of the risk to the fiscal position entailed by expected payouts in respect of contingent liabilities.

—The compilation and reporting of an inventory of contingent liabilities.

—A published fiscal risk analysis as part of the budget.

—A government risk management strategy to guide public sector agencies incurring actual or potential financial liabilities.

—Cost and risk sharing to discourage moral hazard.

—Limits on new guarantees and the incurrence of other contingent liabilities.

—The setting aside of funds to cover calls on guarantees and the cost of other contingent liabilities.[21]

While this is a fairly demanding list of requirements, understanding and appropriately containing the government's overall risk exposure, and thereby limiting the extent to which contingent liabilities are turned unexpectedly into real liabilities, should be an objective of all governments.

Reporting the Public Sector Balance

State-owned banks are not the only entities that undertake quasi-fiscal activities and that are sources of contingent liabilities. Nonfinancial public enterprises that

21. Schick (2002).

are not run on a commercial basis run similar types of operations—and possibly on a larger scale. When public enterprises are largely noncommercial, fiscal statistics, indicators, and targets should cover all their operations.[22] By the same token, this approach could be extended to state-owned banks and other public financial institutions. This could certainly prove to be useful from a transparency standpoint when state-owned banks provide significant directed credit, but the subsidy element entailed by this, and by lending operations more generally, is difficult to identify and quantify. However, there is no consensus regarding the coverage of public financial institutions in fiscal statistics.

The 1993 *System of National Accounts* includes public sector financial corporations as a subcategory of the financial corporations sector and therefore treats their transactions outside the general government. Since the financial sector is broken down along ownership lines, however, it allows for the consolidation of a public sector by putting together general government and "the public subsectors of nonfinancial and financial public corporations."

The 1986 *Manual on Government Statistics,* however, considers that there are "disadvantages . . . in consolidating government and public financial institutions in an overall public sector as this would imply eliminating from the statistics government transactions with public financial institutions."[23] It therefore consolidates the "nonfinancial public sector" but retains the possibility of "building blocks" so that the coverage can be rearranged according to the relevant analytical coverage desired, including public sector financial institutions.

The 2001 manual encourages the compilation of statistics for the public sector, which in turn includes public sector financial institutions.[24] This is mainly because they can carry out operations on behalf of the government, "such as lending to particular parties at a lower-than-market interest rate."[25] One way is to include state-owned banks in the public sector by adding their net operating balance above the line as a proxy for their quasi-fiscal activities. However, this lumps together public policy–based and market-based activities and may distort the true size of the deficit.

Whether fiscal statistics should cover state-owned banks should be decided by reference to the noncommercial nature of their operations, which would require an assessment of their ownership, control, and market orientation. However, any such assessment is necessarily subjective, although certain factors—such as the fact that these banks do not accept deposits and rely on the government for their

22. International Monetary Fund (2004).
23. International Monetary Fund (1986, p. 7).
24. International Monetary Fund (2001c).
25. International Monetary Fund (2001c, paragraph 2.59).

income or on government guarantees to raise most of their funds—may argue in favor of consolidation.

Conclusions

Directed credit, subsidized lending, or guarantees that benefit specific sectors or economic activity are nontransparent and have potentially large hidden fiscal costs. However, if they cannot be avoided, the best-practice treatment would be disclosure as a basis for approval by parliament and provisioning for estimated costs in the budget. Application of these practices would permit a full assessment of fiscal risks and the implications for debt sustainability.

While increased transparency about the operations of state-owned banks would be welcome, transparency is not an end in itself. Transparency, however, is key to subjecting the quasi-fiscal activities undertaken by such banks and the guarantees provided to them—both of which may be legitimate policy instruments—to the same scrutiny as on-budget fiscal activities. Transparency should also lead the government to reconsider the way it uses these banks and should facilitate other policies, such as privatization. Given that the focus on transparency is relatively recent, it is too early to assess its direct impact on policies, although rating agencies are clearly interested in fiscal transparency. Indeed, according to Glennerster and Shin, reports on the observance of standards and codes are being used to inform sovereign ratings and have an influence on borrowing costs for emerging markets.[26] In the aftermath of corporate accounting problems, particular attention is being paid to fiscal accounting and reporting.

This being the case, it is clearly appropriate to highlight the fiscal transparency issues raised by state-owned banks and other public sector financial institutions and to begin paying them more attention in fiscal transparency assessments. That said, more analytical work is needed on assessing, disclosing, and controlling fiscal risks in general.

Appendix: Country Case Studies

Mozambique

The banking system in Mozambique was nationalized two years after independence in 1977 and remained in state hands until the mid-1990s. Former private

---

26. Glennerster and Shin (2003). Reports on the observance of standards and codes are prepared and published, at the request of member countries, by the staffs of the IMF or the World Bank. The reports cover twelve areas, including data, fiscal transparency, and monetary and financial transparency.

banks were merged into either the Banco de Moçambique (operating as the central bank and the largest commercial bank with 90 percent of banking sector assets) or the Banco Popular Desenvolvimento (specializing in agriculture credit). Economic reforms, initiated in 1987 and accelerated at the end of civil war in 1992, led to the separation of the central banking and commercial banking activities of the Banco de Moçambique in 1992. The Banco Comercial de Moçambique—the bank created to take over the commercial activity of the Banco de Moçambique—was privatized in 1996. The Banco Popular Desenvolvimento was privatized a year later, but it was subsequently taken over by the state and reprivatized in 2001.

The banking system had been used to finance loss-making state-owned enterprises and for political lending. The political pressure on financing the state sector intensified with the war, leading to a rapid deterioration of the bank portfolios. The economic program of 1987 started curbing the extension of domestic bank credit to cover operating losses of enterprises, but both the flow and the stock of nonperforming loans continued to be a problem, as the banks were involved in political lending and their capacity remained deficient.

State-owned banks were partially recapitalized at the beginning of the economic program in 1987, but further support was needed in the course of reforms. In 1987, 34 percent of the assets of the Banco de Moçambique and 78 percent of the assets of the Banco Popular Desenvolvimento were recognized as bad loans, and the banks received substantial support from the government. Massive write-offs of the Banco Comercial de Moçambique's loans in 1993 were accompanied by further recapitalization equivalent to 7 percent of GDP. Despite this support, the Banco Comercial de Moçambique ended 1994 with an overdraft from the central bank of nearly 4 percent of GDP because of nonpayments from state-owned enterprises. The majority of the overdraft position was assumed by the new owners after privatization of the Banco Comercial de Moçambique in 1996, but the equivalent of 0.5 percent of GDP was settled by the government. Similarly, the Banco Popular Desenvolvimento was recapitalized before privatization.

The government retained significant shares in the banks and extended further support after privatization, when the scale of nonperforming loans became apparent. These loans were partly inherited from the preprivatization period but were partly related to political and connected lending after the privatization. Further support to the Banco Comercial de Moçambique, equivalent to 1 percent of GDP in government bonds, was extended after a comprehensive audit conducted by the new owners, who acquired the bank in 2000. After privatization of the Banco Popular Desenvolvimento, the government had to step in again in 2001, when the owners handed over their shares to the government after the audit revealed massive nonperforming loans. The bank, renamed Banco Austral, was reprivatized after the government agreed to fully recapitalize it.

Romania

Until 1999 state-owned banks in Romania had a dominant position in the banking system. Commercial banking was established at the outset of transition in 1990, but the sector remained largely state owned and dominated by three banks: Bancorex, Banca Comerciala Romana, and Banca Agricola. State-owned banks accounted for above 70 percent of all banking system assets until 1998. Restructuring, liquidation, and privatization reduced this share to less than 40 percent by 2003.

Subsidized loans by state-owned banks allowed large state-owned enterprises to operate under soft budget constraints. The foreign trade bank, Bancorex, and the bank financing agriculture, Banca Agricola, were the two main institutions providing subsidized credit. Bancorex financed imports of energy and capital goods, subsidizing the energy sector and energy-intensive industry. Banca Agricola lent to the agriculture sector and state-owned agribusiness enterprises.

Political and institutional changes after 1997 revealed that Bancorex and Banca Agricola were insolvent, and were relying on direct central bank credit and a subsidized exchange rate, which both ceased with financial liberalization. In addition, many borrowers became nonviable.

Attempts to recapitalize Bancorex failed. In 1997 the bank received an equivalent of 2 percent of GDP in government securities, but the recapitalization was not accompanied by any serious restructuring attempt. Plans for further recapitalization and privatization were interrupted by a run on deposits in 1999. At the time, the bank accounted for a quarter of banking sector assets, and about 90 percent of its loans were nonperforming. To avoid costly recapitalization, estimated at 6 percent of GDP, the authorities decided to close the bank and to transfer its assets to the asset recovery agency and its liabilities to other banking institutions. The cost of closing the bank was estimated at 4 percent of GDP.

The restructuring of Banca Agricola turned out to be costly—but successful. In 1997, after its nonperforming loans reached 70 percent of the bank's assets, the authorities recapitalized the bank by the equivalent of nearly 1 percent of GDP and downsized its operations. The bank, however, continued generating losses, and nonperforming loans again ballooned. The restructuring process was accelerated after heavy withdrawals of deposits in 1999. Nonperforming loans equivalent to 1 percent of GDP were transferred to the asset recovery agency. Under a new management, and supported by a special credit line from the central bank, the bank was privatized in 2001.

The recapitalization and restructuring of state-owned banks cost the authorities nearly 10 percent of GDP. The costs of bank restructuring in other Central European transition economies were similar: 14 percent of GDP in Bulgaria, 18 percent in the Czech Republic, 12 percent in Hungary, and 6 percent in Poland.

Turkey

State-owned banks have traditionally played a significant, although diminishing, role in the Turkish financial system. Their share of banking sector assets was 35 percent in 2003, compared to over 50 percent before the liberalization of the financial system initiated in the 1980s. The sector has been dominated by the two largest state-owned banks, Ziraat Bank and Halk Bank.

Subsidized lending was the main quasi-fiscal activity conducted by state-owned banks. Ziraat Bank provided subsidized financing to farmers and Halk Bank to small- and medium-scale businesses. The use of banks for political rent distribution had intensified since the mid-1990s.

High profitability of banking operations in Turkey allowed state-owned banks to cover the costs of quasi-fiscal activities until the mid-1990s. They held large government deposits and had a substantial share of the market for deposits and commercial lending, and the spread between their borrowing costs and subsidized lending was relatively low. Entry to the banking system after financial liberalization remained highly politicized, limiting competition and allowing all banks to profit from high-interest margins. High inflation helped to keep the margins high and allowed the banks to benefit from delayed payments to customers (float income).

When the share of state-owned banks in the market diminished and borrowing costs increased, the state-owned banks started accumulating losses. High real interest rates quickly raised the capitalized value of interest-bearing "duty losses," and expectations that all losses would be ultimately covered by the treasury softened banks' budget constraints, leading to a rapid accumulation of unpaid claims. The cash-strapped banks started funding their losses through short-term borrowing, putting pressure on deposit and interbank market rates. The flow of unpaid duty losses increased to 8 percent of GDP in 1999 (from 1 percent in 1994), and the stock reached over 13 percent of GDP.

Subsidized lending was curtailed under the fiscal consolidation program of 2000, but the stock of duty losses was not eliminated until after the 2000–01 crisis. The flow of duty losses declined to 0.1 percent of GDP in 2000, when the interest rate on subsidized lending was linked to treasury bond auction rates. Since 2001 subsidized lending has been allowed only if backed by appropriate allocations in the budget. In May 2001 the treasury securitized all the losses and bad assets. Duty losses were replaced by long-term securities, and cash was also injected to strengthen the banks' capital base. The cost of recapitalization amounted to 15 percent of GDP. Significant restructuring and downsizing under program conditionality further improved the financial position of the banks.

Uruguay

State-owned banks have historically played a key role in Uruguay. Over the period 1996–2000, for example, the two main state-owned banks, Banco de la Republica Oriental del Uruguay, the former central bank, and Banco Hipotecario del Uruguay accounted for 47 percent of the assets of the entire banking system. They have engaged in a variety of quasi-fiscal activities, mainly lending at subsidized rates. As a result of its flat interest rate policy (whereby, within each line of credit, lending rates do not depend on the riskiness of the borrower), The Banco de la Republica Oriental del Uruguay has ended up, by adverse selection, catering mainly to poorer credit risks in the agriculture sector and to a lesser extent in other sectors in crisis. The Banco Hipotecario del Uruguay provided mortgages to low-income groups and, at least until early 2000, has shielded them from currency risk by providing loans indexed to a local wage index—at a high cost for its solvency, as most of its deposits were in dollars.[27]

As a result, the profitability and financial strength of these banks have chronically lagged those of their private competitors. For example, while the after-tax return on equity for private banks averaged 12 percent in 1995–2000, it averaged only 4.7 percent for the Banco de la Republica Oriental del Uruguay and –1 percent for the Banco Hipotecario del Uruguay. Similarly, before the 2002 crisis, nonperforming loans were 5.6 percent of total loans for private banks and 42 percent for state-owned banks.[28]

The macroeconomic impact of these quasi-fiscal activities was potentially large. Table 4A-1 shows that, depending on the estimation methodology and underlying assumptions on the recoverability of these banks' private sector loans,

27. While this policy was changed in early 2000, the mismatch on the outstanding stocks put the bank under severe stress when the peso depreciated in 2002.

28. Besides lending to ex-ante less creditworthy borrowers, state-owned banks also experienced difficulties in collecting their dues. At times, the political clout of their debtors led to the approval of laws, like the so-called Law on Borrowing at the end of 1998, forcing state-owned banks to grant debt forgiveness or restructuring (just this law was estimated to cost the Banco Hipotecario del Uruguay about 0.7 percent of GDP in terms of the present value of the decrease in future income).

Table 4A-1. *Uruguay: Quasi-Fiscal Activities of State-Owned Banks, 1996–2002*[a]
Percent

	1996	1997	1998	1999	2000	2001	2002
Overall balance	−1.5	−1.4	−1.0	−4.1	−4.1	−4.1	−4.6
Flow of quasi-financial activities[b]							
Assuming 80% recovery	1.2	0.8	0.8	−0.2	1.6	0.4	1.1
Assuming 70% recovery	1.8	1.2	1.2	−0.2	2.3	0.6	1.7
Addendum							
Change in equity value[c]	−0.1	0.0	0.0	0.0	−4.8	−0.8	−6.5
BROU	−0.1	0.0	0.0	0.0	−1.4	−0.2	−1.9
BHU	0.0	0.0	0.0	0.0	−3.4	−0.6	−4.6

Source: Banco Central del Uruguay (BCU); and staff estimates.

a. Uruguay's two state-owned banks are Banco de la Republica Oriental del Uruguay (BROU) and Banco Hipotecario del Uruguay (BHU). This table is based on the assumption that a certain fraction of credit extended by these state-owned banks to the private sector will not be recovered. The addendum shows the change in the value of their equity. This measure is backward looking in that the fiscal cost is assessed in the year in which bank capital is found to have eroded, presumably because the bank charged below-recovery rates on its loans. When the two state-owned banks underwent their first external audit, in 2000, their capital was revised downward by an amount equivalent to 5 percent of GDP.

b. Estimate based on assumed recovery rates on the change in credit to nonfinacial private sector.

c. Net worth data for 2001–02 are from audited balance sheets; for previous years, from BCU.

quasi-fiscal activities may have cost between 0.8 and 1.2 percent of GDP on average in the period 1996–2002. For comparison, the recorded overall deficit of the consolidated nonfinancial public sector averaged 3 percent over the same period.

References

Claessens, Stijn, and Daniela Klingebiel. 2001. "Measuring and Managing Governments' Contingent Liabilities in the Banking Sector." In *Government at Risk: Contingent Liabilities and Fiscal Risk,* edited by H. Polackova Brixi and Allen Schick, pp. 311–34. Washington: World Bank.

Daniel, James. 1997. "Fiscal Aspects of Bank Restructuring." Working Paper 97/52. Washington: International Monetary Fund.

Daniel, James, and Matthew Saal. 1997. "Macroeconomic Impact and Policy Response." In *Systemic Bank Restructuring and Macroeconomic Policy,* edited by W. Alexander and others, pp. 1–41. Washington: International Monetary Fund.

Glennerster, Rachel, and Yongsok Shin. 2003. "Is Transparency Good for You, and Can the IMF Help?" Working Paper 03/132. Washington: International Monetary Fund.

International Monetary Fund. 1986. *A Manual on Government Finance Statistics.* Washington.

————. 2000. *Issues in Fiscal Accounting.* Washington.

————. 2001a. *A Manual on Fiscal Transparency.* Washington.

————. 2001b. *Code of Good Practices on Fiscal Transparency.* Washington.

————. 2001c. *Government Finance Statistics Manual.* Washington.

————. 2004. "IMF Executive Board Holds Informal Seminar on Public Investment and Fiscal Policy." Press Information Notice 04/45. Washington.

Kopits, George, and Jon Craig. 1998. *Transparency in Government Operations.* Occasional Paper 158. Washington: International Monetary Fund.

Leviatan, Oded. 1993. "Impact of Public Financial Institutions on the Fiscal Stance." In *How to Measure the Fiscal Deficit,* edited by M. I. Blejer and A. Cheasty, pp. 259–76. Washington: International Monetary Fund.

Mackenzie, George A., and Peter Stella. 1996. *Quasi-Fiscal Operations of Public Financial Institutions.* Occasional Paper 142. Washington: International Monetary Fund.

Organization for Economic Cooperation and Development. 2000. *Best Practices of Budget Transparency.* PUMA/SBO(2000)6/Final. Paris.

Schick, Allen. 2000. "Conclusion: Towards a Code of Good Practice on Managing Fiscal Risk." In *Government at Risk: Contingent Liabilities and Fiscal Risk,* edited by H. Polackova Brixi and Allen Schick, pp. 461–71. Washington: World Bank.

System of National Accounts. 1993. Commission of the European Communities/Eurostat, International Monetary Fund, Organization for Economic Cooperation and Development, United Nations, World Bank.

U.S. Congressional Budget Office. 1989. *Credit Reform: Comparable Budget Costs for Cash and Credit,* December.

World Bank. 1989. *World Development Report.* Washington.

NICHOLAS R. LARDY 5

State-Owned Banks in China

C HINA'S TRANSITION TO a market economy has proceeded gradually over the past twenty-five years. Perhaps it is not surprising that progress across product, labor, and capital markets has been highly differentiated. As outlined in this chapter, in sharp contrast to the situation twenty-five years ago, when only a tiny fraction of farm output was sold at market prices outside of state procurement channels, transactions in product markets are now almost entirely at market-determined prices. This is true not only for agricultural output and consumer goods but even for steel, machinery, and other investment goods. The system of lifetime employment—in which jobs in the modern sector were assigned to individuals when they completed their schooling (whether primary, secondary, or tertiary), the wage structure was determined by government bureaucrats, and job turnover and geographic mobility of workers were rare—largely has given way to a labor market characterized by voluntary contracting between workers and employers, wage flexibility, significant geographic mobility of labor, and substantial labor turnover.

Despite these changes, the role of the market in the allocation of capital has expanded at a painfully slow pace. Whether through banks, equity markets, or bond markets, the role of the government remains in many ways pervasive. This chapter begins by outlining the relatively rapid progress toward the market allocation of resources in product and labor markets and then turns to a more detailed analysis of the market for capital, where progress has been much slower.

93

It then analyzes the economic implications of the dominant role of government in the allocation of capital.

The Expanding Role of Markets

At the outset of economic reform in the late 1970s the role of markets in resource allocation in Chinese agriculture was limited to a small number of rural free markets where peasants were able to sell output they produced on their small private plots. About 95 percent of the output that was not directly consumed by members of the rural collective units responsible for farm production was sold to state procurement agencies at prices fixed by the government. Starting in the late 1970s this system began to break down, as the government abandoned collective organization of farm production and eased restrictions on rural markets. For example, the number of rural free markets expanded from 33,302 in 1978 to 44,775 in 1982. More important, the volume of transactions on these markets almost tripled to reach RMB 32.8 billion.[1] The system of government procurement of grains and other crops at fixed prices, however, remained in place; the government shifted the responsibility for delivery requirements from farm collectives to individual producers. As a result, even after a decade of rural reform, 46 percent of farm-gate transactions still occurred at prices fixed or "guided" by the government. But in the 1990s the government further reduced the scope of state procurement, and a growing share of farm sales to government procurement agencies occurred at market, rather than state-fixed, prices. By 2001 the share of farm-gate transactions occurring at market-determined prices reached 94 percent.[2]

The liberalization of the market for farm products was central to the rapid growth of output and productivity in the farm sector in the first decade of reform. Without the opportunity to market, farmers would have remained locked into the pattern of self-sufficiency that had developed during the decade of the Cultural Revolution, when the watchword in agricultural development policy was grain self-sufficiency, not just at the provincial level but also all the way down to the local level. With the rise of marketing, comparative-advantage cropping patterns reemerged in the first half of the 1980s, making possible a period of record growth of farm productivity and output.

The expansion of the role of the market in the allocation of consumer goods followed a path similar to that in agriculture. At the outset of reform, virtually all retail sales occurred in state-owned retail establishments at prices fixed by state price

1. China State Statistical Bureau (1983, p. 386).
2. Beijing Normal University, Economics and Resource Management Research Institute (2003, p. 118); Lardy (2002, p. 25).

agencies. Liberalization proceeded gradually, with the share of retail transactions at market prices rising steadily to 69 percent by 1991 and 96 percent by 2001.[3]

The government was more reluctant to give up its ability to allocate investment goods at fixed prices. This was perhaps not surprising given that the power to allocate investment goods was at the heart of the system of planning that had played such a large role in the allocation of resources since the First Five-Year Plan (1953–57). The key innovation providing the breakthrough to expand the role of the market in the allocation of producer goods was the dual-track system.[4] This policy allowed enterprises to sell what was referred to as the above-plan portion of their output at market-determined prices. Firms still had to meet targets to deliver fixed amounts of coal, steel, machinery, and other producer goods to the state at fixed prices, but they were allowed to sell overquota amounts of output on the market. Most of these firms also received planned allocations of the inputs they needed to meet their own planned levels of production. But with the introduction of the dual-track system in 1983, for the first time firms had the option of turning to the market to purchase additional inputs so that they, in turn, could produce output in excess of their planned levels. This overquota output could be sold at market-determined prices. At the same time, firms were given rights to retain a share of the profits they generated, modifying the traditional system in which most profits were turned over to the state treasury. Thus for a growing number of firms and commodities, marginal decisions on what and how much to produce were potentially influenced by market-determined prices and the profit incentive.

As the state planning agencies adjusted quota levels of output upward only gradually, the share of producer goods sold on the market expanded steadily to reach 46 percent by 1991. While that reflected a significant liberalization for investment goods, it was well below the share of farm-gate or retail transactions occurring at market-determined prices. In the 1990s the dual-track system was gradually dismantled, and the share of producer goods sold at market-determined prices reached 90 percent in 2001.[5] Government allocation at fixed prices remained important for a handful of commodities: coal, petroleum, and refined petroleum products. The government continued to set prices for some utilities and services, such as electricity and water and passenger and freight transport. The role of the market in the allocation of some of the goods distributed at state-fixed

---

3. Beijing Normal University, Economics and Resource Management Research Institute (2003, p. 118); Lardy (2002, p. 25).

4. Byrd (1987, pp. 295–308); Wu and Zhao (1987).

5. Beijing Normal University, Economics and Resources Management Research Institute (2003, p. 36); Lardy (2002, p. 25).

prices, however, was considerable. For example, beginning in June 1998 the government adopted a policy of adjusting the price of crude oil to bring it in line with
the international price. Two years later it began pricing refined petroleum products
in line with international prices, adjusting prices every month.[6]

One indicator of the growing role of market-determined prices in the distribution of products is the convergence of measures of profitability of different
branches of industry.[7] At the outset of reform, profitability in manufacturing varied widely across sectors. On the one hand, firms producing goods requiring primarily agricultural inputs achieved extraordinarily high rates of profitability. This
reflected not efficiency in production but the state's policy of extracting resources
from the agricultural sector by forcing collective units—and later, individual
farmers—to sell their output to the state at relatively low prices. Returns in the
food processing, textile, apparel, and cigarette industries were boosted by the
effect of relatively low farm-gate prices for grains, fiber crops, and tobacco. On the
other hand, profitability in sectors in which agricultural inputs were not used
tended to be below average.

As farm-gate prices became increasingly market determined over the course of
the 1980s, the terms of trade between the farm sector and manufacturing improved and the hyperprofitability of manufacturing sectors dependent primarily
on agricultural inputs fell. As a result, rates of profitability of various branches of
manufacturing tended to converge. The spread of market-determined prices and
the resulting tendency for profit rates to reflect efficiency rather than pricing decisions of bureaucrats contributed to greater efficiency in the allocation of investment resources.

The reason is that retained earnings are the single largest source of investment
funds throughout the reform period. In the early years of reform, reinvested profits did not contribute to the efficiency of allocation of resources since profit generation reflected systematic pricing distortions. Over time the efficiency of allocation of investment resources improved for two reasons. First, as pricing distortions
were eliminated, the distribution of retained earnings increasingly reflected efficiency of resource use rather than arbitrary pricing decisions. Firms that were more
efficient in production were able to finance more fixed investment. Second, the
share of total investment in fixed assets financed from retained earnings rose, while
the share financed through the state budget fell dramatically. Despite all of the
shortcomings of intermediation through the banking system discussed later in this

---

6. Lardy (2002, p. 26).

7. The measure used here is pretax profits relative to assets, where assets are the sum of working capital and the depreciated value of fixed assets.

chapter, the relatively large role of retained earnings as a source of investment finance played a powerful, positive role.[8]

Tracing the growing role of the market in the allocation of labor is more difficult, but there is little doubt that the traditional system began to break down in the 1980s as the role of the market and flexible wages expanded. One indicator is the rapid growth in the number of workers who are self-employed or who work for private enterprises in urban areas. Private firms (including self-employment) were virtually unheard of when reform was getting under way in the late 1970s. In 1978, for example, private firms in urban areas employed only 150,000 workers, accounting for 0.15 percent of urban employment. By 2002 these firms employed almost 43 million workers, accounting for 17 percent of all employment in urban areas.[9] Another indicator of the dismantling of the system of lifetime employment was the rising share of what are referred to as contract workers. Employers were substantially less committed to these workers than to regular employees, remuneration was more flexible than for permanent workers, and traditional benefits such as pensions and health care were invariably less generous. This system was first introduced in the mid-1980s, and in 1984, 1.8 percent of all workers and staff were hired on a contractual rather than a permanent basis. By 1997 contract workers accounted for just over half of all workers in the modern sector, even in state-owned manufacturing establishments.[10]

In contrast to goods and labor, with the important exception of retained earnings, the role of the market in the allocation of capital remained relatively limited. The analysis that follows focuses on banks, equity markets, and bond markets.

The importance of banks as mediators of capital in China is difficult to overstate. Despite the creation of stock and bond markets more than a decade ago and the subsequent development of important regulatory and other infrastructure to support such markets, the role of capital markets in resource allocation remains tiny, indeed almost insignificant. In 2003, for example, the sum of domestic and foreign currency–denominated loans outstanding from banks in China increased by RMB 2.99 trillion.[11] In contrast, the total amount of funds raised on domestic

8. In 2002 the sources of total investment in fixed assets of RMB 4.5 trillion were as follows: retained earnings, 49 percent; bank loans, 20 percent; state budget, 7 percent; and other (not specified), 18 percent. Thus retained earnings were two and a half times as important as bank loans as a source of funding of investment. National Bureau of Statistics of China (2003, pp. 187–88).

9. National Bureau of Statistics of China (2003, pp. 126–27).

10. National Bureau of Statistics of China (1998, p. 151).

11. People's Bank of China (2003b, p. 18: www.pbc.gov.cn [February 24, 2004]). This number, like other data on loans released by the People's Bank of China since the first quarter of 2002, includes the increase in loans outstanding by foreign banks operating in China.

equity markets (including initial public offerings, secondary offerings, rights issues, and the sale of convertible bonds) was only RMB 81.96 billion, or less than 3 percent of the increase in the stock of bank loans outstanding.[12] Net funds raised by the nonfinancial sector through the issuance of corporate bonds in 2003—RMB 33.6 billion—were barely more than 1 percent of the increase in the stock of bank loans outstanding.[13] In short, funds raised in capital markets (not counting treasury debt or financial policy bonds) in 2003 were the equivalent of less than 4 percent of the increase in the stock of bank loans outstanding.

Even in Asia, where financial systems traditionally have been bank dominated, China is an outlier for two reasons. First, there is no indication of any decline in the role of banks in financial intermediation. Indeed, the role of banks in 2003 was greater than a decade earlier, when capital markets were first created. In 1992, for example, the funds raised by nonfinancial corporate entities through domestic equity and bond markets totaled RMB 53.9 billion. That amount was equivalent to 10.5 percent of the increase in bank loans outstanding in the same year, more than twice the relative role of the capital market in raising funds for the nonfinancial sector of the economy in 2003.

Second, in the aftermath of the Asian financial crisis, several countries in the region have moved away from their historic reliance on banks to finance the corporate sector. In Korea and Thailand, for example, the share of corporate funding from capital markets has grown, while reliance on bank financing has shrunk. In short, while other countries in the region have reduced their reliance on bank intermediation in recent years, China's reliance on banks has actually increased slightly.

The four largest state-owned banks, which remain wholly owned by the Ministry of Finance, continue to have an outsized role in China's banking system. But their share of new lending has fallen to 50 percent in recent years, compared to an average of 70 percent in 1994–98. Although they still accounted for 55 percent of all assets in the financial system at the end of 2003, their share was down significantly from 70.1 percent, which they held at the end of 1997.[14] Closely related are three policy banks created in 1994 to take over the policy lending previously handled by the large state-owned commercial banks. By the end of 2003,

12. Of this amount, RMB 63.9 billion was in equity and RMB 18.06 billion was in convertible bonds. Equity here excludes funds raised on international equity markets.

13. People's Bank of China (2003b, pp. 14, 17–18: www.pbc.gov.cn [February 24, 2004]). This is the net value of corporate bonds issued. Issuance of corporate debt was RMB 35.8 billion, and the value of maturing debt was RMB 2.2 billion.

14. Nan (2004); People's Bank of China (2003a, p. 96; 1998, p. 58).

their assets were RMB 2.1 trillion, accounting for 7.7 percent of all assets in the financial system.[15]

The second tier of China's banking system comprises eleven banks that are legally organized as shareholding companies. This group includes banks created in two waves: 1987–88 and 1992–95. These banks now account for about 14 percent of all bank assets.[16] The ownership form of these banks differs from that of the big four banks, which are wholly state owned. Five of these shareholding banks—China Merchant's Bank, Huaxia Bank, Minsheng Bank, Pudong Development Bank, and Shenzhen Development Bank—are listed on China's A-share domestic stock market. Although these banks have a large number of owners rather than a single owner, most of the share owners are government entities, with two exceptions. The exceptions are Minsheng Bank, in which nongovernment entities control 70 percent of the shares, and Shenzhen Development Bank, in which nongovernment entities control 72 percent of the shares. Government entities are the dominant share owners for the other shareholding banks, both listed and nonlisted.

The third tier of the banking system—city commercial banks—was created in the 1990s through the merger of individual urban credit cooperatives within each of roughly 110 municipalities. Lending by city commercial banks also has been growing rapidly, but by the end of 2003 they accounted for only 5 percent of the assets of the entire financial system.[17] While none of the city commercial banks is yet listed on the domestic A-share equity market, like the second tier of the banking system, they too appear to be legally organized as shareholding companies. But most of the shareholders are municipal entities. Only 30–40 percent of their share capital is owned by nongovernment entities. And even when, as in the case of the largest of these institutions—the Bank of Shanghai—foreign institutions have been able to acquire a minority stake in ownership and even representation on the board of directors, the appointment of bank management remains in the hands of the party state apparatus rather than the board. In short, the rights of minority shareholders are limited.

State ownership of banks suggests that the market has a limited role in the allocation of capital; this is confirmed by the limited ability of banks to price risk. In a market economy, the price of capital—the interest rate—is set in a competitive market. In China the central bank—the People's Bank of China—has historically

15. Nan (2004).
16. Nan (2004).
17. Nan (2004).

fixed all interest rates for loans and deposits offered by commercial banks and other financial institutions. This includes the specific interest rates that banks can offer on deposits of each of several available maturities as well as the interest rates that banks can charge borrowers for loans of various types and maturities. The central bank began to allow some flexibility in the posted lending rates beginning in 1990, when banks were allowed to make working capital loans to individuals at rates up to 20 percent greater than the central bank posted rate, for the first time giving them some ability to price lending risk.[18] Subsequently, limited flexibility was introduced for a broader range of lending transactions.[19] The central bank policy is to introduce flexibility on longer-term rates before short-term rates; on foreign currency transactions before domestic currency transactions; on large transactions before small; and on lending rates before deposit rates. For example, the central bank has liberalized entirely the rates that banks pay on foreign currency deposits in excess of the equivalent of $3 million. In 2003 rates on these deposits for different maturities varied considerably over the year. For example, for one-year deposits the rate was at a low of 0.8341 percent in June and a peak of 1.2822 percent in November, compared with a fixed rate of 0.8125 percent paid on one-year deposits of less than $3 million.[20] But generally the flexibility was highly circumscribed until the beginning of 2004, when the central bank increased to 70 percent the margin of upward adjustment that banks were allowed to make on all loans. That meant, for example, that the maximum rate that could be charged on a one-year working capital loan, when the posted rate was 5.31 percent, rose from 5.84 to 9.03 percent.

In the first half of the 1990s, the Chinese state explicitly acknowledged that banks, particularly the four large state-owned banks, were not free to base their lending decisions on commercial, rate of return, and risk considerations but had to lend funds to help the state in meeting certain policy objectives. These loans became known as policy loans. While the banks did not disclose the magnitude of these loans on any systematic basis, through 1993 policy loans typically accounted for a third of the lending of the four largest state-owned banks.[21]

In the mid-1990s the state adopted several policies to encourage banks, particularly the four largest banks, to operate on commercial principles. In 1995 the State Council promulgated the commercial bank law that included a provision then regarded as revolutionary: Banks should be responsible for their own profits

18. Chinese Banking and Finance Society (1992, p. 509).
19. However, during the Asian financial crisis this flexibility was suspended.
20. Chinese Banking and Finance Society (2003, p. 497); People's Bank of China (2002, p. 5).
21. Lardy (1998, p. 85).

and losses. To facilitate this objective, the government created three new policy banks—the Agricultural Development Bank, the China Development Bank,[22] and the Export-Import Bank—that were expected to take over the responsibility for policy lending, thus relieving the big four state-owned banks of the obligation to extend loans for policy purposes, even when there was little prospect that the borrowers could amortize the loans.

Despite these policies, nonperforming loans of state-owned banks increased rapidly in the mid-1990s. In 1994 nonperforming loans of the four largest state-owned banks stood at RMB 630 billion and constituted 20 percent of their total loans. By 1997 these numbers had jumped to RMB 1.36 trillion and 25 percent of their loans.

Improving Bank Intermediation?

In the wake of the Asian financial crisis, the government undertook a number of important organizational and regulatory reforms designed to encourage state-owned banks to operate on a more commercial basis. The central bank in 1998 dropped its management of bank lending through mandatory lending quotas and substituted indirect management through the promulgation of a number of prudential norms such as the ratio of assets to liabilities.[23] In the same year, the central bank created a series of nine supraprovincial regional offices, modeled loosely on the U.S. federal reserve system of twelve district offices. In an attempt to reduce political interference in bank lending at the provincial level, the heads of these new offices outranked provincial officials. Finally, the government created four asset management companies to serve as workout units for RMB 1.3 trillion in nonperforming loans on the books of the four largest state-owned banks and an additional RMB 100 billion in nonperforming loans of the China Development Bank. The banks received interest-bearing bonds from the asset management companies equivalent to the face value of the loans they surrendered, dramatically improving their financial position.

The central bank also tightened regulatory standards. In an important move, beginning in 1998, for example, the central bank gradually reduced the period in which banks were allowed to accrue unpaid interest on outstanding loans. Before 1998 the central bank allowed banks to count interest due on loans as income

22. Initially, this institution was known as the State Development Bank of China. Although its Chinese name remained the same, beginning in 2000 the translation of this name was changed to China Development Bank.
23. Lardy (1998, p. 208).

even if it went unpaid for as along as three years. Beginning on January 1, 1998, the State Council reduced the accrual period from two years to one.[24] The central bank shortened the accrual period to 180 days in 2000 and to 90 days in 2002, the international standard.[25] Thus when interest on a loan remains unpaid for three months, it must be backed out of the lender's income statement. Moreover, beginning in 2001 the Ministry of Finance required the major state-owned banks to write off, over a five-year period, all previously unpaid interest that was carried on their balance sheets as a receivable.[26]

Various indicators suggest that, in response to the regulatory and institutional changes, Chinese banks, particularly the four largest banks, made substantial progress in developing a commercial credit culture and that their financial performance began to improve. One indicator was a substantial reduction in the organizational structure of the four largest state-owned banks. Through the mid-1990s these banks opened an increasing number of branches and subbranch offices in order to compete for deposits to finance their loan growth. By 1995 the four largest banks operated a total of about 158,000 offices. But after 1995 China's largest banks stabilized their organizational structure, and beginning in 1998 the banks began to close offices at a fairly rapid pace. By the end of 2002, the largest four banks had closed more than a third of their offices.

A second indicator of improved bank performance is the rise of lending to households, starting in 1998. Chinese banks historically relied heavily on household deposits as a source of funding but lent overwhelmingly to state-owned companies. An early effort by the China Construction Bank in 1996 to diversify and improve the quality of their customer profile by offering car loans to individuals was thwarted by the central bank, which seemed unwilling to allow banks to lend predominantly to customers other than state-owned companies.[27] As recently as 1997, loans outstanding to households stood at only RMB 17 billion and accounted for less than 0.2 percent of the loan portfolio of Chinese banks. In the wake of the Asian financial crisis, however, the People's Bank of China recognized that allowing banks to choose their customers was essential if the central bank was to require banks to operate on a commercial basis. The central bank also recognized that consumer lending might contribute to improved bank earnings. Loans to households grew steadily and, by year-end 2003, totaled more than RMB

24. See "Notice Concerning Changing the Calculation of the Years of Accrued Interest and Setting Aside Provisions for Bad Debts of Financial Institutions," in Chinese Banking and Finance Society (1999, pp. 311–12).

25. See "Financial Supervision Review," in Chinese Banking and Finance Society (2002, p. 10).

26. Bank of China (2001, p. 83).

27. Lardy (1998, p. 82).

1.5 trillion, or 9.9 percent of all renminbi loans outstanding from the banking system. Of this amount, home mortgages accounted for RMB 1.2 trillion. Most of the balance was accounted for by car loans.

Growing lending to households is a potential good omen for two reasons. First, almost all Chinese bank lending to households is for mortgage and auto loans; very little is for unsecured credit card debt. Thus to date Chinese banks have avoided the problem encountered by Korean banks, which also sought to diversify their borrowers after the Asian financial crisis but by 2003 encountered massive losses in unsecured credit card lending. Historically, rates of default on mortgages on owner-occupied housing in most Asian countries have been quite low. Thus the growing role for mortgage loans in China may improve the quality of bank assets and contribute to higher earnings. Second, the emergence of significant lending to the household sector almost certainly reflects a reduction in the share of new lending going to state-owned companies, historically the major source of nonperforming loans for Chinese banks. Unfortunately, Chinese banks do not systematically disclose the breakdown of borrowers by form of ownership. But in 1995 loans to state-owned firms accounted for 83 percent of all bank loans outstanding.[28] The relatively quick ramp up in the share of new lending going to households—from 1.1 percent in 1998 to an average of 20.2 percent in 1999–2002 and then dropping slightly to 18.4 percent in 2003—means that the share of new loans going to other forms of ownership must have declined significantly.[29] It is very likely that the historically high share of loans claimed by the state sector is declining, which bodes well for the quality of bank assets.

The third indicator of improving efficiency of bank intermediation is that banks appear to have become more selective in their lending, starting in 1998, when the central bank gave commercial banks more flexibility to determine their levels of lending. One measure of this is the rate at which the stock of loans outstanding increased relative to gross domestic product (GDP) over the past fifteen years. In the expansionary cycle that led to a peak in the rate of investment in 1993 and a peak in inflation a year later in 1994, the annual increase in loans outstanding relative to GDP rose from about 12.5 percent in 1989 to a peak of 19 percent in 1993. By mid-1993 China's leadership recognized that excessive lending growth was causing unacceptably high levels of inflation and was leading to a growing accumulation of risks in the banking system. Vice Premier Zhu Rongji assumed the governorship of the People's Bank in July 1993 and began to institute a more restrictive monetary policy. Lending growth gradually trended

28. Lardy (1998, p. 83).
29. *Jinrong shibao* [Financial News], August 2, 2002, p. 3; People's Bank of China (2002, p. 5; 2003b, p. 2: www.pbc.gov.cn [February 24, 2004]).

downward, with the exception of 1997, when the leadership, worried that the Asian financial crisis would have a serious deleterious effect on Chinese growth, authorized increased monetary expansion. But in the wake of the Asian financial crisis in the four years from 1998 to 2001, the annual increase in the stock of loans outstanding relative to GDP remained consistently at 15 percent or less, despite the rapid growth of lending to households, which were just beginning to emerge as a significant market at the time.

A final indicator of improving bank efficiency is the decline in nonperforming loans in 2001–03. Naturally nonperforming loans fell dramatically in 1998–99, as the asset management companies assumed responsibility for RMB 1.4 trillion in nonperforming loans on the books of the four largest state-owned banks and the China Development Bank. But, subsequently, nonperforming loans first stabilized and then began to fall slightly in absolute amount for two reasons. First, a few of the stronger banks began to aggressively write off nonperforming loans from their own earnings. The Bank of China, for example, in the three years from 2001 through 2003, set aside RMB 74.5 billion in pretax earnings for provisions to be used to write off nonperforming loans. In addition, the bank wrote off RMB 24 billion in old accrued interest in 2002–03. By the end of 2003, the bank had reduced the nonperforming loans on its balance sheet to RMB 343.8 billion, or 15.9 percent of its loan book, compared with RMB 436 billion, or 27.5 percent of its loans two years earlier.[30] Second, at least for some banks, the increasing use of commercial criteria in the loans extended after 1998 appears to have significantly reduced the rate at which new loans became nonperforming.[31]

Retrogression in 2003

Bank lending increased massively in 2003, suggesting that the indicators discussed above may not reliably reflect the emergence of a more commercially oriented banking system. In 2003 loans outstanding increased by RMB 2.99 trillion, compared with an average increase of RMB 1.2 trillion in 1998–2001. Although loan growth moderated in the fourth quarter of 2003, the increase in loans outstanding relative to GDP rose to 25 percent, well above the previous historic high of 19 percent in 1993.

The extraordinarily rapid growth of loans, which got under way in the fourth quarter of 2002, appears to be the result of two factors. First, the banks may have

---

30. These numbers are based on the new more forward-looking five-category loan classification system first used at the Bank of China in the late 1990s. Bank of China (2001, p. 58; 2002, p. 15; 2004: www. bank-of-china.com/news/news200404_006.html [January 20, 2004]).

31. This was particularly evident for the Bank of China.

responded to pressure to reduce the share of their nonperforming loans by dramatically increasing the size of their loan portfolios. Second, the new leadership that assumed political power at the Sixteenth Party Congress in 2002 appears determined to sustain China's rapid growth and, if possible, to increase the pace of job creation compared to their predecessors. They were strongly supported by local government and party officials who shared these goals.

Zhou Xiaochuan, the central bank governor, and Liu Mingkang, the chairman of the newly created China Bank Regulatory Commission, in contrast, became increasingly concerned over the course of 2003 that the rapid pace of loan growth would undermine the goal of creating a financially sound, commercially oriented banking system. As early as June 2003 the central bank issued a circular restricting the real estate lending of commercial banks. And in July the central bank governor, at the central bank's biannual conference, expressed the view that the rapid growth of lending was creating higher risks for the financial system.[32] The bank raised the reserve requirement for commercial banks by 1 percentage point effective September 21, 2003, in an attempt to slow the growth of lending. In the same month, the Central Bank Regulatory Commission announced that it would evaluate the sufficiency of banks' risk controls to deal with the surge in lending.[33]

Government Liabilities

What are the implications of China's state-owned banking and financial system for fiscal sustainability? Will the government be able to ensure the stability of the banking and financial system even as nonperforming loans continue to accumulate? Answering these questions starts with a broader look at the government's liabilities, both explicit and contingent.

Treasury Debt

Treasury debt has grown rapidly since 1994, when the Ministry of Finance adopted a policy of financing the entire government budget deficit through the sale of bonds. As reflected in table 5-1, gross issuance of treasury bonds rose from an annual average of less than RMB 40 billion in 1991–93 to more than RMB 300 billion in 1997–98 and is anticipated to reach RMB 702 billion in 2004. Because much of this debt is relatively short term, treasury bond issuance net of maturing treasury debt is much smaller—for example, RMB 352.5 billion in

32. "Zhou Xiaochuan at the Central Bank Work Conference Promotes Taking the Important Thoughts of the 'Three Represents' to Lead Financial Macroeconomic Adjustment," *Jinrong shibao* [Financial News], July 15, 2003.
33. Phelim (2003).

Table 5-1. *Treasury Debt, 1986–2004*
Billions of renminbi, unless otherwise noted

Year	Issued	Redeemed	Outstanding	
			Amount	*Percent of GDP*
1986	6.251	0.665	29.307	2.87
1987	11.687	1.841	39.153	3.27
1988	18.877	2.166	55.864	3.74
1989	22.391	1.322	76.933	4.55
1990	19.723	7.622	89.034	4.80
1991	28.125	11.160	105.999	4.90
1992	46.078	23.805	128.272	4.82
1993	38.131	12.329	154.074	4.45
1994	113.755	39.189	228.640	4.90
1995	151.086	49.696	330.030	5.66
1996	184.777	78.664	436.143	6.43
1997	241.179	126.429	550.888	7.37
1998	380.877	155.084	776.570	9.74
1999	401.500	123.870	1,054.200	12.87
2000	465.700	217.900	1,302.000	14.56
2001	488.400	228.600	1,561.800	16.28
2002	593.430	221.620	1,933.610	18.88
2003	628.000	275.500	2,286.110	19.59
2004	702.200	n.a.	n.a.	n.a.

Source: China Securities Regulatory Commission (2003, pp. 14–15); People's Bank of China (2003c); Jin Renqing (2004); National Bureau of Statistics of China (2003, p. 55); National Bureau of Statistics of China, press release, January 20, 2004 (www.stats.gov.cn/tjdt/gjtjjdt/200401200061.htm).
n.a. Not available.

2003. Nonetheless, the stock of treasury debt outstanding at year-end 2003—about RMB 2.3 trillion—was more than twenty times the RMB 106 billion outstanding at year-end 1991. But because of rapid economic growth, the size of this debt relative to GDP increased only threefold, from 4.9 percent at year-end 1991 to 9.7 percent in 1998 and to 19.6 percent at year-end 2003.

Contingent Liabilities

In addition to explicit treasury debt, several types of debt can be regarded as contingent government liabilities. These include the indebtedness of provincial and local governments, debt issued by state policy banks, nonperforming assets of state-owned financial institutions, and the unfunded pension liabilities of government and government-controlled entities, especially state-owned companies. The magnitude of some of these contingent liabilities is known with confidence, while some, because of a lack of transparency, can only be estimated, sometimes with a potentially wide margin of error.

STATE-OWNED POLICY BANKS. Information on the debt of China's state-owned policy banks is published regularly. Debt issuance by the Agricultural Development Bank, the China Development Bank, and the Export-Import Bank increased sharply, from an average of RMB 125 billion in 1996–97 to RMB 452 billion in 2003.[34] Most of this debt is not sold on commercial terms but is placed with the four largest state-owned banks at interest rates that are unfavorable to debt holders. At year-end 2002, the reported value of policy financial bonds outstanding was RMB 1 trillion.[35] The value of these bonds outstanding at year-end 2003 was an estimated RMB 1.3 trillion.[36]

STATE-OWNED ASSET MANAGEMENT COMPANIES. A second category of contingent government debt is the bonds issued by the four state-owned asset management companies created in 1998. These institutions purchased RMB 1.4 trillion of nonperforming loans from state-owned banks at face value. The purchase of the assets was financed by the issuance of bonds with a face value of RMB 820 billion and the assumption of existing loans from the central bank to individual state-owned banks valued at about RMB 600 billion. The bonds issued reportedly carry an interest rate of 2.25 percent and have a maturity of ten years. The loans assumed from the central bank carried an interest rate of 3.78 percent in 1999, but presumably this declined to 3.24 percent starting in February 2002.[37]

Estimating the size of the contingent liability of asset management company bonds and loans is extremely difficult because of the lack of transparency of these institutions. Although Chinese news media cover the efforts of the asset management companies to recover on the bad loans they hold, the institutions do not issue annual or other periodic reports of their financial position. Thus it is difficult to know the extent to which their recoveries on nonperforming loans are in

34. China Securities Regulatory Commission (2002, pp. 10–11). RMB 452 billion excludes the $500 million bond issue of the State Development Bank sold on the international market in 2003. People's Bank of China (2003b, p. 14: www.pbc.gov.cn [February 24, 2004]).

35. National Bureau of Statistics of China (2003, p. 707).

36. The estimate of bonds outstanding at year end 2003 is based on the amount of new bonds issued in 2003 (People's Bank of China 2003b, p. 14) and the assumption that the average maturity of the stock of bonds outstanding was the same in 2003 as in 2002. China Securities Regulatory Commission (2003, pp. 14–15).

37. People's Bank of China (2003a, p. 71).

excess of their operating costs. Through the end of 2003, they had disposed of RMB 509.4 billion in loans and recovered RMB 99.4 billion in cash.[38] If this recovery rate of about 20 percent could be sustained as additional assets are sold, the total cash recovery of the asset management companies would be RMB 310 billion.

Recently, however, Xie Ping, director of the Financial Stability Bureau of the central bank, disclosed that the RMB 310 billion in recoveries is a gross figure, which does not include the operating costs of the asset management companies. He estimates that their costs will be RMB 175.5 billion, meaning that their net recovery will be only RMB 134.5 billion. The Ministry of Finance will have to use budgetary funds to redeem the asset management company bonds when they mature in 2009 or roll them over and finance them like regular treasury debt.[39] Thus the contingent liabilities of the asset management companies as a group are RMB 1,265.5 billion.[40]

NONPERFORMING LOANS IN THE FINANCIAL SYSTEM. Data on nonperforming loans of banks and other financial institutions have been released frequently in recent years (see table 5-2 for 2003). China is currently in transition from its traditional four-tier classification system, in which loans are classified based primarily on payment status, to its newer five-tier classification system, which is more forward looking and closer to international standards for classifying nonperforming loans. On the five-tier classification system, nonperforming loans of major financial institutions at year-end 2003 stood at RMB 2.44 trillion, an amount equivalent to about 18 percent of the loans of these institutions and 21 percent of GDP. Other portions of the financial system have not yet adopted the five-tier reporting system, so for the entire banking and financial system, nonperforming loans are reported on the older, four-tier loan classification system. If the five-tier classification system were used, nonperforming loans for the entire financial system at year-end 2003 would have been between RMB 2.9 trillion and RMB 3.1 trillion.[41]

---

38. Jin Yan (2004, p. 11).

39. Liu (2004, p. 9).

40. This number, however, may be a substantial underestimate. It appears that Xie Ping's estimate of the cost of asset recovery does not include the interest cost of the bonds issued by the asset management companies and the interest on the central bank loans that the asset management companies have assumed. In 2002 this interest cost was an estimated RMB 37.9 billion. Assuming that the disposal of loans is completed at the end of 2006, that the asset management companies are unable to prepay any of the bonds issued in 1999, that they are unable to repay any of the loans outstanding from the central bank, and that the interest rate on borrowing from the central bank remains unchanged, the cumulative costs to the asset management companies for interest alone would be RMB 303 billion.

41. If the ratio of 1.2 of nonperforming loans measured by the five- and four-tier classification systems in the four largest state-owned banks is a reasonable conjecture of the same ratio for the entire financial sys-

Table 5-2. *Nonperforming Loans, China's Banking and Financial System, Year End 2003*

Institution	Amount (billions of renminbi)	Percent of total loans	Percent of GDP
State-owned commercial banks			
Five tier	1,920	20.36	16.4
Four tier	1,590	16.86	13.6
State policy banks (five tier)	336	17.39	2.9
Joint stock banks (five tier)	188	7.92	1.6
Major financial institutions (five tier)[a]	2,440	17.8	20.9
City commercial banks	n.a.	n.a.	n.a.
Urban credit cooperatives	n.a.	n.a.	n.a.
Rural credit cooperatives	n.a.	n.a.	n.a.
Nonbank financial institutions	n.a.	n.a.	n.a.
Banking and financial system (four tier)	2,400	15.19	20.6

Source: Zhuo (2004); National Bureau of Statistics of China (2004, p. 11).
n.a. Not available.
a. Includes state-owned commercial banks, state policy banks, and joint stock banks.

The size of the contingent government debt associated with the accumulation of nonperforming loans in the banking and financial system depends on three critical variables. First is the earning power of each of the several categories of financial institution. If nonperforming loans can be written off over time from robust earnings of financial institutions, the size of the government's contingent liability is reduced. Second is the willingness of the government to impose a portion of the losses on depositors. The greater the ability and willingness of the government to pass on the losses to savers, the smaller the size of the government's contingent liability associated with nonperforming loans. Third, the higher the rate of recovery that can be achieved when nonperforming loans are sold or otherwise disposed of, the smaller the contingent liability associated with these bad loans. None of these factors favors the government.

---

tem, then nonperforming loans for the system as a whole are an estimated RMB 2.9 trillion. For the four largest state-owned banks, however, this ratio has fallen substantially over time, probably because of a tightening of the standards used in the four-tier classification scheme. For example, in 2002 the ratio for the four largest state-owned banks was 1.4. It is not clear that other parts of the financial system, particularly rural credit cooperatives and nonbank financial institutions, have instituted increasingly stringent classification standards within the four-tier system.

The ability of banks and other financial institutions to write off nonperforming loans from their own financial resources is heavily constrained by their relatively low earnings. For example, the after-tax earnings of the four largest state-owned banks in 2001 and 2002 were RMB 22.4 billion and RMB 26.7 billion, respectively. That represented 1.0 and 1.3 percent of the outstanding nonperforming loans of those institutions in the same years. The earning power of some other parts of the financial system, particularly rural credit cooperatives and non-bank financial institutions, is even more limited than that of the four largest state-owned commercial banks. In short, the earnings of most of China's financial institutions are so small that there is little prospect that these institutions will be able to reduce nonperforming loans on their own. It is more realistic to regard non-performing loans as a government contingent liability.

Similarly, the Chinese government historically has shown little willingness to pass on losses of the financial system to depositors, which in the Chinese banking system are predominantly households. The easiest way to shift part of the cost to savers is through an inflation tax. If the rate of interest on deposits remains relatively constant when inflation rises, the real value of bank liabilities (that is, deposits of savers) declines. But in the periods September 1988 through December 1991 and July 1993 through April 1996, when the rate of inflation rose sharply, the government offered savers so-called value guarantee deposits designed to insulate longer-term savings from the corrosive effects of inflation.[42] In short, the appetite of the government for imposing losses on depositors historically has been minimal. There is no reason to believe that this preference has changed in more recent years.

The third factor determining the share of nonperforming loans that should be regarded as a government contingent liability is the likely rate of recovery that can be achieved when the nonperforming loans are transferred to asset management companies for liquidation or are resolved by internal workout units of the banks themselves. At one point, there was some optimism on this front. But, as discussed, for the nonperforming loans transferred from banks to asset management companies in 1998 and 1999, it appears that the recovery rate, net of costs, will be less than 10 percent of the face value of the loans. Absent evidence that the quality of nonperforming loans currently held by the banks and other financial institutions is any higher than the nonperforming loans transferred from banks to asset management companies in 1998–99, the net recovery is assumed to be no more than 10 percent.

42. Lardy (1998, pp. 107–15).

With all three of these factors combined, 90 percent of reported nonperforming loans in the financial system should be regarded as a government contingent liability.

GOVERNMENT DEBT. The debt of provincial and local governments is the most difficult component of government contingent liabilities to estimate. China's 1994 budget law precludes these governments from running budget deficits and from issuing bonds. Nonetheless, these governments have incurred significant debts. This debt takes the form of direct bank loans, defaults on loans guaranteed by local governments, wage and pension arrears, and so forth. The magnitude of this debt can be estimated from sporadic reports in the Chinese press. Fortunately, at least some of these reports quote authoritative figures. Unfortunately, even fragmentary information on debt at the provincial and prefectural levels is not available. According to the director of the Institute of Finance of the Ministry of Finance, the total debt of township-level governments in 2001 was RMB 370 billion. Although the director acknowledged that this is a "preliminary estimate" and "the actual situation might be more serious," it is used as an estimate of the debt of township governments in China.[43] According to the head of China's national auditing office, the debt of forty-nine counties and county-level cities located in ten western and central provinces in mid-2003 was RMB 16.3 billion, or RMB 333 million per administrative unit.[44] China had a total of 2,860 administrative units at the county level at year-end 2002, suggesting that county government indebtedness was RMB 952 billion.[45] Prefecture-level governments traditionally have supplied relatively modest levels of social services and have been responsible for few investment initiatives, suggesting that their indebtedness is relatively low.

Provinces, in contrast, undertake significant expenditures, especially for investment. And, given their political leverage, particularly over state banks operating in their jurisdiction, they may have more ability to accumulate debt than lower levels of government. But estimated debt of RMB 1 trillion at the provincial level and RMB 200 billion at the prefecture level should be regarded as not much more than placeholders, to be replaced with better estimates in the future.

China's unfunded pension liabilities also should be regarded as a contingent government liability. According to a World Bank study, various Chinese estimates made in the mid-1990s placed unfunded pension liabilities at as much as three to

43. Jia (2004, p. B2).
44. Jia (2004, p. B2).
45. National Bureau of Statistics of China (2003, p. 3).

Table 5-3. *Summary of Government Liabilities, China, Year End 2003*
Billions of renminbi

Type of debt	Amount
Explicit treasury debt	2,300
Contingent debt	7,660–860
Financial institution bonds	1,275
Asset management company indebtedness, net of recovery	1,265
Provincial and local government debt	2,520
Province	1,000
Prefecture	200
County	950
Township	370
Nonperforming loans of financial institutions, net of recovery	2,600–800
Total explicit and contingent debt	9,960–10,160

four times GDP. The World Bank, largely on the basis of rule-of-thumb comparisons with other countries, suggests that the amount was substantially less: no more than 50 percent of GDP.[46] Given the uncertainties of estimating these contingent liabilities, especially in light of the dramatic reduction in the number of workers in the state-owned sector, this obligation is not included in the estimate of total government contingent liabilities.[47]

Summary of Government Contingent Liabilities

The estimates of various types of government contingent liabilities are summarized in table 5-3. Government contingent liabilities at year-end 2003, not including unfunded pension obligations, totaled between RMB 7.66 trillion and RMB 7.86 trillion.[48] Explicit and contingent government debt combined was about RMB 10 trillion, an amount equivalent to about 85 percent of GDP in the same year.

---

46. World Bank (1997, p. 32).

47. When state-owned firms go through bankruptcy or are reorganized, some workers who lose their jobs receive a lump-sum severance payment in lieu of a previously promised pension on retirement.

48. There may be some double counting in this estimate. For example, some provincial and local government debt is debt owed to banks. If provincial and local governments have not been servicing this borrowing, the lenders should have classified it as nonperforming. Lacking any information both on the share of government debt that reflects borrowing from banks and on the share of nonperforming loans extended to government borrowers, no adjustment is made for this potential double counting.

Table 5-4. *Overall Budgetary Balance, China, 1996–2004*

Year	Budget deficit as percent of GDP
1996	−1.6
1997	−1.8
1998	−3.0
1999	−4.0
2000	−3.6
2001	−3.1
2002	−3.3
2003[a]	−2.8
2004[a]	2.2

Source: International Monetary Fund (2000, p. 5; 2003a, p. 6; 2004, p. 6).
a. IMF staff projection.

Fiscal Sustainability

By most conventional indicators, government debt in China does not pose much of a fiscal challenge. China's budget deficit as a percentage of GDP in recent years, shown in table 5-4, remains significantly higher than in the mid-1990s. But it has been declining since reaching a peak of 4 percent of GDP in 1999.

Interest expenditures on the domestic debt as a percentage of central government expenditures, shown in table 5-5, similarly have been trending downward from their peak in 1998. By 2002 the burden had declined to less than 10 percent of central government budgetary expenditures. In short, while treasury debt outstanding as a percentage of GDP in 2002 was more than quadruple that in 1993, the interest burden of servicing that debt in 2002 was only two and a half times that in 1993.

While these two indicators are useful measures for an initial assessment of China's fiscal position, they are hardly a basis for optimism concerning China's long-term fiscal sustainability for three reasons. First, real interest rates on government debt have declined significantly and are at relatively low levels.[49] Were interest rates to rise to levels of only a few years ago, the interest burden of servicing the

---

49. Ten-year government book entry bonds sold in 1997 at an interest rate of 9.78 percent. In the first half of 2002 ten-year bonds were issued with an interest rate of 2.54 percent. The consumer price index rose 2.8 percent in 1997 and fell 0.8 percent in 2002, suggesting that the real interest rate paid on government bonds of ten-year maturity fell by roughly half over the five-year period.

Table 5-5. *Interest Outlays on Domestic Treasury Debt, China, 1993–2002*
Billions of renminbi unless otherwise indicated

Year	Interest outlays	Central government expenditures	Interest burden (percent)[a]
1993	5.2	136	3.8
1994	12.5	188	6.6
1995	28.2	228	12.4
1996	38.7	254	15.2
1997	49.1	302	16.2
1998	74.6	387	19.2
1999	57.6	473	12.2
2000	69.0	552	12.5
2001	75.8	577	13.1
2002	64.5	677	9.5

Source: BNP Paribas, Deutsche Bank, and UBS Investment Bank (2003); National Bureau of Statistics of China (2003, p. 288); Lardy (2003, p. 76).
a. As share of central government expenditures.

debt would increase significantly.[50] Second, central government expenditure as a share of GDP increased substantially over the past decade. Absent that favorable change, the interest rate burden would have grown significantly.[51] If the growth of central government expenditures as a percentage of GDP were to taper off, the interest burden of treasury debt would rise significantly, even if interest rates remained relatively low. Third, and perhaps most important, government expenditures do not yet reflect the cost of financing most of the implicit government debt. Eventually this must change.

A crude sense of China's fiscal sustainability can be obtained by assuming that all contingent liabilities are made explicit and have to be financed. The estimated interest cost of financing estimated year-end 2003 contingent liabilities in 2004 is about RMB 200 billion.[52] This represents about 7 percent of total expenditures in the combined central and local budgets for 2004.[53] At least in the short run, this

50. The rise in the interest burden in this circumstance would be relatively rapid since the average maturity of China's treasury debt is relatively short, about four years.

51. Because of revenue buoyancy, total government revenues as a percentage of GDP rose dramatically from 10.7 percent in 1995 to 18.6 percent in 2003. Over the same period, the central government share of total budgetary expenditures increased 1 percentage point, reinforcing further the effect of revenue buoyancy. Absent these two effects, interest payments of RMB 64.5 billion in 2002 would have absorbed 16.5 percent of central government expenditures, three-quarters more than they actually absorbed.

52. Based on the average interest rate of 2.6 percent paid on treasury bonds of varying maturities in the first quarter of 2004 (People's Bank of China 2004, p. 67).

could be financed through some combination of lower expenditures on other items and a somewhat higher budget deficit financed by issuing more treasury bonds.

However, over any significant period of time, this will result in a further increase in public debt. Normally such a rising ratio of debt to GDP suggests that the government's fiscal position is not sustainable. This is particularly relevant for China, since its ratio of public domestic debt to GDP already is about two times the average level of emerging markets.[54]

The results of two scenarios designed to explore China's fiscal sustainability on a more systematic basis appear in table 5-6. These scenarios assume that gross domestic product expands at an average annual rate of 7 percent; that the government pays interest of 6 percent on its treasury debt and the new debt issued by the asset management companies, that government revenue as a share of gross domestic product grows at half a percent a year, and that the growth of noninterest expenditure is restrained to absorb only half of the expansion of revenues.[55] The base line is the government's fiscal position in 2003, adjusted to include budgetary financing of the interest cost of the RMB 1.4 trillion in obligations assumed by the state-owned asset management companies in 1999.[56] The two scenarios each begin with the assumption that the asset management companies at end-of-year 2003 removed RMB 3,000 trillion in nonperforming loans from the financial system in exchange for interest-bearing bonds, much as it did in the initial hiving off of RMB 1,400 trillion in nonperforming loans in 1998–99, when the asset management companies were first created.

Both scenarios assume that, despite improvements in the credit culture of the banks in recent years, a significant portion of the huge increase in loans outstanding from the fourth quarter of 2002 through the first quarter of 2004 becomes nonperforming during the years 2005 through 2008. The reason is that the massive increase in credit from the fourth quarter of 2002 through the first quarter of 2004 fueled an investment boom that is not sustainable. As the growth

---

53. Jin Renqing (2004).

54. This comparison is based on a definition of public sector domestic debt that includes the liabilities of the central government, subnational governments, and public sector enterprises but excludes contingent liabilities of the government such as public sector pension liabilities and the potential costs of bank recapitalization. International Monetary Fund (2003b, p. 116).

55. The scenarios assume that when the asset management company bonds issued at 2.25 percent interest in 1999 mature in 2009 they will be rolled over and the interest rate on the new bonds will be the same as the 6 percent paid on treasury debt.

56. The implicit assumption here is that the process of recovery of nonperforming loans has not provided the asset management companies with funds sufficient to pay the interest on the bonds they issued to the banks. Cinda asset management company is believed to have paid a portion of the interest due on its bonds, but the other asset management companies appear to be in a much weaker position.

Table 5-6. *Two Fiscal Scenarios, China, 2003–13*

Scenario	2003	2004	2005	2006	2007	2008	2009	2010	2011	2012	2013
20 percent scenario											
Government revenue											
(% of GDP)	0.186	0.191	0.196	0.201	0.206	0.211	0.216	0.221	0.226	0.231	0.236
Government expenditure											
(% of GDP)	0.214	0.237	0.242	0.248	0.252	0.256	0.261	0.264	0.266	0.268	0.270
Noninterest	0.205	0.208	0.210	0.213	0.215	0.218	0.220	0.223	0.225	0.228	0.230
Interest	0.009	0.029	0.032	0.035	0.037	0.038	0.041	0.041	0.041	0.040	0.040
Budget balance	−0.028	−0.046	−0.046	−0.046	−0.046	−0.045	−0.046	−0.043	−0.040	−0.037	−0.034
Total debt-to-GDP ratio	0.339	0.603	0.663	0.703	0.727	0.735	0.732	0.727	0.720	0.710	0.697
Memo (billions of RMB)											
Budget deficit	324	576	613	665	705	732	797	803	804	797	782
Government debt	3,956	7,532	8,856	10,054	11,114	12,023	12,820	13,624	14,427	15,224	16,007
Treasury debt	2,286	2,862	3,830	4,762	5,644	6,464	7,262	8,065	8,869	9,666	10,448
Existing AMC debt	1,400	1,400	1,400	1,400	1,400	1,400	1,400	1,400	1,400	1,400	1,400
New AMC debt	0	3,000	3,355	3,622	3,800	3,889	3,889	3,889	3,889	3,889	3,889
Special treasury debt	270	270	270	270	270	270	270	270	270	270	270

40 percent scenario

Government revenue											
(% of GDP)	0.186	0.191	0.196	0.201	0.206	0.211	0.216	0.221	0.226	0.231	0.236
Government expenditure											
(% of GDP)	0.214	0.237	0.243	0.252	0.258	0.263	0.268	0.271	0.273	0.275	0.277
Noninterest	0.205	0.208	0.210	0.213	0.215	0.218	0.220	0.223	0.225	0.228	0.230
Interest	0.009	0.029	0.033	0.039	0.043	0.045	0.048	0.048	0.048	0.047	0.047
Budget balance	−0.028	−0.046	−0.047	−0.051	−0.052	−0.052	−0.053	−0.050	−0.047	−0.044	−0.041
Total debt-to-GDP ratio	0.339	0.603	0.718	0.796	0.842	0.860	0.857	0.851	0.842	0.831	0.817
Memo (billions of RMB)											
Budget deficit	324	576	634	725	795	843	921	934	942	944	938
Government debt	3,956	7,532	9,588	11,379	12,884	14,083	15,004	15,938	16,881	17,825	18,763
Treasury debt	2,286	2,862	4,207	5,465	6,615	7,636	8,557	9,491	10,434	11,378	12,316
Existing AMC debt	1,400	1,400	1,400	1,400	1,400	1,400	1,400	1,400	1,400	1,400	1,400
New AMC debt	0	3,000	3,711	4,244	4,599	4,777	4,777	4,777	4,777	4,777	4,777
Special treasury debt	270	270	270	270	270	270	270	270	270	270	270

of fixed-asset investment moderates, economic growth likely will decline significantly over a period of several years. Overall corporate profitability is likely to decline, with particularly sharp declines in sectors in which "blind expansion and low-quality, duplicate construction projects" have led to significant excess capacity.[57] Borrowers in these sectors, which the central bank has identified as including property, steel, aluminum, and cement, may be unable to service the debts taken out to finance their investment projects, thus leading to an increase in nonperforming loans. The same phenomena occurred following the last credit boom of 1989–93. The first scenario assumes that 20 percent of the increase in the stock of loans becomes nonperforming; the second assumes that 40 percent of the increase becomes nonperforming.

These scenarios suggest that the Chinese government has the fiscal capacity to assume the responsibility for the entire estimated RMB 3 trillion in nonperforming loans in the banking system at year end 2003 as well as to absorb substantial additional nonperforming loans that might emerge over the next few years. In the first scenario the government budget peaks at 4.6 percent of GDP and then declines steadily, reaching 3.4 percent of GDP in 2013. The debt-to-GDP ratio reaches a peak of 74 percent and then very gradually ebbs. In the second, less favorable, scenario these ratios peak at somewhat higher levels but also decline in the out years of the scenario. In short, in neither scenario do we see the unambiguous signals of lack of fiscal sustainability—ever-expanding budget deficits and a steadily rising ratio of the stock of debt relative to gross domestic product.

Conclusions

The scenarios suggest that the fiscal burden of absorbing the poor lending decisions of Chinese banks and other financial institutions is sustainable. However, China's overall fiscal position is probably more challenging than the scenarios summarized in table 5-6 suggest. This judgment is based on several factors:

—First, the scenarios may be too bullish on revenue growth. Government revenue as a share of GDP has risen strongly since the mid-1990s but revenue buoyancy in the future could fall below the assumed rate.

—Second, the assumption that the government can limit the annual growth of noninterest expenditure to an amount equal to only half the growth of revenue may be too optimistic. China's political leaders face growing pressure to expand government programs to improve health care and education, mitigate environmental degradation, and meet other urgent social needs. If expenditures on these

57. People's Bank of China (2003b, p. 30: www.pbc.gov.cn [February 24, 2004]).

programs expand more than assumed in the scenarios, annual budget deficits will be larger and the debt-to-GDP ratio potentially higher.

—Third, the scenarios focus on the fiscal implications of the banking and financial system. The cost of financing provincial and local government debt and unfunded state pension obligations is excluded from the analysis. Unfunded pension liabilities, for example, could be financed from the gradual sale of state assets. If this proves infeasible for any reason the fiscal burden would be much greater than suggested by the scenarios.

—Fourth, the scenarios assume that banks are far enough along on the transition to operation on a commercial basis that any loans made after the recent credit boom that become nonperforming will be written off from internal earnings. This assumption could prove too optimistic—meaning that the scenarios understate the government's fiscal burden.

References

Bank of China. 2001. *Annual Report 2001*. Beijing.
———. 2002. *Annual Report 2002*. Beijing.
———. 2004. "Bank of China Realizes RMB 57 Billion Yuan in Operating Profit in 2003 [in Chinese]." Beijing.
Beijing Normal University, Economics and Resource Management Research Institute. 2003. *A Report on the Development of China's Market Economy* [in Chinese]. Beijing: Chinese Ministry of Foreign Economics and Trade Publishing House.
BNP Paribas, Deutsche Bank, and UBS Investment Bank. 2003. "People's Republic of China % Bonds." Preliminary Offering Circular, October 15.
Byrd, William. 1987. "Impact of the Two-Tier Plan/Market System in Chinese Industry." *Journal of Comparative Economics* 11 (September): 295–308.
China Securities Regulatory Commission. 2002. *China Securities and Futures Statistical Yearbook 2002*. Beijing: Baijia Publishing House.
———. 2003. *China Securities and Futures Statistical Yearbook 2003*. Beijing: Baijia Publishing House.
China State Statistical Bureau. 1983. *China Statistical Yearbook 1983* [in Chinese]. Beijing: Statistical Publishing House.
Chinese Banking and Finance Society. 1992. *Almanac of China's Banking and Finance 1992* [in Chinese]. Beijing: China Financial Publishing House.
———. 1999. *Almanac of China's Banking and Finance 1999* [in Chinese]. Beijing: China Financial Publishing House.
———. 2002. *Almanac of China's Banking and Finance 2002* [in Chinese]. Beijing: China Financial Publishing House.
———. 2003. *Almanac of China's Banking and Finance 2003* [in Chinese]. Beijing: China Financial Publishing House.
International Monetary Fund. 2000. "IMF Concludes Article IV Consultation with China." Public Information Notice 00/71, September 1. Washington.

———. 2003a. "IMF Concludes 2003 Article IV Consultation with the People's Republic of China." Public Information Notice 03/136, November 18. Washington.

———. 2003b. *World Economic Outlook: Public Debt in Emerging Markets.* Washington.

———. 2004. "IMF Concludes 2004 Article IV Consultation with the People's Republic of China." Public Information Notice 04/99, August 25. Washington.

Jia Hepeng. 2004. "Local Government Debts Sound Warning." *China Daily Business Weekly,* April 5–11, p. B2.

Jin Renqing. 2004. "Report on the Implementation of the Central and Local Budgets for 2003 and on the Draft Central and Local Budgets for 2004." Paper delivered at the Second Session, Tenth National People's Congress, March 6. *China Economic News,* Supplement 4, May 24.

Jin Yan. 2004. "Banks Fighting to Bring Down NPLs." *China Daily,* March 24, p. 11.

Lardy, Nicholas R. 1998. *China's Unfinished Economic Revolution.* Brookings.

———. 2002. *Integrating China into the Global Economy.* Brookings.

———. 2003. "When Will China's Financial System Meet China's Needs?" In *How Far across the River? Chinese Policy Reform at the Millennium,* edited by Nicholas C. Hope, Dennis Tao Yang, and Mu Yang Li, pp. 67–96. Stanford University Press.

Liu Ping. 2004. "Disposal of Nonperforming Loans to End." *China Economic News,* January 5.

Nan Ke. 2004. "Assets in China's Banking and Financial System Exceed RMB 27 Trillion." *Jinrong shibao* [Financial News], March 10.

National Bureau of Statistics of China. 1998. *China Statistical Yearbook 1998.* Beijing: China Statistics Press.

———. 2003. *China Statistical Yearbook 2003.* Beijing: China Statistics Press.

———. 2004. "Statistical Communiqué of the People's Republic of China on National Economic and Social Development in 2003." *China Daily,* February 27, p. 11.

People's Bank of China. 1998. *Quarterly Statistical Bulletin 1.* Beijing.

———. 2002. *Report on Implementation of Monetary Policy in China in 2002* [in Chinese]. Beijing.

———. 2003a. *Quarterly Statistical Bulletin 4.* Beijing.

———. 2003b. *Report on Implementation of Monetary Policy in China in 2003* [in Chinese]. Beijing.

———. 2003c. *Quarterly Monetary Policy Report 2003 Q4.* Beijing.

———. 2004. *Quarterly Statistical Bulletin 2.* Beijing.

Phelim Kyne. 2003. "Chinese Regulator to Probe Surging Growth in Lending." *Wall Street Journal,* September 11.

World Bank. 1997. *Pension Reform in China: Old Age Security.* Washington.

Wu Jinglian and Zhao Renwei. 1987. "The Dual Price System in Chinese Industry." *Journal of Comparative Economics* 11 (September): 309–18.

Zhuo Fu. 2004. "Why We Must Emphasize Capital in the Third Why of the Shareholding Transformation of State-Owned Commercial Banks." *Jinrong shibao* [Financial News], March 23, p. 3.

III

Country Analysis: Indonesia and India

P. S. SRINIVAS
DJAUHARI SITORUS

6

State-Owned Banks in Indonesia

A S IN MUCH of the rest of the developing world, state-owned banks in Indonesia originated with the government's objectives to channel resources to "priority" sectors of the economy as well as to provide financial services to underserved parts of a widely dispersed country. Each of the banks was also established with a mandate to finance a specific sector of the economy. For much of the country's history, these banks have played a major role in the country's economy—at times controlling over three-fourths of deposits and assets of the banking system—and they continue to control almost half the assets and deposits of the banking system. Also in line with many developing countries, the banking sector dominates the country's economy, accounting for over 80 percent of the financial sector.

The role of state-owned banks has, however, evolved over time. After starting as agents for channeling subsidized credit (provided principally through rediscounting facilities from the central bank, Bank Indonesia) to specific sectors of the economy, these banks have become full-fledged commercial banks. While their privileged access to cheap funding from Bank Indonesia has declined over time, as Indonesia implemented reforms in the financial sector, and while their reported performance in terms of profitability and capital adequacy has improved since the 1997 crisis, they continue to face the usual gamut of problems associated with state ownership. Weak governance and susceptibility to political pressure is a major issue, while the implicit government guarantee (with or without the current blanket guarantee on deposits) to depositors in these banks weakens incentives to focus on performance. Despite efforts by the regulator, state-owned banks also face problems of weak regulation and supervision, given the political considerations involved. As Indonesia extricates itself from the devastating effects of the 1997 crisis and looks ahead, a key challenge is to squarely address the role of these banks in its economy going forward.

Much has been written about the Indonesian financial sector. Nasution and Balino and Sundararajan provide detailed overviews of the Indonesian financial sector before and during the early 1980s and Indonesia's first efforts at financial sector reform.[1] Nasution and Woo focus on the issue of international debt in Indonesia's economy and discuss the political economy of state-owned banks in the 1980s.[2] Cole and Slade review the Indonesian financial sector development between the 1960s and the late 1980s.[3] Hanna and Binhadi assess various financial sector reform packages in Indonesia from 1983 to 1991 and study their effects on the real economy.[4] Harris, Schiantarelli, and Siregar focus on the impact of financial liberalization in Indonesia on corporate sector financing.[5] During the mid- to late 1990s, much of the literature focusing on the East Asian financial crisis also discussed the Indonesian case at length.[6] More recently, Santoso provides an in-depth review of Indonesian financial and corporate sector reform.[7] Enoch and others, Kenward, and the World Bank provide excellent overviews of the evolution of banking crisis and its management.[8] Boediono assesses the political economy of the International Monetary Fund's (IMF) support programs under three Indonesian presidents and its impacts on financial sector reform.[9] Redway assesses the role of the Indonesian Bank Restructuring Agency (IBRA) in reforming Indonesia's banking sector.[10] McLeod reviews the letters of intent from the government of Indonesia to the IMF and evaluates the crisis recovery program.[11] Hofman and Rodrick-Jones provide an analysis of the institutional weaknesses

---

1. Nasution (1983); Balino and Sundararajan (1986).
2. Nasution and Woo (1989).
3. Cole and Slade (1990, 1996).
4. Hanna (1994); Binhadi (1995).
5. Harris, Schiantarelli, and Siregar (1992).
6. See for example Claessens, Djankov, and Klingebiel (1999).
7. Santoso (2000).
8. Enoch and others (2001, 2003); Kenward (2003); World Bank (1998, 2000).
9. Boediono (2002).
10. Redway (2002).
11. McLeod (2003).

underlying Indonesia's rapid growth before the onset of the crisis and address banking sector issues as part of the country's overall institutional framework.[12]

Given the major role of state-owned banks in the Indonesian financial sector, many of the publications cited above necessarily touch upon issues related to these banks. This chapter's contribution is as an analysis of recent developments regarding state-owned banks after a survey of the literature. We examine the rationale for establishing state-owned banks in Indonesia and their early role. We then trace the impacts of various financial sector reforms on these banks and discuss their evolving roles, focusing on the impact of the 1997 financial crisis and on the role of these banks in the mid-2000s and into the future. The chapter considers only the large, national state-owned banks, those that dominate the banking system. It does not focus on regional development banks nor on the details of the 1997 financial crisis.[13] IBRA and its role in the resolution of the crisis is also touched upon only in the context of state-owned banks (for details on this issue, see the publications in note 13). More recent policy issues such as the financial sector safety net, including the proposed deposit insurance scheme to replace the blanket guarantee, the creation of a unified financial supervisory authority, and the new banking landscape proposed by Bank Indonesia are touched upon only in the context of their relevance to state-owned banks.[14]

A Rationale for a Government Role in the Banking Sector

Why do governments own banks? Two broad views—the development view and the political view—help to explain the role of governments in the financial sector.[15] The development view focuses on the necessity of financial development for economic growth. Observers have argued that, while in some industrial countries private banks have been important vehicles of channeling private savings into industrial development, in others—especially developing countries—economic institutions were not sufficiently developed to play this critical role. In such countries the governments could step in, set up financial institutions, and through them help both financial and economic development. This view is broadly in line with the strand of literature in development economics that advocates government

12. Hofman and Rodrick-Jones (2004).

13. For comments on the crisis, see Enoch and others (2001, 2003); Kenward (2003); World Bank (1998, 2000); *Survey of Recent Developments* (2004).

14. For more on recent developments in the financial sector, see World Bank (2003) as well as monthly financial sector updates posted on www.worldbank.org.id.

15. See La Porta, López-de-Silanes, and Shleifer (2002) and the references therein.

ownership of firms in strategic economic sectors. Shleifer provides a review of literature relating to government ownership of firms.[16] Lewis advocates government ownership of banks as part of the "commanding heights" of the economy.[17] Governments could develop strategic industries through both direct ownership of industries and ownership of banks. Myrdal supports government ownership of banks in India, since government as owner has the incentives to take a longer term view of development than private banks can.[18] These ideas were obviously influential as governments across the developing world either nationalized existing commercial banks or started new ones in the 1960s and 1970s.

An alternate view of government ownership of banks is the political view, which emphasizes politicians' desire to control investment in the economy for political objectives. Governments control banks (and other enterprises) in order to provide employment, subsidies, and other benefits to their supporters. The beneficiaries in turn support politicians through votes, political contributions, and bribes. Much academic work supports this view through documenting the inefficiency of state enterprises, the political motivation behind the public provision of services, and the benefits of privatization.[19]

There are various ways in which governments can participate in the financing of activities they consider desirable. They can provide subsidies directly from the budget, they can encourage private banks to lend to desired sectors through regulation, or they can own financial institutions. There are distinct advantages of governments owning banks, as opposed to regulating banks or to owning projects or firms. Bank ownership allows the government control over the choice of projects being financed while leaving the execution of the projects to the private sector. In this manner, governments can meet both their development and their political objectives. Ownership of banks allows governments to both collect savings and direct them toward "strategic" projects. Through such financing the governments overcome institutional failures that undermine private capital markets and foster economic growth. In the development view, these projects would be socially desirable but would not get private financing. The political view states that state financing would fund politically desirable—though not necessarily socially desirable—projects.

La Porta, López-de-Silanes, and Shleifer test these theories using global data and conclude that government ownership of banks is large and pervasive across

16. Shleifer (1998).
17. Lewis (1950).
18. Myrdal (1968).
19. See, for example, Megginson, Nash, and van Randenborgh (1994); La Porta and López-de-Silanes (1999).

the world.[20] It is higher in countries with low levels of per capita income, poorly developed financial systems, interventionist governments, and poor protection of property rights. They find more support for the political view of government ownership; higher government ownership of banks is associated with slower subsequent development of the financial system and lower economic growth. Hanson also highlights the large role that state-owned banks play around the world and argues that these banks' performance has been poor and has impeded financial and economic development.[21]

Indonesia's experience with state-owned banks exhibits elements of both political and development views of state ownership. The historical roots of these banks lie in the development view, wherein the banks were established with mandates to provide financing to segments of the economy that were considered socially desirable but that the government felt would not be financed by the private market. Over time, however, the political view took over, with the banks being used to finance politically important projects as opposed to development objectives. The repeated recapitalizations that these banks required over time—as well as the 1997 crisis—exposed the true extent of the losses incurred by the state as a result of such politically connected financing.

An Overview of State-Owned Banks

The modern banking system in Indonesia has its origins in Law 14/1967 on the principles of banking. The law characterizes the banking system as an instrument of national development to improve economic growth, equitable distribution of wealth, and national stability, clearly the development view. Depending on their core business, banks were classified under the law as general banks (or commercial banks), savings banks, and development banks. State-owned banks spanned all three categories. General banks could finance themselves with current and time deposits and engage in short-term lending. Savings banks were permitted to finance themselves though savings deposits and had to invest in marketable securities. Development banks could fund themselves through time deposits and issue medium- and long-term paper and engage in medium- and long-term credit provision.

Before the 1997 financial crisis, Indonesia had seven state-owned banks. Bank Rakyat Indonesia (BRI)—established in 1895—was the oldest. Bank Negara Indonesia (BNI) was established in 1946. Four others—Bank Bumi Daya (BBD),

---

20. La Porta, López-de-Silanes, and Shleifer (2002).
21. Hanson (2003).

Bank Dagang Negara (BDN), Bank Ekspor Impor Indonesia (Bank Exim), and Bank Pembangunan Indonesia (Bapindo)—were created in 1967–68 under the Banking Act and associated legislation. Bank Tabungan Negara (BTN) was established in 1950. After the crisis, four of these banks—BBD, BDN, Bank Exim, and Bapindo—were merged into the newly created Bank Mandiri in 1998. (See appendix for further details on the origin of each bank.)[22]

As was common in several countries at the time, these banks were established largely under the development view of state ownership of banks. They were to be instruments of promoting overall national economic development, and each was assigned a specific sector of the economy in which it would operate or to which it would give priority. BRI was to provide agricultural and rural credit, which later evolved into microcredit. BBD's mandate was to focus on the provision of credit to entities involved in the development of Indonesia's food and nonfood crop resources, such as agricultural, forestry, plantation, and fisheries.[23] BDN was mandated to focus on the provision of credit to entities involved in the development of Indonesia's mineral resources.[24] Bank Exim focused on providing credit to Indonesian entities involved in importing and exporting activities.[25] Bapindo's focus was on the provision of medium- and long-term credit to entities involved in large-scale development projects in the areas of manufacturing, transport, and tourism.[26] BNI functioned as the country's central bank before it was converted into a commercial bank focusing on the manufacturing industry. BTN was established as a housing bank and continues to provide housing loans to low-income families.

Over time, many of these banks began lending in sectors that were not their focus areas, initially due to pressure from clients who had diversified into other activities but preferred not to change banks and later due to the banks' own strategic decisions to get involved in what they thought were attractive opportunities in corporate lending. The government also played a role, directing the credit of these banks to state-owned enterprises and politically connected private groups.

---

22. Bank Ekspor Impor Indonesia was started in 1999 to channel bilateral aid funds to specified projects. It is not allowed to take deposits and remains a small bank in the overall financial system.

23. BBD was Indonesia's sixth-largest bank at the time of acquisition by Bank Mandiri.

24. BDN was the fourth-largest bank in late 1998, at the time of acquisition by Bank Mandiri.

25. Bank Exim was one of the country's leading trade financiers in 1998, although by this time it was also funding Indonesia's large private sector corporations.

26. In 1993 Bapindo was defrauded of Rp 1.3 trillion via a credit scam involving one of Indonesia's large private sector corporations connected to the Suharto regime. Its capital base diminished in the subsequent years leading up to the Asian crisis, and the bank was almost nonexistent in the market at the time of its merger with Bank Mandiri.

The banking reform package of 1992 eliminated all distinctions between private banks and state-owned banks (except for the status of the owner) and formalized the role of state-owned banks as full-fledged commercial banks. This situation continues at present. Beginning with BNI's partial privatization in 1996, the government has since sold minority stakes in Bank Mandiri (30 percent) and BRI (41 percent) to the public.[27] BTN remains fully government owned.

Tables 6-1 through 6-4 provide an overview of the structure of the Indonesian banking system since 1981. Until the early 1980s, Indonesia's financial sector was relatively small, with total assets of the financial system being around 50 percent of gross domestic product (GDP). In 1981 the system was dominated by seven state-owned banks, which controlled almost 80 percent of banking system assets and deposits and about 85 percent of the system's loans. These banks in turn obtained the majority of their funding from BI.[28] They had a wide network of branches throughout the country (almost two-thirds of all bank branches are those of state-owned banks).

A series of reforms in the 1980s and early 1990s significantly expanded the role of private banks in Indonesia; consequently, the share of assets controlled by state-owned banks declined to about 41 percent just before the crisis. As a result of several actions taken during the crisis, the role of state-owned banks expanded; by 2000 they owned more than half of banking system assets. As the economy has begun to grow again and the role of private banks expands, the share of banking system assets in state-owned banks has begun to drop. Banks continue to dominate Indonesia's financial sector; as of December 2003, 80 percent of financial sector assets were controlled by banks, and 36 percent of these assets were in state-owned banks (table 6-5).

The Role of Bank Indonesia

The evolution of state-owned banks in Indonesia has been strongly influenced by the role and policies of Bank Indonesia. Central Bank Law 13/1968 created BI as the national central bank. At the apex of the banking structure lay the monetary board chaired by the minister of finance, with government representatives constituting a majority of the board. The governor of BI was a member of the board. BI was originally conceived of as very much a part of the government; central

---

27. BNI sold 25 percent of its equity to the public in November 1996. During its recapitalization after the crisis, this was diluted to 0.1 percent.

28. See Cole and Slade (1996) and further discussion below.

Table 6-1. *Number of Banks and Branches, Indonesia, by Bank Type, 1981–2003*

	Number of banks					Number of branches				
Year	State owned	National private	Foreign joint venture	Regional development	Total	State owned	National private	Foreign joint venture	Regional development	Total
1981	7	74	11	26	118	838	311	32	180	1,361
1982	7	73	11	27	118	854	326	35	196	1,411
1983	7	72	11	27	117	874	353	36	203	1,466
1984	7	71	11	27	116	898	386	37	213	1,534
1985	7	71	11	27	116	909	429	37	222	1,597
1986	7	67	11	27	112	952	466	37	229	1,684
1987	7	67	11	27	112	992	538	37	235	1,802
1988	7	66	11	27	111	1,004	631	35	270	1,940
1989	7	90	21	27	145	1,009	1,493	41	341	2,884
1990	7	109	28	27	171	1,018	2,145	48	352	3,563
1991	7	129	29	27	192	1,044	2,742	53	408	4,247
1992	7	144	30	27	208	1,066	2,855	56	425	4,402
1993	7	161	39	27	234	1,076	3,036	75	426	4,613
1994	7	166	40	27	240	1,171	3,203	83	431	4,888
1995	7	165	41	27	240	1,301	3,458	83	446	5,288
1996	7	164	41	27	239	1,379	3,964	86	490	5,919
1997	7	144	44	27	222	1,527	4,150	90	541	6,308
1998	7	130	44	27	208	1,602	3,976	121	555	6,254
1999	5	92	40	27	164	1,579	3,581	93	554	5,807
2000	5	81	39	26	151	1,506	3,228	95	550	5,379
2001	5	80	34	26	145	1,522	3,332	92	574	5,520
2002	5	77	34	26	142	1,590	3,411	88	585	5,674
2003	5	76	31	26	138	1,761	3,821	101	666	6,349

Source : Indef (2003); Bank Indonesia (various years).

Table 6-2. *Market Share and Deposits Growth, Indonesia, by Bank Type, 1981–2003*
Percent

Year and deposits in trillions of rupiahs	Share				Growth				
	State owned	National private	Foreign joint venture	Regional development	All banks	State owned	National private	Foreign joint venture	Regional development
1981	8.0	76.0	10.7	9.0	4.4	. . .	. . .	. . .	. . .	. . .
1982	8.7	71.1	13.7	10.5	4.7	7.8	0.9	37.7	25.8	17.4
1983	12.3	68.1	17.2	10.6	4.0	41.8	35.8	78.5	44.1	20.9
1984	15.4	65.2	19.6	10.6	4.6	24.9	19.7	42.4	24.3	40.8
1985	20.0	64.4	22.7	8.8	4.1	30.4	28.8	50.6	8.5	17.9
1986	23.3	65.2	23.1	8.3	3.4	16.2	17.6	18.6	9.0	-3.4
1987	29.1	62.2	27.4	7.1	3.3	25.0	19.2	48.3	7.5	19.7
1988	37.5	60.1	29.7	6.7	3.5	28.7	24.4	39.5	21.7	36.3
1989	54.0	54.8	36.0	6.1	3.1	44.3	31.6	74.9	30.2	28.8
1990	81.6	49.7	40.5	6.6	3.1	51.0	36.9	69.9	65.7	52.3
1991	95.1	44.0	45.4	7.3	3.4	16.6	3.1	30.4	27.9	26.6
1992	111.4	47.2	42.8	6.7	3.3	17.1	25.8	10.5	7.7	14.5
1993	142.5	43.3	47.2	6.1	3.4	27.8	17.3	41.2	16.3	29.4
1994	170.4	37.7	52.2	6.5	3.6	19.6	4.2	32.1	26.9	29.3
1995	214.8	35.4	54.7	6.3	3.6	26.0	18.1	32.1	23.3	26.3
1996	281.7	32.1	58.6	6.3	3.0	31.2	18.1	40.5	30.9	9.1
1997	357.6	37.2	49.5	10.8	2.5	26.9	47.1	7.4	117.0	3.2
1998	573.5	47.3	41.1	9.7	1.9	60.4	104.1	33.0	43.7	24.3
1999	625.6	45.8	40.4	11.6	2.2	9.1	5.5	7.3	30.4	28.2
2000	720.4	45.6	38.7	12.9	2.8	15.1	14.7	10.3	28.6	41.9
2001	809.1	45.6	37.8	12.0	4.6	12.3	12.4	9.5	4.6	86.4
2002	845.0	44.6	40.1	9.9	5.4	4.4	2.0	10.8	14.0	23.9
2003	888.6	41.7	42.4	10.0	5.9	5.2	(1.8)	11.2	6.5	15.0

Source : Indef (2003); Bank Indonesia (various years).

Table 6-3. *Market Share and Assets Growth, Indonesia, by Bank Type, 1981–2003*

Percent

Year and deposits in trillions of rupiahs	Share				Growth				
	State owned	National private	Foreign joint venture	Regional development	All banks	State owned	National private	Foreign joint venture	Regional development
1981	12.5	79.8	9.4	6.9	3.9	...	...	...	...	...
1982	15.3	79.6	9.9	6.9	3.6	22.3	22.0	28.7	21.3	13.3
1983	19.9	77.0	11.2	8.6	3.2	30.6	26.3	47.0	64.2	15.7
1984	26.5	74.8	13.9	7.8	3.5	32.7	28.9	64.9	20.2	45.5
1985	33.7	73.4	15.3	7.8	3.5	27.2	24.9	39.6	27.4	27.3
1986	40.8	72.1	17.6	6.9	3.4	21.2	19.0	40.1	7.4	17.3
1987	48.2	71.3	19.5	6.2	3.0	18.1	16.9	30.3	6.3	6.0
1988	63.3	66.8	24.0	5.1	4.1	31.3	23.1	61.7	6.9	79.3
1989	93.0	59.0	31.9	5.5	3.6	47.0	29.8	95.4	60.2	28.5
1990	132.6	53.3	36.4	7.4	2.9	42.6	28.8	62.9	90.3	15.4
1991	153.2	50.6	37.9	8.5	3.0	15.5	9.6	20.5	32.4	19.5
1992	180.1	51.8	36.9	8.4	2.9	17.6	20.5	14.2	16.1	14.3
1993	214.0	46.8	41.0	9.2	3.0	18.8	7.2	32.1	30.4	23.0
1994	248.1	41.9	45.6	9.4	3.2	15.9	3.7	28.8	18.9	21.1
1995	308.6	39.6	47.6	9.7	3.2	24.4	17.6	29.9	28.5	23.3
1996	387.5	36.4	51.7	9.2	2.8	25.6	15.4	36.4	18.4	10.0
1997	528.9	37.5	46.2	14.0	2.3	34.5	42.9	23.8	110.8	14.4
1998	762.4	39.6	45.7	12.8	1.9	44.2	50.9	41.5	31.3	18.6
1999	789.4	48.7	36.3	12.7	2.3	3.5	28.5	-17.1	3.7	29.2
2000	984.5	50.3	34.9	12.2	2.5	24.7	29.0	20.2	20.0	35.1
2001	1,039.9	46.6	35.8	13.6	4.0	5.6	2.4	13.4	23.1	76.7
2002	1,059.8	47.3	38.0	9.4	5.3	1.9	-2.7	9.9	-7.1	25.5
2003	1,213.5	45.8	38.0	10.7	5.5	14.5	10.9	14.6	29.8	18.2

Source: Indef (2003); Bank Indonesia (various years).

Table 6-4. *Market Share and Loans Growth, by Type of Banks, 1981–2003*

Year and deposits in trillions of rupiahs	Share				Growth				
	State owned	National private	Foreign joint venture	Regional development	All banks	State owned	National private	Foreign joint venture	Regional development
1981 11.4	85.8	7.3	4.8	2.2	...	...	...	...	...
1982 11.5	80.8	10.4	5.8	3.1	0.9	-4.90	43.5	21.5	44.5
1983 15.0	79.0	12.5	5.7	2.7	30.3	27.5	57.5	29.3	15.1
1984 20.9	78.0	14.6	5.0	2.4	38.9	37.1	61.4	21.5	24.1
1985 24.9	76.7	16.5	4.3	2.6	19.4	17.3	34.9	2.6	25.5
1986 30.3	75.3	18.2	4.0	2.5	21.3	19.1	34.1	12.2	19.7
1987 41.7	67.8	25.2	4.2	2.7	37.9	24.3	91.4	44.8	49.7
1988 50.4	71.3	22.5	3.8	2.4	20.9	27.1	7.7	9.8	4.3
1989 62.9	62.9	29.6	5.0	2.6	24.7	10.0	63.8	62.8	35.9
1990 97.0	55.2	36.1	6.4	2.4	54.2	35.2	88.1	98.3	41.7
1991 112.8	53.1	37.1	7.5	2.3	16.3	11.8	19.6	37.8	13.6
1992 122.9	55.5	34.4	7.6	2.5	8.9	14.0	1.2	9.6	15.3
1993 150.3	47.6	40.2	9.8	2.4	22.3	4.8	42.8	57.9	17.9
1994 188.9	42.4	45.7	9.7	2.2	25.7	11.8	42.8	24.7	18.2
1995 234.6	39.8	47.6	10.3	2.2	24.2	16.8	29.4	32.0	24.8
1996 292.9	37.2	51.2	9.4	2.2	24.9	16.5	34.3	13.8	23.2
1997 378.1	40.5	44.6	12.9	2.0	29.1	40.7	12.5	76.2	16.8
1998 487.4	45.3	39.7	13.7	1.4	28.9	44.0	14.6	37.3	-12.9
1999 225.1	49.9	24.9	22.2	3.0	-53.8	-49.0	71.0	-25.0	4.0
2000 269.0	37.9	30.6	27.7	3.8	19.5	-9.1	47.2	48.7	48.8
2001 307.6	38.1	33.1	23.8	5.0	14.4	14.7	23.6	-1.6	52.6
2002 365.4	40.0	37.5	16.7	5.9	18.8	24.7	34.5	-16.8	39.6
2003 440.5	39.5	40.0	13.8	6.7	20.4	19.2	28.5	-0.3	36.2

Source: Indef (2003); Bank Indonesia (various years).

Table 6-5. *Structure of the Financial System, Indonesia, End of 2003*

Type of institution	Number of institutions	Assets in trillions of rupiahs	Percent of total assets	Average asset size in trillions of rupiahs
Banks	138	1,213.5	80.5	8.9
10 largest banks[a]	10	850.6	56.4	85.1
State-owned	4	551.2	36.5	137.8
Ex-IBRA-owned[b]	5	275.6	18.3	55.1
Foreign and joint venture	1	23.7	1.6	23.7
128 other banks	128	362.9	24.1	2.8
State-owned	1	4.9	0.3	4.9
Regional development	26	66.4	4.4	2.6
Private domestic	71	186.1	12.3	2.6
Foreign and joint venture	30	105.5	7.0	3.5
Nonbank financial institutions[c]	10,237	295.0	19.7	. . .
Finance companies	120	29.8	2.0	0.2
Insurance companies	159	88.6	5.9	0.6
Life	52	29.3	1.9	0.6
Nonlife[d]	107	59.3	3.9	0.6
Pension funds	332	37.4	2.5	0.1
Securities firms	157	10.1	0.7	0.1
Pawnshop (state-owned)	1	2.7	0.2	2.7
Rural institutions[e]	9,106	9.3	0.6	. . .
Mutual funds	131	69.5	4.6	0.5
Venture capital companies[f]	60	2.7	0.2	0.0
Private bond issuers[g]	171	44.9	3.0	0.3
Total	10,375	1,508.5[h]	100.0[i]	. . .

Source: Bank Indonesia (various years); Bapepam; Asian Development Bank (2003); authors' estimates.
a. Bank Mandiri, BCA, BNI, BRI, Danamon, BII, Bank Permata, BTN, Bank Lippo, and Citibank.
b. Banks already privatized.
c. Data as of end September 2003 unless stated otherwise.
d. Includes Jamsostek, Taspen, and Asabri.
e. Include rural and nonrural credit agencies, funds, and institutions.
f. Data as of end 2002.
g. Nonfinancial issuers only.
h. Includes Rp 60 trillion of double counting, as most assets of insurance companies and pension funds are held as deposits in banks.
i. Sums to more than 100 due to rounding.

bank independence in Indonesia would come much later.[29] The law stipulated that if the governor of BI disagreed with the position of the board and was not supported by the cabinet, he could publish his views. However, the cabinet had the right to veto that publication in order to protect national interests. Second, the law required BI to lend money to the treasury on demand. The act stated, "the Bank shall, whenever the Minister of Finance deems it necessary to temporarily strengthen the Treasury funds, be bound to advance the Republic of Indonesia monies in current account against sufficient treasury bonds." Lending limits originally were set at 30 percent of treasury revenue (in the previous budgetary year); they were then raised to 50 percent and later ignored in practice. Early financial sector policies in Indonesia were generally subordinated to the needs of funding large government budget deficits.[30]

While the Banking Act delegated to BI responsibility for the guidance, control, and supervision of all financial institutions, the role of BI in the Indonesian economy historically has been much broader than that of a traditional central bank. It has taken the lead in furthering national development by directly financing public enterprises and by promoting special credit programs (providing refinancing facilities) to banks, thus enabling them to finance investments in priority sectors. In this way, BI became an important source of funds to the banking sector and therefore to the state-owned banks, since the latter formed the vast majority of the banking sector. Until the June 1983 financial sector reforms, state-owned banks had essentially unrestricted access to all BI facilities. BI also functioned for much of its history as an arm of the government: Its lack of independence significantly limited its supervisory and regulatory oversight of state-owned banks, which in turn contributed to the weak performance of these banks over the years. This supervisory system, created by the banking law of 1968, contained the seeds for the weak governance of state-owned banks, a problem that has plagued these banks ever since.

Bank Indonesia as Credit Provider

Bank Indonesia was created through the nationalization of De Javasche Bank in 1951 and the enactment of Central Bank Law 11 in 1953. Under this law, BI acted as both a central bank and a commercial bank, essentially continuing the

---

29. BI's lack of independence from the government would raise alarms repeatedly as banking and financial developments became more complex over the next three decades. In fact recommendations to create an independent central bank feature regularly in World Bank reports issued between 1968 and May 1997. In the end, an independent central bank was not created until May 17, 1999 (Law 23/1999 on Bank Indonesia), after the damage to the financial sector by the 1997 crisis was done.

30. Hofman and Rodrick-Jones (2004).

practice that had prevailed before July 1953, when De Javasche Bank performed both these functions. The dual functions were deemed necessary, as the government at the time had only one other national commercial bank (BNI, established in 1946) to carry out its policies. Understandably, over time, this role of BI led to direct competition between BI and other commercial banks.[31]

After several changes to the structure of BI and BNI in the 1960s (see appendix for details), BI's role in 1968 was formally limited to that of a central bank, albeit under a broad definition of central bank. BI's credit provision role continued, as it remained part of the government and was its agent in implementing government economic policy. This role was carried out through the provision of direct credits to borrowers and through provision of liquidity credit to commercial banks, functions well beyond a lender of last resort. BI's direct credit was used to finance large projects that could not be financed by commercial banks or government economic programs.[32] Liquidity credit (better known as KLBI) was given through commercial banks (mostly state-owned banks) to finance special programs in prioritized sectors as outlined in the government's five-year economic plans. Table 6-6 provides an illustrative list of programs supported by BI through liquidity credits. During the oil boom years from 1974 to 1982, abundant government revenues were channeled into the domestic economy through more BI credits and through policies on credit ceilings and credit allocation. Liquidity credits were allocated among the state-owned banks in accordance with their mandates as agents of development in their sectors.

Table 6-7 shows the evolution of the role of BI in credit activities both directly and through financing banking sector credit. In 1963 its direct lending accounted for more than 46 percent of loans of commercial banks. The share decreased after that, primarily because BI transferred ownership of many of these loans to state-owned banks.[33] From 1974 until the early 1980s liquidity credits became the major source of loans for the banking sector. The share of liquidity credit to total loans of commercial banks reached 19 percent in 1974 and rose to 36 percent in 1982. As most of these loans were provided by state-owned banks, their share in total loans of state-owned banks also increased during that period. Liquidity credits accounted for 26 percent and 65 percent of the loans of state-owned banks in

31. BI's commercial banking operation was once even considered the strongest and most prestigious commercial bank at the time. See Rindjin (2003) and references therein.

32. Examples of these were loans to Krakatau Steel (the state steel factory), loans for the import of sugar and wheat, and loans to BIMAS, the government-sponsored rice program.

33. For instance, in 1984 BI's direct loans to BULOG (the national food buffer stock maintenance company) were transferred to BRI, and its loan to PERTAMINA (the state oil company) was transferred to BDN.

1974 and 1982, respectively.[34] BI also supported the operations of state-owned banks in other ways in order to increase their term lending and improve their credit evaluation capacities. BI set up a project appraisal department to monitor the appraisal quality of the individual banks and helped provide training programs on project evaluation.

The decline in oil prices and the world recession of the early 1980s led to the introduction of a series of financial sector reforms (see below). As part of these reforms, BI reduced its liquidity credit both in volume and in terms of sectors targeted. It introduced Sertifikat Bank Indonesia (BI's certificate) in 1984 and permitted commercial banks to issue Surat Berharga Pasar Uang (SBPU, or money market securities) in 1985. These short-term securities were the new tools for BI to conduct open-market operations. This policy, coupled with policies to remove credit ceilings and permit banks to freely set loan and deposit rates, increased competition for state-owned banks. The series of bank deregulation measures of the late 1980s and early 1990s further limited both types and numbers of BI credit programs. However, the preferred position of the state-owned banks, particularly their access to BI funding and BI's regulation of most of the interest rates they could charge (until 1983), effectively insulated them from competition and diminished the stimulus for these banks to emphasize operational efficiencies.

Bank Indonesia as Regulator and Supervisor of State-Owned Banks

Bank Indonesia has been the supervisor of the banking sector since 1953, and its role was further clarified in Central Bank Law 13 of 1968. However, until the early 1980s, there were a relatively small number of commercial banks, and state-owned banks dominated the sector (see table 6-1). BI therefore rarely gave its supervisory function much importance, and its powers over the state-owned banks were rarely exercised. Following the October 1988 deregulation package, the number of banks and their branches increased significantly (see table 6-1). The amounts of loans and deposits soared as well (see tables 6-2 through 6-4). This prompted the government to introduce a number of prudential measures aimed at enhancing bank soundness, such as enhanced capital requirements (based on capital, asset quality, management, equity, and liquidity), limits on net open positions, and stricter loan provisioning requirements. Together with these measures also came sanctions for violations. However, BI's enforcement of sanctions was weak, especially in dealing with state-owned banks.

34. Rahardjo and others (1995).

Table 6-6. *Bank Indonesia's Liquidity Credit Programs*[a]

Program	Recipient	Terms	Tenure	Objective
Working capital credit for farmers (Kredit Usaha Tani–KUT)	Farmers and families	According to necessity	1 year	To increase farmers' income
Credit for members of primary cooperatives (Kredit Kepada Koperasi Primer Anggotanya–KKPA)	Cooperative members	Maximum Rp 50 million	1–15 years	To increase capital quality
Credit for cooperatives (Kredit Kepada Koperasi–KKOP)	Cooperatives	Rp 350 million	1–10 years	To facilitate working capital and cooperative investment
Working capital credit for development of People's Credit Banks and Syariah Bank (Kredit Modal Kerja Pengembangan BPR/Syariah)	Banks	Rp 15 million	Maximum 1 year	To support People's Credit Banks
Credit for primary cooperative members in sugarcane plantations (Kredit Kepada Koperasi Primer untuk Anggota Tebu Rakyat)	Sugarcane farmers	Maximum Rp 50 million	2 years	To facilitate working capital for cooperatives involved in sugarcane plantation intensification
Credit for primary cooperative members who are transmigrated farmers in east Indonesia (KKPAPIR Trans Kawasan Timur Indonesia)	Small-scale farmers in east Indonesia and new transmigration areas	Rp 50 million	3 years	To facilitate working capital for plantations

Program	Target	Ceiling	Term	Objective
Credit for primary cooperative members who are Indonesian laborers abroad (KKPA Tenaga Kerja Indonesia)	Indonesian workers abroad	Maximum 85 per-cent of total cost in organizing workers to go abroad	...	To prepare the Indonesian labor force that works abroad
Credit for cooperative members based on profit sharing (KKPA Bagi Hasil)	Small-scale entrepreneurs	Maximum Rp 50 million	11–15 years	To provide working and investment capital for small-size entrepreneurs under a profit-sharing scheme
Credit for small-size entrepreneurs (Kredit Pengusaha Kecil and Mikro/KPKM)	Small-scale entrepreneurs	Maximum Rp 25 million	5 years	To develop small-scale industries
Credit for applied technology (Kredit Penerapan Teknologi Tepat Guna/KPTTG)	Poorest segment of society	Rp 50 million each group	1 year	To eradicate poverty
Working capital credit for small- and medium-sized enterprises (Kredit Modal Kerja Usaha Kecil dan Menengah)	Cooperatives and small- and medium-sized enterprises	Rp 3 billion each customer	1 year	To develop small-scale entrepreneurs
Credit for applied technology in prime provincial manufactured products (Kredit Penerapan Teknologi Produk Unggulan Daerah)	Cooperatives and small- and medium-sized enterprises	Rp 400 million	1 year	To develope primary provincial manufactured products

Source: Bank Indonesia (various years); Center for Financial Policy Studies (2000).
a. Programs available after 1999.

Table 6-7. *Bank Indonesia's Credit Activities, Selected Years, 1963–2003*

Year	Bank Indonesia[a]	State-owned banks	Other	Total, state-owned banks and other	Liquidity credit[a]
1963					
Amount (Rp billions)	56	59	6	121	75
Share (%)	46.4	48.4	5.2	100	61.9
1974					
Amount (Rp billions)	233	1,135	206	1,574	294
Share (%)	14.8	72.1	13.1	100	18.7
1978					
Amount (Rp billions)	1,933	2,832	559	5,324	682
Share (%)	36.3	53.2	10.5	100	12.8
1982					
Amount (Rp billions)	2,519	7,291	1,691	11,500	4,086
Share (%)	21.9	63.4	14.7	100	35.5
1990					
Amount (Rp billions)	763	53,544	43,456	97,000	1,978
Share (%)	0.8	55.2	44.0	100	2.0
1991					
Amount (Rp billions)	777	59,897	52,114	112,800	2,026
Share (%)	0.7	53.1	46.2	100	1.8
1995					
Amount (Rp billions)	n.a.	93,375	141,236	234,611	10,423
Share (%)	0.0	39.8	60.2	100	4.4
1997					
Amount (Rp billions)	n.a.	153,258	224,876	378,134	15,112
Share (%)	0.0	40.5	59.5	100	4.0
2000					
Amount (Rp billions)	. . .	102,059	166,941	269,000	9,736
Share (%)	0.0	37.9	62.1	100	3.6
2002					
Amount (Rp billions)	. . .	145,981	219,429	365,410	8,507
Share (%)	0.0	40.0	60.1	100	2.3
2003					
Amount (Rp billions)	. . .	177,137	263,368	440,505	7,765
Share (%)	0.0	40.2	59.8	100	1.8

Source: Bank Indonesia (various years); Pangestu (1996); Rahardjo and others (1995); authors' estimates.
a. Not recorded in banks' balance sheet.

BI was clearly conflicted in its dual role as an agent of the government for development and as the regulator and supervisor of banks. This led to the situation of weak supervision, especially of the state-owned banks. Quite often violations of banking regulations by these banks were ignored and left unsanctioned because they were deemed in line with high-level government economic policies. Such forbearance, together with many other types of intervention from various government authorities and officials, had effectively reduced BI's credibility as the supervisor of commercial banks. In addition, BI did not have the necessary supervisory capacity to cope with the implications of the deregulation packages of the late 1980s and early 1990s. Although the economic slowdown of the 1980s provided the opportunity for reform of the banking sector, deregulation of banking was too hurried, was poorly planned, and was too late, coming after the sector had been liberalized for a number of years.

Bank Indonesia and Changes in Regulation and Supervision

The enactment of Central Bank Law 23/1999 in May 1999 repositioned BI as an independent central bank free from interventions by the government or any other parties (article 4). Such independence is also reflected in the provision of the objective of BI to achieve and maintain stability of the value of the rupiah (article 7). The 1999 law freed BI from its earlier objective of assisting the government to "promote smoothness of production and development as well as to expand employment opportunity in order to improve that standard [of] living of the people" (article 7, Central Bank Law 13/1968). The 1999 law ensures that no party can interfere with BI in performing its duties, requiring BI to reject or ignore such interventions (article 9). BI is no longer an implementing agent of government policies and is now positioned as a partner of the government that is to be consulted on various economic, banking, and budget policies and decisions (articles 52–55). Thus the 1999 law effectively removed the role of the monetary board as a bridge between BI and the government. The new law also prohibits BI from providing loans to the government (article 56). And the bank's outstanding or committed liquidity credit was transferred to a new state-owned enterprise, Permodalan Nasional Madani (PNM) (article 74).

The 1997 crisis prompted the need for improved banking regulation and supervision. The letter of intent that the government signed with the IMF in 1998 stipulates a commitment to strengthen the supervision of BI and to strengthen the enforcement of regulations. Since 1998, BI has issued numerous regulations covering licensing and operations, prudential practices, performance rating, self-regulation, reporting, short-term financing, *shariah* banking principles, money laundering, and risk management.[35]

BI developed a master plan for banking supervision complying with the Basel Core Principles.[36] The core program, most of which was put into place during 2000, includes special surveillance, off-site supervision, and on-site supervision of a number of banks that play a significant role in the national economy, including state-owned banks. In practical terms, BI divides the supervision into normal supervision, intensive supervision, and special supervision based on the health of the particular bank. Based on an independent assessment of its compliance with the Basel Core Principles, BI declared that it was fully compliant with two principles, largely compliant with twenty, and noncompliant with three.[37]

BI's willingness to enforce regulation and perform its role as banking supervisor has significantly improved since the crisis. For instance, in August 2002, BI publicly placed two private national banks under special surveillance due to their inability to meet the required 8 percent capital adequacy ratio. After both banks' managements and shareholders took remedial measures deemed adequate by BI, these banks were returned to normal status in October 2002.[38] In another instance, BI denied forbearance to a state bank regarding bypassing the limit on buying nonperforming loans from IBRA and on required loan-loss provision for such loans. In other cases, BI has also shown keen interest in working with other institutions in the country, as evidenced by its cooperation with the capital market supervisory authority (BAPEPAM) in the latter's investigations on alleged publications of misleading financial statements and with Indonesia's anti-money-laundering authority and financial intelligence unit (PPATK) on investigations of suspected money-laundering transactions.[39] More recently (in April 2004) BI shut down two relatively small banks (Bank Asiatic and Bank Dagang Bali), citing their noncompliance with prudential capital requirements and weak capital adequacy.

---

35. *Shariah* principles are those based on the Koran. A complete list of BI's banking regulations can be viewed at its website, www.bi.go.id.

36. The Basel Core Principles for effective banking supervision, developed by the Basel Committee on Banking Supervision, are a set of twenty-five basic principles that need to be in place for a banking supervisory system to be effective. The principles are considered minimum requirements and may need to be supplemented by other measures designed to address particular conditions and risks in the financial systems of individual countries.

37. Bank Indonesia (2000).

38. These banks are Bank CIC and Bank IFI. Further information is available at BI's website, www.bi.go.id.

39. The case involves a dubious valuation of foreclosed assets at Bank Lippo, which let its capital adequacy ratio fall below the minimum level. Market manipulation of the bank's share price was alleged.

Financial Sector Reforms and State-Owned Banks

In the early 1980s Indonesia recognized that it would need to support the economic growth and development of the real economy, with a financial system that would be able to provide resources cheaply and efficiently. In the decade of 1983–92 it implemented a series of financial sector reforms aimed at liberalizing the financial sector. Liberalization, combined with rapid economic growth, poor corporate governance, and weak regulation and supervision of the banking sector, led to the extremely rapid growth of banks with poor asset quality. By the mid-1990s several banks had failed, and the rest of the system was beginning to show signs of weakness. The economic and political crisis in 1997 exposed the full extent of the problems in the banking sector. The government implemented a series of policy packages during 1997–99 aimed at bringing the banking sector back to health, including many actions focusing on insolvent and weak banks. By 2000 the major process of restructuring the banking sector had largely been completed, although the sector had still a long way to go before it could begin to function effectively. Since 2000 efforts have focused on further strengthening regulation and supervision, continuing divestment of intervened banks and assets, strengthening the governance of state-owned banks, and (partially) privatizing them.

This section presents a brief overview of the various reform measures implemented over the last two decades in the financial sector and their impact on the evolution of state-owned banks.

Before the 1983 Reforms

As briefly discussed above, BI's liquidity credit programs played a key role in the early evolution of state-owned banks. Under the scheme, banks obtained refinancing at a low interest rate from BI for credit extended to certain borrowers. Directed credit programs were an important part of the government's overall development strategy, especially as the need to present a domestic balanced budget and to recycle large government revenues from oil and gas exports provided a powerful stimulus to the growth of extrabudgetary lending. However, this facility was provided only to state-owned banks and selected private banks, which satisfied certain minimum criteria related to soundness ratings. This limitation discouraged banks from mobilizing funds from the public, because the deposit interest rates were less competitive compared to interest rates for the liquidity support scheme. By 1982 the total assets of all banks were only 25 percent higher than the total assets of BI, indicating the high degree of dependence of the banks on BI.[40]

---

40. Cole and Slade (1996).

In 1982, for example, deposit rates for rupiah-denominated deposits was 6 percent a year at state-owned banks and 19 percent a year at private banks, while the range of BI's subsidized interest rates were 3–6 percent. Lending rates for eligible borrowers under BI schemes averaged 12 percent at state-owned banks and at private banks were 9–20 percent. Lending rates for normal credit were 15–21 percent at state-owned banks and 21–36 percent at private banks (table 6-8). Because of this policy, subsidized credits from government accounted for over half of total bank credits.[41] This dominance of subsidized credits was backed up by a government-financed credit guarantee agency that guaranteed banks (and BI) against defaults.[42]

The policies of this early period affected state-owned banks in various ways. First, they had little incentive to gain experience in mobilizing deposits, since much of their financing came from BI. Second, they developed little expertise in credit evaluation but simply acted as channels to provide government-subsidized credits to selected sectors and customers. Third, the regime ensured that they developed few strengths in overall notions of risk involved in banking. The structure of their operations and of the role of BI ensured that their exposure to credit risks, foreign exchange risks, and interest rate risks was low. The major risk they were exposed to was operational risk.

By the mid-1970s financial development began to be constrained by the imposition of interest rate and credit ceilings on banks. The crunch came in the early 1980s, when the oil price boom abated, and in its wake external payments and fiscal deficits widened considerably. Inflationary pressure were also aggravated. The decline in oil revenue and a consequent deterioration in the balance of payments led to the shrinkage of resources of both the government and the private sector. The mobilization of domestic resources thus became a top priority.

The 1983 Reforms

In 1982—before the first major reforms implemented in the Indonesian financial sector—banking system assets as a ratio of GDP stood at 33 percent. The major deposit money banks, along with BI, dominated the financial system, with a share in total assets of more than 95 percent.[43] Among the deposit money banks, five

---

41. Santoso (2000).

42. Askrindo is a credit insurance company established in 1971 by the Ministry of Finance and BI. It started as a provider of insurance for loans to small and medium-size enterprises provided by commercial banks, but now it also provides credit management services, surety bonds, customs bonds, and letter of credit guarantees.

43. Hanna (1994).

state-owned banks had a dominant position, accounting for about three-fourths of total assets (see table 6-2).

The 1983 reforms were motivated by the difficult balance-of-payments and fiscal situation facing the country after the oil price boom abated in the early 1980s. The government initiated the reform process through a scaling back of the requirement to provide directed credits to some low-priority sectors in August 1982. In June 1983 the government initiated a major financial sector reform, involving the deregulation of state-owned banks' deposit rates on time deposits of longer than six months, the elimination of credit ceilings and their replacement with a system of reserve money management, and the rationalization of the sub-sidized directed credit program. As discussed above, BI also moved to limit its direct lending activities (relying instead on refinancing the banking sector) and introduced the Sertifikat Surat Berharga Pasar Uang Bank Indonesia and the Surat Berharga Pasar Uang for reserve money management.

The 1983 reform resulted in state-owned banks taking their initial steps in moving to more market-based banking (although they were still operating in a highly protected environment). On the funding side, after the reform BI contin-ued to provide refinancing (liquidity support) for small-scale credits and high-priority credits to help weak and small enterprises in improving their role in the economy as well as for lending to support nonoil and gas exports. However, an important aspect of the reform was also that lending to nonpriority sectors would now need to be fully financed through public deposits. This meant that, to finance loans to large borrowers, banks (including state-owned banks) needed to seek an alternative to BI's liquidity support. This meant that state-owned banks would have to learn to compete with private banks in attracting public deposits—that they would need to manage their own funds to comply with minimum reserve requirements without using interest rate subsidies from the government. These banks responded to this challenge by increasing their interest rates on three-month and twelve-month time deposits, although they continued to maintain them at levels lower than the private banks (see table 6-8).[44] State-operated banks' extensive branch network, as well the public's perception that these institutions were less risky than private banks, led to a rapid increase in their time deposits (mostly deposits of less than twelve months' maturity; see tables 6-1 and 6-2).

With the relaxation of credit ceilings, private banks began to lend more aggres-sively. The share of private banks in total loans doubled over the 1983–87 period (see table 6-4). Much of this market share was lost by the state-owned banks.

44. Cole and Slade (1996).

Table 6-8. *Annual Interest Rates, Indonesia, Commercial Banks, End of Year,*
1982, and 1985–2003
Percent

Item	1982	1985	1986	1987	1988	1989	1990	1991	1992
Nominal deposit rates[a]									
State-owned banks	6.0	16.0	14.7	17.3	18.2	17.2	19.4	22.3	17.3
Private banks	18.5	17.8	15.5	18.5	19.6	18.2	20.0	23.3	18.9
All banks	n.a.	16.9	15.4	18.4	19.0	17.7	19.6	22.7	17.8
Real deposit rates[b]									
State-owned banks	−3.5	11.3	8.9	8.0	10.2	10.8	11.6	12.9	9.8
Private banks	9.0	13.1	9.7	9.2	11.6	11.8	12.2	13.9	11.4
All banks	n.a.	12.2	9.6	9.1	11.0	11.3	11.8	13.3	10.3
Nominal lending rates[c]									
State-owned banks	12.0	15.3	18.5	20.0	20.2	19.7	21.2	25.1	21.2
Private banks	n.a.	24.2	23.0	3.6	23.8	21.7	25.1	28.2	23.1
All banks	n.a.	22.1	21.1	2.1	22.3	21.0	23.0	26.1	n.a.
Real lending rates[b]									
State-owned banks	2.5	10.6	12.7	10.7	12.2	13.3	13.4	15.7	13.7
Private banks	n.a.	19.5	17.2	−5.7	15.8	15.3	17.3	18.8	15.6
All banks	n.a.	17.4	15.3	−7.2	14.3	14.6	15.2	16.7	n.a.
Lending-deposit spread[c]									
State-owned banks	6.0	−0.7	3.8	2.7	2.0	2.5	1.8	2.8	3.9
Private banks	n.a.	6.4	7.5	−14.9	4.2	3.5	5.1	4.9	4.2
All banks	n.a.	5.2	5.7	−16.3	3.3	3.3	3.4	3.4	n.a.
Addendum									
Consumer price									
index	9.5	4.7	5.8	9.3	8.0	6.4	7.8	9.4	7.5

Source: Bank Indonesia (various years); authors' estimates.
a. Rate of rupiah, six-month time deposit.
b. Rate calculated using actual annual inflation rate.
c. Rate of rupiah working capital loan.

Thus as a result of the reforms there was a clear difference between these banks
and private banks. Customers preferred to deposit their money in state-owned
banks, for three reasons: These banks were perceived to be safer, their yields were
higher due to the gradual implementation of a zero interest rate for excess reserves
at BI, and their branch networks were more extensive than those of the private
banks. However, customers preferred to borrow from private banks, because they

1993	1994	1995	1996	1997	1998	1999	2000	2001	2002	2003
12.3	12.5	16.1	16.1	15.7	35.2	14.4	13.4	16.6	13.9	8.0
14.6	14.8	17.8	17.4	19.2	33.3	13.6	13.2	15.6	13.9	8.7
13.1	13.3	17.0	16.8	17.0	36.8	14.3	13.3	16.2	13.8	8.3
2.6	3.9	6.7	8.2	9.5	−23.3	−6.1	9.7	5.0	2.0	1.4
4.9	6.3	8.4	9.5	13.0	−25.1	−7.0	9.5	4.1	2.0	2.1
3.4	4.8	7.5	8.9	10.8	−21.7	−6.3	9.6	4.7	1.9	1.7
18.2	15.5	17.2	16.9	18.5	25.1	26.2	19.9	19.2	18.9	16.2
19.4	18.6	20.5	20.2	23.7	36.4	32.6	17.8	19.2	18.2	14.7
18.7	17.8	19.3	19.0	22.0	32.3	28.9	18.4	19.2	18.3	15.1
8.5	7.0	7.8	9.0	12.3	−33.4	5.7	16.2	7.6	7.0	9.6
9.7	10.1	11.0	12.3	17.6	−22.1	12.0	14.1	7.7	6.3	8.1
9.0	9.2	9.8	11.1	15.8	−26.2	8.3	14.7	7.7	6.4	8.5
5.9	3.1	1.1	0.7	2.8	−10.1	11.8	6.4	2.6	5.0	8.2
4.7	3.8	2.6	2.8	4.6	3.0	19.0	4.6	3.6	4.3	6.0
5.7	4.4	2.3	2.3	5.0	−4.5	14.6	5.1	3.0	4.5	6.8
9.7	8.5	9.4	7.9	6.1	58.5	20.5	3.7	11.5	11.9	6.6

were probably less bureaucratic and also because the transactions costs of dealing with state-owned banks—including the costs of corruption—probably made their effective borrowing rates higher than those at private banks, although nominal lending rates of state-owned banks were lower.

To permit sound reserve management for banks, BI had introduced discount window facilities and Bank Indonesia certificates to help banks to maintain their liquidity.[45] However, there were implementation problems with this liquidity management mechanism, and the interbank call money market became the primary venue of liquidity management for banks.[46] State-owned banks played a key role in this market, largely due to their ability to attract more deposits from the public. Private banks' expansion of loans was not balanced with a corresponding growth of deposits. Interbank call money was the main source of funds for private banks, and state-owned banks were the main suppliers. Because the interest rates in the interbank market were lower than those on deposits, private banks were better off using funds from the interbank call money market. State-owned banks therefore effectively became the financiers of private bank lending.

These banks were also the primary beneficiaries of BI refinancing, as their lending activities continued to focus on channeling subsidized credits (see table 6-7). Subsidized credit programs also kept the financial market fragmented (as characterized by large differences in access to credit and its cost for individual borrowers), adversely affected long-term funds mobilization, contributed to distortions in the use of financial resources, reduced transparency, and weakened financial discipline. Following a deceleration in 1983–84 resulting from the June 1983 reforms, directed credits increased rapidly. However, because total domestic credit rose even more rapidly over the period, the share of directed credit declined, from around 50 percent of total domestic credit in 1982 to about 28 percent in 1989. About 80 percent of all directed credits were channeled through state-owned banks.

The motivation for the deregulation of 1983 was concern about the tighter resource position resulting from weakening oil prices. By allowing greater flexibility in deposit interest rates, the deregulation measures significantly increased the volume of resources mobilized through the financial system. However, success in other areas was limited, and several issues remained unresolved. First, despite the reform, competition remained weak due to regulatory restrictions on operations, branching, and entry. The state-owned banks enjoyed preferential treatment on branching, capital and loan-loss provision requirements, and access to deposits from public enterprises (which were restricted from dealing with private financial institutions). Lack of competition was reflected in relatively high intermediation costs (see table 6-8). Second, the expansion of directed credit lending further fragmented the financial market and adversely affected long-term fund mobilization. Third, the ability of state-owned banks to refinance a substantial proportion of their loans with BI at subsidized rates and liberal credit insurance

45. These certificates are used to absorb excess liquidity of banks, while discount window facilities provide a mechanism for banks to borrow funds from BI when they are short of liquidity. BI also maintained 15 percent reserve requirements.

46. For more on problems with reserve management, see Santoso (2000).

provisions for these loans resulted in perfunctory credit analysis, which led to weak portfolio performance of some of these banks. Finally, the legal, information, and regulatory framework for the financial sector remained weak, and the pace of financial innovation was slow.

After the implementation of the June 1983 reform, state-owned banks still dominated the market share in total assets, deposits, and loans. In 1987, before the next round of reforms, these banks held two-thirds of the total deposits and loans and 71 percent of the total assets of the banking system. However, private banks had nearly doubled their share in deposits, loans, and assets in the system. Interest rates on deposits paid by both kinds of banks began to converge. The stability of the banking industry was sensitive to interest rate risk (stemming from the liberalization of interest rates) and credit risk (stemming from the rapid credit expansion by private banks). State-owned banks were exposed to private bank credit risks through their interbank lending.

The 1988–97 Period

During October–December 1988 the government introduced a comprehensive set of reform measures aimed at further enhancing financial sector efficiency and significantly lowering barriers to entry. The major reforms aimed at the banking sector were

—Permitting the entry of new private banks, including joint ventures with foreign banks.

—Allowing domestic banks to open branches throughout Indonesia.

—Permitting new rural banks to be established in districts outside the capital.

—Easing the requirements for a bank permitted to transact foreign exchange.

—Allowing state enterprises to place up to 50 percent of their bank deposits with private banks and nonbank financial institutions.

—Stipulating loan concentration ratios for banks and nonbank financial institutions that limited lending to a single borrower or group.

—Specifying minimum capital requirements for banks.

—Eliminating differential reserve requirements for banks by establishing a uniform and lower rate of 2 percent and removing restrictions on interbank borrowings.

—Extending the maturities of BI certificates and money market securities and taking steps to develop a secondary market for them.

—Determining the swap premiums on the interest rate differentials between domestic and international markets.

—Reducing the discrimination against public holding securities market instruments as compared to holding term deposits with the banks.

—Permitting banks and nonbank financial institutions to raise capital from the securities market.

—Allowing banks to have as subsidiaries multiservice financial companies (providing leasing, factoring, consumer finance, and venture capital).

Further reforms were introduced in subsequent years. In March 1989 regulations were issued that clarified aspects relating to lending limits, joint venture bank capital requirements, bank mergers, definition of bank capital, reserve requirements, and bank investments in stocks. Absolute limits on external borrowings for banks were replaced with restrictions on net open positions in foreign exchange (maximum of 25 percent of equity). Banks no longer needed BI approval for offshore lending. This implied that banks could borrow freely abroad as long as they covered their positions by lending in foreign exchange. In January 1990 directed credit programs were further reduced. Priority programs were reduced from thirty-seven to four.[47] One important sector excluded from directed credit was export finance. Interest rates were moved closer to the market level, and the portion of credit available for refinancing was lessened. Mandatory, subsidized credit insurance was abolished. All these measures were additional incentives for the originating banks to more carefully select and monitor their borrowers. As a political compromise, the elimination of directed credit programs for small businesses was replaced by a requirement that 20 percent of a bank's loans be made to small borrowers. The next set of reforms, announced in March 1991, returned once again to prudential regulations. New professional standards were set for bank directors. Loan-loss provisioning standards were overhauled, now involving a financial analysis of customers rather than simply a check of whether their payments were current. A new, more quantitative evaluation of bank soundness, based on capital, asset quality, management, equity, and liquidity, was implemented. Finally, banks were obliged to adopt the Basel Agreement's risk-based capital adequacy standards by the end of 1993 (subsequently extended to 1994). The banking law issued in early 1992 eliminated all legal distinctions between private banks and state-owned banks other than status of the owners, although the law also required that the government retain a 51 percent share of all state-owned banks.

The 1988 reforms had a strong positive impact on the diversification of the country's financial structure. They also set the stage for extremely rapid expansion of the banking sector within the context of a weak regulatory and supervisory

47. The four programs were investment and working capital credits to members of rural and primary cooperatives; one-year credits to rural cooperatives to finance procurement and other productive activities; credits to BULOG; and investment credits of a minimum five-year maturity by development banks and plantation credits through commercial banks.

framework and an even weaker structure of enforcement. By the mid-1990s state-owned banks as well as several private banks began to show signs of weakness. Well before the 1997 crisis, several banks in Indonesia had begun to fail.

The easing of entry restrictions increased competition for state-owned banks considerably. The number of private and joint-venture banks increased from 77 in 1988 to 206 in 1994, while the number of state-owned banks remained at 7 (see table 6-1). Branches of private and joint-venture banks increased from 666 in 1988 to 3,286 in 1994, while those of state-owned banks increased from 1,004 to 1,171 over the same period. The share of state-owned banks in total loans decreased from over 71 percent in 1988 to less than 40 percent in 1995. In terms of total assets, the share of state-owned banks declined from over 66 percent in 1988 to under 40 percent in 1995. Correspondingly, the share of private banks in total assets nearly doubled between 1988 and 1994, from 24 to 48 percent (see tables 6-2 through 6-4). Deposit rates at state-owned banks converged to match those at private banks (see table 6-8), as state-owned banks tried to attract more deposits.

The reform of the subsidized directed credit system was particularly important for its resource allocation effects. The stock of outstanding liquidity credits declined by 20 percent, to Rp 14 trillion by October 1991, and their share in total domestic credit declined from 28.4 percent in 1989 to 12.6 percent in 1991. State-owned banks continued to remain the dominant suppliers of BI liquidity credits, although the importance of liquidity overall declined. Liquidity credits had formed 41 percent of total loans in 1982; by 1995 they accounted for less than 6 percent.[48]

The reduction in liquidity credits, the greater competition from private banks, and the newly imposed capital requirements exposed the weak state of state-owned banks' balance sheets. These banks had been accustomed to lending at the behest of the government, with little credit analysis, and accustomed, too, to not taking credit risks adequately into consideration, practices that left their capital levels far below those required under the new capital adequacy ratios. The government committed to recapitalizing these banks to bring them up to the full 8 percent ratio by 1992; however it did not adequately recognize the extent of capital infusions that these banks would require.[49] Given that the government was facing budgetary constraints at the time, it did not want to finance the recapitalization through budgetary resources. A solution was therefore structured whereby the World Bank would provide a loan of $300 million to the government, which the latter would use toward the recapitalization. In addition, earlier loans from the World Bank to these banks (which had been provided for the purposes of lending

48. Bank Indonesia (1995); Pangestu (1996); Rahardjo (1995).
49. Cole and Slade (1996).

to specific sectors) would be converted to government equity. Thus recapitalization could take place with no infusion of fresh cash from the government. It was expected that after this recapitalization no further calls would be made on government, as the banks were expected to raise fresh capital either from retained earnings or from the capital market. Such expectations implied the possibility of privatization of these banks, but in the event, even partial privatization did not come until after the 1997 crisis, during which the government would once again be forced to recapitalize these banks.

Another impact of this round of reforms was that state-owned banks no longer focused purely on development activities. This shift of focus had been in the making over the years; the regulatory removal of all distinctions between private banks and state-owned banks simply formalized the situation. The activities of state-owned banks were now much more in line with the political view than the development view of state ownership. For example, they extensively funded politically connected projects and persons. Several examples of such funding were discovered during the investigation that preceded recapitalization under the World Bank loan. A relatively small group of conglomerates with strong political connections had availed themselves of large loans from state-owned banks and had not serviced them. These loans were therefore nonperforming, although they had not been classified as such and exceeded the prudential regulations for borrower concentration established by BI. In mid-1993 newspaper reports listed fifty of the largest of these borrowers; many had political connections.[50]

The weak governance of state-owned banks—which had always been a problem—worsened after the liberalization of the banking sector. Many of the scandals involved mismanagement and allegations of corruption. Until some high-profile chief executive officers were replaced or jailed in the early 1990s, many of them were considered politically untouchable, and BI did little to rein them in.

Before the crisis in 1997, state-owned banks still played a major, though no longer a dominant, role in the banking system. At the end of 1996 these banks controlled 36 percent of assets, 37 percent of loans, and 32 percent of deposits in the system.

The Impact of the 1997 Crisis on State-Owned Banks

Credit quality in banks had been deteriorating for many years before the crisis of 1997. Lack of credit analysis was the main problem for state-owned banks, as credit decisions were largely made at the behest of the government or top gov-

---

50. A highly publicized case of the politicization is the Bapindo–Golden Key scandal involving a loan of Rp 1.3 trillion.

ernment officials. Nonperforming loans at private banks were normally related to loans extended to the group that owned the bank. BI's enforcement of the legal lending limit was very weak due to its lack of independence. In 1995, for example, state-owned banks accounted for 40 percent of total loans of the banking system (see table 6-4) but about 73 percent of total classified loans (see table 6-8).[51] By April 1997, before the crisis, state-owned banks accounted for 36 percent of total loans but 66 percent of classified loans. By December 1998 their classified loans had reached 49 percent of their loan portfolios.[52]

A combination of poor loan portfolios, outright fraud, asset-liability mismatches, lending to group companies by private banks, unhedged foreign exchange positions, and deficiencies in bank supervision led to a series of bank failures before the 1997 crisis. Bapindo essentially collapsed in 1993, after the well-publicized Golden Key scandal, in which the sponsors of the borrowing firm disappeared after taking loans from Bapindo of more than 140 percent of the bank's capital. Complicity by bank officials was alleged, highlighting the weak state of governance of the state-owned banks as well as the inadequate supervision that permitted Bapindo to be so exposed to a single borrower. An assessment by the World Bank in mid-1997, before the crisis, revealed that BBD was also in trouble, and the authorities announced a merger of BBD and Bapindo in June 1997 (a merger not implemented until the 1999 merger of both these banks with Bank Mandiri). It was in this context that Indonesia encountered the economic and political crisis of 1997, a crisis that had a major impact on the state-owned banks of Indonesia.[53]

As the crisis broke and deepened in 1997 and the first half of 1998, audits were conducted of all commercial banks by well-reputed international auditors and BI as part of IMF-supported programs. These audits revealed that much of the banking system was insolvent and that the level of nonperforming loans was much higher than had been anticipated by the authorities—both in state-owned banks and in private banks (table 6-9). Credit defaults were at the root of the problems of almost all banks within the context of a corporate sector that had borrowed heavily in foreign currency and was now faced with a depreciation of the rupiah from Rp 2,500 to the dollar to over Rp 15,000 to the dollar at one stage in the crisis. The main cause of private banks' nonperforming loans was connected lending, with these banks being used to channel credits to bank owners. In the case of

---

51. Classified loans include substandard, doubtful, and bad debt.

52. Private bank loan portfolios had also been deteriorating for several years before the crisis. See Santoso (2000).

53. For background on the crisis, see Enoch and others (2001); Kenward (2003); World Bank (1998, 2000); *Survey of Recent Developments* (2004).

Table 6-9. *Classified Loans, Indonesia, by Bank Type, 1995–2003*[a]

Type of loan	1995	1996	April 1997	December 1997	December 1998	December 1999	December 2000	December 2002	December 2003
Total loans (in trillions of rupiahs)	234.6	292.9	350.0	378.1	487.4	225.1	269.0	365.4	440.5
Classified loans as a percent of total									
Substandard loans	2.7	2.6	2.8	2.6	10.4	10.2	7.8	2.4	2.9
Doubtful loans	2.4	3.3	3.5	2.5	15.2	12.8	4.6	2.1	1.1
Bad debt	3.3	2.9	2.3	3.2	23	9.9	7.7	3.0	2.7
Percent distribution of classified loans, by bank ownership									
State-owned banks	72.7	67	65.9	52.7	38.9	52.6	33.1	32.6	43.4
Private banks	16.3	22.8	24.5	42.3	52.7	23.1	22.7	28.0	31.3
Regional development banks	5.5	4.9	4.8	0.43	0.1	1.2	1.6	1.5	1.6
Foreign and joint venture banks	5.5	5.3	4.8	4.6	8.4	23.2	42.6	37.9	23.6
Classified loans as percent of total credit, by bank ownership									
All banks	...	10.4	8.8	8.3	48.6	32.9	20.1	7.5	6.8
State-owned banks	...	16.6	13.4	4.4	18.9	17.3	17.4	6.0	7.3
Private foreign exchange banks	...	3.7	4.3	2.8	21.1	7.3	16.2	5.8	5.5
Private nonforeign exchange banks	...	13.8	1.1	0.7	4.5	0.3	4.2	4.5	3.6

Source: Santoso (2000); Bank Indonesia (various years).

a. Classified loans include substandard and doubtful loans and bad debt.

state-owned banks, the main cause was state-directed lending to unviable projects. Interestingly, in only one state-owned bank—Bank Exim—were foreign exchange losses the proximate cause of insolvency.[54] Supervision by BI was ineffective and weak. In some cases the supervisors lacked adequate capacity; in others, they were politically constrained from carrying out their functions.

In response to the findings of these audits, the government announced a series of steps that directly affected the banking sector. For private banks, the government adopted an approach wherein banks were classified in terms of their capital adequacy ratios into three categories, which determined whether they would be left unintervened, recapitalized, or closed.[55] State-owned banks, however, were thought to be too big to fail and hence would be recapitalized by the government after undertaking certain operational changes.[56] As of June 1997 these banks accounted for about 40 percent of the banking system's assets. By the end of the bank restructuring process, they would absorb over two-thirds of the recapitalization resources spent by the government (table 6-10). Each state-owned bank entered into performance contracts with the government, contracts that laid out the operational steps that were to be undertaken and the changes that were to be made in management in return for the government's recapitalization.

As the crisis intensified, depositors initially shifted funds from private banks to state-owned banks, perceiving them to be safe havens. The share of deposits in these banks increased from 32 percent in 1996 to 48 percent in 1998. By late 1997, given the uncertainties in the banking system, a group of twenty-four banks—including all state-owned banks and some well-known foreign and private banks—were transacting almost exclusively among themselves, resulting in a situation of excess liquidity for this group, while the rest of the system faced increasing rates in the interbank market.[57] While Bank Indonesia's liquidity support was extensively used (and often misused) by the private banking system, the state-owned banks (with the sole exception of Bank Exim) needed almost no liquidity support throughout the crisis. Bank Exim suffered losses of about Rp 20 trillion in failed foreign exchange derivative transactions, and BI provided it with liquidity of an equivalent amount. After the announcement of a blanket

54. There was speculation at the time that Bank Exim's foreign exchange trading losses were part of a failed government attempt to shore up the value of the rupiah.

55. Private banks whose ratio was over 4 percent were considered sound, those with a ratio between 4 percent and minus 25 percent were considered for recapitalization, while those with a ratio less than −25 percent were to be closed.

56. Audits revealed that most of these banks were insolvent. Had the authorities adopted the same criterion for state-owned banks as they did for private banks, most state-owned banks would have been classified in the weakest ratio category and would have been closed.

57. Enoch and others (2001).

Table 6-10. *Cost of Banking Sector Restructuring, Indonesia, 2000*

Bank type	Trilllions of rupiahs	Percent of recapitalization cost	Percent of gross domestic product[a]
State-owned banks	282.6	66	22.4
Mandiri	178.0	41	14.1
BNI	61.8	14	4.9
BRI	29.0	7	2.3
BTN	13.8	3	1.1
Taken-over banks (14)	109.3	25	8.7
Recapitalized banks (7)	36.9	9	2.9
Regional banks (12)	1.2	0	0.1
Subtotal, recapitalization cost	430.0	. . .	34.1
Guarantee program	218.3	. . .	17.2
Government credit program	10.0	. . .	0.8
Total cost	658.3	. . .	52.1

Source: Bank Indonesia (various years); authors' calculations.
a. Gross domestic product was Rp 1,264.9 trillion in 2000.

guarantee of deposits, the government also used its banks (largely BNI) as receivers of deposits of closed banks, with matching government bonds on the asset side. The management personnel of private banks taken over by IBRA was replaced by management personnel from the state-owned banks.

As the macroeconomic condition stabilized in late 1998, the authorities put in place a comprehensive strategy to restore the health of the banking system. For state-owned banks this strategy involved merging four of the weakest of these banks—as well as the corporate loans of BRI—into the newly created Bank Mandiri, which would control about 25 percent of the banking system's assets.[58] Mandiri was recapitalized in late 1999, and its capital adequacy ratio was brought up to 4 percent (tier 1) and 8 percent (total). Nonperforming loans of the component banks were transferred to IBRA. Nonperforming loans of other state-owned banks were also moved to IBRA, and these banks were recapitalized. Recapitalization of the component banks of Bank Mandiri cost the government Rp 178 trillion (41 percent of the total cost of recapitalization of the banking system). BNI absorbed 14 percent of the total recapitalization resources, while the

58. Bank Mandiri initially operated as a holding company for the shares of the four state-owned banks. The formal merger was completed in 1999.

remaining two state-owned banks accounted for less than 10 percent of the total cost (see table 6-10).

The recapitalization of state-owned banks has been one of the most expensive elements of the Indonesian bank restructuring efforts. Their recapitalization cost the government Rp 283 trillion (compared to private bank recapitalization of Rp 147 trillion). This cost can be attributed to both their weak asset portfolios and the incentive effects of the too-big-to-fail principle. Their management personnel had little incentive to collect on loans, and as a result their nonperforming loans grew substantially.[59] Deposit rates at these banks were also the highest, as they were indifferent to resulting negative spreads. For the first time in their history, state-owned banks were paying higher interest rates than private banks on their deposits (see table 6-9). Systemwide loan-to-deposit spreads had fallen from 6 percent in the early 1990s to minus 20 percent in 1998, although there was not much lending occurring in 1998 (figure 6-1). Their loan-to-deposit ratios also began to fall, even before the recapitalization by the government, as deposits rose more than proportionately to loans until 1998 (table 6-11). BNI, which had a loan-to-deposit ratio of 103 percent in 1997, had a ratio of 87 percent in 1998. Subsequently, the recapitalization by the government would further dramatically reduce these ratios.

The Current Role of State-Owned Banks

Within the context of the systemic bank restructuring since the crisis, state-owned banks continue to play a major role in the banking system. The number of banks in the system was reduced to 138 in 2003, from its peak of 240 before the crisis.[60] This reduction has largely occurred due to closures of several banks and mergers of smaller banks with larger ones. Banks continue to dominate the financial system. As of December 2003 the banking sector represented 80 percent of financial system assets (see table 6-5). Also at the end of 2003, state-owned banks controlled 46 percent of assets, 42 percent of deposits, and 38 percent of loans. Viewed from their precrisis levels, the restructuring process has led to an increase in the role of state-owned banks in the banking system. The two largest of these banks—Bank Mandiri and BNI—account for nearly one-third of total assets (the four state-owned banks together control over 46 percent of system

59. It is very likely that some of this growth was the result of poor credit decisions made before the crisis. However, it is difficult to disentangle such loans from those that went bad due to poor incentives.

60. Two relatively small private banks were closed in April 2004.

Figure 6-1. *Yearly Interest Rate Spreads, Indonesia, 1992–2003*

Interest rate (percent)

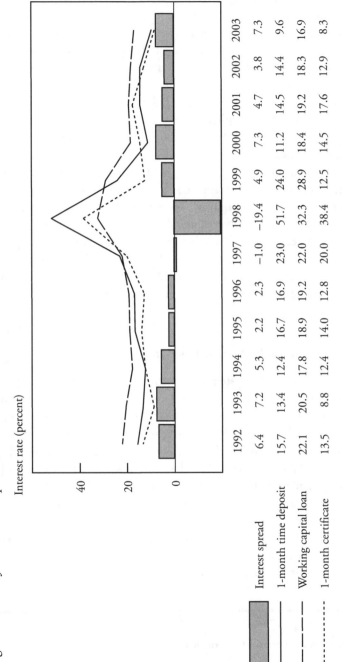

	1992	1993	1994	1995	1996	1997	1998	1999	2000	2001	2002	2003
Interest spread	6.4	7.2	5.3	2.2	2.3	−1.0	−19.4	4.9	7.3	4.7	3.8	7.3
1-month time deposit	15.7	13.4	12.4	16.7	16.9	23.0	51.7	24.0	11.2	14.5	14.4	9.6
Working capital loan	22.1	20.5	17.8	18.9	19.2	22.0	32.3	28.9	18.4	19.2	18.3	16.9
1-month certificate	13.5	8.8	12.4	14.0	12.8	20.0	38.4	12.5	14.5	17.6	12.9	8.3

Source: Bank Indonesia (various years),

Table 6-11. *State-Owned Banks, Indonesia, Loan-to-Deposit Ratio, 1994–2003*

Percent

Bank	1994	1995	1996	1997	1998	1999	2000	2001	2002	2003
BNI	103.6	89.9	93.3	102.7	87.3	51.7	36.1	34.4	37.7	43.6
BTN	190.3	180.9	202.0	177.9	75.9	54.2	46.1	44.0	50.2	58.3
BRI	130.3	141.6	137.6	124.1	99.9	62.3	52.2	55.1	55.2	62.3
Mandiri	. . .	. . .	. . .	. . .	. . .	28.6	25.4	23.3	32.5	41.6
BBD[a]	129.6	123.0	98.2	112.4	n.a.	. . .	. . .	. . .	. . .	. . .
BDN[a]	139.1	137.0	133.3	126.9	n.a.	. . .	. . .	. . .	. . .	. . .
Bank Exim[a]	74.9	76.7	78.3	n.a.	n.a.	. . .	. . .	. . .	. . .	. . .
Bapindo[a]	n.a.	230.3	193.1	201.9	n.a.	. . .	. . .	. . .	. . .	. . .

Source: Banks' annual reports.

a. Merged into Bank Mandiri in 1999.

assets, compared to 37 percent before the crisis). Bank Mandiri alone controls one-fifth of all assets. The government has begun the process of privatization of the largest of these banks and has sold 30 percent of the equity of Bank Mandiri and 40.5 percent of the equity of BRI in initial public offerings. The government also intends to undertake a significant secondary offering of the equity of BNI during 2004.[61] BTN continues to be fully government owned, and there are no plans yet for its privatization. The overall reported performance of state-owned banks has improved since the crisis. Despite these efforts, however, these banks continue to face significant challenges.

As Indonesia recovers from the 1997 crisis, the environment in which the banking sector operates is undergoing profound transformations. Interest rates on BI's certificates have come down from 40 percent in 1998 to 7.5 percent in April 2004. In line with this, nominal deposit rates at state-owned banks have come down from their high of under 35 percent in 1998 to under 10 percent by the end of 2003. Lending spreads have, however, not declined in line with declines in interest rates in the rest of economy. State-owned banks continued to enjoy a spread of almost 700 basis points on their working capital loans, higher than those of private banks (see table 6-8 and figure 6-1).

The restructuring process of both the banking sector and the economy since the crisis has had a significant impact on the structure of the balance sheets of state-owned banks. As of December 2003, for the overall banking system nearly 30 percent of assets are government securities, while for state-owned banks nearly 40 percent of their assets are in government bonds (table 6-12). Liquid assets and BI certificates account for a quarter of the assets of the overall banking system. On the liability side, deposits account for 75 percent of all liabilities of the overall banking system and for two-thirds of those of state-owned banks. Before the crisis of 1997 the holdings of government bonds in the banking system were zero, and loans accounted for over three-quarters of the assets of the system. Loans accounted for more than 70 percent of the 1996 assets of state-owned banks. The ratio of government bond holdings to total assets for the banking system has been declining from its peak of more than 43 percent in 2000 to 30 percent in 2003, as banks began lending again.[62] For state-owned banks these ratios declined from 62 percent to 40 percent over the same period.

---

61. There is ongoing speculation about the government's intention to merge Bank Mandiri and BNI, which would create a state-owned bank three times as big as its nearest competitor.

62. Some part of this decline is also due to banks selling government bonds to mutual funds (*reksadanas*). The size of the mutual fund industry at the end of 2003 was Rp 70 trillion.

The flip side of large government bond holdings is low loan-to-deposit ratios. The banking system's loan-to-deposit ratio, which was more than 103 percent in 1996, declined to 38 percent in 2002 and rose to nearly 50 percent at the end of 2003 (see table 6-12). State-owned banks have faced similar declines (see table 6-11). BNI had a loan-to-deposit ratio of 93 percent in 1996 and 44 percent in 2003. BRI's ratio declined from 138 percent to 62 percent over the same period. All banks experienced a significant rise in this ratio since 2001.

As mentioned above, the overall banking system as well as state-owned banks are also highly liquid in terms of their holdings of cash and liquid assets. This liquidity increases further if government bonds are counted as being liquid (table 6-13).[63] This high level of liquidity combined with a revival of economic growth provides the incentive for banks to look for new lending opportunities. Data for the overall banking system indicate that credit has grown in real terms since 2001 (table 6-14), although much of the new lending is retail consumer loans (mainly financing durable goods and housing), and the overall level of credit is still below 1998 levels. Consumer lending increased from 15 percent of loans in 2000 to 25 percent by the end of 2003, while investment loans remained stable at 22–23 percent of loans, and working capital loans have declined from 61 to 53 percent of loans. For state-owned banks, consumer lending is beginning to show signs of rapid growth recently (table 6-15), although working capital and investment lending remain the bulk of their portfolios. Despite the growth in credit, a significant share of approved loans are unused. Loans at the end of 2003 equaled Rp 440 trillion; the banking sector had off-balance-sheet (approved but undisbursed) credit lines of a further Rp 103 trillion. State-owned banks have about a third of the system's total approved but undisbursed credit lines (see table 6-15).

Banks consider consumer loans to be less risky than corporate lending. This is borne out by the past good experience of BRI in its microfinance lending. Even at the peak of the crisis in 1998–99, BRI's nonperforming loans from its microfinance lending were less than 6 percent, compared to corporate loans, in which nonperforming loan ratios were much higher.[64] Corporate sector lending has not yet revived for a variety of reasons: incomplete corporate restructuring, possible low capacity utilization in certain sectors, poor experience with corporate lending, consumer spending being the leader of economic growth, and the view that large

---

63. It is not clear how liquid recapitalized bonds would be, especially if there were to be a large demand for liquidity.
64. Robinson (2000).

Table 6-12. *Commercial Banks, Indonesia, Summary Data, End of Year, 1996–2003*[a]
Trillions of rupiahs unless otherwise indicated

Item	1996	1997	1998[b]	1999	2000	2001	2002	2003
Number of banks	238	222	208	164	151	145	142	138
	(7)	(7)	(7)	(5)	(5)	(5)	(5)	(5)
Total assets	387.5	528.9	762.4	762.4	984.5	1,039.7	1,059.8	1,213.5
	(178.8)	(243.9)	(230.7)	(357.7)	(455.4)	(492.1)	(488.0)	(556.2)
Government bonds	0	0	0	281.8	431.8	435.3	419.4	344.6
	(0)	(0)	(0)	(214.2)	(282.3)	(256.3)	(244.6)	(207.4)
Loans	292.9	378.1	487.7	225.1	269.0	307.6	365.4	440.5
	(124.5)	(169.6)	(198.3)	(116.1)	(109.4)	(126.6)	(151.0)	(177.2)
Deposits	281.7	357.6	573.5	625.6	720.4	809.1	845.0	888.6
	(106.9)	(143.7)	(196.8)	(284.1)	(325.8)	(384.8)	(388.1)	(368.5)
Equity	37.1	46.7	–98.5	–21.6	50.6	66.8	93.7	112.4
	(11.1)	(12.0)	(–97.4)	(–31.3)	(23.3)	(23.0)	(29.3)	(48.3)
Nonperforming loans	22.8	32.9	276.7	92.0	56.9	38.7	27.8	29.9
	n.a.	n.a.	n.a.	(17.2)	(18.4)	(8.8)	(9.1)	(13.0)
Profit before tax	4.7	–1.5	–178.6	–75.4	10.5	13.1	21.9	28.9
	(2.2)	(1.9)	(–152.8)	(–35.0)	(1.2)	(6.9)	(10.1)	(12.7)
GDP at current prices	532.6	627.7	955.8	1,099.7	1,264.9	1,449.4	1,610.0	1,786.7
Addendum (percent)								
M1 over GDP[c]	12.0	12.5	10.6	11.3	12.8	12.3	11.9	12.5
M2 over GDP[d]	54.2	56.7	60.4	58.8	59.1	58.2	54.9	53.5
Bank assets / GDP	72.8	84.3	93.7	91.5	81.5	75.9	69.1	67.9

Government bonds / GDP	⋯	⋯	⋯	25.6	34.1	30.0	26.0	19.3
Loans / GDP	55.0	61.7	57.1	25.2	25.3	24.7	25.5	24.7
Loans to private banks / GDP[e]	n.a.	57.3	18.4	18.9	20.3	20.2	21.5	23.4
Deposits / GDP	52.9	57.0	60.0	56.9	57.0	55.8	52.5	49.7
Gross nonperforming loans to total loans ratio	7.8	8.7	48.6	32.8	18.8	12.1	8.3	6.8
Loans to deposits	103.9	105.7	72.4	26.2	33.2	33.0	38.2	49.6
Capital/risk-weighted assets	12.2	4.3	-15.7	-8.1	12.5	20.5	22.5	19.4
Profit after tax/equity	7.6	11.8	437.2	110.8	3.0	13.9	15.0	20.4
Profit after tax/assets	0.7	1.4	18.8	6.1	0.6	1.3	2.0	1.9

Source: Bank's financial statements, Bank Indonesia (various years); authors' calculations.

a. Numbers in parentheses are those of state banks.

b. 1998 figures for state banks are estimated figures, because Bank Exim, BDN, Bapindo, and BBD did not publish 1998 financial statements. Bank Exim also did not publish a financial statement in 1997.

c. Currency outside banks + demand deposits.

d. M1 + quasi money.

e. Total loan minus loan to government entities and state-owned enterprises.

Table 6-13. *Commercial Banks, Indonesia, Summary Balance Sheets,*
End of Year, 1997–2003
Trillions of rupiahs

Item	1997	1998	1999	2000	2001	2002	2003
Claims on BI certificates	17.4	34.2	42.7	49.7	49.0	56.9	72.3
Holdings of BI certificates	16.5	58.8	86.9	58.8	102.6	76.9	101.4
Foreign assets	46.8	115.7	94.5	102.2	109.8	90.1	77.3
Liquid assets-1[a]	80.7	208.7	223.5	238.7	301.0	258.3	285.8
Government bonds	1.0	0.7	268.7	429.7	408.9	378.3	344.6
Liquid assets-2[b]	81.7	209.4	492.2	668.4	709.9	638.6	630.5
Credit	378.4	487.5	225.1	269.0	307.6	365.4	410.5
Other assets[c]	68.8	65.5	72.1	47.1	22.4	57.8	142.5
Total assets/total liabilities	528.9	762.4	789.4	984.5	1,039.9	1,059.8	1,213.5
Deposits	357.6	573.5	625.6	720.4	809.1	845.0	888.6
Borrowing from BI	23.1	112.9	33.4	16.5	15.2	12.7	10.9
Foreign liabilities	70.4	97.8	74.6	92.7	68.4	51.9	31.5
Other liabilities[d]	48.5	76.7	55.8	104.3	80.4	56.5	170.2
Equity	46.7	(98.5)	(21.6)	50.6	66.8	93.7	112.4
Addendum (%)							
Liquid assets-1	22.6	36.4	35.7	33.1	37.2	30.6	32.2
Liquid assets-2	22.8	36.5	78.7	92.8	87.7	75.3	71.0
Loans to deposit	105.7	72.4	26.2	33.2	33.0	38.2	49.6

Source: Bank Indonesia (various years); Asian Development Bank (2003); BI balance sheet.

a. Claims on BI and interbank claims.

b. Liquid assets-1 + government bonds.

c. Fixed assets and other marketable securities, determined as residual. Other liabilities mostly consist of borrowings.

d. Determined as a residual.

borrowers are bad credit risks while small borrowers usually are not.[65] To the extent that corporate lending is implemented, the usual form is working capital loans.

The reason that the banking system holds such a large share of its assets in government bonds is that the worst nonperforming loans of state-owned banks—and of many private banks, too—were transferred to IBRA and replaced by govern-

65. Firm data on capacity utilization across industrial sectors are not available. Current estimates range from 50 percent in certain industries to 70 percent in others. It is also likely that a portion of the capacity is now obsolete.

ment bonds. Nonperforming loans for all banks declined from almost 50 percent of outstanding loans at the end of 1998 to their precrisis level of 8 percent at the end of 2002 (see table 6-12). State-owned banks were the most affected: In 1998 their nonperforming loans stood at 48 percent of outstanding loans.[66] These loans declined to 6 percent by 2002, although they rose to 7 percent by 2003 (see table 6-12). Banks also set aside substantial provisions (more than 11 percent of outstanding loans at the end of 2002; table 6-16), with state-owned banks setting aside more than 9 percent of total loans as provisions. Net nonperforming loans for these banks stood at –2 percent at the end of 2003.

This percentage needs to be interpreted with some caution, as it likely overstates the true quality of asset portfolios. Bank Mandiri and BNI, for example, carry a substantial portion of their "restructured" assets on their balance sheets (table 6-17). Some of these loans were taken over by IBRA, in return for which the banks obtained government bonds. They bought some of these loans back from IBRA at steep discounts, even though they were effectively not restructured in any real sense: BI loan classification rules allow such loans to be considered to be performing for one year from the date of purchase. The rest of the restructured loans were restructured by the banks themselves, usually through rollovers, maturity extensions, or debt-to-equity conversions. Reports indicate that some of these so-called restructured loans may be nonperforming again.[67] In addition, some banks include as performing assets in their restructuring deals foreclosed assets and equity received. If these types of loans are reclassified as nonperforming, those numbers—especially for Bank Mandiri and BNI—get substantially worse.[68] Table 6-17 shows an analysis of two scenarios, with either 50 percent or 100 percent of restructured loans considered nonperforming. The net increases from –2.3 percent to 7.0 percent and 16.3 percent, respectively.[69] This implies that if a significant fraction of the restructured loans were to turn nonperforming again, state-owned banks would be significantly underprovisioned. Commercial banks reported capital adequacy ratios of nearly 20 percent in 2003 (see table 6-12). The reported capital adequacy ratios of state-owned banks are similarly high (see

66. The precise level is difficult to estimate. These numbers are drawn from BI's 1998–99 annual report. Some observers quote higher numbers.

67. For example, Bank Mandiri bought from IBRA a loan of a large debtor (Kiani Kertas) with a face value of Rp 1.7 trillion at a discount of 80 percent. This loan is reported to be nonperforming again.

68. Ratios of nonperforming loans for some private banks also increase quite substantially.

69. Some market analysts disagree with the view that restructured loans could be a source of problems for state-owned banks and express the view that these loans were bought at such steep discounts that they will be profitable. However, all of the restructured loans have not yet been reclassified based on the standard classification rules. Only after this is done will the true performing status of restructured loans be known.

Table 6-14. *Outstanding Credit, Indonesia, by Type of Lending and Bank, End of Year, 1998–2003*

| | 1998 | | 1999 | | | 2000 | | |
Credit source	Rp trillion	Percent	Rp trillion	Percent	Real growth (percent)	Rp trillion	Percent	Real growth (percent)
Investment	141.5	29	57.7	26	–21.1	65.3	23	9.5
State banks	89.1		37.6			34.4		
Regional banks	0.9		0.7			0.8		
Private domestic banks	38.7		13.1			19.9		
Foreign and joint								
venture	12.8		6.2			10.2		
Working capital	314.2	64	143.4	64	–21.1	163.6	61	10.4
State banks	115.9		61.3			50.8		
Regional banks	3.4		3.3			2.7		
Private domestic banks	142.6		36.8			49.3		
Foreign and joint								
venture	52.2		41.9			60.9		
Consumption	31.8	7	24.1	10	–20.8	40.1	15	62.7
State banks	15.7		13.4			16.8		
Regional banks	2.2		2.8			6.6		
Private domestic banks	12.1		6.1			13.3		
Foreign and joint								
venture	1.7		1.8			3.4		
Total	487.4	100	225.1	100	–21.1	269	100	15.8
Annual inflation								
rate (percent)				20.5			3.7	

Source: Bank Indonesia (various years).

table 6-17). One reason for this high ratio is that many of the worst loans were taken over by IBRA and replaced with government bonds, which have a zero risk weight. Another reason is that, as stated above, banks have been reporting that they are overprovisioned for their current level of nonperforming loans. If restructured loans are more conservatively provided for, the capital adequacy ratio changes significantly. For example, for Bank Mandiri if 50 percent of the restructured assets on the balance sheets are considered to be nonperforming, the capital adequacy ratio falls from nearly 28 percent to about 17 percent. If all the

	2001			2002			2003	
Rp trillion	*Percent*	*Real growth (percent)*	*Rp trillion*	*Percent*	*Real growth (percent)*	*Rp trillion*	*Percent*	*Real growth (percent)*
73.5	24	1.1	82.9	23	0.9	95.8	22	8.9
38.6			43.5			49.6		
1.3			2.2			3.1		
24.5			30.5			37.7		
9.1			6.7			5.3		
175.7	57	−4.1	202.7	55	3.5	233.5	53	8.6
56.1			73.2			83.7		
3.6			5.8			7.5		
56.8			76.1			95.7		
59.3			47.6			46.6		
58.4	19	34.1	79.8	22	24.8	112.1	25	32.8
22.4			29.3			43.8		
10.6			13.5			17.8		
20.6			30.5			41.1		
4.8			6.5			8.6		
307.6	100	2.8	365.4	100	6.9	440.5	100	14.0
	11.5			11.9			6.6	

restructured assets were to be nonperforming, Bank Mandiri's ratio falls to just under 6 percent.

Both state-owned and many private banks have experienced improved profitability since 2000 (see table 6-12). State-owned banks (which reported a loss of Rp 35 trillion, before taxes, in 1999) reported a profit before taxes of Rp 12.7 trillion in 2003. In terms of returns on assets, these banks have been improving their performance in terms of profit after taxes, increasing from 0.56 percent in 2000 to 2.3 percent in 2003 (table 6-18). For the system as a whole, the proportion of

Table 6-15. *Lending by State-Owned Banks, Indonesia, 2000–03*

Type of lending	Nominal (trillions of rupiahs)				Share (percent)				Growth (percent)		
	2000	2001	2002	2003	2000	2001	2002	2003	2001	2002	2003
Bank Mandiri	43.0	27.7	39.5	75.9	100.0	100.0	100.0	100.0	-35.6	42.5	92.2
Working capital[a]	23.0	13.1	21.9	37.9	53.5	47.2	55.5	49.9	-43.1	67.5	72.9
Investment	12.7	9.8	11.4	25.8	29.5	35.4	28.8	34.0	-22.8	16.2	126.3
Consumer[b]	0.8	1.0	1.9	4.1	1.9	3.6	4.9	5.5	20.0	94.9	113.6
Other[c]	6.5	3.8	4.2	8.1	15.0	13.8	10.7	10.6	-40.8	11.1	90.4
BRI	27.0	33.5	39.4	47.5	100.0	100.0	100.0	100.0	24.0	17.4	20.7
Working capital[a]	16.3	21.1	24.0	29.5	60.4	63.0	61.0	62.0	29.3	13.8	22.8
Investment	2.3	2.9	2.8	3.4	8.6	8.6	7.1	7.2	24.4	-3.6	22.2
Consumer[b]	5.6	7.8	10.0	11.2	20.8	23.2	25.5	23.6	38.3	29.1	11.6
Other[c]	2.8	1.8	2.5	3.4	10.2	5.2	6.4	7.2	-36.5	44.5	35.8
Bank BNI	32.0	35.4	37.8	46.4	100.0	100.0	100.0	100.0	10.7	6.8	22.8
Working capital[a]	16.0	19.3	21.7	26.5	50.1	54.6	57.5	57.1	20.6	12.6	21.9
Investment	13.4	12.6	11.3	13.4	41.8	35.5	29.9	28.8	-6.0	-10.1	18.4
Consumer[b]	1.9	2.7	4.2	5.9	5.9	7.6	11.2	12.7	43.4	56.7	39.6
Other[c]	0.7	0.8	0.5	0.6	2.2	2.3	1.4	1.4	16.7	-35.3	20.8

BTN	7.6	8.4	10.2	11.1	100.0	100.0	100.0	100.0	10.2	21.4	8.6
Working capital[a]	0.2	0.3	0.5	0.5	3.0	3.5	4.9	4.2	26.4	73.0	-6.9
Investment	0.0	0.0	0.1	0.0	0.2	0.1	0.8	0.0	-70.5	1,577.0	-97.8
Consumer[b]	7.4	8.1	9.6	10.6	96.8	96.5	94.3	95.8	9.8	18.7	10.3
All state-owned banks	109.7	105.1	126.9	181.0	100.0	100.0	100.0	100.0	-4.2	20.8	42.6
Working capital[a]	55.6	53.8	68.2	94.4	50.7	51.2	53.7	52.1	-3.2	26.7	38.4
Investment	28.4	25.3	25.6	42.6	25.9	24.0	20.1	23.5	-11.1	1.1	66.6
Consumer[b]	15.7	19.6	25.8	31.9	14.3	18.6	20.4	17.6	24.6	31.9	23.4
Other[c]	9.9	6.4	7.3	12.2	9.1	6.1	5.8	6.7	-35.5	14.2	66.4
Undisbursed credit lines	64.7	70.5	81.1	103.0	100.0	100.0	100.0	100.0	9.0	14.9	27.0
Mandiri	8.1	6.6	10.4	17.0	12.5	9.3	12.8	16.5	-18.7	58.4	63.5
BRI	3.9	4.3	8.4	7.6	6.1	6.1	10.4	7.3	10.5	94.8	-10.5
Bank BNI	3.2	3.7	4.9	7.4	4.9	5.3	6.1	7.2	18.0	32.2	50.2
BTN	0.3	0.2	0.2	0.3	0.5	0.3	0.3	0.3	-41.7	27.1	34.0
Other banks	49.2	55.7	57.1	70.7	76.1	79.0	70.4	68.7	13.2	2.4	23.9

Source: Banks' annual reports and financial statements; figures include channeling loans.
a. Includes syndicated loans.
b. Includes loans to employees.
c. Mostly program or export loans.

Table 6-16. *Loan-Loss Reserves and Provisions, Indonesia, Selected Years, 1982–2003*

Percent

	1982	1988	1989	1990	1991	1995	1997	2000ᵃ	2003
Loan-loss reserve to total loans									
State-owned banks	3.2	4.2	2.3	4.4	4.5	2.8	2.7	18.9	14.9
Private foreign exchange banks	1.7	1.2	1.0	0.8	1.1	2.8	2.0	9.1	8.8
Private nonforeign exchange banks	0.7	0.7	0.5	0.6	0.9	1.3	2.2	3.3	3.8
Foreign banks	0.6	2.0	1.6	1.4	1.9	2.2	3.5	22.4	13.3
All banks	2.7	3.3	3.3	2.7	2.8	2.0	2.4	16.3	11.3
Provision expense to total loans									
State-owned banks	n.a.	1.2	0.6	1.3	0.9	1.2	1.3	-2.0	2.5
Private foreign exchange banks	n.a.	1.0	0.7	0.8	0.7	0.6	1.8	1.1	2.7
Private nonforeign exchange banks	n.a.	0.9	0.7	0.6	1.2	0.7	1.1	1.5	1.0
Foreign banks	n.a.	1.1	0.7	0.6	0.8	1.4	3.6	1.5	0.0
All banks	n.a.	1.1	1.0	1.0	0.8	0.9	1.7	0.3	1.4
Provision expense to interest margin									
State-owned banks	n.a.	44.9	36.0	35.5	47.3	26.2	38.7	-4.5	22.2
Private foreign exchange banks	n.a.	20.7	16.3	18.1	14.9	12.9	38.9	26.3	26.3
Private nonforeign exchange banks	n.a.	17.1	16.7	13.4	27.2	12.0	15.0	10.5	10.5
Foreign banks	n.a.	17.2	12.8	8.7	14.6	16.7	45.0	0.0	0.0
All banks	n.a.	29.2	28.2	22.3	23.4	18.6	38.4	13.4	13.4

Source: Bank Indonesia (various years); banks' financial statements; authors' calculations.

a. Ratios are negative or small because of reverse loan-loss provisions.

Table 6-17. *State-Owned Banks, Indonesia, Nonperforming Loans and Capital Adequacy, End of Year, 2003*
Trillions of rupiahs unless otherwise indicated

Item	Mandiri	BNI	BRI	BTN	Total
Assets	245.8	131.2	94.7	26.8	498.6
Loans	73.3	45.9	47.5	11.2	177.9
Category 1	55.8	35.7	41.2	9.0	141.8
Category 2	11.0	7.6	3.4	1.7	23.7
Category 3	1.6	1.3	1.4	0.2	4.5
Category 4	1.4	0.9	0.6	0.1	3.0
Category 5	3.4	0.5	0.9	0.2	4.9
Nonperforming[a]	6.5	2.6	2.9	0.4	12.4
Loan-loss provision	9.0	2.4	4.3	0.7	16.5
Nonperforming loans (percent)					
Gross ratio	8.8	5.7	6.0	3.8	7.0
Net ratio	–3.5	0.5	–3.0	–2.5	–2.3
Provision	139.6	91.8	150.4	164.9	132.8
Share of assets	29.8	35.0	50.2	41.6	35.7
Restructured assets					
Restructuring loans, category 1	14.0	2.4	0.7	0.1	17.3
Restructuring loans, category 2	5.9	4.8	1.2	...	12.0
Foreclosed assets	0.1	0.3	0.0	...	0.5
Equity from restructuring	0.1	3.3	0.0	...	3.4
Under 50 percent restructuring	10.1	5.5	1.0	0.0	16.6
Net ratio, 50 percent restructuring (percent)	10.3	12.4	–1.0	–2.2	7.0
Net ratio, 100 percent restructuring (percent)	–3.5	0.5	–3.5	–2.5	–2.3
Addendum					
Risk-weighted assets	91.9	66.2	46.2	6.6	
Capital	25.5	12.0	9.6	0.8	
Published capital adequacy ratio (percent)	27.7	18.2	20.9	12.1	
Capital adequacy ratio					
Under 50 percent restructuring (percent)	16.7	9.9	18.7	11.6	
Under 100 percent restructuring (percent)	5.8	1.7	16.6	11.1	

Source: Bank Indonesia (2003); authors' calculations.
a. Categories 3, 4, and 5.

Table 6-18. *Share of Bank Costs and Margins, Indonesia, by Bank Type, Selected Years, 1982–2003*
Percent

	1982	1988	1989	1990	1991	1995	1997	2000	2002	2003
Interest income										
State-owned banks	1.42	9.57	10.48	11.25	13.57	10.60	10.02	9.89	12.80	9.40
Private foreign exchange banks	1.59	15.82	14.32	16.48	20.59	13.07	13.91	9.73	11.70	9.70
Private nonforeign exchange banks	0.91	16.92	14.81	19.56	25.13	14.48	19.89	11.45	16.40	14.40
Foreign banks	4.45	11.71	12.05	12.52	12.99	11.59	7.58	8.07	8.30	7.10
All banks	1.60	11.17	11.60	13.18	16.03	11.99	11.91	9.76	12.00	9.50
Interest expense										
State-owned banks	4.10	7.40	7.77	8.08	11.43	7.66	7.73	8.02	9.20	5.70
Private foreign exchange banks	7.95	11.90	10.81	12.49	16.14	9.98	10.83	7.38	8.20	5.80
Private nonforeign exchange banks	9.74	12.64	11.49	15.03	20.09	10.66	14.68	7.01	11.50	8.50
Foreign banks	9.15	7.57	7.97	6.95	7.83	6.11	3.45	4.05	4.00	2.60
All banks	4.82	8.25	8.83	9.29	12.60	8.82	9.02	7.38	8.20	5.50
Net operating margin										
State-owned banks	2.55	2.45	2.63	2.84	1.31	0.92	0.85	-1.76	0.30	0.80
Private foreign exchange banks	4.00	2.89	2.37	2.26	2.24	1.33	0.91	1.61	0.60	1.40
Private nonforeign exchange banks	3.67	1.78	1.37	1.93	1.87	0.69	1.41	1.34	1.80	2.30
Foreign banks	4.51	3.70	3.64	3.98	4.53	4.02	2.97	1.90	2.60	2.70
All banks	2.99	2.64	2.57	2.91	1.98	1.22	1.07	-0.06	0.80	1.40
Pretax return on assets										
State-owned banks	2.40	1.40	1.55	1.78	0.31	0.96	0.74	0.56	2.00	2.30
Private foreign exchange banks	3.60	1.93	1.68	1.39	1.24	1.44	0.92	0.67	1.10	1.80
Private nonforeign exchange banks	3.08	1.29	0.78	0.97	0.91	1.09	1.30	1.51	2.10	2.40
Foreign banks	4.32	1.78	2.80	3.02	3.39	4.13	2.89	2.79	4.50	4.10
All banks	2.81	1.68	1.67	1.99	0.97	1.32	1.01	1.01	2.00	1.90

Source: Bank Indonesia (various years); banks' financial statements; authors' calculations.

banks' income from interest on government bonds has been reduced to 17 percent of total income in 2003 (compared to 22 percent in 2002). The majority of the banking sector's income already comes from loans. It is, however, difficult to evaluate bank profitability given the uncertainty about nonperforming loans, as discussed earlier. State-owned banks continue to depend heavily on recapitalized bonds for their income. In addition, some of these banks carry high-cost deposits on their balance sheets, with low ratios of core deposits to total deposits, which make ongoing profitability a challenge.

The Governance of State-Owned Banks

It is well recognized that governance plays a key role in the effective functioning of financial institutions.[70] Banks—state-owned banks in particular—face special problems of governance.[71] As discussed above, governance issues have played a major role in the banking crisis in Indonesia.[72] Given the importance of this issue, this section presents a brief discussion on the evolution and current governance of state-owned banks in Indonesia.

In Indonesia such banks traditionally viewed themselves as agents of development and as arms of the government, with a correspondingly weak credit culture, inadequate provisioning, and poor risk management. They were subject to weak supervision by BI, but sanctions were rarely imposed due to political considerations. The banks also operated in an environment in which they had no real "owner." Although the Ministry of Finance has always been their legal owner, since 2001 this ministry has delegated day-to-day oversight to the Ministry of State-Owned Enterprises. This joint responsibility has created further potential for difficulties in governance. Historically, selected individuals within the banks controlled the banks. The banks were also influenced directly and indirectly by Parliament as well as by the Supreme Audit Authority.

Before the 1997 crisis, the organizational structure of a bank typically consisted of a board of directors and a board of commissioners. The board of directors consisted of one president director and a number of directors (the number varying across banks). These directors were appointed for five-year tenures by the president of Indonesia upon the recommendation of the minister of finance. Members of the board of directors were typically career state bankers. The board of commissioners was chaired by one president commissioner and usually had

70. Litan, Pomerleano, and Sundararajan (2002).
71. Caprio and Levine (2002).
72. For discussion, see Enoch and others (2001); World Bank (1998, 2000); Grenville (2003); Santoso (2000); Asian Development Bank (2003).

two other commissioners. President commissioners were usually retired military officers or police officers appointed by the president of Indonesia. Commissioners were usually drawn from active senior officials of the Ministry of Finance or retired BI officials. While technically the commissioners were mandated to represent the owner (the state) and the directors were responsible for day-to-day operations, in practice their mandates were often unclear and had overlapping responsibilities. Given the composition and the unclear mandates, the board of commissioners usually did not effectively safeguard the interest of the owner and in general had weaker bargaining positions and political power than the board of directors. Membership on boards of commissioners was often viewed as a sinecure, with the real power resting with directors, who were an integral part of the bank's management.

After the financial crisis of 1997 many efforts were made to improve the governance and the quality of management of state-owned banks by all parties involved—the government, BI, and after their partial privatization, Bapepam. Governance structures were reformed, and commissioners and directors were appointed with greater considerations given to professionalism, experience, and technical skill. The boards now are appointed based on five-year contracts, with clear business plans and quantifiable performance indicators.

As part of the restructuring process—and to keep itself better informed about developments in the banks—the Ministry of Finance appointed a Monitoring and Governance Unit to aid the government in exercising its rights as a shareholder of the state-owned banks.[73] (The unit has concluded its operations and no new mechanism has been installed in its place.) The unit reported to both the Ministry of Finance and the Ministry of State-Owned Enterprises. In August 2001 the Ministry of State-Owned Enterprises became responsible for day-to-day oversight, but the Monitoring and Governance Unit stayed within the Ministry of Finance. The minister of finance signed recapitalization agreements, under which the banks are required to perform according to agreed upon business plans and performance contracts.[74] The Ministry of Finance retains the right to approve changes in the banks' corporate structure.

Regulations issued by BI and Bapepam—with the latter playing a role after the banks' partial privatization—require the appointment of independent commissioners as well as audit committees. Since 1999 BI also requires directors and

---

73. The work of this unit was financed by a grant from the Australian government.

74. The banks' directors and the commissioners signed these agreements as equal signatories, a further indication of the lack of clarity of the roles of these two bodies.

commissioners to pass "fit and proper" tests. BI's efforts to improve prudential supervision reinforce this requirement, particularly through compliance directors (since September 1999), on-site supervisors, and the quarterly accounts publication. However, significant weaknesses in governance and internal controls remain. BNI faced losses of over $200 million in a scandal involving letters of credit honored by branch officials, in collusion with politically connected parties. BRI reported losses of Rp 300 billion in another case of fraud.[75] In the BNI case, the bank admitted to failure of its internal control systems, and as a result the government largely replaced the board of directors.

Another key governance issue is that, despite partial privatization of three of the four state-owned banks, the government continues to retain a "golden share," giving it complete authority with regard to the boards of commissioners and directors. This structure provides little incentive for bank management to change from its traditional view of themselves as agents of development and as acting at the behest of politicians to a view in which commercial considerations and maximization of shareholder value plays a greater role.

Therefore, although the government has taken many steps in the right direction in improving the governance of these banks, they continue to face significant challenges with regard to governance. Although BI is now an independent regulator, it still faces challenges when trying to supervise the banks. International evidence shows that government ownership of banks is negatively associated with development of the banking sector and positively associated with several measures of bank inefficiency.[76] Research also shows that countries enjoy better developed financial systems with a lower likelihood of crises when private sector entities can monitor banks better, a situation that is unlikely in Indonesia unless there is a significant reduction in the share of government ownership of the sector.

Conclusion

Much progress has been made in regard to the state-owned banks in Indonesia. In addition to recapitalization and restructuring, the government has begun reducing its stake in these banks through initial public offerings of minority equity stakes in Bank Mandiri and BRI. The financial performance not only of state-owned banks but also of the overall banking sector shows signs of improvement. BI's regulation

---

75. In addition, the IMF has expressed concern over the rapid expansion of lending by certain banks. "Banks Considered Too Aggressive" (2004).

76. Barth, Caprio, and Levine (2001a, 2001b).

and supervision of the sector has been strengthened substantially. However, fraud charges as well as concerns that banks are being too aggressive in new lending raise continuing questions regarding the extent to which reforms have taken root and the fragility of the banking sector. Much remains to be done in the financial sector overall, in the banking system in particular, and among state-owned banks specifically.

Arguably the first issue that the government needs to address is the role of the state in state-owned banks, which have a long history of weak governance and poor performance and have had to be recapitalized repeatedly. When these banks moved from their development focus, the ensuing crisis exposed the full extent of the political nature of their operations. BI has faced continuing difficulties in supervising these banks. Many attempts have also been made to improve their governance without relinquishing the state's role as owner. Keeping all these issues in mind, there is little rationale for the government to continue to be a shareholder in these banks. The government made significant progress in cleaning up the rest of the banking sector after the crisis, having sold the majority of intervened banks to foreign investors. Retaining majority ownership of state-owned banks weakens their incentives for performance and exposes the government to the risk of future recapitalizations in case of weak performance. Full privatization of these banks, along with a change in incentive structures that accompanies privatization, would strengthen the financial sector. International experience with state-owned banks also points to the benefits of such action. While capital markets do focus more on the performance of these banks as a result of their partial privatization, there is little that they can do to effect change as long as the government continues to retain its share and the right to appoint and change management. Giving up its golden share would require legislative action but is critical to attracting private strategic investors who could promote proper governance and improve management of the banks. There could also be difficulties in finding buyers for the two largest state-owned banks, Bank Mandiri and BNI. However, these institutions could be restructured—including downsizing—to make them more attractive to investors.

Some observers argue that BRI is well managed and hence presents a case in which the state may not necessarily have to relinquish its role. BRI was built on government-subsidized programs for the rural sector in the belief that commercial banks would not venture into this area. In other words, it was built with the social objective of making banking services available to the rural poor. With its good performance in this niche, BRI has become one of the more attractive and profitable banks in Indonesia. Another view, however, is that now that this niche has proved profitable—and commercial banks could also play a role—the government should relinquish its control over BRI.

Full privatization of state-owned banks will likely take some time. In the interim, one focus of the government needs to be to further improve the governance of these institutions through closer involvement in the design and execution of their corporate strategies, holding them accountable to their shareholders (the largest being the government) and monitoring their performance on an ongoing basis. The government should also consider renewing and, importantly, enforcing performance contracts at these banks. BI's supervision of these banks needs to be brought in line with the supervision of private banks and its regulations better enforced. Another focus is on the new—and competitive—lending environment as economic growth resumes. Trends indicate that this new lending environment favors small- and medium-sized enterprises and consumers and will require state-owned banks to acquire new credit assessment and delivery skills as well as to upgrade their risk management expertise.

Indonesia's financial sector is at a crossroads. It has been rescued from a debilitating crisis at a huge cost to the taxpayer. Much of the crisis management work is done. The focus now needs to be on developing a strong diversified sector that is able to finance economic growth on a sustainable basis. The emphasis in the banking sector needs to be on developing a banking system that avoids destabilizing crises, provides secure payments, offers savers secure deposits, intermediates efficiently between savers and investors, and provides access to financial services. The state-owned banks should contribute to this process. Indonesian history and international experience suggest that a good way to achieve this objective is to reduce the role of the state-owned banks in the Indonesian banking sector.

Appendix: Indonesia's State-Owned Banks

Bank Negara Indonesia 1946

BNI 1946 was established in July 5, 1946, to assume the role of a central bank for Indonesia. However, in 1951 the government nationalized De Javasche Bank, a de facto central bank during the Dutch colonial era, and made this bank the central bank of the country. De Javasche Bank changed its name to Bank Indonesia (BI) in 1953. Since 1955, BNI 1946 has operated as a commercial and development bank. In 1965 the government merged BI, BNI 1946, Bank Koperasi Tani dan Nelayan, and Bank Tabungan Negara to become Bank Negara Indonesia (BNI). The operations of BI and BNI 1946 were put under BNI Unit I and BNI Unit III, respectively. In 1968, under Laws 13 and 17, BNI Unit III was spun off, and Bank Negara Indonesia 1946 was recreated. In 1992, BNI 1946 changed its name to Bank BNI and continues to operate as a commercial bank.

Bank Rakyat Indonesia

BRI was officially formed in 1946, although its history can be traced back to the formation of Bank Priyayi in 1896. In 1958 the government also established Bank Koperasi Tani dan Nelayan and merged this bank with BRI in 1960. Also in that year the government nationalized Nederlandsche Handles Maatschappij (NHM) and merged it into Bank Koperasi Tani dan Nelayan. In 1965 Bank Koperasi Tani dan Nelayan was acquired by BNI. BRI's operation was placed under BNI Unit II for the rural sector; NHM's operation was under BNI Unit II as an import bank. Under Law 13 of 1968, the two units were spun off again. BNI Unit II for rural development became Bank Rakyat Indonesia, based on Law 21 issued in 1968, whereas BNI Unit II for exports and imports became Bank Ekspor Impor Indonesia (Bank Exim), based on Law 22 of 1968. BRI is still in existence; Bank Exim was merged into Bank Mandiri in 1998.

Bank Dagang Negara

BDN was created when the Indonesian government nationalized Escompto Bank in 1960. BDN was given a mandate to operate as a commercial bank since its establishment. In 1965 the government decided to merge BDN into BNI, but in practice the two banks kept operating independently. BDN continued to operate as a commercial bank until it was merged into Bank Mandiri in 1998.

Nationale Handelsbank

In 1959 the Indonesian government nationalized Nationale Handelsbank, changing its name to Bank Umum Negara. It operated as a commercial bank. In 1965 Bank Umum Negara was acquired by BNI and became BNI Unit IV. After that— in 1968—BNI Unit IV became a separate bank, Bank Bumi Daya. Bank Bumi Daya continued to operate as a commercial bank until 1998, when it was merged into Bank Mandiri.

Bank Pembangunan Indonesia

Bapindo was originally Bank Industri Negara, which was created in 1951. Law 21 of 1960 changed Bank Industri Negara to Bapindo.

Bank Tabungan Negara

BTN has its origin in the Dutch Postpaarbank, which was formed in 1934. In 1950 the bank changed its name to Bank Tabungan Post and in 1963 to Bank Tabungan Negara. In 1965 BTN was acquired by BNI, becoming BNI Unit V. In 1968 it was separated from BNI again and finally—through Law 20—was established as Bank Tabungan Negara.

References

Asian Development Bank. 2003. "Indonesia: An Overview of Recent Developments and Pending Issues in the Financial Sector." Jakarta.

Balino, Tomas J. T., and V. Sundararajan. 1986. "Financial Reform in Indonesia." In *Financial Policy and Reform in Pacific Basin Countries,* edited by H. S. Cheng. Singapore: Oxford University Press.

Bank Indonesia. Various years. *Annual Report.*

"Banks Considered Too Aggressive, IMF Warns BI." 2004. *Bisnis Indonesia,* March 5, 2004, p. 1.

Barth, James, Gerard Caprio, and Ross Levine. 2001a. "Bank Regulation and Supervision: A New Database." In *Brookings-Wharton Papers on Financial Services,* edited by Robert E. Litan and Richard Herring. Brookings.

———. 2001b. "Bank Regulation and Supervision: What Works Best." Policy Research Working Paper 2725. Washington: World Bank.

Binhadi. 1995. *Financial Sector Deregulation, Banking Development, and Monetary Policy: The Indonesian Experience.* Jakarta: Institut Bankir Indonesia.

Boediono. 2002. "The International Monetary Fund Support Program in Indonesia: Comparing Implementation under Three Presidents." *Bulletin of Indonesian Economic Studies* 38, no. 3: 385–91.

Caprio, Gerard, and Ross Levine. 2002. "Corporate Governance in Finance: Concept and International Observations." In *Building the Pillars of Financial Sector Governance: The Roles of the Private and Public Sectors.* Brookings.

Claessens, Stijn, Simeon Djankov, and Daniela Klingebiel. 1999. *Financial Restructuring in East Asia: Halfway There?* Financial Sector Discussion Paper 3. Washington: World Bank.

Cole, David C., and Betty F. Slade. 1990. *Financial Development in Indonesia.* Washington: World Bank.

———. 1996. *Building a Modern Financial System: The Indonesian Experience.* Cambridge University Press.

Enoch, Charles, and others. 2001. "Indonesia: Anatomy of a Banking Crisis, Two Years of Living Dangerously." Working Paper 01/52. Washington: International Monetary Fund.

———. 2003. "Indonesia's Banking Crisis: What Happened and What Did We Learn?" *Bulletin of Indonesian Economic Studies* 39, no. 1: 75–92.

Grenville, Stephen. 2003. *Strengthening the Indonesian State-Owned Banking Sector.* Washington: World Bank.

Hanna, Donald P. 1994. *Indonesian Experience with Financial Sector Reform.* Discussion Paper 237. Washington: World Bank.

Hanson, James A. 2003. "Public Sector Banks and Their Transformation." Working Paper. Washington: World Bank.

Harris, John R., Fabio Schiantarelli, and Miranda G. Siregar. 1992. "How Financial Liberalization in Indonesia Affected Firms' Capital Structure and Investment Decisions." Policy Research Working Paper 997. Washington: World Bank.

Hofman, Bert, and Ella Rodrick-Jones. 2004. "Indonesia: Rapid Growth, Weak Institutions." Working Paper. Washington: World Bank.

Indef. 2003. *Restrukturisasi Perbankan di Indonesia: Pengalaman Bank BNI.* Jakarta.

Kenward, Lloyd. 2003. *From the Trenches: The First Year of Indonesia's Crisis 1997/98 as Seen from the World Bank's Office in Jakarta.* Jakarta: Center for International and Strategic Studies.

La Porta, Rafael, and Florencio López-de-Silanes. 1999. "The Benefits of Privatization: Evidence from Mexico." *Quarterly Journal of Economics* 114: 1193–242.

La Porta, Rafael, Florencio López-de-Silanes, and Andrei Shleifer. 2002. "Government Ownership of Banks." *Journal of Finance* 57, no. 1: 265–301.

Lewis, W. Arthur. 1950. *The Principles of Economic Planning.* London: Allen and Unwin.

Litan, Robert E., Michael Pomerleano, and V. Sundararajan, eds. 2002. *Financial Sector Governance: The Roles of the Public and Private Sectors.* Brookings.

McLeod, Ross. 2003. "Dealing with Banking System Failure: Indonesia, 1997–2002." Technical Working Paper in Trade and Development 2003/05. Australian National University.

Megginson, William L., Robert C. Nash, and Mathias van Randenborgh. 1994. "The Financial and Operating Performance of Newly Privatized Firms: An International Empirical Analysis." *Journal of Finance* 49: 403–52.

Myrdal, Gunnar. 1968. *Asian Drama.* New York: Pantheon.

Nasution, Anwar. 1983. *Financial Institutions and Policies in Indonesia.* Singapore: Institute of Southeast Asian Studies.

Nasution, Anwar, and Wing Thye Woo. 1989. "Indonesian Economic Policies and Their Relation to External Debt Management." In *Developing Country Debt,* vol. 3, edited by J. Sachs and S. Collins, 101–20. University of Chicago Press.

Pangestu, Mari, ed. 1996. *Economic Reform, Deregulation, and Privatization: The Indonesian Experience.* Jakarta: Center for Strategic and International Studies.

Rahardjo, M. Dawam, and others. 1995. *Bank Indonesia Dalam Kilasan Sejarah Bangsa.* LP3ES. Jakarta: Lembaga Penelitian, Pendidikan dan Penerangan Ekonomi dan Sosial.

Redway, Jake. 2002. "An Assessment of the Asset Management Company Model in the Reform of Indonesia's Banking Sector." *Bulletin of Indonesian Economic Studies* 38, no. 2: 241–50.

Rindjin, Ketut. 2003. *Pengantar Perbankan dan Lembaga Keuangan Bukan Bank.* Jakarta: Gramedia Pustaka Utama.

Robinson, Marguerite. 2000. *The Microfinance Revolution.* Washington: World Bank.

Santoso, Wimboh. 2000. "Indonesia's Financial and Corporate Sector Reform." Jakarta: Bank Indonesia.

Shleifer, Andrei. 1998. "State versus Private Ownership." *Journal of Economic Perspectives* 12: 133–50.

Survey of Recent Developments. 2004. Special issue, *Bulletin of Indonesian Economic Studies.* April.

World Bank. 1998. *East Asia: The Road to Recovery.* Washington.

———. 2000. *East Asia: Recovery and Beyond.* Washington.

———. 2003. *Indonesia: Beyond Macroeconomic Stability.* Brief for the Consultative Group on Indonesia. Washington.

URJIT R. PATEL

7

Role of State-Owned
Financial Institutions in India:
Should the Government
"Do" or "Lead"?

A DEEP AND EFFICIENT financial sector is necessary for the optimal allocation of resources. Governments have been involved in the financial sectors—in intermediation, if not directly as the owners of intermediaries—of many countries, even currently developed ones, during various stages of their growth. In many countries, development financial institutions have been major conduits for channeling funds to particular firms, industries, and sectors during their development. Many studies (more recently by Allen and Gale, and by Levine) identify the importance of development financial institutions in the South Korean and Japanese process of industrialization.[1] In some developed countries, such as Germany, especially in the post–World War II era, this (command) mode of financial intermediation has been used in national reconstruction as well. In many developing countries, the government traditionally has had a strong presence in the sector, usually through a combination of either directly owning these entities or indirectly mandating the rules for allocating credit. This has followed a line of thinking emanating from the works of Gerschenkron and Lewis that advocated a "development" role for state-owned intermediaries.[2]

The author would like to thank Saugata Bhattacharya for collaborating on work that forms the basis of this paper.
    1. Allen and Gale (2001); Levine (1997).
    2. Gerschenkron (1962); Lewis (1955).

Arguably, compelling arguments have been made for this involvement in the initial stages of a country's development. It is in the financial sector that market failures are particularly likely to occur.[3] In addition, the significant asymmetries of information characterizing the sector, as well as the lack of commercial viability of lending to most pioneering or small-scale projects, generate a bias in bank loan portfolios away from areas deemed vulnerable but identified as priority areas for development. As a result, governments have often established development-oriented intermediaries to nurture infant industries and have also occasionally resorted to bank expropriations and nationalizations in order to advance social goals like expanding the reach of banking—in other words, addressing market failures. Even in countries without a high level of direct government ownership of financial intermediaries, the involvement of governments in intermediation has been significant.

Reflecting the erstwhile predominance of the public sector in most areas of economic activity, government involvement in the financial sector has been devised implicitly to assume counterparty risks. This cover was adequate in the past given the relative simplicity of transactions then prevalent. As economic activity became increasingly commercial, however, the government-dominated financial systems of most developing countries were ill equipped to tackle the new risks arising from increasingly complex transactions. Nor did there exist the robust clearing systems needed to support new financial products, the accounting and hedging mechanisms to deal with the significant counterparty risks that now permeated the system. The consequence was a large increase in both institution-specific as well as systemic moral hazard, manifested in repeated bailouts and recapitalizations.

Worldwide experience suggests that, in the case of public sector institutions, the owner—the government—typically lacks both the incentive and the means to ensure an adequate return on its investment.[4] Political decisions, as opposed to rate-of-return calculations, are often important in determining resource allocation. In many instances, as well as across a wide spectrum of countries, this involvement has led to fragility of the financial sector, occasionally resulting in macroeconomic turbulence as well. One thread of explanations for this stems from the political theories advanced, for instance, by Kornai, by Shleifer and Vishny, and by others.[5] Directed lending to projects that might be socially desirable but not privately profitable is not likely to be sustainable in the long run. These weaknesses go beyond the normal crises that have characterized the finan-

3. Events over the past half decade have provided numerous examples of these failures spanning geographic areas as well as various types of economic systems.

4. La Porta, López-de-Silanes, and Shleifer (2000).

5. Kornai (1979); Shleifer and Vishny (1994).

cial sector.[6] A conflict of interest arises between the development goals of government-directed credit flows and the absence of commercial discipline that gradually percolates the lending process.

The issue of incentives is especially relevant in India's financial reforms, particularly given the current importance of these government-owned financial enti ties that cover almost all segments. India is one of a number of countries whose governments have used intermediaries to allocate and direct financial resources to both the public and the private sector. Government ownership of banks in India is the highest among large economies, barring China.[7] Beside the standard problems of the financial sector that result from information asymmetry and agency issues, moral hazard might be *aggravated* in countries like India with high government involvement because both depositors and lenders count on explicit and implicit guarantees.[8]

The high degree of government involvement gives rise to a belief on the part of depositors and investors that the system is insulated from systemic risk and crises by engendering a sense of confidence, making deposit runs somehow unlikely even when the system becomes insolvent. While selective regulatory forbearance might be justified to balance the likely panic following news of runs on troubled institutions, a blanket guarantee by government makes forbearance difficult to calibrate and sharply increases systemwide moral hazard. Depositors, borrowers, and lenders all know that the government is guarantor. Since for all intents and purposes all deposits are covered by an umbrella of implicit government guarantees, there is little incentive for depositors to practice due diligence, which further erodes any semblance of market discipline for lenders in deploying funds; this was witnessed most recently in the case of cooperative banks in India. The regularity of sector restructuring packages (for steel and textiles and proposed most recently for telecommunications), on the other hand, diminishes the incentives for borrowers to mitigate the credit risk associated with their projects.

Just as important, India now has a banking sector whose indicators (in terms of standard norms like profitability and spreads) are prima facie more or less comparable to the standards of its international peer group. This sector is also

6. They are explored in detail in Patel (1997b).

7. Hawkins and Mihaljek (2001) outline the characteristics of financial systems that are dominated by government ownership of intermediaries.

8. The term *aggravated* is distinguished from *enhanced*: The former is a parametric shift of the underlying variables, while the latter is a functional dependence. More explicitly, increasing moral hazard enhances the incentives of banks to accumulate riskier portfolios, whereas an aggravated moral hazard results in a failure to initiate corrective steps to mitigate the enhanced hazard: for example, higher requirements of capital, proper risk weighting, project monitoring, and so forth.

complemented by relatively well-developed capital markets, which are playing an increasingly important role in the resource requirements of commercial entities.

This chapter draws heavily on recent work by Bhattacharya and Patel, and by Patel and Bhattacharya.[9] It argues that the useful role of public sector financial institutions in resource intermediation in India is now very limited. After a brief sketch of the status of the sector, it highlights infirmities and weaknesses of the system that are engendered by the high degree of government involvement in the sector, takes a critical look at the areas often claimed to be the residual (but legitimate) domain of intervention by the government, and examines the merits of the arguments advanced.

The Financial Sector and Current Infirmities

From independence to the end of the 1960s, India's banking system consisted of a mix of banks, some of which were government owned (the State Bank of India and its associate banks), some private, and a few foreign. The political class felt that private banks, which concentrated mainly on high-income groups and whose lending was security rather than purpose oriented, were failing to encourage the development of a wider entrepreneurial base, thereby stifling economic growth. Hence the government decided to nationalize twenty large private banks in two phases—in 1969 and 1980—with the objectives of promoting broader economic goals, achieving better regional balance of economic activity, extending the geographic reach of banking services, and diffusing economic power. Significant financial deepening took place over the three decades since the 1970s (see table 7-1). The ratio of M3 to gross domestic product (GDP) increased from 24 percent in 1970–71 to 70 percent in 2003, and the number of bank branches increased eightfold, with much of the expansion in rural and semiurban areas, which now account for 71 percent of total branches.

After a hiatus of two decades, private banks were allowed to be established in 1993, but their share in intermediation, albeit increasing, continues to be low. The largest growth in savings since 1997–98 has been in bank deposits, which now account for half of financial savings.

Public Sector Involvement in the Financial System

Banking intermediaries continue to dominate financial intermediation (see table 7-2 for details).[10] Much of this segment is publicly owned and accounts for

---

9. Bhattacharya and Patel (2002, 2003b); Patel and Bhattacharya (2003).

10. See Patel (2000) for a detailed exposition.

Table 7-1. *Indicators of Financial Deepening in India*

Indicator	1970–71	1980–81	1990–91	2000–01	2002–03
Ratio of M3 to GDP (percent)	24	39	47	63	70
Number of bank branches per 1,000 population	0.02	0.05	0.07	0.07	0.07

Source: Reserve Bank of India (various issues).

an overwhelming share of financial transactions (see table 7-3 for a thumbnail view). Moreover, the extent of government ownership of banks is quite high in India compared to international levels (see figure 7-1). The Reserve Bank of India, moreover, has a majority ownership in the State Bank of India, the largest public sector bank.

The shortcomings of the banking system in India are now relatively well known. Efforts have been made to tackle these issues, predominantly by adopting a regulation-centric approach. There is also a move to transform the major development financial institutions into entities approximating commercial banks.[11] But another large section of intermediaries—government-sponsored systemically important financial institutions—has not attracted requisite attention.[12] Specifically, inadequate attention has been devoted to the role of market discipline for institutions like Life Insurance Corporation of India (LIC) and Employees' Provident Fund Organisation (EPFO). A particular cause of concern is the opacity of their asset portfolios, a shortcoming that is especially serious in the case of EPFO.

As of March 2003, LIC had investible funds of Rs 2.9 trillion (which, to provide perspective, was 11.9 percent of GDP in 2002–03).[13] The book value of LIC's "socially oriented investments," mainly government securities and social sector investments, amounted to Rs 1.8 trillion—that is, 71 percent of a total portfolio value of Rs 2.7 trillion (10.9 percent of GDP).[14] A staggering 87 percent of this portfolio comprised exposure to the public sector.

11. In India, development financial institutions are a subgroup of intermediaries termed all-India financial institutions.

12. The classification of systemically important financial institutions used here is somewhat different from the government's view, enunciated in the Reserve Bank of India's monetary and credit policy (Reserve Bank of India 2003c), which referred to "large" intermediaries, including banks like State Bank of India and ICICI Bank.

13. IDBI (2003, app. tables 117–19).

14. Social sector investments include loans to state electricity boards, housing, municipalities, water and sewerage boards, state road transport corporations, roadways, and railways. These, however, account for about a fifth of the portfolio of socially oriented investments, with the balance accounted for by government and government-guaranteed securities.

Table 7-2. *Comparative Profile of Financial Intermediaries and Markets in India*

Indicator	1990–91	1998–99	2002–03
Gross domestic savings			
Amount (billions of rupees)	1,301	3,932	5,500
Percent of GDP	24.3	22.3	24.0
Bank deposits outstanding			
Amount (billions of rupees)	2,078	7,140	13,043
Percent of GDP	38.2	40.5	50.1
Small savings deposits, Public Provident Funds, and others			
Amount (billions of rupees)	1,071	3,333	3,810
Percent of GDP	20.0	19.1	15.4
Mutual funds (assets under management)			
Amount (billions of rupees)	253	858	1,093
Percent of GDP	4.7	4.9	4.2
Public and regulated NBFC deposits			
Amount (billions of rupees)	174[a]	204	178
Percent of GDP	2.4	1.2	0.7
Total borrowings by development financial institutions (outstanding)			
Amount (billions of rupees)	. . .	2,108	901
Percent of GDP	. . .	12.0	3.5
Annual stock market turnover[b] (Bombay Stock Exchange and National Stock Exchange)			
Amount (billions of rupees)	360[c]	15,241	9,321
Percent of GDP	5.6	79.0	35.8
Stock market capitalization[b]			
Amount (billions of rupees)	845[c]	18,732	11,093
Percent of GDP	15.8	97.1	42.6
Turnover of government securities through SGL[d] (monthly average)			
Amount (billions of rupees)	. . .	310	2,287
Percent of GDP	. . .	1.8	9.0
As percentage of stock market turnover (annual)	. . .	24	276
Volume of corporate debt on National Stock Exchange[e]	. . .	9	58

a. End of March 1993.
b. Stock Exchange, Mumbai (BSE), and National Stock Exchange.
c. Pertains only to BSE.
d. Excluding repos.
e. Excluding commercial paper.

Table 7-3. *Share of Public Sector Institutions in Segments of the Financial Sector*[a]
Percent, unless otherwise noted

Type of institution	Public sector share	Private sector share	Total value (billions of rupees)
Scheduled commercial banks[b]	75.6	24.4	16,989
Mutual funds[c]	48.2	51.8	1,093
Life insurance[d]	99.9	[e]	2,296

Source: Reserve Bank of India (2003d); SEBI (2003); IRDA (2002).

a. Banking and mutual fund data are as of the end of March 2003. Insurance data are as of the end of March 2002.

b. Total assets. Private banks include foreign banks.

c. Total net assets of domestic schemes of mutual funds (public sector includes Unit Trust of India).

d. Life insurance policy liabilities. Public sector insurance includes LIC and State Bank of India Life.

e. Negligible.

Figure 7-1. *Government Ownership of Banks, Selected Countries*

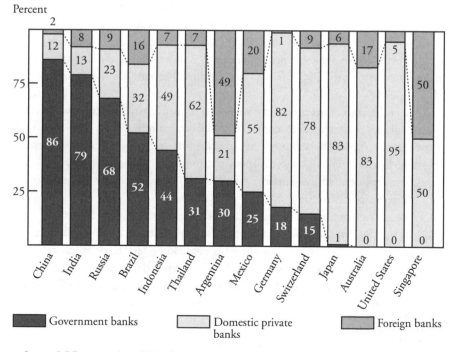

Source: BCG presentation, CII Banking Summit, 2003.

Compared to those of LIC, the accounts of EPFO are, simply, opaque. Cumulative contributions to its three schemes—the Employees' Provident Fund (EPF), Employee Pension Scheme (EPS), and Employees' Deposit Linked Insurance (EDLI)—up to the end of March 2002, amounted to Rs 1.3 trillion (5.1 percent of GDP). Total cumulative investments of these three schemes were Rs 1.4 trillion (5.6 percent of GDP), with EPF being the largest. EPFO does not come under the purview of an independent regulator, with oversight resting on three sources: the Income Tax Act (1961), the EPF Act (1952), and the Indian Trusts Act (1882).

More important, the government's involvement in intermediation is much wider than mere ownership; its ambit stretches across mobilization of resources, direction of credit, appointments of management, regulation of intermediaries, provision of "comfort and support" to depositors and investors, as well as influence over the lending practices of all intermediaries and the investment stimuli of private corporations. These practices include treating banks as quasi-fiscal instruments, the consequent preemption of resources through statutory requirements, directed lending, administered interest rates applicable to select savings instruments, encouraging imprudent practices like cross-holding of capital between intermediaries, continual bailouts of troubled intermediaries, control and manipulation of smaller intermediaries like cooperative banks, weak regulatory and enforcement institutions, and unwarranted levels of government-controlled deposit insurance.[15] Bhattacharya and Patel have developed a set of indexes to quantify the extent of this involvement.[16] Figure 7-2 shows that, after having declined almost secularly until 1995–96, the degree of involvement has risen fairly sharply after 1997–98.

One of the arguments previously advanced to justify government ownership of intermediaries was related to concerns about systemic stability. The argument went that an implicit government net of "comfort and support" to both depositors and lenders deterred the prospect of financial runs. Until 2001–02, the explicit component of this support translated into a cumulative infusion of Rs 225 billion into banks.

The government also engineered many other indirect forms of bailouts. Financial interventions in the US-64 scheme of the Unit Trust of India—India's largest mutual fund—are examples. Following the recommendations of an expert committee constituted after an earlier payments crisis in 1998, the government decided to exempt for three years the US-64 from a 10 percent dividend tax

---

15. Buiter and Patel (1997).

16. Bhattacharya and Patel (2002). The appendix to this chapter describes the index construction methodology.

Figure 7-2. *Index of Density of Government Involvement in the Financial Sector (IDGI-F) for India*

Index

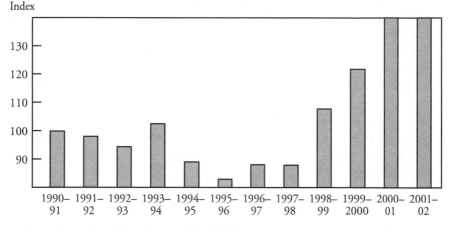

Source: Updated from Bhattacharya and Patel (2002).

(deducted at source) that other equity mutual funds were required to pay. Data on dividend income distribution and the dividend tax for US-64 for 1999–2000 indicate forgone tax revenue of around Rs 2 billion. Under the special unit scheme of 1999, the government did a buyback of public sector unit shares at book value, higher than the prevailing market value, effectively transferring Rs 15 billion to investors. After the second US-64 payments crisis in 2001, under a repurchase facility covering 40 percent of the assets of US-64, investors were allowed to redeem up to 3,000 units at an administratively determined price, with the government making up the gap between this price and the net asset value of a unit. Eight public sector banks "offered" liquidity support to Unit Trust of India in the event of large-scale redemptions. Recognizing that this support was not viable and that the probability of an ultimate default on these loans was high, these banks sought comfort through government guarantees to help in easy provisioning against the loans and avoid violating the norms of lending without collateral. Even more than the actual losses to the exchequer, these implicit safety nets create an insidious expectation of government support to investors, weakening their commercial judgment.

Weaknesses of the Financial System

Certain structural characteristics and institutional rigidities further weaken the mechanisms for prudent derisking of portfolios. The absence of effective bankruptcy procedures, leading to a lack of exit opportunities for both intermediaries and the firms that they lend to, forces intermediaries to roll over existing substandard debt or convert it into equity, thereby continually building up the riskiness of their asset portfolio. The government's use of intermediaries to "divert" funds for purposes that are not entirely commercially motivated reinforces the decline in the quality of assets. A prominent reason is an attempt by government to boost investment, both by direct spending and indirectly via credit enhancements, like guarantees, partially to counter low private investment. In combination with the frequently observed "tunneled" structure of many corporations,[17] which facilitates connected lending and diversion of funds between group companies, institutional rigidities (especially weak foreclosure laws), and regulatory forbearance (including inadequate disclosure requirements and other lending practices), the outcome is a disproportionate buildup of the riskiness of intermediaries' asset portfolios.

Incentive Distortions Arising from Public Ownership of Intermediaries

In the process, the incentive structures that underlie the functioning of intermediaries are blunted and distorted to the extent that they override the safety systems that have nominally been put in place. The large fiscally funded recapitalizations of banks in the early and mid-1990s were designed to prevent a systemwide collapse at a time when the sector had been buffeted by the onset of reforms and had not had time to develop risk mitigation systems. Moreover, the overall reforms were designed to enhance domestic and external competition, which was bound to have an adverse impact on past loans to industry, affecting these banks' balance sheets. The nascent state of capital markets at that time was seen as a hindrance in accessing capital, especially capital without large attached risk premiums. The impact of this support, though, has been considerably reduced, if not eliminated, by the series of ongoing bailouts, with seemingly little by way of (binding) reciprocating requirements imposed on intermediaries to prevent a repeat of these episodes. It needs to be recognized that the only sustainable method of ensuring capital adequacy in the long run is through improvement in earnings profile, not government recapitalization or even mobilization of private capital from the market.

A singular aspect of financial sector reforms in India has been that, while the "look and feel" of organizations associated with intermediation have altered, the focus of the changes has revolved around the introduction of stricter regulatory standards. Caprio argues that regulation-oriented reforms cannot deliver the desired outcome unless banks are restructured simultaneously; this includes the

---

17. See Johnson and others (2000).

introduction of measures that empower banks to work the new incentives into a viable and efficient business model and encourage prudent risk taking.[18] These mechanisms are also meant to, inter alia, mitigate the "legacy costs" that continue to burden intermediaries even after restructuring. Some of these costs, apart from the consequences of public ownership, are well known, including weak foreclosure systems, weak legal recourse for recovering bad debts, and ineffective exit procedures for both banks and corporations. In addition, during difficult times, fiscal stress is sought to be relieved through regulatory forbearance; there are demands for (and occasionally actual instances of) lax enforcement (or dilution) of income recognition and asset classification norms. A multiplicity of economic regulators, most of them not wholly independent, deters enforcement of directives.[19]

Other than structural changes in the patterns of corporate resource raising, commercial lending is inhibited, inter alia, by distortions in banks' cost of borrowing and lending structures arising from interest rate restrictions. Continuing floors on short-term deposits and high administered rates on bank depositlike small savings instruments (national savings certificates, post office deposits) artificially raise the cost of funds for intermediaries. Lending constraints relate to various guidelines concerning the prime lending rate for small-scale industries and other priority-sector lending. This constellation of factors has made treasury operations an important activity in improving banks' profitability.[20] Over and above the regulatory oversight of the Reserve Bank of India, the role of government audit and enforcement agencies—like the comptroller and auditor general, Central Vigilance Commission, and Central Bureau of Investigation—in audits of decisions made by loan officers at banks undermines "normal" risk taking associated with lending.[21]

The outcome of this environment is "lazy banking"; banks in India seem to have curtailed their role in credit creation.[22] Outstanding assets of commercial

18. Caprio (1996).

19. See Bhattacharya and Patel (2002) for an analysis of how regulators have looked at financial market failures. For instance, cooperative banks have been lax in implementing Reserve Bank of India notifications on lending to brokers.

20. Declining interest rates increased trading profits (in securities) of public sector banks in 2001–02 more than two and a half times that of the previous year and accounted for 28 percent of operating profits (Reserve Bank of India 2002, table II.14).

21. Loan officers have complained about being harassed, if not penalized, for taking on "good" credit risks, whereas risks not warranted by sound commercial practices have often been foisted on them by the political owners of these institutions.

22. The term *lazy banking* was coined by one of the current deputy governors of the Reserve Bank of India.

Figure 7-3. *Cumulative (Quarter-wise) SLR Securities Investment-Deposit Ratio of Scheduled Commercial Banks, 2001–04*[a]

Ratio of securities investment to deposits (percent)

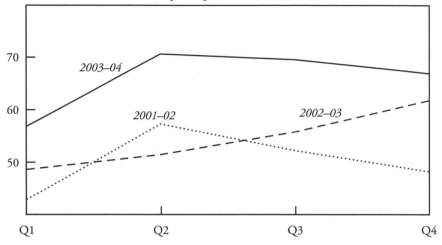

Source: Reserve Bank of India (2003b); weekly statistical supplements.
a. Q4 2003–04 figures are as of March 5, 2004.

banks in government securities are, as of March 5, 2004, much higher (just over 46 percent) than the mandated statutory liquidity ratio (SLR), of 25 percent.[23] As figure 7-3 shows, a large fraction of bank deposits are being deployed for holding government securities. This ratio, as is evident, has been increasing steadily over the last seven quarters and, more pertinently, has persisted over the last two quarters despite a strong economic rebound and, presumably, a consequent increase in demand for credit.

This phenomenon constitutes rational behavior by banks given the incentive structure described above. In deciding on a trade-off between increasing credit flows and investing in government securities, the economic, regulatory, and fiscal environment is stacked against the former. An unintended consequence of the increasingly tighter prudential norms that banks will be forced to adopt has been

23. It is also noteworthy that 51 percent of the outstanding stock of central government securities at the end of March 2002 was held by just two public sector institutions: the State Bank of India and the Life Insurance Corporation of India (sourced from the government of India receipts budget, Reserve Bank of India 2003d, and investment information on LIC's website).

a further shift in the deployment of deposits to government securities and other investments that carry a comparatively lower risk weight.[24]

Residual Roles of Government in Intermediation in a Market Economy: A Critical Look

Given the scenario described in the previous section, primarily driven by distorted incentives for public sector involvement, there is a robust case for the government to exit from actual intermediation. This section takes a critical look at the functions often claimed to be the residual (but legitimate) domain of intervention by the government and examines the merits of the arguments advanced. Even though the chapter analyzes the specific activities that are claimed to be the residual arenas of government involvement in a commercial environment, it in no way provides a blanket endorsement of these actions in India.

The chapter adapts an institution-specific framework explored by Rodrik—formulated in the context of general economic development—as a touchstone for this analysis.[25] Rodrik groups the shortcomings and required actions related to market-driven reforms into four components: market stabilization, market regulation, market creation, and market legitimization. This chapter relates to the last two aspects, primarily through the lens of a fifth component: market completion. Table 7-4 provides a schematic layout as an organizing scaffold for drawing together the threads of various aspects of the role of the government in creating new markets that are necessary for facilitating transactions as well as dealing with issues that are a corollary of a move toward commercial orientation of economic activity.

Facilitating Transactions and Deepening Markets

Given the significant information asymmetries that normally characterize capital markets and because, consequently, there are specific risks that individual intermediaries (or even groups) might not be able to bear, there are often inefficiencies in market transactions or in the inability of institutions to catalyze certain

24. Banks were advised in April 2002 to build up an investment fluctuation reserve of a minimum 5 percent of their investments in the categories "held for trading" and "available for sale" within five years. As of the end of June 2003, the total investment fluctuation reserve amounted to only about Rs 100 billion (that is, 1.7 percent of investments under relevant categories). While twelve banks are yet to make any provisions for an investment fluctuation reserve, twenty have built one up to 1 percent, but only sixty-five have a reserve exceeding 1 percent (Reserve Bank of India 2003c). Seventeen public sector banks have investment fluctuation reserves of 2 percent or more (Reserve Bank of India 2003d).

25. Rodrik (2002).

Table 7-4. *Matrix of Institutional Processes in the Reform of the Indian Financial Sector*

Institutions' role	*Objective*	*Mapping to the Indian (financial) context*	*Addressing specific shortcomings*
Market stabilization	Achieve stable monetary and fiscal management	Profligate fiscal environment	Preemption of resources by government; efficacy of central bank functions
Market regulation	Mitigate the impact of scale economies and informational incompleteness	Regulatory forbearance; public ownership of institutions	Appropriate prudential regulation; imposition of market discipline; transparency and information disclosure
Market creation	Enable property rights and contract enforcement	Public ownership of institutions	Enforcement of creditor rights; effective dispute resolution mechanisms
Market legitimization	Ensure social protection; conflict management; market access	Profligate fiscal environment; regulatory forbearance; public ownership of institutions	Mixing of social and commercial objectives (for example, rural branch requirements for banks); appropriate insurance for depositors; capital markets enforcement; effective redress of investor grievances
Market completion	"Span states of nature"	Shallow or nonexistent markets	Lack of institutions and products to mitigate specific (market-making) risks that hamper formation of markets; inadequate old-age income safety nets

specialized economic activities. Market institutions that minimize transaction costs, often in the nature of a quasi-public good, may not necessarily emerge as a rational collective outcome of the individual players involved. These activities usually share characteristics of public merit goods. The government has an important role in developing institutions that serve as platforms for correcting market deficiencies and failures as well as for facilitating transactions, increasing market liquidity, and improving clearing and settlement systems.

Dealing with the commercial consequence of the new set of risks, however, demands the presence of specialized institutions. Debt markets in developed countries both complement intermediaries' loans to corporations and offer innovative structured financial instruments. In India, on the other hand, the fragmented nature of debt markets had entailed significant counterparty risk, thereby becoming a barrier to market integration and further hindering the formation of benchmark yield curves. This resulted in large and distorted spreads on rates of interest on debt instruments. As a consequence, the market-disciplining effect of capital markets on intermediaries' loans, especially to corporations, has tended to be mitigated.

Recognizing the need for a financial infrastructure for clearing and settlement of government securities, foreign exchange, money, and debt markets (to make the transaction settlement process more efficient and insulate the financial system from shocks emanating from operations-related issues), the Reserve Bank of India initiated a move to establish the Clearing Corporation of India Limited (CCIL), with the State Bank of India playing a lead role. CCIL was incorporated in October 2001. CCIL takes over and mitigates counterparty risks by "novation" and "multilateral netting."[26] The risk management system at CCIL includes a settlement guarantee fund (SGF) composed of collateral contributed by the members, liquidity support in the form of prearranged lines of credit from banks, and a procedure for collecting initial and mark-to-market margins from the members to ensure that the risk on account of members' outstanding trade obligations remains covered by their respective contributions to SGF.

The Securities Trading Corporation of India, which participates, underwrites, makes a market, and trades in government securities, was sponsored by the Reserve Bank of India jointly with public sector banks and all-India financial institutions.[27] Its main objective is to foster the development of an active secondary market for government securities and bonds issued by public sector undertakings.

26. *Novation* is the term used for replacing the original contract between the two counterparties by a set of two contracts—in this case, between CCIL and each of the two counterparties, respectively.

27. These comprise the development financial institutions, investment institutions like LIC and Unit Trust of India, other specialized financial institutions, and refinance institutions (NABARD and the National Housing Bank).

In the equity markets, an important component of the government's reform program in the 1990s consisted of creating three new institutions—the National Stock Exchange, the National Securities Clearing Corporation Limited (NSCCL), and the National Securities Depository Limited (NSDL)—to facilitate trading, clearing, and settlement. The National Stock Exchange has been the most successful and was, in fact, the progenitor of the other two. Promoted in 1993 by some all-India financial institutions (at the behest of the government) as an alternative to the incumbent Stock Exchange, Mumbai (BSE), the National Stock Exchange has since become a benchmark for operations characterized by innovation and transparency. It has overtaken the BSE in spot transactions and has spearheaded the introduction of derivative instruments, where it now accounts for 95 percent of trades.

The NSCCL, a wholly owned subsidiary of the National Stock Exchange, was incorporated in August 1995 to provide counterparty risk guarantees and to promote and maintain short and consistent settlement cycles. The National Securities Clearing Corporation has had a trouble-free record of reliable settlement schedules since early 1996, having evolved a sophisticated "risk containment" framework.

To promote dematerialization of securities, the National Stock Exchange, Industrial Development Bank of India (IDBI), and Unit Trust of India set up the National Securities Depository Limited, which began operations in November 1996, to gradually eradicate physical paper trading and settlement of securities. This eliminated the risks associated with fake and bad paper and made the transfer of securities automatic and instantaneous. Dematerialized delivery today constitutes 99.99 percent of all delivery-based settlements.

A point worth noting is the inherent profitability of many of these institutions. Volumes at the National Stock Exchange, in both the spot and derivatives segments, have grown significantly. The annual compound growth in turnover at the National Stock Exchange between 1995–96 and 2002–03 was 73.1 percent[28] and is likely to have increased significantly in this fiscal year, 2004–05. The government (indirectly, through the sponsoring financial institutions) stands to increase its returns from the volumes in these markets (not to mention the service taxes that directly accrue to it).

Catalyzing Niche Economic Activities

As the government begins to open up areas of economic activity to the private sector that had hitherto been the exclusive domain of government, many processes

---

28. National Stock Exchange (2003).

and institutions have to develop that can mitigate and allocate the attendant risks through appropriate financial structures, innovative products, resource syndication, and project facilitation. Without these institutions, the probability of private sector operations not succeeding increases, leading to the political risk of renationalization of at least some of these activities. In addition, individual initiatives depend on attaining a critical mass in certain "supporting" areas, which are analyzed next.

EXPORT-IMPORT FINANCING. Although commercial banks in developed markets have the capability of financing (and refinancing) most trade-related transactions, there remains—even in developed countries—a residual role for a state-sponsored export-import bank for underwriting sovereign-related risks, as well as advancing matters that are strategic in nature, apart from the traditional role in building export competitiveness. In developing countries, in addition, commercial banks may not have sufficiently diversified portfolios of assets to be able to adequately cover the foreign exchange risks that are necessarily an adjunct of trade financing.

The Export-Import Bank of India (Exim Bank) was established in 1982 for the purpose of financing, facilitating, and promoting foreign trade. It is the principal intermediary for coordinating institutions engaged in financing foreign trade transactions and accepting credit and country risks that private intermediaries are unable or unwilling to accept. The Exim Bank provides export financing products that fill gaps in trade financing, especially for small businesses, in the areas of export product development and financing export marketing, besides information and advisory services.[29] As Indian corporations increasingly invest in foreign countries, there is also a need for political risk insurance, which the Exim Bank might provide.

The Exim Bank's loan assets rose from Rs 20.3 billion in 1993–94 to Rs 87.7 billion in 2002–03 (an increase of 340 percent), and its guarantee portfolio rose from Rs 7.5 billion to Rs 16.1 billion (113 percent). India's manufacturing exports increased from Rs 685 billion to about Rs 2.3 trillion (234 percent) during this period.

INFRASTRUCTURE AND PROJECT FINANCING. Universally considered a pivot for economic growth, infrastructure is one of the two large segments that have traditionally been under the rubric of the state (the other is the financial sector). The gradual recognition of the inefficiencies inherent in public provision of

---

29. The Exim Bank's role in export promotion, besides extending lines of credit, consists of educating exporters about market potential, banking facilities, payment formalities, and similar matters, which has a bearing on the country risk they might face.

utility services, as well as the inability of the exchequer to cope with the large investments needed to upgrade, refurbish, and build assets, made the government amenable to introducing private participation in the sector (in the early 1990s). Bhattacharya and Patel detail the necessity of developing sound regulatory structures in emerging economies for encouraging private investment in infrastructure.[30] The unique requirements of project finance necessary for financial closure of private infrastructure projects were recognized early on, but this of itself was soon found to be insufficient. After years of effort—and initial failure in most sectors—the government understood the importance of sound policy and regulatory frameworks to complement specialized financial products and markets.

As an outcome of this understanding, the Infrastructure Development Finance Company (IDFC) was established to "lead private capital into commercially viable infrastructure projects." Apart from its responsibility in structuring finances for infrastructure to lower the cost of capital, the IDFC was tasked with rationalizing the existing policy regimes in sectors as diverse as electricity, telecommunications, roads, ports, and water and sanitation. Its policy advocacy initiatives in the telecommmunications and civil aviation sectors are good examples of the success in "developing sectors," in contrast (and in addition) to merely financing individual projects. The IDFC has also had an impact in bringing funds into projects through innovative financial products like take-out financing and the use of various risk-guarantee instruments, as well as financing structures such as the annuity method for road projects. These initiatives have orchestrated a significant quantum of private investment into infrastructure projects.

Channels and Instruments for Social Objectives

The original rationale for nationalization of banks, as well as for the establishment of development financial institutions, was the failure of private sector intermediaries to extend the reach of banking to rural and remote areas, as well as perceived inadequacies in channeling credit to what were then deemed critical areas of industrialization. Although understandable, and even recommended, in a specific context, the justification for a continuation of these policies has been largely eroded. For some of these objectives, India already has specialized intermediaries, including the National Bank for Rural Development (NABARD), the Small Industries Development Bank of India (SIDBI), and state finance corporations. These institutions have quite obviously failed to live up to their mandates, given the periodic exhortations of the government and supplementary mechanisms that

30. Bhattacharya and Patel (2003a).

are proposed to advance their stated objectives.[31] This section looks at individual components of these objectives and argues that using bank intermediaries to achieve them is suboptimal.

INTERMEDIATING RURAL FINANCIAL RESOURCES. Rural banking is rife with inefficiencies. Commercial banks, especially public sector banks, have an inordinately large presence in rural and semiurban areas. While only 33 percent of their deposits are sourced from (and 21 percent of credit is disbursed in) these areas, a full 71 percent of their branches are located there (see table 7-5). Reserve Bank of India's licensing conditions for new private sector banks stipulate that, after a moratorium of three years, one out of four new branches has to be in a rural area, which significantly raises operating costs in an intensely competitive environment.

This is the case despite the prevalence of a large network of post offices that is the predominant channel for small savings, as well as specialized Regional Rural Banks, cooperatives, and other intermediaries working through NABARD. India had around 155,000 post offices at the end of March 2002, including about 139,000 in rural areas.[32] The Post Office Savings Bank, operated as an agency of the Ministry of Finance, besides being a conduit for National Small Savings Schemes, also offers money order and limited life insurance schemes. The ambit of these outlets, many already operating in partnership with commercial banks and insurance companies, can be further expanded in rural areas to address the shortcomings of credit delivery (the problematic aspect of rural intermediation). Although the potential of a reorganized post office network in India as the main channel of delivery for rural credit has not been explored, an instructive report is that of the Performance and Innovation Unit of the British government, whose post office organizational structure is similar to that of India.[33]

The needs of rural banking might be "narrower" in nature, and alternative credit delivery mechanisms—which might be better suited and more cost-effective—perhaps should be considered. The other side of the coin is the reported shortcomings of credit delivery through institutions like NABARD, which is validated through the casual empiricism of a periodic refrain by the government to disburse funds to the agricultural sector at administratively mandated rates of interest.[34] These administrative directives not only distort the lending decisions of individual banks (through the implicit cross-subsidies) but also systematically

31. There is a proposal in the interim budget 2004–05 for a fund for small-scale enterprises, but the objective and disbursement mechanisms are not clear.

32. India Post (2003).

33. Performance and Innovation Unit (2000).

34. For instance, the recent directive to banks in December 2003 to disburse farm credit at 2 percent below their respective prime lending rates.

Table 7-5. *Trends in Indian Banking in Urban and Nonurban Areas,*
as of March 31, 2003

Type of bank	Bank branches		Deposits		Credit		Ratio of credit to deposits (percent)
	Number	Percent	Amount (billions of rupees)	Percent	Amount (billions of rupees)	Percent	
Scheduled commercial banks							
Urban centers (including							
metro centers)	19,379	29	8,619	67	5,998	79	70
Metro	8,664	13	5,719	45	4,745	62	83
Top 100	15,066	23	7,603	61	5,758	75	74
Nonurban centers							38
Semiurban	14,813	22	2,405	19	847	11	35
Rural	32,244	49	1,763	14	748	10	42
All India	66,436		12,787	...	7,592	...	59
Regional rural banks	14,462	21[a]	498	4[a]	221	3[a]	44

Source: Culled from Reserve Bank of India (2003a).

a. Percentages for regional rural banks represent shares relative to those for all-India scheduled commercial banks.

undermine financial sector reforms. The success of operations of certain self-help groups and microcredit institutions (the Self-Employed Women's Association being a prime example) has also demonstrated the viability and higher sustainability of these alternative channels. The use of minimum subsidy bidding to achieve some of the government's social objectives might be more cost-effective.

LENDING TO "PRIORITY SECTORS." Dilution of the credit creation role of banks has raised concerns about underlending. This worry is especially high for agriculture and small-scale industries. According to Reserve Bank of India guidelines, banks have to provide 40 percent of net bank credit to priority sectors, which include agriculture, small industries, retail trade, and the self-employed. Within this overall target, 18 percent of the net bank credit has to be to the agriculture sector and another 10 percent has to be to the weaker sections. Commercial banks have been consistently unable to attain these targets, and the expedient of channeling the shortfalls to the Rural Infrastructure Development Fund (under NABARD's administrative ambit) has led to concerns about its relatively nontransparent procedures of disbursement and the potential of future nonperforming assets.

One of the arguments for mandating lending to the priority sectors at interest rates lower than market rates is to mitigate the higher risk premiums for the (supposedly) inherently risky nature of this lending. An outcome of this risk is the level of nonperforming assets. Although credit appraisals for small firms are definitely more difficult to conduct than appraisals for large firms, the argument that a large portion of nonperforming assets are found in priority sectors may need to be nuanced (even if just a little) in light of the sectoral origins of the nonperforming assets of public sector banks. While the share of priority-sector nonperforming assets in the total was about 47 percent[35] for public sector banks at the end of March 2003, their total loans outstanding to the priority sectors (as a percentage of total loans) was about 43 percent.[36] At the same time, the high nonperforming assets of development financial institutions remain a pointer to the perils of administrative mandates in advancing social goals as well as reliance on state government-guaranteed lending.[37]

SOCIAL SECURITY NETS. The provident fund system is the most important component of the social security net but covers a meager 11 million persons, all

---

35. Reserve Bank of India (2003e, table 7.2).

36. Reserve Bank of India (2003d, para. 3.93). This includes transfers to the Rural Infrastructure Development Fund and the Small Industries Development Bank of India, among others.

37. Net nonperforming assets of development financial institutions were 18.8 percent of advances in 2002–03 (Reserve Bank of India 2003d).

of them in the organized sector. An important component of the Employee Provident Fund scheme of EPFO is the administratively determined markup for the returns provided on deposits into the fund, justified on the basis of providing an adequate livelihood for pensioners and others on limited fixed incomes. The average real annual compound rate of return over the period 1986–2000 was an estimated 2.7 percent.[38]

One of the worries, apart from concerns about investment efficiency, is the sustainability of this method. The average markup between the returns provided by the Employee Provident Fund and ten-year government securities since 1995–96 has been 120 basis points.[39] The various tax exemptions that are granted to these deposits throughout their life make the effective rate of return even higher. One back-of-the-envelope calculation indicates that the Employee Pension Scheme was actuarially insolvent, and EPFO's reluctance to make public its actuarial calculations does little to assuage this conclusion.[40] Other than issues of sustainability, concerns remain of these and other national small savings schemes regarding the distorting effects on the yield curve (term structure of interest rates). As table 7-2 shows, small savings outstanding accounted for more than 15 percent of GDP in 2002–03, dwarfing all other intermediaries but banks.

Deposit Insurance to Enhance Systemic Stability

Other than instituting a sound regulatory mechanism and facilitating efficient and seamless transactions, a major aspect of the government's role in imparting stability to the financial system is the constitution of an *appropriate* safety net for depositors. The current system has a built-in bias that leans toward using taxpayer funds to finance bank losses, thus undermining even limited market discipline and encouraging regulatory forbearance.

India has a relatively liberal deposit insurance structure, compared to international norms.[41] Depositors in India do not have to bear coinsurance on the insured deposit amount, and the ceiling insured amount (Rs 100,000) is five times per capita GDP, which is high by international standards. This encourages some depositors to become less concerned about the financial health of their banks and for banks to take on additional (and commercially nonviable) risks.

The Deposit Insurance and Credit Guarantee Corporation (DICGC) came into existence in 1978 as a statutory body through an amalgamation of the erst-

---

38. Asher (2003).

39. The rate of return on the EPF scheme was set at 12 percent a year from 1989–90 onward, until July 2000, when it was progressively reduced to the current 9 percent.

40. See Patel (1997a).

41. Demirgüç-Kunt and Kane (2001).

while separate Deposit Insurance Corporation (DIC) and the Credit Guarantee Corporation (CGC). DICGC extended its guarantee support to credit granted to small-scale industries beginning in 1981, and in 1989 the guarantee cover was extended to priority-sector loans. However, since 1995 housing loans have been excluded from the purview of guarantee cover. As of 2001–02 about 74 percent of the total (accessible, that is, excluding interbank and government) deposits of commercial banks were insured.[42] Banks are required to bear the insurance premium of Re 0.05 per Rs 100 per year (depositors are not charged for insurance protection).

The government recognizes the issues raised by an overly generous deposit insurance structure. Some of the major recommendations of the 1999 working group constituted by the Reserve Bank of India to examine the issue of deposit insurance are to withdraw the function of credit guarantee on loans from DICGC and to institute risk-based pricing of the deposit insurance premium instead of the present flat-rate system. A new law, superseding the existing one, supposedly must be passed in order to implement the recommendations.

Conclusions

Despite the institution of market reforms in India since the early 1990s, government interests in the financial sector have not diminished commensurate with its withdrawal from most other aspects of economic activity. The continuing presence is too large to be justified solely on considerations of containing systemic risk.

There might have been justifiable reasons for government ownership of intermediaries in the early years of India's development, but these have now been rendered redundant, and possibly even damaging. India now has a relatively well-developed intermediation network, with intermediaries that are becoming increasingly commercially oriented. The raison d'être of the development finance institutions is also now obsolete, with the continuing development of project finance skills of banks and the maturing of capital markets.

A combination of directing resources of intermediaries in fulfilling a quasi-fiscal role for government, extra-commercial accountability structures, and regulatory forbearance (arising out of an implicit overarching guarantee umbrella) has mitigated the essential corrective effect of market discipline in both lending and deposit decisions. Coupled with persisting government involvement in intermediation and an implicit scaffold of support, this has resulted in an *aggravation* of the problem of moral hazard that is a normal feature of financial systems.

42. DICGC (2002).

A cycling analogy is the most apt to describe the outcome of these deficiencies. The set of actions that increasingly aggravate moral hazard, through visible and invisible props to keep the edifice from falling, is like riding a bicycle without brakes down a hill: Attempting to stop or pedaling harder will lead inexorably to a wreck. The prudent escape is to look for a soft spot to crash to minimize damage and then get the brakes repaired.

India is unlikely to suffer a full-blown systemic crisis, such as that witnessed in different contexts in various countries. Its financial sector inefficiencies are likely simply to simmer, with occasional payments crises, like the one at the dominant mutual fund over the last five years. However, the cumulative inefficiencies and grim fiscal outlook, with the concomitant regulatory forbearance that public involvement inevitably entails, are certain to retard India's transition to a high-growth trajectory. The persistent unease with the state of the system, it can be speculated, arises from recognition that the perceived safety of intermediaries is due more to the "social contract" between the government and depositors than to the underlying robustness in the health of the sector.

The system of intermediation will not improve appreciably in the absence of any serious steps toward changing incentives blunted by public sector involvement (of which ownership is an important aspect). To sharpen these incentives, outright privatization may not be sufficient, but it *is* necessary. It is the first step toward a true relinquishing of management control, which remains far beyond the scope envisaged in the Banking Companies (Acquisition and Transfer of Undertakings) Bill tabled in Parliament in 2002 (and still languishing). The bill was designed to reduce government holding in nationalized banks to 33 percent, while allowing them to retain their "public sector character" by maintaining effective control over their boards and restricting the voting right of nongovernment nominees. Attempts to shed the commercial risks of investors, borrowers, and depositors (through implicit bailout and other means of accommodating fragility) will almost certainly lead to economic risks during slowdowns, creating a new kind of instability.

Old habits, unfortunately, die hard. There has reemerged in official thinking an ambiguity about the perceived role of financial institutions as a tool of financial policy. On the one hand, the extensive restructuring of the development financial institutions is under way, through mergers and redefinitions of their statutory status. Yet, on the other hand, various aspects of financial sector reforms are either being rolled back (directives for lending to target groups) or not being addressed (artificially high rates of interest for small savings schemes). Various decisions that strengthen the development financial institution model, including directed disbursements at lower-than-market interest rates and use of public sector intermediaries for interventions in capital markets, have recently been taken. More than anything else, the cardinal mistake is to confuse outcomes with mechanisms and processes. Both, after a brief period of increasing emphasis on commercial viability, are again becoming target driven.

Given the increasing integration of financial markets, there is also a need to shift the focus of reform from individual intermediaries to a system level. An important component in this shift is enhancing the ability of intermediaries to de-risk their asset portfolios. Undoubtedly, the Securitisation and Reconstruction of Financial Assets and Enforcement of Security Interest Act of 2002 is a crucial step forward in addressing bad loans, but on its own it is limited in scope and even this is beset by various legal challenges. Establishing asset reconstruction companies, even under private management, will serve only to tackle the overhang of existing bad assets and do little to correct the distortions in incentives that are intrinsic to large parts of the system.

However, there remain some aspects of intermediation that are in the nature of public goods. One is the establishment of specific "platforms" for facilitating transactions. Another is to catalyze certain economic activities that are in the nature of testing the waters or else are pioneering financial services. The government has constituted diverse bodies to fulfill these roles; the most successful have been institutions with no direct intermediation functions. The state might have other legitimate social objectives, such as extending the reach of intermediation in rural and remote areas and providing social security nets; these, though, would be better achieved through the use of existing networks like post offices rather than commercial banks.

Appendix: The Index of Density of Government Involvement in the Financial Sector

This appendix enumerates the constituent groupings of the index of density of government involvement in the financial sector (IDGI-F) and an associated weighting system. The weights are uniform, being simply +1 or −1, depending on the appropriate definition of the respective series vis-à-vis the definition of impact on involvement.

Constituents

A. The share of public sector banks and financial institutions in total financial intermediation is the share in resource mobilization (as a sum of the following):

—Net demand and time liabilities of public sector banks (as a percentage of financial savings)

—Resources mobilized by development financial institutions through bond is-sues (as a percentage of financial savings)

—Premiums of Life Insurance Corporation and amounts mobilized by Unit Trust of India (as a percentage of financial savings)

B. The lending practices and use of funds consist of the following:

—Investments in government securities by banks and financial institutions (as a percentage of their incremental lendable resources)

—Excess deposits deployed by public sector banks in priority sectors (as a per-centage of net bank credit, in excess of minimum prescribed norms)

C. Trends in the government's preemption of financial resources consist of the following:

—Share of public investment in overall investment (for example, 7.7 percent out of 26.8 percent in 1995–96 and 6.9 percent out of 23.7 percent in 2001–02)

—Gap between public sector savings and investment (as a percentage of GDP)

—Public sector fiscal (or resources) gap (a proxy for the public sector borrow-ing requirement as percentage of GDP)

—Outstanding explicit liabilities of the (central and state) governments (as a percentage of GDP)

—Outstanding contingent liabilities (guarantees and other off-balance-sheet items) of the (central and state) governments (as a percentage of GDP)

Methodology of Construction

The IDGI-F is a simple weighted average of the rates of change of "synthetic" (subindex) constituent series. These synthetic subindex series are constructed using the (observed) rates of change of the constituent variables, with the values of variables of the individual series each being normalized to 100 in 1990–91.

References

Allen, Franklin, and Douglas Gale. 2001. "Comparative Financial Systems: A Survey." New York University and University of Pennsylvania, Wharton School.

Asher, M. G. 2003. "Reforming India's Social Security System." National University of Singa-pore, May.

Bhattacharya, Saugata, and Urjit R. Patel. 2002. "Financial Intermediation in India: A Case of Aggravated Moral Hazard?" Working Paper 145. Stanford University, Stanford Center for International Development, July. (Revised version forthcoming in *Proceedings of Third Annual Conference on the Reform of Indian Economic Policies*, edited by T. N. Srinivasan. Stanford University).

———. 2003a. "Markets, Regulatory Institutions, Competitiveness, and Reforms." Working Paper 184. Stanford University, Stanford Center for International Development, September.

————. 2003b. "Reform Strategies in the Indian Financial Sector." Forthcoming in the proceedings volume of IMF-NCAER conference on India's and China's experience with reform and growth, New Delhi, November.

————. Forthcoming. "New Regulatory Institutions in India: White Knights or Trojan Horses?" In *Public Institutions in India: Performance and Design,* edited by Devesh Kapur and Pratap Mehta.

Buiter, Willem H., and Urjit R. Patel. 1997. "Budgetary Aspects of Stabilisation and Structural Adjustment in India." In *Macroeconomic Dimensions of Public Finance, Essays in Honour of Vito Tanzi,* edited by Mario Blejer and Teresa Ter-Minassian, 363–412. London: Routledge.

Caprio, Gerard. 1996. "Bank Regulation: The Case of the Missing Model." Paper presented at Brookings–KPMG conference on sequencing of financial reform, Washington.

Demirgüç-Kunt, Aslı, and E. J. Kane. 2001. "Deposit Insurance around the World: Where Does It Work?" Paper prepared for World Bank conference on deposit insurance, Washington, July.

DICGC (Deposit Insurance and Credit Guarantee Corporation). 2002. *Annual Report 2001–02.*

Gerschenkron, Alexander. 1962. *Economic Backwardness in Historical Perspective: A Book of Essays.* Harvard University Press.

Hawkins, John, and Dubravko Mihaljek. 2001. "The Banking Industry in the Emerging Market Economies: Competition, Consolidation, and Systemic Stability." BIS Paper 4. Geneva: Bank for International Settlements, August.

India Post. 2003. *India Post Annual Report 2002–03.* Mumbai.

IDBI (Industrial Development Bank of India). 2003. *Report on Development Banking in India, 2002–03.*

Interim Budget, India, 2004–05.

IRDA (Insurance Regulatory and Development Authority). 2002. *Annual Report 2001–02.*

Johnson, Simon, Rafael La Porta, Florencio López-de-Silanes, and Andrei Shleifer. 2000. "Tunnelling." Working Paper 7523. Cambridge, Mass.: National Bureau of Economic Research, February.

Kornai, Janos. 1979. "Resource-Constrained vs. Demand-Constrained Systems." *Econometrica* 47, no. 4: 801–19.

La Porta, Rafael, Florencio López-de-Silanes, and Andrei Shleifer. 2000. "Government Ownership of Banks." Harvard University.

Levine, Ross. 1997. "Financial Development and Economic Growth: Views and Agenda." *Journal of Economic Literature* 35, no. 2: 688–726.

Lewis, W. A. 1955. *The Theory of Economic Growth.* Homewood, Ill.: Irwin.

National Stock Exchange. 2003. *National Stock Exchange Factbook 2002–03.*

Patel, Urjit R. 1997a. "Aspects of Pension Fund Reform: Lessons for India." *Economic and Political Weekly* 32 (September 20–26): 2395–402.

————. 1997b. "Emerging Reforms in Indian Banking: International Perspectives." *Economic and Political Weekly* 32 (October 18–24): 2655–60.

————. 2000. "Outlook for the Indian Financial Sector." *Economic and Political Weekly* 35 (November 4–10): 3933–38.

Patel, Urjit R., and Saugata Bhattacharya. 2003. "The Financial Leverage Coefficient: Macroeconomic Implications of Government Involvement in Intermediaries." Working Paper 157. Stanford University, Stanford Center for International Development.

Performance and Innovation Unit. 2000. "Counter Revolution: Modernising the Post Office Network." Performance and Innovation Unit Report. U.K. Government Cabinet Office, June.

Reserve Bank of India. 2002. *Report on Trends and Progress of Banking in India, 2001–02.* Mumbai.

———. 2003a. *Banking Statistics: Quarterly Handout, March 2003.* Mumbai.

———. 2003b. *Handbook of Statistics, 2002–03.* Mumbai.

———. 2003c. *Mid-Term Credit and Monetary Policy, 2003.* April. Mumbai.

———. 2003d. *Report on Trends and Progress of Banking in India, 2002–03.* Mumbai.

———. 2003e. *Statistical Tables Relating to Banks in India, 2002–03.* Mumbai.

———. Various issues. *Report on Trends and Progress of Banking in India.* Mumbai.

Rodrik, Dani. 2002. "After Neo-Liberalism, What?" Harvard University, June.

SEBI (Securities and Exchange Board of India). 2003. *Annual Report 2002–03.*

Shleifer, Andrei, and Robert Vishny. 1994. "Politicians and Firms." *Quarterly Journal of Economics* 109 (November): 995–1025.

PART IV

Managing and Regulating

LEWIS MUSASIKE
TED STILWELL
MORAKA MAKHURA
BARRY JACKSON
MARIE KIRSTEN

8

Lessons from Southern Africa

THE STATE HAS always played a role in the economies of both developed and developing nations, although the dominance of that role has changed over time in response to globalization, privatization, and the perceived efficiencies of the private sector. The establishment of the Bretton Woods institutions was a landmark in the reshaping of the international financial system—the development financial system in particular.

In the 1960s, as former colonies gained nationhood and independence from western nations, regional economic and political groups established their own development institutions, such as the African Development Bank, the Asian Development Bank, and the Inter-American Development Bank. Subregional and national development financial institutions gained prominence with the support of the Bretton Woods institutions. A number of these institutions were created for political reasons, but they also addressed development challenges related to the provision of basic services, the creation of jobs, the promotion of foreign exchange earnings, and the building of infrastructure.

In most developing nations there was no dividing line between public finance and development finance, with governments often using development financial institutions as conduits for fiscal transfers—and in reverse, using them to fund budgetary deficits. The result was that over time these institutions became a drag on the treasury of many governments and were finally allowed to disappear. Their demise at national and even subregional levels was precipitated by the structural reforms of the 1980s and 1990s (as dictated by the Bretton Woods institutions), the privatization trends that began in the mid-1980s in developed nations, and mismanagement and corruption. As the role of the state was reduced, so was the influence of state-owned enterprises reduced, with the exception of those deemed of strategic importance to the well-being of the state.

African performance has lagged behind other regional groupings, which has led to a reexamination of the challenges facing African countries in their quest for development and to the birth of the New Program for Africa's Development (NEPAD). Politically, the transformation of the Organization of African Unity to the African Union revealed the determination of Africans to promote good governance and to resolve civil strife. Regional integration is a principal feature of the NEPAD strategy, which argues that, to improve international competitiveness, African countries need to pool their resources and enhance regional development and economic integration. NEPAD emphasizes Africanness and African responsibility while recognizing the need for support from, and partnerships with, other regions of the world. In 2003 the United Nations General Assembly accepted NEPAD as the basis for all UN engagements with Africa, in effect significantly elevating the standing and credibility of NEPAD's approach.[1] The UN resolution also implies that all multilateral and bilateral agencies and organizations that include Africa adopt the same overarching strategy. NEPAD's strategy, it goes without saying, also affects development financial institutions in Africa.

Development Financial Institutions in Perspective

Development financial institutions are post–World War II, postcolonial developments designed to provide focused financial support to national and regional development efforts and to bolster economic growth.[2] Development finance is that set of financial flows, largely of a capital nature, that involves investments in both public and private income-producing development projects that operate on the basis of commercial profitability and full cost recovery.[3]

These institutions address market, political, or bureaucratic imperfections and asymmetry arising from perceived or actual financial risk by delivering a structured package of support to their clients. Their classic role is to fill the gaps in the domestic fiscal and term-lending capabilities of underdeveloped and developing countries. They seek to address capital market inefficiencies, wherein private cap-

1. "World Body Endorses NEPAD" (2003) (www.un.org/ecosocdev/geninfo/afrec/vol16no4/164nepd1.htm).
2. Diamond (1957).
3. Hoffmann (1998).

Figure 8-1. *Market Niche, Development Financial Institutions*

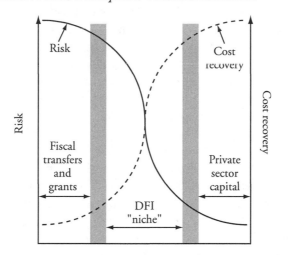

ital is unwilling or unable to provide capital to countries, projects, or clients not considered creditworthy. They further seek to fill the fiscal gap between capital for pure public goods provided by the state and commercial projects for which there is cost recovery.[4] This particular role in support of development finance is illustrated in figure 8-1.

The figure implies that by and large pure public goods and projects that lack sufficient income-generating capability do not constitute a substantial part of the loan portfolio of a development financial institution. Special fiscal, grant, and concessionary funding vehicles are required to meet many basic human needs and social services, with the institutions and the private sector supplementing these efforts with loan funding on the basis of cost recovery from beneficiaries. The interface areas may vary from sector to sector and client to client depending on the institution's financial model, funding sources, and ability to access resources and concessionary finance from multilateral and bilateral agencies. The figure further illustrates the potential for cofunding with the private sector and for various tripartite funding modalities.

Development finance is usually applied to investments in revenue-generating enterprises, public or private. These enterprises may be commercially profitable; they may involve full-cost recovery autonomous to the enterprise or partial cost

4. Mistry (undated).

recovery with an explicit subsidy provided by government. Application is generally confined to the initial capital outlay (or first cycle of working capital).[5] The capitalization of these enterprises usually consists of public sector equity and fiscal transfers, often augmented by loan or grant capital from private and donor sources. As governments face more budgetary constraints and as development aid declines, development financial institutions have been forced to become less dependent on central governments and to use their financial strength to intermediate between the providers of capital (financial markets and international funders) and users of capital who cannot access this capital directly. By intermediating, these institutions can substantially reduce the cost of capital to borrowers by the partial transfer of a subsidy through interest rate or tenure (maturity and grace periods), through asset and liability matching, or through stipulating less onerous collateral requirements. Further, the institutions have a good understanding of developmental risk, a high risk appetite, and a strong risk rating, all of which they can use to benefit poorer or unrated clients. The inclusion of commercially oriented projects in their portfolios also allows them to cross-subsidize development projects in poor areas.

Recently, public-private partnerships have materialized as important financial instruments through which development financial institutions can structure their development banking portfolios by mobilizing resources in partnerships with private sector players. These products and services include equity, quasi-equity instruments, senior debt, subordinated debt and guarantees, syndication underwriting, and arranging. Through their willingness to take political and general country risks that private sector investors have less appetite for, nonfinancial constraints on private sector investment in what are perceived to be economically depressed areas are mitigated and market comfort brought to fruition. This leveraging accelerates the pace at which development backlogs can be addressed.

A second, complementary function of these institutions is development assistance. This function is additional, and often nonrecoverable, but complements development banking by improving information flow, enhancing borrower capacity, and improving the prospects of debt servicing. In this way banking and development assistance functions become mutually reinforcing. The institutions value development per se, but they also depend on the servicing of debt. Private financial institutions are concerned with repayments and enforce more onerous financial requirements (higher collateral, capacity, and tenure) up front. The development banking and development assistance functions are bundled together, since the skills required for assessing potential investment projects are similar to those

5. Kritzinger-van Niekerk (2002).

required for addressing capacity building and development needs and for preparing borrowers for project lending. This implies the existence of economies of scope in the provision of these two services. Of late, emphasis on development financial institutions as knowledge brokers has also increased.

The nature and role of development finance is continuously changing due to developments in global capital markets over the last decade, global constraints on public finance, the narrowing definition and range of public goods and services, and the reduced direct role of the state in the market (for example, increasing privatization). The borders between public finance on the one hand and private commercial finance on the other have become blurred, thus shifting the nature, scope, and role of development finance in a rapidly changing macroeconomic environment.

Moreover, experience with development finance and its institutions in the past has led to skepticism about the efficacy of development finance, especially where state-owned banks are used for noncommercial, quasi-fiscal purposes (thus posing a risk to macroeconomic and financial sector stability of economies in transition).[6] Development finance cannot compensate for deficiencies in regional and national policy gaps and institutional capacities, which make development finance a weak mechanism for unfunded public sector redistributive mandates.

The intermediation function of development financial institutions requires sound banking principles to ensure that scarce capital is obtained at an affordable cost and allocated efficiently, consistent with both risk and return (in development and financial terms). Cost-effective intermediation is key for the institution's customers, who generally cannot afford high interest rates and often cannot access commercial bank services. Nationally based institutions that are required to be self-sustaining—must increasingly raise funds independent of government guarantees—have to pay special attention to their credit ratings and adopt prudent risk management policies and practices. The outcome is that these institutions end up prioritizing their financing activities, and certain high-risk segments of the market go unserved. However, some institutions establish special-purpose grants and soft loans to reach the unserved without compromising basic functions and sustainability.[7]

The fundamental role of development finance in a market economy—to fill the gap between capitalizing pure pubic goods and capitalizing pure commercial projects—means that such institutions should not be permanent; they should work toward their own demise by transforming both development financing and funding.

6. Sherif, Borish, and Gross (2003).
7. Development Bank of Southern Africa (2004).

The Development Bank of Southern Africa

The Development Bank of Southern Africa (DBSA), which is wholly owned by the South African government, was established in 1983 under the apartheid government to channel fiscal transfers from the central government to the so-called homeland governments, or Bantustans. The transformed bank was created under an act of Parliament, the DBSA Act, as amended in 1997 (Act 13 of 1997). The bank does not fall under the Banks Act and is therefore not directly supervised by the Reserve Bank. It however complies with applicable provisions of the Companies Act and the Public Finance Management Act of 1999.

Governance of the DBSA

Articles 5 through 10 of the DBSA Act of 1997 provide for the governance of the bank. Ten to fifteen directors are appointed by the minister of finance "on the grounds of their ability and experience in relation to socio-economic development, development finance, business, finance, banking and administration." At present the board of directors consists of twelve members from the private sector and one from the public sector. (Until recently there were two public sector members.) All but one of the directors are independent and nonexecutive. That the majority of directors are from the private sector indicates the arm's-length relationship between the South African government, as shareholder, and the bank. The board of directors controls the business of the bank and directs its operations.[8] The board is assisted in its strategic oversight by a number of functionally focused committees, namely the Audit and Finance Committee, the Credit Committee, the Knowledge Strategy Committee, and the Remuneration Committee. Although the DBSA does not legally report to the Reserve Bank, it nonetheless provides it with regular information regarding its funding and asset and liability management practices.[9]

The DBSA Act notes that the bank was "to be a leading change agent for socio-economic development in southern Africa" and its mission, accordingly, "to contribute to development by providing finance and expertise to improve the

---

8. In execution of their duties the directors subscribe to the King Report (2002) and the South Africa Public Finance Management Act, 1/1999 (www.gov.za/acts/1999/a1-99.pdf). Reviews of the effectiveness of the board were conducted during the 2003–04 financial year.

9. The Public Finance Management Act lays out a framework for an effective corporate governance for the public sector, introducing generally recognized accounting practices, uniform treasury norms and standards, measures to ensure transparency in expenditure in all spheres of government; and operational procedures for borrowing, guarantees, and procurement of services. The bank reports quarterly to the National Treasury and provides specific information to the Reserve Bank on its borrowings and currency management policies.

quality of life of the people of southern Africa, mainly through the provision of infrastructure." Before 1994 the bank funded projects in all sectors, including agriculture, industrial development, and small- and medium-size enterprises. In the period between 1994 and 1996 the government streamlined the development funding system, which resulted in the refocusing of the five national institutions that narrowly constitute the development financial system: the DBSA on infrastructure, the Landbank on agriculture, the Industrial Development Corporation on industry, Khula Enterprise on small- and medium-scale lending, and the National Housing Finance Corporation on housing.

During its first ten years, as a publicly funded body, the DBSA stressed its role of encouraging private sector lending by describing itself as a "lender of last resort." Since 1994 the newly elected African National Congress (ANC) government supported the continuation and transformation of the DBSA with the intention that public sector borrowers, such as local authorities, be subject to the discipline of the market. In 1995 the government ceased fiscal transfers to the DBSA and required it to be financially self-sustaining.

For the DBSA, *infrastructure* is broadly defined to comprise economic, institutional, and social infrastructure. Examples of economic infrastructure include water, sanitation, roads, drainage, telecommunications, and energy (figure 8-2). Like many of its peers, the bank is mandated to accelerate the delivery of basic services and economic growth while maintaining financial sustainability. Consequently it must operate on sound banking principles and resolve any conflict among these underlying principles.

To galvanize its interventions, the bank adopted further guiding principles:
—Partnerships with government, the private sector, and civic society
—Innovation, risk taking, and risk management
—Knowledge management
—Reward of performance
—Focus on its mandate.

Products and Services of the DBSA

The bank is predominantly a debt provider, but it invests in equity instruments as guided by its risk management policies. In recent times it has widened its scope of funding instruments to include such powerful tools as arranging syndication and underwriting. Within the broad operational framework of the DBSA's mandate, it plays a triple role of financier, partner, and adviser. These roles are complementary and mutually reinforcing.

As financier the bank mobilizes funds, makes grants, makes loans, invests, underwrites ventures, and arranges financing. As partner the bank acts as a catalyst

Figure 8-2. *Cumulative Loan and Equity Approval, Development Bank of Southern Africa, by Sector, August 2004*[a]

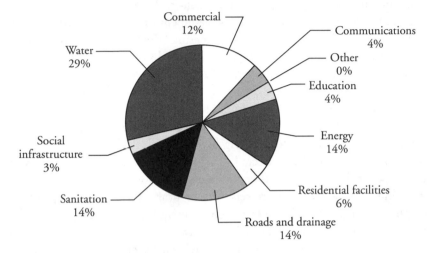

Source: Development Bank of Southern Africa, working document.
a. Shares exclude guarantees and equity investments.

and an agent, provides leverage, and facilitates development. As adviser the bank provides policy analysis, advocacy, training, capacity, research, evaluation, and information.

The bank's lending and investment instruments consist of fixed-rate and floating-rate loans based on rands as well as U.S. dollars and euros. In broader terms, the lending modalities are similar to those of other development financial institutions, but its lending and investment operations, as noted, are focused on infrastructure. Projects must be sustainable from a development impact and financial perspective. In arriving at a lending or investment decision, the appraisal process considers the economic, financial, technical, social, institutional, and environmental effects (factors similar to those used by multilateral development institutions). Risk management tools and practices are applied and weighted accordingly. As part of its development assistance, the bank offers technical assistance to address constraints at the project or client level that may negatively affect the success of the project.

Infrastructure projects are by nature long term, and cash flows are not always positive at the outset. The bank offers long-term loans that match the lives of the projects or underlying assets, while at the same time structuring the project to

Figure 8-3. *Lending and Investment to Countries of the Southern African Development Community, August 2004*

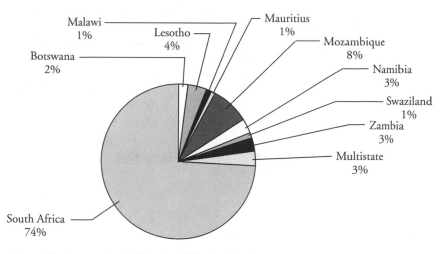

Source: Development Bank of Southern Africa, working document.

include the private sector, which might not be in a position to assume certain risks without the involvement of a development financial institution. In this regard, the DBSA regularly applies project finance and syndication techniques to encourage the participation of the private sector.

The bank's lending and investment operations extend to other Southern African Development Community (SADC) countries but with an overall exposure limit of one-third of total portfolio (figure 8-3). In the rest of the SADC region, the bank finances not only projects of an infrastructural nature but also economic growth sectors that are drivers of the economic development plans of these countries. In addition, projects and programs that promote the development of local capital markets are encouraged and so is support to financial institutions through lines of credit. The bank's operations in SADC countries are not all guaranteed by the respective governments, nor does the bank enjoy preferred creditor status. It operates through memorandums of understanding and within the context of treaties and other bilateral agreements between South Africa and these countries.

For South African–based activities, the major clients are local authorities (municipalities) and utilities (box 8-1). In 1996 the bank established its private sector partnering for development projects. This portfolio now amounts to $690,000 and is one of the fastest growing parts of the bank's business. The development finance

Box 8-1. *Msunduzi Urban Development Program*

As part of its drive to extend municipal services to the previously disadvantaged areas, the Msunduzi Municipality (formerly Pietermaritzburg) designed an infrastructure renewal program: the Msunduzi Urban Development Program. The program was divided into phases and involves the development and extension of infrastructure in three key sectors—roads, electricity, water, and sanitation.

At the start, the municipality used its own capital budget, but because of the magnitude of the program it approached the Development Bank of Southern Africa toward the end of 1997. The bank gave approval for the first loan in 1998. Phases 1 and 2 were completed in 1999 and 2000, respectively. By December 2002 the bank's financial contribution to the whole program was R 154.3 million. Meanwhile, work continued on the remaining phases of the program.

(banker) role of the DBSA is the nexus of its long-term sustainability and of its independence from periodic government recapitalization.[10]

The bank's sources of funding are domestic and international financial and capital markets, international development financial institutions and partners, internal cash generation, and callable capital of $700 million (2004 prices). Among other factors, investment-grade credit ratings put the bank in a position to mobilize funds efficiently and cost-effectively. As the bank looks forward to raising its profile in international capital markets, these credit ratings underpin its borrowing strategy. Its regulations stipulate a maximum debt-equity ratio of 250 percent.

During the transformation of the national development finance system, certain of the bank's loan portfolios to homeland governments were taken over by the national government in exchange for liquid government bonds at a higher coupon rate. This effectively added another capitalization layer. Furthermore, in 1997 the government committed itself to callable capital of R 4.8 billion to support the expansion of the bank's borrowing to fund its lending operations. The bank has further strengthened its capital base through the net surpluses it has earned since inception. Its capital base now stands at around R 11 billion ($1.75 billion).

The bank maintains a portfolio balance to mitigate risk in terms of country spread, sector spread, and single-obligor limits. Country limits are reviewed on an

10. The rating agencies Fitch, Moody's Investors Service, and Standard and Poor's have reaffirmed the bank's investment ratings for 2003–04. Fitch reaffirmed the AAA domestic ratings in 2003–04; international ratings by Moody's were Baa2 and were BBB by Standard and Poor's. These ratings reflect, among other factors, strong shareholder support from the South African government, a solid financial position, and prudent risk management policies.

annual basis and presented to the board of directors for approval. Total exposure to SADC countries (excluding South Africa) cannot exceed 33 percent of the bank's portfolio. The bank's exposure to countries outside South Africa was 25 percent at the end of August 2004 (see figure 8-3) and within the limits set by the directors.

The bank is by policy not unduly exposed to single obligors, who are limited to 10 percent of shareholders' interest, including the R 4.8 billion callable capital for South Africa. The public sector single-obligor limit for clients outside South Africa is 10 percent of shareholders' interest excluding callable capital. No more than 10 percent of shareholders' aggregate interest may be invested in equity or quasi-equity.

Interest rate subsidies to clients tend to distort financial markets and crowd out local and foreign direct investment. Client subsidies are better applied through the development assistance functions of development financial institutions, such as the DBSA's advisory (capacity-building) and partnership roles. The bank's policy is thus to charge market-related interest rates and to create opportunities for private capital through its project loan financing. The interest rates applied to project finance are determined in accordance with the bank's interest rate policy, approved from time to time by the board of directors, and implemented by executive management. This policy determines, inter alia, that lending rates are based on the cost of funding plus a margin for risk and an internal overhead charge.

In the development of its risk management policies and methodologies the bank has consistently endeavored to benchmark against best practice in the development finance industry as well as others in the banking industry.[11] Additionally, the bank, using grant financing provided by the World Bank, engaged consultants to benchmark its risk management practices against international best practice. As a result of these policies the bank has maintained the quality of its loan book, its low rate of defaults, its efficient and effective procedures for defaults, its low cost of funding, and its premier credit ratings.

In the bank's involvement with NEPAD, with Africa south of the Sahara, and more specifically with the SADC countries, its strategic thrust is to establish partnerships with multilateral and bilateral development financial agencies and, as part of its advisory role, with knowledge partners (box 8-2). The bank's partnership role helps reduce transaction costs and risks through better knowledge management and capacity building and enables the realization of synergies and positive externalities,

11. The International Finance Corporation (IFC) and the African Development Bank (AfDB) loan pricing spread resemble that of DBSA. The IFC currently applies lending spreads between 125 and 500 basis points. The AfDB aggregates its risk pricing also to a maximum of 500 basis points for unsecured private sector loans in high-risk countries.

Box 8-2. *The Mozal Aluminum Smelter*

The Mozal aluminum smelter near Maputo is the biggest industrial development project ever undertaken in Mozambique. When completed, the smelter will produce 2 percent of the world's annual consumption of aluminum. Total cost of the smelter is estimated at $2.2 billion, with financing by the Development Bank of Southern Africa equaling $103 million.

The bank became involved in the project to support the Maputo development corridor and the economic development programs of Mozambique and the region. This decision has been justified by the performance of the first phase, Mozal I, which has contributed around $160 million a year to the country's gross domestic product, generated export earnings of $430 million a year (an increase of more than 150 percent), and added about $4 million a year to tax revenue. The Mozambican government's shareholding in the first phase has generated dividend income of $5 million a year. Investor confidence in the country has risen significantly, and the prospects for further investment are strong, with a number of substantial projects in the pipeline.

The economy has also benefited from the establishment of related infrastructure, including improved roads and bridges, telecommunications networks, water and sewage systems, harbor facilities, and electricity supply. Mozal has initiated a social development program, implemented through the Mozal Community Development Trust, for communities within a ten-kilometer radius of the smelter. The company funds the trust with $2 million a year. The trust focuses on small business development, agriculture, education and training, health and the environment, culture and sports, and community infrastructure.[1]

1. New Program for Africa's Development/Development Bank of Southern Africa (2003).

thus achieving developmental leverage beyond the bank's own means. This is consistent with efforts by development agencies and enhances the role of nontraditional partners in development, such as the private sector, regulators, and civil society.

As the bank has become known for its institutional capacity, there have been more and more requests for it to play an agency role in implementing projects on behalf of others. These requests come from institutions such as governments, donors, and other development stakeholders who lack the specific local and regional capacity to implement programs. The bank in turn has increasingly recognized that it needs to play a more enabling role in development. The idea of providing agency services has therefore developed over time and is now included in the bank's range of standard products. Agency activities allow the bank to enhance development in South Africa and the rest of the continent by negotiating new partnerships and strengthening existing ones with other development stakeholders.[12]

As an adviser the bank addresses clients' shortfalls in borrowing capacity. The bank does this by building clients' institutional capacity to manage projects in terms of good governance, the systems in place (both organizational procedures and management information hardware and software), and individuals' knowledge and skills. A knowledge organization, as defined by the bank, is an organization that values, generates, and shares knowledge; applies and internalizes knowledge in business processes and client-focused products and services; pursues focused knowledge outreach to stakeholders; and has the architecture and infrastructure to capacitate the organization for learning and leveraging skills and information. This organizational structure gives equal importance to knowledge and function (operations, private sector investment, treasury and special projects).

Development banking has always been a knowledge-based business, but in the past this has been largely implicit since the skills required for assessing potential investment projects are similar to those required for addressing capacity building and development needs and for preparing borrowers for project lending. As a regional organization the DBSA is uniquely endowed with a developmental track record of twenty years. With new frameworks for knowledge management, and the more explicit recognition that the bank has a huge pool of development finance knowledge, a concerted effort is being made to recognize and characterize the knowledge that the bank possesses and to put structures and processes in place to enable its widespread exploitation. This is especially important as the DBSA's own triple role of financier, partner, and adviser has matured. The approach has been to build solid foundations for the sustained delivery of knowledge by first improving internal capabilities to deliver on the knowledge vision and then to deploy as widely as possible through its marketplace the extensive, domain-specific knowledge that the bank has built up.

The bank has developed a knowledge strategy by propagating and entrenching a knowledge culture in the organization; by helping it become a learning organization; by exchanging and sharing knowledge in communities of practice and

12. Currently, the bank has twenty-two agency projects on its books, with a funding value of about $7 million in financial year 2002–03. These projects are diverse in nature and include joint ventures, independent contractor assignments, and management contracts. Some of the important agency functions are the African Connection project, the Carbon Finance Intermediary Agreement (with the World Bank), the International Development Research Council (sponsored by the Canadian Research Centre), the Environmental Capacity Building Unit (with the South African government), the Job Creation Trust, the Timbuktu Manuscript and Infrastructure Restoration Project (with the governments of Mali and South Africa), and the Low-Cost Housing Infrastructure Fund (funded by Kreditanstalt für Wiederaufbau).

stakeholders; by evaluating and assessing effective deployment of knowledge; and by building smart institutional partnerships for knowledge building and brokering. The bank thus continues to invest in knowledge networks and communities of practice within and outside the organization. It is currently setting up and operationalizing a specialized training academy and working closely with such partners as universities and multilateral and bilateral development agencies to tackle social, financial, and technological challenges of development economies.

The bank also assists its clients through its Development Fund, a nonprofit company incorporated in December 2001 to address sustainable capacity building at the municipal level and to support municipalities in enhancing service delivery and local economic development. The core business of the Development Fund is to maximize the impact of development finance through grants that address the human, institutional, and financial constraints on rural and urban development, thereby promoting service delivery and local economic development. This is done through a mix of products and services, including

—Funds: Supporting capacity-building funding through grants, development credits, and other financial instruments

—Expertise: Consulting and advisory services for institutional and human capacity building to ensure that basic services are delivered to disadvantaged communities

—Development facilitation: Ongoing technical support and sharing of knowledge to ensure that clients gain the necessary experience to manage the functions and processes of service delivery.

With the Development Fund operational in all nine provinces of South Africa, progress has been made in helping local government institutions build capacity and formulate integrated development plans. In its first year of operation the fund approved technical support grants to 134 municipalities and provincial departments totaling $1.1 million and has now been capitalized with the transfer of $50 million from the DBSA's operational surpluses. Through its operational units the DBSA frequently provides technical assistance to its clients for project preparation to the point at which a bankable project proposal is submitted to the bank for consideration for development finance.

Development Impact of the DBSA

Through its sound governance and fiscal and outreach policies the bank has had a considerable impact in southern Africa (table 8-1). The bank also leverages third-party funding into the development process, an approach that has led over the ten-year period 1993–2003 to a 1–3.4 participation ratio, with the bank alone supporting projects to the value of $3,723 million and cofunders providing

Table 8-1. *Loan Approvals, Development Bank of Southern Africa,*
by Annual Report Indicator, 1993–2003
Millions of dollars, except as indicated

Indicator	Total loan approvals, including cofunders	Total DBSA loans approved
Project funding	10,889	3,723
Contribution to GDP	7,940	2,176
Employment creation (number of jobs)	527,874	143,904
Skilled	51,250	15,355
Semi-skilled	227,027	63,100
Unskilled	249,597	65,449
Impact on low income households	968	328

Source: Development Bank of Southern Africa (2004).

an additional $7,166 million. Furthermore, projects supported by the bank and cofunders contributed $7,940 million to the region's gross domestic product over the period.

Unemployment in the region is a concern, and through its funding the bank has contributed to part-time and permanent employment in the region. The table indicates the impact of disbursements on the income of low-income households. The impact is considerably smaller than the impact on gross domestic product because of the capital-intensive nature of most infrastructure projects.

Ongoing Challenges for the DBSA

The environment in which the DBSA operates creates certain tensions among its triple roles of financier, partner, and adviser, giving rise to a number of challenges to its directors and executive in balancing priorities. While the objectives and mandate of the bank are clearly developmental, tensions arise between the need to retain favorable credit ratings and the need to deliver development outcomes, such as combating poverty and creating employment. A careful balance must be struck between investments with high returns and less secure or less attractive investments in pursuit of the government's development agenda. Continuous strategic analysis, careful financial modeling, review of key performance areas, and value engineering have become crucial to the management of the bank.

There is also a tension in the imperative to encourage private sector lenders to be involved in development lending. Ideally the DBSA should not compete with the private sector when the private sector is willing to invest. However the bank needs to have some good quality loans in its book, which means that this area needs to be managed carefully to avoid discouraging private sector investments. When the bank has a number of financial products, such as special purpose grants, and soft loan windows, such as the DBSA's Development Fund, it needs clear policies on when to use each in order to reach the unserved in a manner that does not compromise the basic functions and sustainability of the bank. In the same vein, the bank can use these products (in appropriate amounts) and its knowledge role to build capacity among hitherto nonbankable clients and so "graduate" them to a position from which they can take up loans from the DBSA, thus increasing the bank's loan book and scope of its development finance operations.[13]

Conclusions

An overview of the development financial system and the background, nature, and practice of the DBSA in addressing development challenges lead to a number of guiding principles for the successful management of development financial institutions:

—Governments must provide an environment conducive to the development of financial markets. For example, NEPAD emphasizes transparency and good governance as crucial for Africa's recovery.

—The institution needs autonomy of governance to maintain an appropriate distance from both the government and the institution's clients. Prescriptions regarding whom to fund and on what financial terms and conditions lead to ineffectiveness, to a weakening of the institution's ability to raise private capital, and to a crowding out of private capital.

—The institution should have the flexibility to focus on regional and local circumstances as a development partner with multilateral and bilateral agencies, as the institution has a better understanding of local and regional developmental risk and is able to match its risk appetite accordingly.

—The institution can achieve enormous leverage beyond its capitalization by establishing smart partnerships with multilateral and bilateral agencies, private capital, knowledge institutions, and nongovernmental organizations.

—Prudent management of systemic risk requires that the institution's portfolio be diversified. The sustainability of the institution depends on its spreading risk across different types of client and sector.

—Interest rates and tenure should be market related to avoid crowding out private capital. Client subsidies are better applied through the institution's development assistance functions, such as advisory services and capacity building.

13. The DBSA established the Vulindlela Academy and the Knowledge Portal for this purpose.

—The institution should be subject to strict commercial norms and practice. Systemic risk as related to funding structure (as reflected in balance sheet ratios) should be minimized by applying commercial risk principles.

—Public-subsidy-dependent areas and sectors (for example, basic social services) in the portfolio should generally be pursued as an off-balance-sheet agency arrangement entered into with the relevant government ministry or multilateral and bilateral donors.

—For a development financial institution to succeed within the rapidly changing global and regional environment, it must have sound governance and financial management, flexibility, and an ability to balance cost-effective intermediation and risk management with outreach through smart partnerships, capacity building, and knowledge management.

References

Development Bank of Southern Africa. 2004. "Ten-Year Review." Midrand, South Africa.

Diamond, W. 1957. *Development Banks.* Johns Hopkins University Press.

Hoffmann, S. L. 1998. *The Law and Business of International Project Finance.* London: Kluwer Law International.

King Report (King Report on Corporate Governance for South Africa). 2002. Johannesburg, South Africa: Institute of Directors in Southern Africa (www.idosa.co.za).

Kritzinger-van Niekerk, Lolette. 2002. "The Role of Development Finance in Alleviating the Constraints to Private Capital Flows." Paper presented at Development Bank of Southern Africa workshop, Financing Africa's Development: Enhancing the Role of Private Finance. Midrand, July 2002.

Mistry, Percy. Undated. "Realigning the Development Finance System in South (and Southern) Africa: Issues and Options." Midrand, South Africa: Development Bank of Southern Africa.

New Program for Africa's Development/Development Bank of Southern Africa. 2003. *Financing Africa's Development: Enhancing the Role of Private Finance.* Development Report. Midrand, South Africa: Development Bank of Southern Africa.

Sherif, Khaled, Michael Borish, and Alexandra Gross. 2003. *State-Owned Banks in the Transition: Origins, Evolution, and Policy Response.* Washington: World Bank.

"World Body Endorses NEPAD: UN Negotiations Bring Agreement to Back African Initiative." 2003. *Africa Recovery* 16, no. 4: 6.

PAK RUDJITO
HENDRAWAN TRANGGANA

9

Lessons from Indonesia

INDONESIAN STATE-OWNED enterprises are major actors in national economic development. The activities managed by these enterprises cover almost all sectors in Indonesia, and almost all people must deal with them in one way or another.

The economic crisis in Indonesia in 1997–98 caused the financial performance of many state-owned enterprises with a strong position in the national economy to severely drop, with a lessening of the contribution of these enterprises to the country's revenue. As an illustration, the contribution (taxes and dividends) of fourteen of the top state-owned enterprises in 2000 was only Rp 13.6 trillion, while total government revenue was Rp 187 trillion.[1] Thus the contribution of these enterprises to government revenue was only 7.3 percent.

Several experts believe that the crisis in Indonesia stemmed mainly from the cumulative results of weaknesses in the banking institutional framework:

—Unseparated functions among owners, regulators, management, and supervisors

—The lack of good corporate governance (risk management, transparency, accountability, and compliance)

—The dominance of state-owned banks, the number of new banks, and the minority role of the capital market in these banks.

---

1. Sukardi (2002).

The crisis saw banks' capital adequacy ratio fall below zero and the ratio of high-performance loans to third-party liabilities dramatically decrease. Therefore, when the crisis hit it inevitably led to a deterioration of Indonesia's banking infrastructure.

The crisis affected most business people, especially those whose business involves imports. Many corporate-scale companies went stagnant, most of them declaring bankruptcy because of the sudden increase of debt brought on by the fall of the Indonesian rupiah against the U.S. dollar and the weakness of domestic demand. These two factors increased Indonesia's level of country risk, leading to the deterioration of banks' management and asset quality.

However, if state-owned enterprises are managed professionally, they can be productive, profitable, and even worldwide actors. Of thirty-seven sectors involving 161 state-owned companies, 124 of these companies (or 77 percent) are competitive, and only 11 companies (or 7 percent) are monopolistic.[2] Sectors that have the potential to become worldwide actors are financial services, agroindustry, consumer goods, energy, tourism, telecommunication and media, and mining.[3]

Government Recovery Efforts

Since the beginning of the crisis, the government has worked hard to improve its banking sector. On January 27, 1998, the Indonesian Bank Restructuring Agency (IBRA) was created to take over the claims deriving from Bank Indonesia's facilities and to replace them with government bonds. The Jakarta Initiative Task Force assisted IBRA in restructuring most of the private sector's debt. The liquidity of Bank Indonesia was underwritten with Rp 21.6 billion in order to maintain people's confidence. Of the country's 237 banks, 66 were liquidated. Its seven state-owned banks were merged into five. A number of banks were recapitalized. All of this effort cost Rp 650 trillion, with interest rates in 2002 close to 90 percent and a deficit budget reaching –47 percent in 1999 (figures 9-1 and 9-2).

In addition to these efforts, the government has passed a series of laws with the aim of restructuring state-owned banks.[4] After the recapitalization program, tax revenue increased as well as revenue from IBRA, and bank stock prices continued to improve through early 2004 (figures 9-3 and 9-4).

Economic growth in 2003 was 4.2 percent, higher than the 3.7 growth rate of 2002. The 2003 exchange rate was Rp 8,465 to the U.S. dollar. The 2003 infla-

---

2. "Master Plan Badan Usaha Milik Negara Tahun, 2002–2006" (2002).
3. Ahmadjajadi (2002); "BUMN Incorporated Dalam Rangka Memperkuat Strategi Bisnis" (2003).
4. The laws are People Assembly's Decree IV/MPR/1999; People Assembly's Decree X/MPR/2001; People Assembly's Decree VI/MPR/2002; Law 25/2000; Law 19/2001; Presidential Decree 22/2001; State-Owned Enterprise Minister Decree 35/2001; Law 19/2003.

Figure 9-1. *Interest Payments by Indonesian Government, 1998–2003*

Percent

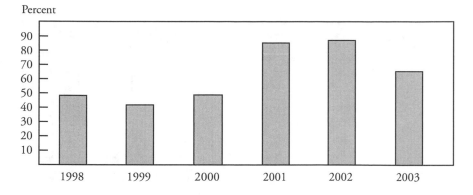

tion rate was 5.06 percent, compared with 10.03 percent in 2002. The 2003 interest rate was 8.3 percent, compared with 12.9 percent in 2002.

Bank deposits and credits increased in approximately balanced amounts. Third-party fundraising up to September 2003 was Rp 952 trillion, an increase of around 3 percent over that of January 2003 (Rp 924.6 trillion). Assets also improved: By January 2003, total loans outstanding were Rp 402.6 trillion, which increased to Rp 454.2 trillion by September 30, 2003, indicating that the banks were doing their job as intermediary institutions. This can also be seen in the 2003 lending-to-deposit ratio, which reached 53.70 percent; the 2002 ratio was 49.19 percent. In addition, between 2000 and 2001 state-owned banks

Figure 9-2. *Country Deficit Budget, Indonesia, 1998–2003*

Percent

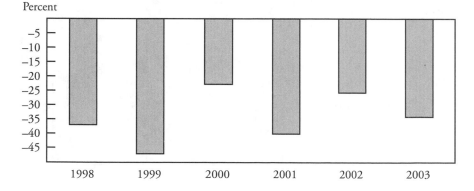

Figure 9-3. *Revenue after Recapitalization, Indonesia, 1998–2003*

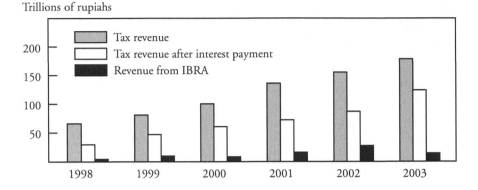

Trillions of rupiahs

showed a significant increase in tax contributions to the country, for a total improvement between 2000 and 2001 of 68 percent (table 9-1).

The data above show that, by 2000, the Indonesian bank structure had dramatically changed compared with that before the crisis. Recapitalization and bank mergers become the starting point of a move toward a highly competitive banking industry. Most of the big banks are owned by the government due to the recapitalization process. However, currently some recapitalized banks have been sold to the public and to strategic partners.

As the bank structure changed, the business environment also changed. Several regulations were introduced, most of them focusing on the implementation of good corporate governance, which had not been taken into account before the

Figure 9-4. *Stock Prices, Bank Rakyat Indonesia, December 2003 to March 2004*

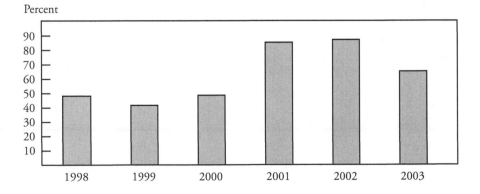

Percent

Table 9-1. *Tax Contribution from State-Owned Banks, Indonesia, 2000 and 2001*

	Tax		Increase	
Banks	2000	2001	Rupiahs	Percent
Bank Mandiri	1,570,400	1,805,289	234,889	15
Bank Negara Indonesia	518,829	1,112,684	593,855	114
Bank Rakyat Indonesia (Persero)	196,676	828,137	631,461	321
Bank Ekspor Indonesia	74,116	165,725	91,083	124
Bank Tabungan Negara	13,639	69,722	56,083	411
Total	2,373,660	3,981,557	1,607,897	68

Source : Sukardi (2002).

crisis. Over the ten-year period beginning in 2004, Bank Indonesia is gradually implementing a new concept of banking, called Arsitektur Perbankan Indonesia, which is based on six fundamental pillars:[5]

—A robust, internationally competitive, banking structure to support economic development

—A strong internal banking industry

—An effective regulation system to anticipate the development of a domestic and international money market

—An independent and effective banking supervisory body

—A strong and supportive bank infrastructure

—A system to protect and empower customers.

Based on Arsitektur Perbankan Indonesia and the market conditions, the banks will probably be categorized into four classifications: In category 1 are rural banks and banks with limited operations, which will provide financial services to small-scale, active, but poor customers; these banks will have a minimum equity of Rp 100 billion. In category 2 are banks that focus on regional, corporate, retail, and other customers; these banks will operate with a minimum equity of Rp 10 trillion. In category 3 are the national banks; these operate nationally, with a minimum equity of Rp 50 trillion. In category 4 are the international banks, which operate worldwide, with a minimum equity above Rp 50 trillion. These classifications aim to create a sound banking structure and are expected to enable the banks to compete nationally and internationally. They are also expected to allow

5. "Arsitektur Perbankan Indonesia" (2003); Sabirin (2003).

banks to determine their own market, based on their competencies, so that there will be no overlapping in market target, and competition among banks in each category will be encouraged. It can be seen that one of the distinctive features of Arsitektur Perbankan Indonesia is the formulation of a vision and a mission for banks based on their core competencies. This situation is totally different from that of the boom era, in which anybody was able to open a bank without considering its competencies.

After recapitalization, domestic banks were immediately hit by stiff competition at the regional and international level. The banks responded with a variety of products and services to help them keep their customers. As customer satisfaction increased, information technology became the most important bank service offered. Almost all banks in Indonesia have implemented online banking, phone banking, automatic teller machines (ATMs), mobile banking, and Internet banking.

From the financial point of view, banking conditions are getting better. However, there are still lots of problems to be solved in the short term—and in the long term—in order to bring Indonesian banks into a competitive position in the global market.

Bank Rakyat Indonesia

The history of Bank Rakyat Indonesia (BRI) began on December 16, 1895, when Aria Wiriaatmadja, an indigenous person, established a small bank in Purwokerto, Central Java, by using mosque funds to help the poorest citizens of Purwokerto and to help them avoid the high interest rates of local loan sharks. Under BRI Law 1968, the bank legally belonged to the government, with a specific program for agriculture. The bank, as the government's agent for development, channeled government funds through 300 BRI rural branches to farmers to enable them to become self-supporting rice growers. After one decade, the self-supporting—and supply driven—rice program was successful, even though most of the loans were doubtful.

In 1984, after banking deregulation in 1983, the government and the management of BRI transformed the BRI rural units from supply driven to demand driven and based loans on the market and on customer needs. The bank introduced

—Simplicity: The products were pared down to general rural loans and rural savings.

—Accessibility: BRI unit offices were moved closer to the businesses they serve.

—Transparency: Reporting became more transparent.

—Independence: BRI unit managers were was given full authorization without central intervention.

—Human resource building: BRI uses recruitment, training, reward, and punishment to build a skilled staff.

—Technology building: BRI has computerized its work.

After eighteen years of consistently following these guidelines, the BRI unit system, with its demand-driven policy and its leadership by committed managers, was named the model of commercial microscale banking.

The Restructuring Program

In response to the banking reforms, the government sought to recapitalize a number of state-owned banks, including BRI. In exchange for the nonperforming loans in the portfolio that were transferred to IBRA, the government injected additional capital into BRI. These funds were immediately used to purchase government recapitalization bonds totaling Rp 29,149.0 billion, of which Rp 20,404.3 billion was issued on July 25, 2000, and Rp 8,744.7 billion was issued on October 31, 2000. All of the government recapitalization funds were issued as fixed-rate bonds.

Under the recapitalization program, BRI and the government entered into a management contract (a temporary contract on July 28, 2000, and the final contract on February 28, 2001). The government acted through the Ministry of Finance; the members of BRI's board of directors and board of commissioners acted for the bank. Pursuant to the management contract, BRI adopted a business plan establishing certain performance targets and related time frames for, among other things, the strict control of overhead expenses, the divestment of nonagribusiness corporate loans and share ownership in other companies, the reduction of nonperforming loans, the implementation of a new information technology system, and the privatization of BRI.

Under the management contract, BRI's board of directors and board of commissioners are required to ensure that BRI is operated in accordance with the business plan; if it is not, and if the reasons for nonachievement are beyond the control of—or correction by—either board, the targets may be adjusted. The management contract is to expire on December 31, 2004, however.

Maximizing Profit

During restructuring, banks often do little in the way of expansion. However, during its more than three-year restructuring program (July 2000 to December 2003), BRI was able to maximize profit as well. Its capital adequacy ratio in December 2003 was 20.87 percent, well above the minimum standard of 8.0 percent set by

Bank Indonesia. In 2001 its profits were Rp 1.0 trillion, in 2002 they were Rp 1.5 trillion, and in 2003, Rp 2.5 trillion. Net nonperforming loans in December 2003 were only 3.3 percent, below the BI target 5.0 percent.

During its restructuring BRI faced both external and internal competition, primarily from regional banks, other large commercial banks, and foreign banks. BRI also faces indirect competition from finance and securities companies, saving cooperatives, leasing and factoring companies, and venture capital companies, as well as certain government-owned or -affiliated entities that provide industrial development funding and export-import lending and services. However, BRI has strong competitive advantages:

—It has the most extensive branch network in Indonesia.

—It has strong positions in the micro-, small-, and medium-scale business sectors and in the low- to middle-income consumer loan markets.

—It has good quality assets and a strong capital base.

—It is well positioned for continued growth amid improving macroeconomic conditions.

—It has an experienced and professional management team.

Risk Management

BRI's commitment to be a leader in micro-, small-, and medium-scale business sectors is strongly maintained (table 9-2). It is the intermediary between millions of creditors and millions of debtors. Its lending policy of giving a minimum 80 percent of its loans to these business sectors greatly improves BRI's future prospects. This business focus is also strongly backed by the bank's widespread network, which is evident from the following numbers:

—Regional BRI offices: 13

—BRI branches: 325

—BRI subbranches: 147

—BRI *sharia* branches: 8

—BRI units: 4,049

—BRI village service centers: 199

—BRI automatic teller machines: nearly 8,000

—BRI employees: 32,298.

BRI serves more than 30 million customers. Its staff generally come from the unit office's local area, enabling it to provide a local, more human touch when dealing with customers. Along with its grassroots national development, decentralization, and lending policies set by government, BRI is committed to two strategic issues:

Table 9-2. *BRI Reorientation to Business Sectors, 1997–2003*
Percent

Segment	1997	1998	1999	2000	2001	2002	2003
Micro	15	12	23	29	30	31	32
Small	44	40	45	38	43	49	48
Medium	41	48	33	13	11	4	8
Total	. . .	. . .	. . .	80	84	85	88
Corporate	n.a.	n.a.	n.a.	20	16	15	12

Source: BRI, investor presentation, October 2003.
n.a. Not available.

—Empowering the employees by delegating authority for regional branches to unit managers

—Developing a synergy policy, supported by information technology.

BRI's management approach is based on interactive communication and team building. Its profit-setting approach is capital-based, risk-based, and information technology–based.

Regarding its strategy for capital, BRI has high financial leverage, since the biggest part of it liabilities are funds from depositors. Therefore, to cover losses, to support growth for the bank, and to protect against risk, the bank set its minimum capital adequacy ratio at 12 percent. Regarding its strategy for risk, BRI's risk management system covers not only credit risk but also market risk and operational risk. The ability of the bank to manage these risks will determine its profitability and viability. Credit risk management at BRI is adopted from international best practice and is conducted as a part of prudential banking practices. The principles of credit risk management used by the bank are the "four eyes principle" for credit approval (two people must evaluate each loan decision), credit limits and responsibility of managers, maximum-loss tolerance, and risk scoring and a credit risk review for each loan proposal.

Regarding information technology, BRI is forming a new IT architecture based on a centralized system, which embraces the core banking system, a delivery channel, and a management information system. The program had 587 operational networks online in real time in 2003 and added more than 600 more networks in 2004. Since 2002, BRI has delivered services through a trough phone (land line) banking facility that can be used by customers with the BritAma service—a type of BRI account that pays a competitive interest rate, allows free transfers, and includes an ATM card. The use of technology will be expanded to develop debit card, credit card, Internet banking, home banking, and e-commerce services in the near future.

The bank's employee training system is known as the best in the country. BRI operates seven training centers, training about 90,000 people a year. Six of these centers are dedicated to training employees for microlevel banking. The training centers are also responsible for providing continuous training for BRI employees. BRI's training system guarantees that every employee has the opportunity to enroll in a training program at least once a year. This is in line with a central bank policy that calls for each bank to spend 5 percent of its income for the training and development of its employees.

Privatization

BRI has entered the privatization stage, having put its stock on the market in an initial public offering on November 10, 2003. The response to the stock offer, both within Indonesia and overseas, was gratifying. But it is not a surprise, given the superior performance of BRI.

This performance is linked to BRI's core business—that is, its focus on micro-, small-, and medium-scale business sectors. In addition, during the monetary crisis its nonperforming loans in this sector were regarded as very low. BRI has become known for its successful microfinance development and has been called by the World Bank "the world's largest and oldest microfinance institution." Further, Harvard University has termed BRI a world-class example of microfinance in practice.

The initial public offering went well also because of employee faith in the bank. The bank's staff has an inside understanding of the bank's solidity and was enthusiastic about the public offering. The bank ensured employee support for the public offering in several ways. First, the objectives of the offering were explained to them. Second, the bank assured employees that the bank's good reputation externally was due to their hard work and capabilities. Third, the public offering was promoted as significant in not only the short term but also the long term, as the new investors would be monitoring BRI's performance.

The bank's share value in its first year rose almost continuously (figure 9-4). The offering was oversubscribed: The government sold 3 billion stocks and the bank issued 1.7 billion new shares, but demand reached more than 75 billion shares.[6]

November 10 is National Hero Day in Indonesia and was deliberately chosen by the bank as the day to offer BRI stock publicly. The day was established in

---

6. "Dibalik Fenomena Go Public BRI" (2003).

1945 as a day to honor heroes in the struggle for Indonesian independence (independence from the Netherlands was declared on August 17, 1945).

In 2004 democracy was to be established in the country in three stages, with deadlines of April 5, July 5, and September 20, at which time the IMF program was to terminate—with the expectation that the economic picture in Indonesia would be relatively stable. Economic growth was expected to be around 4.2–4.4 percent, the inflation rate around 5.5–7.0 percent, the exchange rate stable at around Rp 8,400–700 to the U.S. dollar, and the interest rate around 8.4–9.0 percent.

Conclusions

BRI began restructuring in 1999 and entered into a management contract on February 28, 2001. Pursuant to the management contract, BRI adopted a business plan establishing certain performance targets and related time frames. Among other targets set in 2003 was the successful initial public offering of its stock. Throughout, BRI had continued to focus on its core business, the micro-, small-, and medium-scale business sectors. When other banks became frustrated with the corporate sector and wanted to serve the same sectors as BRI, that bank became the model for them to follow.

BRI's earlier winning of various awards generated a favorable climate for its initial public offering. In addition, BRI's staff was part of the bank's success, both in its public recognition and in its stock sales.

References

Ahmadjajadi, Cahyana. 2002. *Deputi Bidang Jaringan Komunikasi.*
"Arsitektur Perbankan Indonesia." 2003. Jakarta: Bank Indonesia.
"BUMN Incorporated Dalam Rangka Memperkuat Strategi Bisnis." 2003. Jakarta: Dalam Seminar Sehari.
"Dibalik Fenomena Go Public BRI." 2003. *Business Indonesia.*
"Master Plan Badan Usaha Milik Negara Tahun, 2002–2006." 2002. Kementrian BUMN, February.
Sabirin, Syahril. 2003. "Tantangan dan Peluang Perbankan Nasional." *Bank and Manajemen* 70 (January–February).
Sukardi, Laksamana. 2002. "Privatisasi Menegakkan Martabat Bangsa." *Indonesian Financial Statistics,* October.

JONATHAN L. FIECHTER
PAUL H. KUPIEC

10

Principles for Supervision

W**HEN POLICY DISCUSSIONS** are focused on state-owned financial institutions, economists often suggest privatization as a means for improving economic efficiency and social welfare. In a wide range of settings, competitive market forces promote an efficient allocation of resources. Theory and experience suggest that public ownership and control of productive activities that could be undertaken by privately held competitive enterprises often leads to inefficiencies, market distortions, and governance arrangements that may facilitate the expropriation of government resources for the benefit of specific political interests.

While there may be cases in which specific financial sector needs are chronically undersupplied by the private market, in most instances these activities are relatively specialized in some way. When preconditions create a viable credit culture with enforceable contracts, commercial banking per se is not an activity that private markets underproduce, although pockets of underserved markets may arise (for example, low incomes and sparse population density may limit profitability and branch development in rural areas; cultural and educational barriers may limit access of some parts of the population to "mainstream" banks). In these cases, governments may intervene to support these underserved needs by, for

The authors acknowledge valuable comments and discussions by David Marston, Jan Willem van der Vossen, Aditya Narain, Jody Morris, Julia Majaha-Jartby, Socorro Heysen, Jorge Cayazzo, Inwon Song, Thordur Olafsson, Greta Mitchell-Caselle, and Matthew Jones.

example, allowing state-owned postal saving institutions to provide financial services in localities that might be chronically underserved by private commercial banks. It is also common to use the intermediation activities of state-owned financial institutions to spur growth in other financial sector activities as well. The provision of foreign trade and export finance credit support for agriculture, fishing, housing, small- and medium-sized businesses, industrial development, pension savings services, and insurance underwriting are among the activities often associated with state-owned financial institutions.

The results of a recent survey by the International Monetary Fund (IMF) of a sample of its membership suggest that a large share of IMF member countries includes state-owned financial institutions as an important component of their financial sectors.[1] Of the twenty-two countries that provided detailed responses—including industrialized, transition, and developing countries on all continents—respondents identify 683 of these institutions. While a majority of the institutions (588) are classified as primarily engaged in commercial banking-type activities, the sample includes postal banks, development banks, mutual funds, asset management companies, export credit agencies, pension funds, leasing companies, other nonbank credit institutions, and insurance companies. The survey further suggests that many of the institutions are hybrid, undertaking both commercial banking-type activities and some other forms of policy-directed financial intermediation.

Survey responses suggest that many of the institutions are subject to some form of supervision. State-owned commercial banks typically are subject to supervision by the private sector banking supervisory authority. Others are supervised by their sponsoring ministry (for example, a housing bank is supervised by the ministry in charge of housing), and some development banks appear to be unsupervised. Postal savings banks typically are not formally supervised. And even when institutions are subject to outside supervision, there often are limits on the supervisor's powers relative to those typically exercised over private sector commercial banks.

Without promoting or disparaging the view that privatization is an effective means for improving social welfare, the results of the IMF survey suggest that state-owned financial institutions may well be a durable component of the financial sector in most IMF member countries. With that as a premise, this chapter is intended to open a dialogue on whether there is merit in formulating a framework for the operations and supervision of these institutions. The ultimate objective is the promotion of financial sector efficiency and the mitigation of pruden-

1. See the chapter by David Marston and Aditya Narain, this volume.

tial concerns that may arise from the unique position of such institutions regarding their missions, governance, and access to market funding. As a starting point in this process, we propose ten basic tenets that are useful for formulating the supervision and governance practice for these institutions.

Why Supervise State-Owned Financial Institutions?

The rationale for requiring strong supervision of private commercial banks is rarely disputed. A sound private commercial banking system is typically vital to the maintenance of a country's payment system. By licensing commercial banks to accept deposits (including those of unsophisticated depositors), the government assumes both a political and potentially large fiscal liability. While non-bank state-owned financial institutions are typically not an important component of a country's payment system, their affiliation with the government usually results in a presumption that they are soundly managed and that their liabilities carry the full faith and credit of the government. Such liabilities may include deposits, guarantees, insurance, and debt issued by the institutions. As a result, in many countries these institutions typically represent both a fiscal liability and a reputation risk for the government.

Notwithstanding the potential liabilities posed by such institutions, even large ones often are not subject to formal supervision of the type typically applied to private commercial banks. In principle, many countries' state-owned commercial banks are supervised under the same rules that govern the supervision of private commercial banks. In practice, however, a bank supervisor's powers over state-owned commercial banks may be limited. Moreover, in many countries, the bank supervisor's job is further complicated when state-owned commercial banks are also engaged in policy-directed intermediation activities that, by their nature, may not be subject to banking sector oversight or associated prudential standards.

In addition to state-owned commercial banks, many member countries own nonbank financial institutions with policy-directed intermediation functions. Nonbank institutions often are operated under the supervision of a government ministry. The supervising ministry may also be the executive ministry that selects the institution's senior management and sets its interim policy goals. This governance arrangement may be inimical to fostering an effective supervisory culture.

In the case of commercial banks, whether publicly or privately owned, supervision is necessary to ensure the safety and soundness of the monetary system as well as to mitigate moral hazard and risk-taking incentives created by implicit and explicit depositor protection policies. While maintenance of payments systems, prudential standards, and banking system liquidity are key aspects of supervision, at a basic level the mission of a bank supervisor is to ensure that the banking system continues to operate as efficiently as possible, while protecting taxpayers from direct costs for the losses that may occur as a consequence of the normal course of business.

The prospect of bank runs, depositor protection, and payments system issues often are not associated with a failure in the operation of a nonbank state-owned financial institution. Nevertheless, at a basic level the rationale for independent supervision of these institutions is identical to the case for supervision of commercial banks. In both instances, the supervisor is empowered to take actions to minimize the likelihood of taxpayers' bearing any unexpected (unbudgeted) direct costs for the inevitable losses. At a high level of abstraction, but a reality nonetheless, the supervisor is responsible for protecting the sovereign's credit standing against risks that may arise from the financial sector.

When the benefits of supervision of nonbank state-owned financial institutions are evaluated, clearly costs must be weighed against benefits. The potential systemic cost of a private nonbank financial enterprise in distress may not be large. But the failure of a state-owned nonbank financial institution may pose reputation risks for the government. Moreover, there are many large institutions whose distress could have systemic implications for the national financial system. In these instances, the case for competent and comprehensive supervision may be strong. And the case can be strong even in the absence of systemic exposures. Depending on the size of an institution's market funding and off-balance-sheet activities, if governments are called upon to honor implicit or explicit government guarantees, the taxpayer costs of mismanagement can be substantial. By monitoring and making public information regarding undue risks, poor controls, excessive costs, and activities outside an institution's charter, an efficient supervisor creates strong incentives to promote efficient management.

In addition to limiting the potential liability of taxpayers, inappropriately managed state-owned financial institutions can also inhibit the development of private sector financial intermediaries. Given their preferred status as government-backed borrowers, these institutions have the capacity to easily fund themselves in the credit markets. The public perception of an implicit guarantee removes the market discipline that is imposed on private borrowers, and so it is important that state-owned institutions face limits on their ability to use market funding. Such limits may be set in the form of directed intermediation goals and criteria that specify when parties are eligible for subsidized financial services.

Without independent supervision and oversight, there may be no natural market forces that restrict an institution's intermediation activities. "Mission creep" can be detrimental to the development of private sector financial intermediaries, as many state-owned financial institutions lend on more favorable terms than their private counterparts. Strong supervision that ensures that the state-owned institutions' operations conform to their original mandate can help limit the unintended impact of these institutions on private financial sector opportunities. It is in this sense that the effective supervision of these institutions supports efficiency and development for the entire financial sector.

The importance of state-owned financial institutions in IMF member countries highlights the benefits that might be gained from developing a core set of guidelines for setting minimum supervision, regulation, and governance standards for such institutions. The following section begins this process by proposing ten principles for their effective supervision. These principles draw heavily from the Basel Core Principles for Effective Banking Supervision. They are a distilled and modified compilation of the twenty-five Core Principles of the Basel Committee on Banking Supervision.

The following ten principles could apply to all state-owned financial institutions, including commercial banks. Although state-owned commercial banks fall under the twenty-five Basel Core Principles, there is nothing in these ten principles that conflicts with the Basel Principles. They do, however, differ from the Basel Principles in some respects. In particular, they suggest public disclosure as a tool to overcome the practical limitations that arise when one is supervising a state-owned commercial bank. They also suggest the need for supervisory powers to evaluate and restrict policy-related intermediation activities to those explicitly enumerated in chartering legislation and fiscal budgets. In this sense, the Basel Core Principles' criteria are extended beyond safety and soundness to evaluating suitability and scale of policy operations.

The Proposed Ten Principles

The ten core principles for the effective supervision of state-owned financial institutions are outlined below.

Principle 1: Preconditions

The supervision of a state-owned financial institution would be stronger if certain government preconditions were in place: sustainable macroeconomic policies, a well-developed legal system, and a robust accounting profession. Because of its government affiliation, an institution may not be subjected to effective market discipline, nor does its supervisor have the typical array of resolution powers available to a bank supervisor. The supervisor should have the power to effect safety and soundness changes as well as to seek intervention by a higher authority should supervisory directions be ignored.

The lack of market discipline and the difficulties associated with ensuring compliance with supervisory mandates reinforce the importance of disclosure and financial transparency. The operations of an institution may be undermined or the viability of private market financial firms may be harmed if the state-owned financial institution is not limited to its mandate.

Principle 2: Permissible Activities

The authorizing law should define the permissible activities of a state-owned financial institution, including the institution's mission, its methods of funding, its methods of providing subsidies, its minimum prudential standards (or a grant of authority to a designated supervisory agency to set binding standards), specific standards under which the institution's operations are to be conducted (such as criteria to guide the provision of subsidized intermediation activities), and the criteria and agent responsible for evaluating the institute's performance in achieving its policy goals.

The authorizing legislation should include policies defining the government's responsibilities regarding the provision of capital as well as the policies governing the recognition of operating and capital expenses on government fiscal accounts. The authorization legislation should also specify the policies to be followed in accounting and auditing, including the procedures to be used to value and disclose off-balance-sheet positions and guarantees.

Principle 2 outlines mission-related issues, restrictions, and operational modalities to be considered when a state-owned financial institution is chartered. Because the institution's activities are not constrained by market discipline, they are susceptible to internal incentives and political pressures to expand the scale and scope of activities. As a consequence, authorizing legislation should include detailed restrictions on these institutions' scale and breadth of operations. The scope of authorized activities should be clearly linked to the institution's policy goals defined in the authorizing legislation. Approved methods for providing subsidies to the intended constituency should be articulated, along with the criteria that must be satisfied to qualify for a subsidy.

Authorizing legislation should provide a clear mission statement for the institution and establish a transparent governmental process for setting interim policy and performance goals for the institution. The legislation should specify an agent or agency to evaluate the institution's performance relative to its statement and the interim targets that have been specified. The agent should be required to report the findings publicly.

In the absence of any explicit statement and history to the contrary, the liabilities of these institutions are often presumed to carry a full faith and credit guarantee of the government. The authorizing legislation should specify the responsibilities of the government for providing the institution's initial capital as well as the government's responsibility and commitment to provide additional capital during the course of operations. It must be recognized that, even when the government pledges only limited capital support, investors may still assume that the institution's liabilities are fully guaranteed.

The public perception of an implicit guarantee is difficult to dislodge; an institution's authorizing legislation, therefore, should place limits on the institution's ability to borrow. Funding methods should be described in the authorizing legislation, and limits should be placed on the use of these market resources. Such limits should be set to accommodate the institution's policy goals and should be consistent with the fiscal resources provided in government accounts. Funding usage and existing limits should be reviewed periodically and revised under a fully transparent government process.

Authorizing legislation should establish the accounting policies of each institution, including the selection of an external auditor (government agency or private firm) and of the accounting standards that will apply. The legislation should also specify the methods by which the firm will value any off-balance-sheet positions and guarantees to which it is a counterparty and include a requirement that these values be publicly disclosed in its annual accounts.

Principle 3: Supervisory Objectives

An effective system of supervision would assign clear responsibilities and objectives for each agency involved in the supervision of a state-owned financial institution specified in the authorizing legislation. Each supervising agency should possess operational independence and resources commensurate with its appointed duties. A suitable legal framework would specify ongoing supervisory responsibilities and would include the legal powers to obtain information and address prudential compliance issues and other safety and soundness concerns. The supervisor should provide periodic public reports regarding its assessment of the institution's safety, soundness, and financial performance and issue special reports when appropriate. Adequate legal protections for the supervisor would be necessary. Arrangements for sharing information both with the public and between supervisors, as well as precautions for protecting the confidentiality of sensitive information, should be in place.

The supervisor should be empowered in a monitoring role to ensure that the supervised financial institutions are run efficiently while minimizing the risk to the taxpayers of any unexpected (unbudgeted) direct costs for the inevitable losses that may occur in the normal course of business operations.

The costs of independent supervision may be reduced through economies of scale if supervision of multiple organizations is combined into one entity. The move toward unified financial sector supervision makes it possible that some authorities may empower the independent financial sector supervisor with responsibility for the supervision of state-owned financial institutions. If this approach is adopted, it is important that the supervisor receive adequate additional funding and that the culture of prudential supervision be consistent with the culture used to supervise commercial banks.

While they would not necessarily be required to make a profit, the institutions should be run as pseudocommercial enterprises—required to maintain minimum regulatory capital and prudential standards and directed to maintain their overall annual expenses (including losses) within their allocated fiscal budgets. Supervisory expenses are properly considered a cost necessary to the efficient management of these institutions. Consequently, these costs should be reflected in the fiscal budget as an expense of the institution.

The supervisor should be empowered with the legal means to enforce prudential standards and seek corrective measures when necessary. These legal powers could be reinforced with public disclosure responsibilities. Public disclosure may be an important way to foster effective supervision of state-owned financial enterprises. Public disclosure of supervisory annual assessments could be considered, and the supervisor should have the power to make interim and special issue reports when appropriate. The transparency created by mandatory public disclosure creates a powerful incentive to maintain efficiency and encourage compliance.

Principle 4: The Supervisor's Role

The supervisor should have the right to set criteria and prohibit activities not consistent with minimum prudential standards or the stated goals and scope of activities permitted in the institution's chartering legislation. A lack of market discipline would make it relatively easy for an unsupervised state-owned financial institution to fund inappropriately risky operations outside of its expertise and potentially even outside the scope of its officially sanctioned activities.

The supervisor should have the responsibility of monitoring an institution's activities and of prohibiting new business that may compromise the institution's prudential standards. The supervisor should be required to evaluate the institution's activities according to the institution's mission statement and the specific lines of business its charter legislation empowers it to conduct. The supervisor should be required to formally raise objections and seek administrative injunctions against inadmissible activities should such activities be identified. These objections should be made public in annual reports or in a special interim report, as appropriate.

Principle 5: Capital Adequacy

The supervisor or an institution's authorizing legislation should define regulatory capital and set minimum capital adequacy requirements that reflect the risks that the institution undertakes. Because the institutions do not face market discipline from their creditors, minimum capital standards are an essential tool for enforcing a proper risk management culture. The institutions should be required to continuously satisfy minimum prudential capital standards. These capital standards could be set in the institution's chartering legislation, in the authorizing legislation for the institution's supervisor, or in regulations issued by an empowered supervisor. The prudential capital standards should reflect the risk profile of an institution's primary businesses and provide an adequate buffer against unscheduled needs for fiscal support.

Minimum prudential capital standards do not need to be constructed identically across these institutions. While the level of protection against losses should be comparable across institutions, minimum capital standards should be designed to reflect differences in the nature of the institution's liabilities. Minimum capital regulations should be designed to minimize any externalities that they may create for private sector financial institutions that interact with the state-owned financial institution, including limiting incentives for transactions that are driven solely by differences in regulatory capital treatment.

Principle 6: Evaluations

The supervisor should conduct independent evaluations of an institution's policies, practices, and procedures related to extensions of leases, credits, and financial guarantees; the making of investments; and the ongoing management of the loans, leases, investments, and guarantee portfolios. The supervisor should determine that an institution has in place internal controls adequate for the nature and scale of its business. These should include arrangements for delegating authority and responsibility; for separating the functions that involve committing its capital; for paying out its funds; for accounting for its assets, liabilities, and off-balance-sheet positions; for reconciling these processes; and for safeguarding its assets. The supervisor should ensure that there are appropriate independent internal or external audit and compliance functions to test adherence to these controls—as well as applicable laws.

State-owned financial institutions should have written policies and procedures that guide their operations in conducting approved financial intermediation activities. These include policies that qualify counterparties as to their credit quality and suitability for participation in an authorized government-sponsored financial intermediation program. These policies should be approved and monitored by senior management. The suitability of these policies should be periodically assessed by the independent supervisory agency against criteria specified in the law.

Formal policies and procedures should be in place for managing the portfolio of the institution's financial assets and off-balance-sheet commitments (policies and procedures similar to those recommended in the Basel Core Principles). Formal documentation and organizational plans should include clear lines of managerial responsibility for approval, review, and internal oversight. Activities and responsibilities should be separated internally to avoid managerial conflicts of interest and to maintain the efficacy of internal controls. Organization, procedures, and internal controls should be approved by senior management. The supervisor should assess the adequacy of organizational, managerial, and internal control procedures and communicate to management in a timely manner any safety and soundness issues identified. Significant issues, should they arise, should be discussed in the supervisor's annual report along with proposed remedies.

Institutions should have adequate internal audit processes and resources. Senior management should ensure that these processes and resources, and reporting lines of authority, are in place and respected. The supervisor should review these arrangements, assess their adequacy, and publicly disclose the findings and recommended modifications.

Principle 7: Transparency

The supervisor should ensure that the institution has established and adheres to adequate policies, practices, and procedures for valuing its financial assets, leases, and off-balance-sheet positions, including evaluating the adequacy of loss provisions and reserves. The supervisor should ensure that the institution maintains adequate records, drawn up in accordance with consistent accounting policies and practices, that enable the supervisor to obtain a true and fair view of the financial condition of the institution and the profitability of its business. The institution should publish on a regular basis audited financial statements that fairly reflect its condition.

This principle, consolidated from several Basel Principles, is primarily about ensuring that there is transparency regarding an institution's financial condition. The institution must be subject to accounting standards that ensure that the assets and liabilities of the institution and all off-balance-sheet commitments are valued appropriately. The supervisor must be satisfied that loss provisions represent the true diminution in carrying value of the institution's assets and off-balance-sheet positions. The institution not only should comply with these standards of accounting; it should also periodically disclose its financial condition by issuing audited financial statements. The auditor could be a private sector accounting agency, a government agency, or the supervisory agency specified in the authorizing legislation or related decrees.

The transparency principle is silent as to what accounting standard should apply, be it market value, historical cost, or some other standard or combination of standards. What the principle requires is that the standard be clearly articulated in legislation, regulations, and national accounting board decrees and that the supervisor be satisfied that these standards enable an assessment of the financial condition of the institution, given its business practices and activities. If the supervisor has issues with existing accounting standards, it should have the power to recommend to standard-setting bodies that the standards be modified.

An especially problematic situation may arise when state-owned commercial banks are also the agents of government-directed lending or subsidized financial intermediation. In this case—of the hybrid institution—the level of policy-directed lending may be indistinguishable from a commercially viable lending operation. If appropriate controls and reporting are not in place, the magnitude of an institution's policy-directed activities may not be subject to government budgetary discipline. Policy-directed intermediation often has a competing culture regarding lending practices and prudential standards. The interaction of weak market discipline, noncommercial lending practices, and weak or nonexistent prudential standards may allow excessive growth of directed intermediation. Long-term consequences may include large taxpayer liabilities if excessive growth of policy-directed activities weakens the prudential standing of the state-owned commercial bank.

To improve transparency and safeguard the prudential standing of the commercial banking operations of a hybrid institution, it may be appropriate to separate the financial accounts of its commercial operations from its policy-directed activities. The commercial activities should be fully subject to the Basel Principles, while policy-directed activities should be organized and supervised using the ten principles outlined here.

Principle 8: Risk Management

Principle 8 represents a consolidation of several Basel Principles that address various risk management and measurement processes.

The supervisor should ensure that the institution has in place a comprehensive risk management process (including appropriate senior management oversight) to identify, measure, monitor, and control all material risks, including risks associated with fraud and money laundering.

The institution should have measurement and control processes in place sufficient to keep its material risks within prudent limits. These processes should be adequate for the size and nature of the institutions' activities. They should be reviewed periodically and their adequacy assessed against current best practices, the institution's current business activities, and external market developments. These processes include senior management oversight and guidelines for requiring senior management approval before large or otherwise unusual risk exposures are undertaken.

This principle allows the supervisor to require the use of modern risk-modeling techniques for interest rate, credit, market, foreign exchange, and operational risk when the supervisor decides that business risk levels merit their use. The supervisor should review any risk-modeling technique that the institution employs, whether required or not, and assess its adequacy and discuss any shortcomings that merit attention. The supervisor should ensure that, when an institution uses models, it continuously monitors the model's accuracy, using appropriate techniques, and makes model validation results available to the supervisor.

The institution should have in place an appropriate risk management process for all of its material business risks. This includes policies regarding the exposure limits for business units, macrohedging and limit policies for overall risk control, and adequate processes and procedures that protect against money laundering and related activities. Processes should be in place to prevent the bank from inadvertently assisting a customer in perpetrating criminal or fraudulent activities. The supervisor would be responsible for ensuring compliance and for assessing the adequacy of these processes and risk controls. The supervisor should have the power to recommend changes when weaknesses are detected. The supervisor's annual report should disclose the results of its assessments and any material recommending changes.

Principle 9: Monitoring

An effective supervisory system should consist of both on-site and off-site supervision. Effective supervision requires a thorough understanding of an institution, including safety and soundness monitoring through a combination of on-site and off-site monitoring.

On-site monitoring activities should be conducted either by the supervisor's own staff or by external auditors. On-site monitoring should be adequate to provide independent verification that governance procedures (including risk management and internal control systems) are adequate and to validate the accuracy of information provided by the institution. Off-site work should monitor the financial condition of the institution using prudential reports, statistical returns, and other appropriate information. The mix of on-site and off-site monitoring is likely to be specific to the country and to the nature of the supervised institution. The mix should, however, enable the supervisor to check for compliance with prudential regulations and other legal requirements.

Principle 10: Corrective Action

The supervisor should be able to bring about timely corrective action when an institution fails to meet prudential requirements (such as minimum capital adequacy standards) or when there are regulatory violations. The supervisor should, at a minimum, produce a publicly available annual report that discusses any safety and soundness supervisory measures that it recommended to a supervised institution and the actions that were taken in response to its recommendations.

The supervisor should have the legal authority to take appropriate remedial actions when an institution fails to meet prudential requirements or violates regulations. If management ignores supervisory recommendations, the supervisor should be able to appeal to a higher authority within the government. In some instances, it may be appropriate to provide the supervisor with authority to take public legal actions to secure court-ordered remedies. The range of possible actions includes, inter alia, restricting the current activities of the institution, restricting or suspending dividend payments, barring certain individuals from management, and replacing or restricting the powers of managers or directors. The supervisor should ensure that remedial actions are taken in a timely manner and should not unduly delay in recommending appropriate corrective actions.

The legal powers of the supervisor and his or her ability to use the judicial system may be restricted in some systems. As a consequence, the supervisor should have the legal authority to make its concerns and recommendations public. Indeed, it has an obligation to make its opinions public.

Best-Practice Issues for State-Owned Commercial Banks

The ten core principles proposed above are designed to apply to all state-owned financial institutions, including commercial banks. The Basel Core Principles are intended to apply to all supervised banking institutions in a country regardless of ownership and so apply to state-owned commercial banks.[2] The two sets of core principles are complementary in the case of these banks. The ten core principles include additional dimensions and criteria intended to strengthen the Basel Core Principles when applied to state-owned commercial banks engaged in policy lending.

Banking sector regulations often may appear uniform, but in practice they may compromise the powers of the supervisor of state-owned commercial banks in certain respects. Specific powers related to licensing, fitness and propriety, lending practices, acquisitions, and effecting changes in operations capital and management may be curtailed by complications introduced by state ownership. State-owned banks are often granted their operating licenses in special legislation. Often, such licenses may not be able to be suspended by a banking supervisor.

The personnel of state-owned banks may be employees of the government, and the senior managers of state-owned banks are often selected by ministries without a requirement for supervisory approval or "fit-and-proper" certification. State-owned banks may be required to administer government-directed lending programs and make loans under credit-granting policies that would not be suitable for underwriting commercial loans. Banking supervisors may be powerless to effect changes in these government-directed intermediation policies even if they affect the safety and soundness of the consolidated institution.

In some instances, state-owned banks have been used to acquire other financial institutions that were in danger of failing. Such acquisitions often occur without satisfying the Basel Core Principles' requirement that supervisors approve (or fail to object to) the acquisition.

Differences in the rigor of prudential standards among banks may create distortions in banking sector credit flows that create economic imbalances, undermine financial sector stability, and inhibit the development of private sector intermediaries. When prudential standards are lowered for state-owned banks, financial market distortions may arise because the funding of state-owned banks is not limited by market discipline.

Depositors often view deposits in these banks as implicitly guaranteed by the government and thereby fail to charge a risk premium when placing deposits or purchasing their debts. In addition to funding market distortions, the inability to enforce a common prudential standard on state-owned institutions may erode a

---

2. The Basel Committee on Banking Supervision's *Basel Core Principles for Effective Banking Supervision* (Basel, 1997) states that "supervisors should apply their supervisory methods in the same manner to government-owned commercial banks as they do to all other commercial banks."

supervisor's authority to enforce the national standards on private commercial banks as well. Political fairness issues may compromise a supervisor's ability to impose rigorous standards on private commercial banks. Funding-cost subsidies may allow state-owned banks to use this advantage to subsidize lending rates and gain market share. In the process of expanding, state-owned banks may erode lending margins below fair competitive levels, thereby reducing the profitability of private commercial banks and making it more difficult for them to maintain capital adequacy. For these and other reasons, the authors of the Basel Core Principles were against allowing prudential standards to differ between private and state-owned commercial banks.

The ten core principles described here stress public disclosure as a tool to overcome the practical limitations in supervising a state-owned commercial bank. They recognize differences in capital regimes and also stress the need for supervisory powers to evaluate and restrict policy-related intermediation activities to those explicitly enumerated in chartering legislation and fiscal budgets. In these areas, the Basel criteria are extended to include suitability of capital, business activities, and scale of policy operations. Aside from these prescriptions, the ten principles do not conflict with the Basel Principles.

Conclusions

The IMF survey documents the importance of state-owned institutions in the financial sectors of many IMF member countries. It is important to recognize and accommodate the fact that state-owned financial institutions will likely remain a durable feature of many member countries' financial sectors. Proper supervision and governance of these institutions is necessary to promote fiscal and financial sector integrity and to prevent unintended misallocation of resources.

This chapter is intended to begin a dialogue on the merits of developing a framework to promote proper supervision and governance of these institutions, using the ten principles defined here. No doubt these principles will evolve as they are modified to reflect informed opinions and as they are augmented to address oversights. As a next step in the process, it would be beneficial if interested supervisory agencies were to meet for an exchange of views on supervision and governance standards for state-owned financial institutions. We fully anticipate that the IMF will play an active role in organizing and participating in this congress.

PART V

Preparing for Privatization

ISHRAT HUSAIN

11

Lessons from Pakistan

PAKISTAN'S FINANCIAL SECTOR privatization, which began in the early 1990s and continues today, offers valuable lessons for policymakers in other emerging economies. Pakistan successfully reduced state ownership in the banking sector from 92 percent of assets in 1990 to 18.6 percent in 2004. The government also pushed through a number of very tough policies dealing with overstaffing, overbranching, and nonperforming loans and managed to attract top managers from international banks to bring an infusion of new skills to the sector. This chapter lays out the hurdles Pakistan faced and the measures taken to privatize the banking system.

Nationalization of Pakistan's Financial Sector

In 1974, when the world was being swept by socialism, the Pakistani government decided that the best way to achieve economic development and equitable growth was to nationalize everything: industries, banks, insurance companies, educational institutions, and so forth. Policymakers embraced socialization because they perceived that there was a strong concentration of wealth. But nationalization resulted in a huge economic setback for Pakistan, compared to growth levels under its previous, market-driven, policies. In 1969, for example, exports were higher than the combined exports of Indonesia, Thailand, Philippines, and Malaysia; these were drastically reduced by the nationalization efforts of the 1970s.

Table 11-1. *Preprivatization Structure of the Banking Sector, Pakistan, 1990*

Type of bank	Number	Assets		Deposits		Equity	
		Amount (billions of rupees)	Share (percent)	Amount (billions of rupees)	Share (percent)	Amount (billions of rupees)	Share (percent)
State owned	7	392.3	92.2	329.7	93.0	14.9	85.6
Private	. . .	. . .	. . .	. . .	. . .	. . .	. . .
Foreign	17	33.4	7.8	24.9	7.0	2.5	14.4
Total	24	425.7	100.0	354.6	100.0	17.4	100.0

Source: State Bank of Pakistan, "Financial Sector Assessment, 1990–2000."

By the 1980s the banking sector was dominated by public institutions. The government exerted direct monetary control, controlled credit, directed credit, and determined pricing for financial institutions. Most of the borrowing was done by the government for fiscal deficit financing or meeting the losses of public sector corporations. The relationship between government and the financial sector was incestuous, which led to financial repression, financial sector inefficiency, crowding out of the private sector, and deterioration of asset quality. Further, the central bank could not effectively play any role in the growth of financial institutions or in cleaning up the mess because the Pakistan Banking Council had clipped its wings: The central bank was now directly controlled by the government of Pakistan.

By 1990, 92 percent of the assets, 93 percent of deposits, and 86 percent of the equity in Pakistan's financial sector was in the hands of state-owned financial institutions (table 11-1). There were no private sector banks (except some foreign banks, which played a marginal role because of the restrictions and directed credit controls in place). Pakistan's banks were characterized by high intermediation costs, overstaffing, overbranching, a huge portfolio of nonperforming loans, poor customer service, undercapitalization, and a poorly managed and very narrow product range. The banks' primary business was to serve government organizations, subsidize the fiscal deficit, serve a few large corporations, and engage in trade financing. There was no lending to small- and medium-size enterprises, to the housing sector, or to the agricultural sector, which create most of the growth and employment in Pakistan. Most important, the financial system suffered from political interference in lending decisions and also in the appointment of managers.

Rationale for Financial Sector Privatization

In the early 1990s the government introduced policies to liberalize the economy. At the same time, the World Bank was reporting on financial sector weaknesses in Pakistan and urging liberalization. Pakistan welcomed the Bank's advice and accepted the suggested reform package.

At first the government focused on lowering the fiscal deficit, state-owned enterprises representing the greatest burden. These enterprises' efficiency levels were low, and their production seemed unresponsive to market demand. They were producing goods and services that nobody wanted, and the cost of their continuing losses was being borne completely by the government.

To stem the losses and begin the privatization process, the government established the Privatization Commission in 1991. Its mission was to foster competition and to ensure greater capital investment, competitiveness, and modernization, thereby enhancing employment, improving the quality of products and services to consumers, and reducing the fiscal burden on the state.

The government also aimed to broaden the base of equity capital by divesting the shares of public enterprises through stock exchanges. It was hoped that, as the government's burden lessened, public resources for physical and social infrastructure would be released. These are the reasons that every government since 1991 proceeded with the privatization of public enterprises, including public sector banks.

Pakistan's Approach to Privatization

The Policy of 1998 laid the framework for privatization in the financial sector. Four methods of privatization were described in the law: total disinvestment through competitive bidding, partial disinvestment with management control, partial disinvestment without management control, and the sale and lease of assets and property. The law also required total transparency in the process, because it would be critical to win the support of the political officials as well as the general public, and there could be no hint of insider manipulation. The identification of transactions is also described by the law: A financial adviser is hired through a competitive bidding process and is responsible for the exercise of due diligence.

A number of regulatory and sectoral reforms have facilitated privatization transactions. There are two standard processes, one for the valuation of property and one for prebidding and bidding. Postbidding matters also are sorted out through a well-defined procedure.

In the case of banks, many hurdles had to be passed before they could privatize. The banks certainly were in no condition to be privatized as they were. The first challenge was legal empowerment. The Bank Nationalization Act had created a lot of obstacles to the sale of assets, so disposing of these assets first required amending the act.

Second, banks were burdened with excess staff. No private sector investor interested in profit maximization under a competitive environment would be prepared to accept an overstaffed bank. Nor would an investor be able to get rid of the excess labor, because of the political difficulties the new owner would face. So it was the government's challenge to get rid of the excess labor: It cut almost one-third of the labor force in the three top banks.

A third problem was the unprofitable branches of state banks; almost one-third of the branches (1,646) were closed.

Fourth, the state banks had accumulated losses for over twenty years, which the government had to recapitalize through equity injections in order to make the banks attractive to buyers. To deal with the large stock of nonperforming loans, the Corporate and Industrial Restructuring Corporation, an asset management company, was created in 2000. The CIRC bought some of the nonperforming loans at a discount and auctioned them to third parties. Nonperforming loans worth Rs 47 billion (at that time close to $800 million) were transferred to the CIRC for disposal. Then tax refund bonds were issued.[1]

A fifth problem was the human capital at the state banks. Many in the management teams were political appointees of the government party, lacking professionalism and incapable of running these institutions. Similarly, the boards of directors consisted of government representatives and, as such, not only lacked financial expertise but also were indifferent to the banks' need for both oversight and policymaking. The boards of directors were disbanded and many of the management teams were replaced. Fortunately, Pakistan has a pool of highly skilled international bankers at Citibank, ABN-Amro, and Bank of America. These international managers were brought in and induced to take over the management of the three big state banks. It was also important to attract private sector specialists in chartered accountancy, business, economics, and law who could make significant contributions to the leadership and oversight of the banks. With new boards of directors in place, the quality of the oversight did improve.

1. These measures were undertaken during the Musharraf period at a time when there was no elected government in Pakistan. Although these were tough decisions for the president and his cabinet to make, they would have been harder to make by an elected representative government because of the pressure not to close branches, cut jobs, transfer nonperforming loans, or create tax refund bonds.

Transparency was the sixth challenge. To further improve the transparency of the bank privatizations, a new law was promulgated in 2000, with more stringent information disclosure rules.

Finally—seventh—the repayment ethic among borrowers from state banks was terribly weak. Many borrowers had defaulted on their loans years before; some were enterprises that had ceased operation, but the banks continued to accumulate interest on the books. To encourage loan payments and to promote efficient loan write-offs, the government created an incentive scheme whereby, if loan defaulters could pay the principal amount with a certain percentage of the accumulated interest, the rest of the loan value would be written off.

Role of the State Bank of Pakistan

Fortunately, when the privatization effort got under way in 1997, the government of Pakistan decided to disband the Pakistan Banking Council and provided autonomy and powers to the State Bank of Pakistan as the single supervisor and regulator. The SBP got involved in the sale of state banks because, from the regulatory point of view, it wanted to make sure that the banks would end up in the right hands and not create any subsequent problems for the regulator. The SBP handled the analytic and diagnostic work and participated in the design, monitoring, and implementation of the bank restructuring plan, including reduction of excess labor, removal of incompetent management, reconstitution of boards of directors, injection of capital, and closure of branches.

The World Bank provided financial assistance for a massive voluntary employee separation scheme. Through these efforts, the SBP further reduced the number of state bank employees to levels acceptable to private sector buyers.

The SBP also created fit-and-proper criteria for the appointment of chief executives and boards of directors at state banks. These criteria have become part of the corporate code, so there are no longer subjective, and politically influenced, assessments of managers. If during supervision or inspection the SBP finds a deviation from these criteria, it is empowered to take action. The deviation is exposed rather than permitted.

The SBP also provided important inputs in the documentation for privatization: statements of qualifications, agreements of sale, share transfers, and so forth. Before 2000 every transaction carried out by the Privatization Commission ended up in a court of law because laws were not clear and documentation was ambiguous. The SBP was determined not to expose itself or the banks to litigation risk, which could abort the privatization process.

In addition, the SBP played a key role in the screening and evaluation of strategic investors. According to the fit-and-proper criteria, any investor buying more than 5 percent of the shares in a bank had to be cleared by the central bank. The SBP also handled issues raised by potential investors during the prebidding process. Finally, the SBP took part in the evaluation of bids.

Bank Privatizations, 1991–2004

Since the privatization program began, six large state banks have been privatized: Muslim Commercial Bank, the third largest bank; Allied Bank Limited, the fifth largest bank; Bankers Equity, which was disbanded after privatization because of its fraudulent activities; Bank AlFalah Limited, the former BCCI; United Bank, the third largest bank; and Habib Bank, the largest bank. The National Bank of Pakistan, which is the remaining bank in the public sector, is moving out of state hands; 23.2 percent of its shares have been divested through initial public offerings and the stock market.

Pakistan has now sold off seven state-owned banks, worth Rs 40.9 billion, or $710 million. (Between 1991 and June 2002, four banks were sold, with assets of Rs 5.6 billion; from July 2002 to June 2003, another two banks were sold, with assets of Rs 12.9 billion; between July 2003 and January 2004, another bank, with assets of Rs 22.4, was sold.) Table 11-2 provides a picture of Pakistan's banking sector in 2004. The share of assets held by state-owned banks has been reduced from 92 percent in 1990 to 19 percent. So more than 80 percent of banking assets, deposits, and equity is now in the private sector—probably a rare circumstance among developing countries.

Pakistan's financial sector and economy has benefited greatly from bank privatizations. Competition in the banking sector has intensified so much that the average lending rate has come down from 21 percent to 5 percent. Intermediation costs have come down so significantly that individuals, the prime borrowers, can get loans at a 3–4 percent interest rate. Since inflation is also 3–4 percent, the bank loan interest rate actually equals zero.

Pakistan's experience shows that privatization can be beneficial to the banking sector and to the economy, but it must be handled carefully, and many tough steps need to be taken along the way. Some of the key lessons that have emerged from Pakistan's experience are as follows:

—The legal framework is critical: Central bank independence, the ability to dispose of state-bank assets, and fit-and-proper criteria are a few of the essential legal underpinnings for a successful privatization program.

Table 11-2. *Postprivatization Structure of the Banking Sector, Pakistan, March 2004*

Type of bank	Number	Assets		Deposits		Equity	
		Amount (billions of rupees)	Share (percent)	Amount (billions of rupees)	Share (percent)	Amount (billions of rupees)	Share (percent)
State owned[a]	4	518.8	18.6	379.3	20.1	22.5	17.2
Private	20	1,840.3	66.0	1,292.3	68.5	92.8	70.9
Foreign	13	278.4	10.0	198.0	10.5	26.7	20.4
Specialized[b]	3	149.8	5.4	16.1	0.9	−11.1	−8.5
Total	40	2,787.3	100.0	1,885.7	100.0	130.9	100.0

Source: State Bank of Pakistan, Banking Supervision Department.

a. Three small new banks were set up in the public sector during the 1990s. These included the First Women Bank, set up to provide credit to women entrepreneurs; and two provincial banks: the Bank of Punjab and the Bank of Khyber.

b. These include Zarai Tarqiati Bank Ltd., Industrial Development Bank of Pakistan, and Punjab Provincial Co-operative Bank Limited.

—The government must take tough measures to eliminate excess staff and branches before attempting to sell unprofitable state banks; to accomplish this, political pressure must be overcome.

—International expertise should be welcomed and actively sought; international bank managers and professional specialists will prove an asset to the privatized banks.

—Governments need to deal swiftly and decisively with nonperforming loans and to reverse the weak repayment ethic among borrowers from state banks. This works best when fitted into a broad privatization program for state-owned enterprises and when the repayment ethic is addressed along with government efforts to deepen capital markets as alternative sources of financing for large enterprises.

It is useful to analyze the privatization effects of two representative banks: Muslim Commercial Bank and Allied Bank Limited.

Muslim Commercial Bank was sold to strategic investors, who purchased shares in three successive rounds. In 1991 investors purchased 26 percent of its shares at Rs 56 a share. In February 1992 investors purchased a further 25 percent of its shares. More shares were purchased in 2001. By 2002 Muslim Commercial Bank was fully privatized, and there is no longer any government holding.

The assets, deposits, and advances of Muslim Commercial Bank all show improvement over their performance when the bank was state owned. The bank's

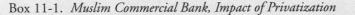

Box 11-1. *Muslim Commercial Bank, Impact of Privatization*

—Assets as a percentage of total assets of nationalized banks grew from 18 percent in 1994 to over 28 percent in 2003.

—Deposits as a percentage of total deposits of nationalized banks grew from 18 percent in 1994 to 27 percent in 2003.

—Advances as a percentage of total advances of nationalized banks grew from 18 percent in 1990 to 27 percent in 2003.

—Nonperforming loans as a percentage of total loans varied between a low of 11 percent in 1997 to a high of 19 percent in 1993.

net nonperforming loan ratio is close to 2 percent. (In the system overall the net nonperforming loan ratio is 5.5 percent.) In addition, returns on assets grew from almost zero to 0.8 percent. The bank therefore appears to be in a much healthier condition now than under state ownership (see box 11-1).

Allied Bank Limited was the second bank to privatize. On September 9, 1991, the government sold 26 percent of the bank's shares to the bank employees' group, the Allied Management Group, at Rs 70 a share. On August 23, 1993, the government sold another 25 percent of the shares to the same group and at the same share price, resulting in the transfer of majority ownership from the government of Pakistan to the bank's employees.

By 1999 one of the major defaulters of Allied Bank Limited had purchased 35–40 percent of the bank's shares from employees. De facto, the bank's defaulter had become its manager! This was obviously a moral hazard and a potential regulatory problem, so in July 1999 the SBP imposed a restriction on the transfer of shares from employees to nonemployees except with the SBP's prior approval. Unfortunately, the damage had already been done, and the SBP found that the chairman and managers were working against the interest of Allied Bank Limited and its depositors. On August 3, 2001, the SBP removed the chairman and the three directors on the board of Allied Bank Limited and replaced the whole board.

As a result of this scandal, the Privatization Commission directed the SBP not to privatize Allied Bank Limited but to merge it with existing financial institutions. By February 2004 six parties had prequalified. But the defaulters, who were affected by this decision, went to a court of law and challenged the merger. The SBP and Allied Bank Limited appealed a high court order to the supreme court. The bank has now been sold to a private investor through an open bidding process.

Box 11-2. *Allied Bank Limited of Pakistan, Impact of Privatization*

—Assets as a percentage of total assets of nationalized banks grew from 10 percent in 1995 to 12 percent by 2002.

—Deposits as a percentage of total deposits of nationalized banks grew from 10 percent in 1995 to 14 percent in 2003.

—Advances as a percentage of total advances of nationalized banks peaked at 16 percent in 1999 but declined to 11 percent in 2003.

—Nonperforming loans as a percentage of total loans jumped from 16 percent in 1993 to 44 percent in 2003.

The impact of privatization of Allied Bank Limited is shown in box 11-2. Assets and deposits, though somewhat higher, have changed very little. Advances have actually gone down, and nonperforming loans have risen to more than 40 percent of the total loan portfolio. Return on assets declined from near zero to −5 percent. Once the SBP removed the board of directors, bank performance started improving. Allied Bank Limited was not transferred to a specific investor but rather to employees, an approach that proved to be even worse than public sector ownership. The 2004 sale to a private sector financial institution through competitive bidding has once again helped reconstitute the bank's capital, raising capital adequacy ratio to 25 percent.

Clearly, the two bank privatization experiences demonstrate that it is critically important that a government privatize state-owned financial institutions in the right way. Otherwise, it will make the situation worse than it was before. And those opposed to privatization will use a particular failure or scandal to try to abort or defeat the whole privatization effort.

LOUIS KASEKENDE # 12

Lessons from Uganda

THE PRIVATIZATION OF the Uganda Commercial Bank (UCB) occurred during a period of comprehensive reforms aimed at introducing market-based mechanisms for resource allocation and price determination, moving away from controls of the 1960s and 1970s. The government recognized early in the process that the reforms were unlikely to achieve their objectives if the banking system remained insolvent and inefficient. This was also likely to undermine the use of open-market operations by the central bank in the context of a market-based monetary policy framework, something the government welcomed in order to ease the burden placed on fiscal policy in the pursuit of macroeconomic stability.

The UCB not only stood in the way of successful financial sector reforms but also posed the greatest threat to government's commitment to achieving sustainable macroeconomic stability and economic growth. Thus while the bank fully recognizes the potential fiscal benefits, the major objectives underlying the privatization of UCB were twofold: First, to improve the effectiveness of monetary policy in contributing to macroeconomic stability; and second, to foster financial sector efficiency in resource intermediation in support of sustainable long-term growth. This chapter discusses the policy issues that the government and the monetary authorities had to grapple with during the privatization process and outlines the lessons learned.

Background

Consistent with the practice of many African governments after gaining political independence in the 1960s, the government of Uganda established a number of financial institutions with the aim of jump-starting economic growth and job creation.

In line with these objectives, public sector banks were mandated to operate branches in all areas of the country with a view to enhancing rural savings and fostering development. As a result, an extensive branch network was developed, which revolutionized the rural payments system and facilitated income transfers. However, rural branches were used mostly for deposit mobilization, while the bulk of lending went to urban customers. At the microeconomic level, therefore, the rural sector was serviced by loss-making branches, whereas the urban branches generally made money. As a result of these social functions, public sector banks combined profitable and nonprofitable business undertakings in a manner that did not necessarily protect the banks' capital position. Thus by the time government was considering the first privatization of UCB, public ownership of financial institutions was as follows:

—Uganda Commercial Bank (UCB): 100 percent

—Foreign banks (five): 49 percent

—Development banks (two): 100 percent

—Post Office Savings Bank (POSB): 100 percent

—National Social Security Fund (NSSF): 100 percent

Besides these institutions, the government also controlled a very large cooperative bank, largely through monitoring the bank's financial performance, appointing and dismissing management, and deciding on loan beneficiaries. This was rather unusual, as cooperatives were legally owned by their members.

This kind of political interference in bank operations was more entrenched in the case of UCB. With 85 percent of all banking branches in the country, 230 branches at one time, UCB accounted for 41 percent of all bank liabilities, half of which were held by small depositors in the rural sector. Almost all government banking transactions were conducted through the bank.

The government was not just the largest borrower but it also influenced credit allocation, mostly for political purposes. The result of these factors, combined with rampant inefficiencies in operating an extensive branch network, was that 56 percent of UCB's assets were nonperforming and increasing by the day.

General Policy Considerations

The policy choices facing government were in four categories: First, there were issues related to the timing of the privatization; second was the question of who should own the bank, taking into account the interests of the people; the third group of issues involved the available sale options; and fourth was the legal framework for the privatization.

The timing of the privatization depended on several factors, the most important being whether sufficient political support could be sustained throughout the process. The sheer size of UCB complicated the policy debate within government. There was serious concern that privatizing UCB could reflect badly on the government; people would view the action in terms of failure not only to manage state resources but also to recognize the debilitating effect such action would have on the banking system and on the lives of people in rural areas. In order to gain public support, therefore, the way forward was either to assure the general public that government would continue to safeguard their interests or to continue rural banking services through the creation of a rural bank to be owned by the people themselves. The latter option obviously required postponing privatization for several months or even years. The second concern related to the credibility of the regulatory and supervisory framework in order to maintain confidence in the banking system and thus mitigating any systemic risks that could culminate in a run on banks.

The background to the credibility question was that government had proceeded in 1993 to amend laws governing the central bank—Bank of Uganda (BoU)—and the banking business in general. Among other things, the new law empowered the central bank to take action in the event of a bank's becoming insolvent. But as the financial condition of UCB deteriorated, BoU failed to implement the letter of the law—largely because of government ownership and the political risks of closing down a bank that catered to nearly 70 percent of the country. There was a real possibility that such a move would have led to loss of confidence in the banking system. BoU was probably more concerned about this than the loss of its own credibility. Nonetheless, the central bank's inaction gave rise to a public debate about the effectiveness of the supervisory authority as well as the condition of the remaining publicly owned banks. Moreover, it was obvious that government had not accorded BoU the necessary political support to carry out its proper functions. In the circumstances, BoU needed some time to reestablish its credibility as bank regulator and supervisor.

Macroeconomic considerations, with the battle against inflation yet to be won, further complicated the timing of the privatization. Also heightening the political stakes was the fact that the existing banking law provided for only minimal compensation to depositors in the event of a bank liquidation. In the circumstances, the government recognized that a failed privatization or a liquidation of UCB would have placed a heavy financial burden on already constrained budgetary resources, particularly as the deposit insurance had not been fully capitalized.

Against the backdrop of these concerns, government had to review its position on foreign ownership of such a big bank. Experience from other countries had shown that foreign banks concentrated on investing in risk-free money market instruments or tended to support foreign companies at the expense of local enterprises. Therefore, government had to consider how best to convince the general public about the long-term benefits of foreign ownership. Fortunately, Uganda's experience with the Africanization of businesses under the Idi Amin regime had been a total disaster. Thus the debate was not as intense as it would have been otherwise. However, the issue is important and was raised in political circles, and it probably explains the slow pace of privatizations in some countries.

Other ownership structures were also considered. The possibility of putting together a group of local buyers as an alternative to a strategic partner was explored, but there were serious concerns about conflict of interest associated with insider lending. Public ownership through a public trust or selling on the stock exchange was considered; however, there were concerns about the ability of a large number of small shareholders to ensure high standards of corporate governance. There could be an argument for a small public trust to ensure that the general public has a chance to acquire shares over time. At the same time, privatizations through stock exchanges have not been good in Africa.

A number of sale options were reviewed. The first option was selling the bank on an "as is" basis or through asset stripping with the possibility of writing off residual assets. Calls for maximizing revenues from privatization necessitated consideration of restructuring the bank before the sale. In this respect, government discussed what to do with the nonperforming assets and overstaffing problems. It considered the option of asset-liability matching to come up with a financially viable entity that could be privatized for a much higher value. But the most contentious issue was reaching consensus on the criteria for selecting a strategic investor. Should anyone with the purchase money be allowed to buy the bank? Or should some sort of due diligence be conducted?

With regard to the legal framework, government had the option of utilizing the law establishing the Privatization Commission or that governing BoU. The two laws provided different due processes in the privatization of a state-owned bank, although both needed to revert to the Company Law with respect to change of ownership. More important, the central bank law provided a much broader scope in dealing with market and financial risks in the course of privatization or liquidation.

Policy Decisions

The financial condition of UCB was so bad that government simply did not have the luxury to delay the privatization pending sufficient political consensus. That also meant the choice of a legal framework was going to be dictated by expediency. Similarly, selling the bank to a reputable strategic investor was considered the most effective way to deliver rural banking services on a sustainable basis. However, in the short run, options provided for subsidies to key branches and the possibility of spinning off a rural bank fell away. Government realized that the macroeconomic situation at the time, while not totally ideal, could only get worse unless the looming banking crisis were forestalled. Government could also not afford to experiment with other innovative ways of privatizing the bank.

In the circumstances, therefore, the government of Uganda decided to proceed cautiously, with a view to assuaging public fears, and to avoid interfering with the payments system. Toward this end, government decided to still hold majority shareholding in UCB and to sell the balance (49 percent) to a foreign strategic partner in accordance with the law governing privatizations. To facilitate the transaction, government decided in 1995 to establish a Nonperforming Asset Recovery Trust (NPART), to which it transferred the bad-debt book of UCB. It downsized the bank in terms of staffing levels and selling off noncore assets. A substantial investment was also made in upgrading computer hardware and operating systems. In addition, government recapitalized the bank.

Results

Investor interest in UCB was very subdued up until 1997, when the Privatization Unit carried out due diligence and recommended sale of government shares to the only available foreign strategic investor. Shortly thereafter, the investor assigned the shares to another investor without consent of the government as majority shareholder. This created an immediate problem, as the regulatory authorities could not clearly distinguish between shareholders and management of the bank. This absence of clear corporate governance resulted in huge losses, with 64 percent of assets in nonperforming status. BoU was therefore forced to intervene in the management and ownership of the bank.

Following the official takeover, it was decided to reprivatize UCB, with BoU in charge of the process. BoU decided to announce the terms and conditions of the second-round privatization, which included plans to resolve immediate financial problems of UCB. Investors were invited to indicate their interest and preferred option. They were informed that while desirous to maintain at least 20 percent ownership, the government was prepared to consider selling 100 percent shareholding of the bank, with five possible options:

—On an "as is" basis

—Without noncore assets

—Stripped of all loss-making branches

—With the key branches necessary to maintain a sound payment system and a minimum rural branch network (with a further option of a negotiated government subsidy for two years)

—A combination of these options.

Based on the results of a market test, it was decided to improve the bank's financial structure before entering into negotiations with interested investors. The first step involved recapitalization, to bring the bank's capital to solvency status. This was followed by management reorganization, staff retrenchments, sale of noncore assets, and new investment in the bank's computer hardware and operating systems. The fiscal costs of this "beautification" exercise were substantial to say the least.

The selected strategic investor in the second-round privatization discounted heavily the investment in information technology, preferring to install a different corporate banking system. This new operating system necessitated further staff retrenchments.

On balance, therefore, the social costs of the two privatizations went beyond government's imagination. To make matters worse, the performance of NPART was equally disappointing. Out of nearly $65 million, the trust managed to collect only $15 million after two to three years of operations. Much of the collected amount went into administrative and legal costs.

Lessons

A number of lessons can be drawn from Uganda's experience with the two privatizations of the same bank.

The first privatization demonstrated that

—The policy decision to maintain majority shareholding in UCB completely undermined the attainment of privatization objectives.

—While BoU was consulted, reliance on the privatization law might have contributed to the perverse outcome.

—A more comprehensive market survey of viable sale options was needed before taking the process forward.

—A thorough due diligence of the investor's market reputation—and not just capital strength—would have helped to avoid perverse investor selection.

—It is important to reach an understanding of the investor's future intentions to strengthen capital and management of a bank.

The second phase of the privatization showed that

—The long-term stability of the monetary and payments systems should take precedence over the revenue considerations of privatizations.

—The "beautification" of a bank prior to privatization may be unduly costly, with little long-term benefit.

—The political aspects of privatization should not be allowed to dictate the final outcome.

Conclusion

Uganda's experience with the privatization of UCB points to the inherent difficulties of trying to privatize a bank that is insolvent but too large to be closed down. In such a case, a number of prior steps to mitigate systemic risks and ensure financial sector soundness need to be taken in a phased and deliberate manner. In this regard, the monetary authorities should be fully involved throughout the privatization of a bank.

PART VI

Achieving
Privatization

GEORGE R. G. CLARKE
ROBERT CULL
MARY SHIRLEY

13

Empirical Studies

STATE OWNERSHIP OF large parts of the banking system is relatively rare in developed countries but widespread in less developed countries (table 13-1). In 1999 governments held controlling shares in banks representing more than 30 percent of banking sector assets in 25 percent of the seventy-eight less developed countries for which we have information, compared to only two (10 percent) of the twenty developed countries for which we have data.

The importance of state-owned banks in these developing countries contrasts worryingly with research findings that state ownership has pernicious effects in general and for banks in particular. A large literature on privatization, summarized in the appendix to this chapter, suggests that privatized firms generally outperform state-owned enterprises, especially in competitive sectors. Much of the literature does not deal with banks, however. A recent set of cross-country studies of bank privatization, summarized below, allows us to contrast the theoretical claims made for state ownership in the financial sector with the—negative—empirical findings. Yet although many low-income countries have begun to reduce their high levels of state involvement in banking, some have resisted, and the levels of state ownership remain high for some of the countries in table 13-1, while others are renationalizing. There is considerable regional variation in state ownership of banks and in privatization, which we also examine below.

To understand the reluctance to privatize and the pressure to renationalize, we need to understand how bank privatization has progressed in individual countries

Table 13-1. *Share of Banking Sector Assets in Majority State-Controlled Banks,
by Country, 1999 and 2003*

Country	1999	2003	Change	Country	1999	2003	Change
Albania	61.4	54.0	–7.4	Egypt	66.6	64.7	–1.9
Algeria	n.a.	95.8	. . .	El Salvador	7.0	4.2	2.8
Argentina	30.0	31.9	1.9	Estonia	0.0	0.0	0.0
Armenia	2.5	0.0	–2.5	Fiji	n.a.	1.1	. . .
Aruba	0.0	0.0	0.0	Finland	21.9	0.0	–21.9
Australia	0.0	0.0	0.0	Gambia	0.0	n.a.	. . .
Austria	4.1	0.0	–4.1	Georgia	0.0	n.a.	. . .
Bahrain	3.7	0.0	–3.7	Germany	42.0	42.2	0.2
Bangladesh	69.9	n.a.	. . .	Ghana	37.9	12.1	–25.8
Belarus	67.3	74.0	6.7	Gibraltar	0.0	0.0	0.0
Belgium	n.a.	0.0	. . .	Greece	13.0	22.8	9.8
Belize	n.a.	0.0	. . .	Guatemala	7.7	3.0	–4.6
Bhutan	60.0	70.0	10.0	Guernsey	0.0	0.0	0.0
Bolivia	0.0	0.0	0.0	Guinea	n.a.	0.0	. . .
Bosnia-				Guyana	19.0	15.0	–4.0
Herzegovina	30.0	n.a.	. . .	Honduras	1.1	0.0	–1.1
Botswana	2.4	0.0	–2.4	Hungary	3.0	9.0	6.0
Brazil	51.5	32.0	–19.5	India	80.0	75.3	–4.7
British Virgin				Indonesia	44.0	n.a.	. . .
Islands	0.0	1.7	1.7	Israel	n.a.	46.1	. . .
Bulgaria	17.6	17.6	0.0	Italy	17.0	10.0	–7.0
Burundi	63.0	n.a.	. . .	Jamaica	56.0	n.a.	. . .
Cambodia	16.0	7.6	–8.4	Japan	1.2	0.0	–1.2
Canada	0.0	0.0	0.0	Jordan	0.0	0.0	0.0
Cayman Islands	0.0	0.0	0.0	Kazakhstan	1.1	n.a.	. . .
Chile	11.7	13.3	1.6	Kenya	n.a.	1.1	. . .
Colombia	n.a.	18.3	. . .	Korea	29.7	40.0	10.3
Costa Rica	n.a.	62.3	. . .	Kuwait	0.0	0.0	0.0
Côte d'Ivoire	n.a.	10.0	. . .	Kyrgyzstan	14.4	16.0	1.6
Croatia	37.0	5.0	–32.0	Latvia	n.a.	3.2	. . .
Cyprus	3.3	4.2	0.9	Lebanon	0.0	2.0	2.0
Czech Republic	19.0	3.8	–15.2	Lesotho	51.0	n.a.	. . .
Denmark	0.0	0.0	0.0	Lithuania	44.0	12.2	–31.8

(continued)

Table 13-1. *Share of Banking Sector Assets in Majority State-Controlled Banks, by Country, 1999 and 2003 (Continued)*

Country	1999	2003	Change	Country	1999	2003	Change
Luxembourg	5.0	5.0	0.0	Singapore	0.0	0.0	0.0
Macau	1.4	0.8	−0.6	Slovakia	25.8	4.4	−21.4
Macedonia	0.5	1.3	0.8	Slovenia	39.6	12.2	−27.4
Malawi	48.9	n.a.	. . .	Solomon			
Malaysia	0.0	0.0	0.0	Islands	10.0	n.a.	. . .
Maldives	75.0	n.a.	. . .	South Africa	0.0	0.0	0.0
Malta	0.0	0.0	0.0	Spain	0.0	0.0	0.0
Mauritius	0.0	0.0	0.0	Sri Lanka	55.0	n.a.	. . .
Mexico	25.0	0.0	−25.0	St. Kitts–Nevis	20.5	n.a.	. . .
Moldova	7.1	13.6	6.6	Sweden	0.0	n.a.	. . .
Morocco	23.9	35.0	11.1	Switzerland	15.0	14.1	−0.9
Namibia	n.a.	0.0	. . .	Taiwan	43.0	n.a.	. . .
Nepal	20.0	n.a.	. . .	Tajikistan	7.4	n.a.	. . .
Netherlands	5.9	3.9	−2.0	Thailand	30.7	30.6	−0.1
New Zealand	0.0	0.0	0.0	Tonga	0.0	0.0	0.0
Nigeria	13.0	4.7	−8.4	Trinidad and			
Oman	0.0	0.0	0.0	Tobago	15.0	14.5	−0.5
Panama	11.6	11.8	0.2	Tunisia	n.a.	42.7	. . .
Peru	2.5	0.0	−2.5	Turkey	35.0	31.8	−3.2
Philippines	12.1	11.2	−0.9	Turkmenistan	97.1	96.0	−1.1
Poland	43.7	23.5	−20.2	Ukraine	n.a.	12.0	. . .
Portugal	20.8	22.8	2.0	United Arab			
Puerto Rico	0.0	0.7	0.7	Emirates	n.a.	35.0	. . .
Qatar	43.4	46.0	2.6	United			
Romania	70.0	41.8	−28.2	Kingdom	0.0	0.0	0.0
Russia	68.0	35.5	−32.5	United States	0.0	0.0	0.0
Rwanda	50.0	6.6	−43.4	Uruguay	n.a.	42.5	. . .
Samoa (Western)	0.0	n.a.	. . .	Vanuatu	n.a.	5.9	. . .
Saudi Arabia	0.0	21.4	21.4	Venezuela	4.9	6.9	2.0
Serbia and				Yugoslavia	90.0	n.a.	. . .
Montenegro	n.a.	3.8	. . .	Zambia	23.0	n.a.	. . .
Seychelles	n.a.	40.0	. . .	Zimbabwe	n.a.	6.1	. . .

n.a. Not available.

Figure 13-1. *Assets Held by State-Owned Banks, Case Studies, 1999*

Percent

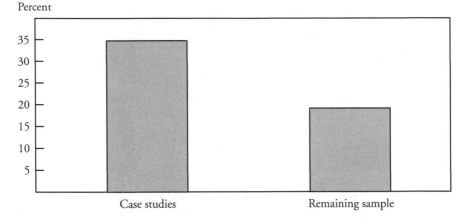

Source: Barth, Caprio, and Levine (2001a).

and how politics has influenced privatization decisions. Recently, bank privatization was studied in twelve countries—Argentina, Brazil, Bulgaria, Croatia, Czech Republic, Egypt, Hungary, Mexico, Nigeria, Pakistan, Poland, and Romania—chosen because they had high levels of state ownership at some point in the 1990s and undertook a relatively high number of privatizations. Some of the privatized banks were small, so the share of total banking sector assets privatized was also small in some cases. Nevertheless, the case study countries appear to have been well selected: They had a much higher share of state ownership in 1999 (35 percent) than the rest of the countries in a wider sample (19 percent) (figure 13-1), and they reduced the banking sector assets held by government-controlled banks more than the other countries (figure 13-2).

The case studies are based on detailed panel data sets for many—in some cases all—banks in each country. These data enable the authors to measure performance gains or losses much more precisely and to compare any improvements in privatized banks with trends for other banks in the country. The similarities we observe in these country cases, reinforced by recent cross-country studies, allow us to explore a set of hypotheses about the effects of privatization choices on bank performance. The detailed case studies also allow us to identify the political factors that determined the design and timing of privatization. In addition, another study examines the cross-country variation in bank privatization to test directly the political and economic factors that lead governments to relinquish control of banks, complementing the political insights drawn from the case studies. The

Figure 13-2. *Change in Assets Held by State-Owned Banks, Case Studies, 1999–2002*

Percent

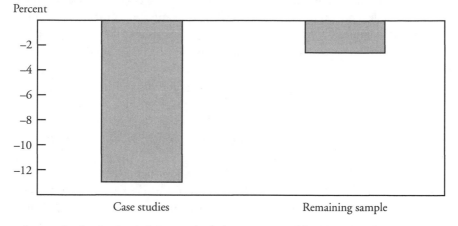

Source: Barth, Caprio, and Levine (2001a); see www.worldbank.org/research/projects/bank_regulation.htm.

analyses form the basis for a set of policy lessons, detailed in the final section of this chapter.

State-Owned Banking: Theoretical Promises, Empirical Observations, and Recent Trends

Why state-owned banks? Theory offers at least three explanations. First, state-owned banks might serve markets that are underserved because of imperfect information or incomplete contracts.[1] Second, private banks might tend to become too concentrated, limiting access to credit to fewer borrowers.[2] Third, private banks might take bigger risks, creating more crises.[3] Because of these potential effects, state ownership of banks offers the promise of greater financial development, leading to faster economic growth and higher productivity.

Recent empirical studies challenge these three assumptions. State-owned banks have been found to be associated with less financial development, slower growth, and lower productivity, and these effects were larger in countries with lower income and weaker protection of property rights.[4] State-owned banks have not

1. Greenwald and Stiglitz (1986).
2. Caprio and Honohan (2001).
3. Caprio and Honohan (2001).
4. Barth, Caprio, and Levine (2001a); La Porta, López-de-Silanes, and Shleifer (2002).

been found to increase access. One study finds no significant link between state ownership and access to credit in 3,000 firms in over thirty countries.[5] Nor is there evidence that state banks serve underserved markets: State banks in Argentina and Chile lend less to small- and medium-size enterprises than other banks.[6] Finally, state-owned banks are not associated with stability; they may instead be a cause of instability. One study finds that state-owned banks are associated with the same risk of systemic banking crisis as private banks, while others find that state-owned banks increase the risk of bank crisis and instability.[7] Given the negative effects of state ownership, one might expect governments to move quickly to phase out state ownership of banks. While some have done so in recent years, others have been reluctant, and the banking crises of the 1990s even led to renationalizations in some countries.

State ownership of banks varies widely by region (figure 13-3).[8] South Asian countries have the highest share of banking sector assets held by government-controlled banks, followed by the transition countries of Europe and Central Asia, Africa, Latin America and the Caribbean, East Asia and the Pacific, the Middle East and North Africa, and finally, the countries of the Organization for Economic Cooperation and Development (OECD). The sample of countries from South Asia is small, and their remarkably high level of state ownership in banking is largely driven by India, Bangladesh, and Pakistan. The lower levels of state ownership in the Europe and Central Asia region and the Latin America and Caribbean region are recent, the result of extensive bank privatization there in the early to mid-1990s.

Some of the averages mask substantial intraregional variation. For example, in the Middle East and North Africa region, Jordan has no government ownership, while Egypt's state-owned banks hold close to two-thirds of sector assets. The average is also misleadingly low because of its country response rate to the survey. The addition of data on four new countries in 2003 raised this region's average level of state ownership to 30 percent, falling between that of Africa and the Europe and Central Asia region.

The extent of privatization of state-owned banks has also varied widely (figure 13-4). From 1999 to 2002, Africa had the steepest reductions in state own-

5. Clarke, Cull, and Martinez Peria (2001).

6. Clarke and others (forthcoming).

7. Barth, Caprio, and Levine (2001a); Beck, Demirgüç-Kunt, and Levine (2003); Caprio and Martinez Peria (2002); La Porta, López-de-Silanes, and Shleifer (2002).

8. The figures in this chapter describe cross-country patterns in state ownership of banking and bank privatization, based on data from the Barth, Caprio, and Levine (2001a) survey of regulators and supervisors, conducted in 1999 and updated in 2003. One hundred thirty countries have state banking ownership data for either 1999 or 2002; eighty-one countries have reliable information for both years.

Figure 13-3. *Assets Held by State-Owned Banks, by Region, 1999*

Percent

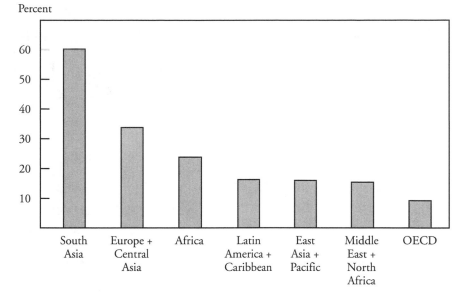

Source: Barth, Caprio, and Levine (2001a).

ership of banks, again ignoring the extensive privatization in the Europe and Central Asia region and the Latin America and Caribbean region earlier in the decade. East Asia and the OECD countries maintained their levels of state ownership, while the South Asia region and the Middle East and North Africa region showed slight increases in state ownership, partly because of state intervention in some troubled private sector banks. Per capita income has a strong and significant negative association with the extent of state ownership of banks (first documented by the World Bank).[9] Lower income countries have substantially more state ownership (figure 13-5), which probably accounts for their relatively greater share of recent privatization activity (figure 13-6).[10]

The Effect of Privatization on Bank Performance

The privatization literature (summarized in the appendix to this chapter) provides good reasons to assume that bank privatization will be beneficial under

9. Caprio and Honohan (2001).

10. The income classification of countries is the one used by the World Bank, which is based primarily, but not solely, on the level of per capita income.

Figure 13-4. *Change in Assets Held by State-Owned Banks, by Region,*
1999–2002

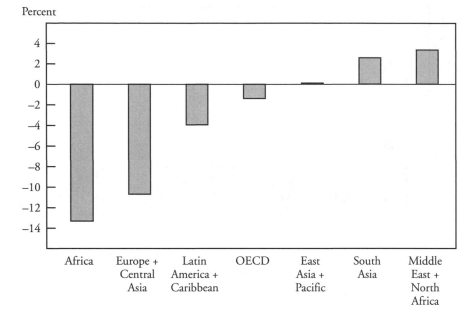

Percent

Source: Barth, Caprio, and Levine (2001a); see figure 13-2.

many circumstances, but few studies deal explicitly with privatization in the
financial sector. Cross-country studies show that state ownership of banks has
serious negative consequences, but once again the question is whether and under
what circumstances the privatization of banks will improve performance over
continued state ownership. To answer this question, we turn to a set of country
case studies and cross-country studies of bank privatization. Most of the case
studies were financed by the World Bank research department.[11]

11. Before the studies described here, there was relatively little published on bank privatization, and
most of it did not rigorously examine performance effects. Some studies describe the technical process of
privatization: Abarbanell and Bonin (1997) for Poland; Unal and Navarro (1999) for Mexico; Meyendorff
and Snyder (1997) for the transition countries. Others are narrative accounts that describe, in addition to
the technical aspects of privatization, the political and economic environment that precipitated the sale and
some postprivatization developments: Bonin and Wachtel (2000) for Czech Republic, Hungary, and
Poland; Baer and Nazmi (2000), Makler (2000), and Ness (2000) for Brazil; and Brock (2000) for Chile.
Rarer are studies that use financial ratios to assess the effects of privatization: Clarke and Cull (1999) for
Argentina; Otchere and Chan (2003) for Australia; and Verbrugge, Megginson, and Owens (2000) for

Figure 13-5. *Assets Held by State-Owned Banks, by per Capita Income, 1999*

Percent

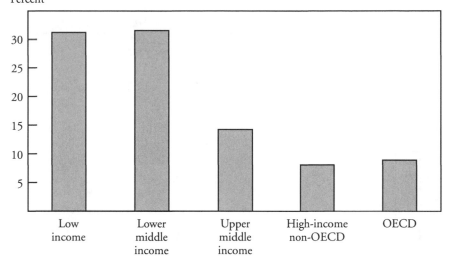

Source: Barth, Caprio, and Levine (2001a).

The studies allow us to explore five hypotheses. First, the general literature on privatization and the cross-country studies of financial privatization summarized earlier lead us to expect that privatization improves bank performance on average. (Bank performance is measured in these case studies by comparing improvements in the financial ratios of privatized banks against their past performance and—sometimes—against other banks in the same country.) Theory assumes that privatization improves performance in part by limiting harmful government intervention in state-owned enterprises. In nonfinancial enterprises, intervention is motivated by politicians' desire to employ or subsidize political constituents or by bureaucrats' desires to expand their power, prestige, and "perks." Harmful government intervention in banks is more likely motivated by a desire to loot or divert the deposits. Banks move money, which makes them a more versatile tool for politicians and makes intervention harder to detect than with nonfinancial firms.

share privatizations, mostly in developing countries. Comparing share price movements for the privatized banks with those of their competitors, Otchere and Chan (2003) assesses the competitive effects of privatization. Finally, aside from the studies on political economy described later, we know of no others that use econometric analysis to test what factors lead governments to privatize their banks.

Figure 13-6. *Changes in Assets Held by State-Owned Banks,*
by per Capita Income, 1999–2002

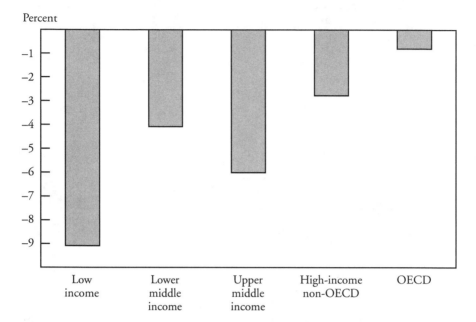

Source: Barth, Caprio, and Levine (2001a); see figure 13-2.

Second, given the temptation to loot, we further expect that retained government shares in banks will reduce the positive impact of privatization by allowing
continued government intervention in lending decisions. Government retention
of shares in nonfinancial entities has been shown to have negative effects in some
studies, and because of the special characteristics of banks as public trust entities
managing other people's money, we expect that retained shares in banks will have
unambiguously negative consequences.[12]

Third, we expect that privatization of banks through sale to foreigners will be
associated with performance gains. Foreign owners have been shown to improve
performance in privatized nonfinancial enterprises in a number of studies.[13]
These studies suggest that foreign buyers bring greater experience and techno-

12. D'Souza, Megginson and Nash (2001), in a sample of 118 firms, do find that performance improves more the less the government's retained shares.
13. Frydman and others (1997); Cull, Matesova, and Shirley (2002); D'Souza, Megginson, and Nash
(2001).

logical knowledge in firm takeovers and operation. It may also be that foreign buyers are associated with performance gains because governments willing to sell to foreigners are willing to forgo intervention in the privatized bank; indeed, foreign investors may participate in sales only when there is low risk of intervention.

Our fourth hypothesis is that sales to one or a few strategic buyers will be associated with greater performance improvements than sales to a larger number of owners through share-issue privatization. In studies of transitional economies performance improvements of privatized nonfinancial firms are attributed to the concentration of ownership in the hands of a strategic investor.[14] The authors of these studies argue that a single, concentrated owner is more motivated and capable of improving operations than many, widely dispersed owners. They draw on the large corporate governance literature, which argues that managers have every incentive to use their control to serve their own purposes at the expense of profitability and owner welfare or even to expropriate investments funds altogether.[15] Information asymmetries may allow managers significant leeway in negotiating contracts.[16] When ownership is dispersed, each individual owner has an incentive to free ride off the costly monitoring efforts of other owners, and a suboptimal level of monitoring will result.[17] Such agency problems are more likely in weak institutional settings, in which information is poor and safeguards of minority shareholders are weak to nonexistent.

Fifth, we expect that, as with nonfinancial firms, expanded competition will lead to performance improvements in banks, at least up to a point. Competition among banks can be harmful when banking supervision is weak or distorted and when there is deposit insurance.[18] When regulation and insurance encourage it, bankers facing strong competition might make risky loans to try to undercut their rivals. However, the emerging empirical evidence suggests strongly that denying entry to new applicants is not a solution to this problem. Cross-country regressions indicate that banking sector stability and development are adversely affected by such restrictions.[19]

14. Frydman, Hessel, and Rapaczynski (1998); Weiss and Nikitin (1998).

15. See Berle and Means (1932); Jensen and Meckling (1976); Fama and Jensen (1983); Vickers and Yarrow (1989); Stiglitz (1993); Shleifer and Vishny (1995); Lin, Cai, and Li (1998); Kane (1999); Dyck (2001); Shleifer and others (1999).

16. See Hart (1983); Willig (1985); Yarrow (1986); Vickers and Yarrow (1989); Stiglitz (1993); Kane (1999).

17. See Furubotn and Pejovich (1972); Yarrow (1986); Vickers and Yarrow (1989, 1991); Shleifer and Vishny (1995); Dyck (2001); Kane (1999).

18. See, for example, Akerlof and Romer (1993).

19. Barth, Caprio, and Levine (2001b); Beck, Demirgüç-Kunt, and Levine (2003).

Case studies do not permit us to distinguish the relative importance of these performance determinants, but they do highlight regularities important for policy. It is not obvious that cross-country analysis would be able to determine the contribution of these performance determinants in any case, since they seem to be highly correlated. Unwillingness to sell most or all government shares or to sell to foreigners may signal government's intention to intervene; it also is likely to reduce the interest of competent strategic investors to purchase shares. Share-issue privatizations may be the preferred sales tactic of governments wishing to loot, especially governments that are also retaining large ownership stakes. Governments that wish to divert bank funds also prefer to limit competition and may privatize in order to confer oligopolistic powers on political cronies. Below we consider evidence from the studies that supports or refutes each hypothesis.

First Hypothesis: Bank Performance Improves after Privatization

Variations across countries and across privatized banks within the same country notwithstanding, there is evidence of postprivatization improvements in performance (box 13-1).[20]

An advantage of case studies is their rich details, which permit us to analyze the role of environmental factors. For example, the second round of privatization in Nigeria suggests that privatization can have a positive effect on performance even in an inhospitable macroeconomic and regulatory environment—and even when the banks being sold are the weakest ones. Although bank-level data are probably somewhat less reliable for Nigeria than for the other countries, there is still significant and robust evidence that privatization in that country was associated with a significant increase in return on equity and a significant decrease in nonperforming loans. But Nigeria's second round also shows how an adverse macroeconomic and regulatory environment limits privatization's positive effects: Privatized banks improved in the first year but made no subsequent gains; the performance of nonprivatized banks was not improved by the stimulus from privatization; and banks that focused on retail lending performed worse than banks investing in government bonds and other nonlending activities.

The similarities and differences between Nigeria's privatized banks and those in Argentina's provinces are instructive. In both cases, profitability and loan port-

---

20. Although less widely studied, privatization of banks may also have positive effects on related industrial firms. Djankov, Jindra, and Klapper (forthcoming) find that the sale of banks to foreign buyers is associated with a premium in the value of related firms over the long run because of the value that investors put on the effects of foreign capital and expertise. Conversely, the Czech Republic's initial failure to privatize majority control over its banks may explain the poor performance of its larger privatized firms that were the banks' preferred customers: Cull, Matesova, and Shirley (2002).

folio quality improved. Unlike in Nigeria, however, Argentina's improvements were reflected only in measures of profit efficiency; cost efficiency did not improve.[21] In Nigeria, although the data were not sufficiently detailed to conduct efficiency analyses, the ratio of overhead costs to total assets increased at the time of privatization but slowly declined thereafter.

Argentina is also the only case study that documents the changes in lending strategy associated with these efficiency improvements. In particular, privatized banks reduced overall lending and lending in local currency, both signs of greater prudence. There were also substantial initial reductions in mortgage lending and agricultural lending. Subsequently, loans to both of these sectors increased, but their quality was much higher than in the preprivatization period, presumably because screening of potential borrowers had improved. The design of the privatization, including restrictions on firing and branch closing and perhaps changes in lending strategy, made it difficult for the provincial banks to lower their costs, but this was more than offset by increases in revenue.

Second Hypothesis: Government's Retained Shares Reduce Performance Gains

As we expected, privatization produced few or no performance benefits in cases in which the government retained majority control or even a sizable minority ownership of the bank (see box). The same conclusion emerges when we compare the first unsuccessful round of privatization in the Czech Republic and Poland (when the governments maintained relatively large ownership stakes) with the second (when the governments divested more or all of their shares). In Poland's initial round of privatization the Polish treasury retained a 30 percent stake, employees purchased up to 20 percent of the shares on preferential terms, and the remaining shares were divided between a large- and small-investor tranche.[22] The performance of privatized Polish banks improved somewhat, but the subsequent divestiture of all government shares led to unambiguous performance gains.

In the first round of sales, the Czech Republic distributed shares through a voucher privatization program; most voucher shares were invested in funds, many of the largest being created by banks.[23] These investment funds acquired large stakes in both financial and nonfinancial firms, which resulted in interlocking ownership between the banks and their clients. The state also retained substantial influence over the banks' operations. The banks' soft lending practices for many

---

21. Berger and others (forthcoming).
22. Bonin, Hasan, and Wachtel (forthcoming b).
23. Cull, Matesova, and Shirley (2002) provide details of the privatization program.

Box 13-1. *Bank Performance after Restructuring or Privatization,*
by Extent of Government Ownership

In cases in which the government kept *no shares* of stock in the banks

Five showed notable improvement

—Argentina (direct sale to strategic investor)
—Brazil, privatization (direct sale to strategic investor)
—Hungary (direct sale to strategic investor)
—Poland, second phase of privatization (direct sale to strategic investor)
—Australia (sale via share offering)

Two showed some improvement

—Mexico, second phase of privatization (direct sale to strategic investor)
—Nigeria, second phase of privatization (share offering, foreign ownership not permitted)

Only one showed no improvement

—Mexico, first phase of privatization (direct sale, foreign ownership not permitted or discouraged)

In cases in which the government kept a *minority share* of stock in the banks,

Four showed some improvement

—Bulgaria (direct sale to strategic investor)
—Croatia (sale via share offering and direct sale to strategic investors)

---

of their large clients eventually resulted in a deterioration of bank performance; government bailouts were required before foreign investors could be attracted to the second round of bank privatization.[24] Again, performance improved in the second round.

Comparing banks in Brazil and Nigeria leads to a similar conclusion: Government ownership is associated with weaker bank performance. Brazil fully divested some banks and retained complete control of others that it attempted to restructure. Performance improved in Brazil's fully privatized banks but remained unchanged in the state-owned restructured banks.[25] Nigeria maintained a minority interest in some of its privatized banks. There was some improvement in profitability and portfolio quality in those Nigerian banks in which the government

---

24. Bonin, Hasan, and Wachtel (forthcoming a); Cull, Matesova, and Shirley (2002).
25. Beck, Crivelli, and Summerhill (forthcoming).

—Czech Republic, second phase of privatization (direct sale to strategic investor)

—Pakistan (direct sale to strategic investor)

One showed no improvement

—Nigeria, first phase of privatization

In cases in which the government kept a *majority share* of stock in the banks

One showed some improvement

—Poland, first privatization (share offering, foreign ownership not permitted)

Four showed no improvement

—Brazil, restructuring

—Czech Republic, first privatization (share offering, foreign ownership not permitted)

—Romania (direct sale to strategic investor)[a]

—Egypt (sale via share offering)

Source: Beck, Demirgüç-Kunt, and Levine (2003); Bonin, Hasan, and Wachtel (forthcoming b); Omran (2003); Haber (forthcoming); Bonaccorsi di Patti and Hardy (forthcoming); Berger and others (forthcoming); Bauhmol-Weintraub and Nakane (forthcoming); Otchere (forthcoming).

a. It is perhaps too early to judge the case of Romania.

fully divested its shareholdings, but when the government retained minority shareholdings performance was substantially worse than in the fully privatized banks and nearly as bad as that of the state-controlled banks for some measures of profitability.[26] In short, the Nigerian case highlights the negative performance effects of even minority ownership by government, while the Brazilian case offers reasons to be skeptical of state restructuring of government-controlled banks.[27]

26. Beck, Cull, and Jerome (forthcoming). Berger and others (forthcoming) also illustrates the negative effects of state control of banks in Argentina. We do not reflect this in box 13-1, because our focus is not static government control of banks but rather changes in state control or organization. In the Brazilian case, there were presumably organizational changes associated with state restructuring. In Nigeria, minority ownership is interesting because the sate had already relinquished some control (if not full).

27. One might be worried that selection effects are driving these results. However, the preprivatization performance of those banks in which the government fully relinquished its shareholdings was worse than that of the restructured banks in Brazil and the minority government-owned banks in Nigeria.

Cross-country analysis also indicates that bank privatization outcomes are best when government fully divests its ownership stake. Using a sample of twenty-one share-issue privatizations in nine developing countries (Croatia, Egypt, Hungary, India, Jamaica, Kenya, Morocco, Philippines, Poland), one study finds that the shares of the privatized banks underperformed vis-à-vis the market and that there was no statistically significant improvement in their operating performance.[28] Empirical tests indicate that the proportion of ownership retained by the government significantly explains the underperformance of the privatized banks.

The Hungarian case is further evidence that fully privatized banks perform better than state-owned banks, but it also supports the more sobering conclusion of the broader privatization literature: Privatized enterprises often do not perform as well as de novo private firms. The de novo foreign banks in Hungary have long outperformed the state-owned banks sold to foreign buyers. The de novo banks are much smaller, to be sure, but their stronger performance provides further evidence that changing the performance of weak former public-sector banks is difficult, often more difficult than setting up a good performer from scratch.

Third Hypothesis: Privatizations to Strategic Investors Result in Concentrated Ownership and Increase Performance Gains, but Share-Issue Privatizations Result in Dispersed Ownership and Reduce Performance Gains

The cases in box 13-1 suggest that in weak institutional environments direct sales to concentrated owners are preferable to share-issue privatizations, which disperse shares widely. The only case in which a sale to a strategic investor is not associated with performance improvement is that of Romania, and this outcome largely results from its very late start in bank privatization. Over time, performance of Romania's newly privatized banks could improve. The most notable exception to this general pattern is the share-issue privatization of the Commonwealth Bank of Australia, which outperformed a control group of existing private banks on multiple financial ratios and share prices.[29] The Australian case suggests that share-issue privatization can successfully spur performance improvement but only in an environment in which the stock market and the associated market monitoring by informed investors are well developed.

By contrast, share-issue privatizations in less developed countries—the Czech Republic (first privatization), Egypt, Poland (first privatization), and Nigeria (second phase)—were less successful. Only in the Nigerian and Polish cases did the banks show even meager performance improvements. In Poland and the Czech

28. Otchere (forthcoming).
29. Otchere and Chan (2003).

Republic the first privatizations used share issues and the second, more successful, privatizations used direct sales.[30] Fully disentangling the cause of performance differences between the first and second privatizations in Poland and the Czech Republic is difficult. As we discuss above, the governments maintained sizable shareholdings in the first rounds; they also largely precluded foreign participation in the initial privatizations. Cross-country analysis also shows few or no performance gains in banks sold through share-issue privatization.[31]

The strong association between share-issue privatization and large government ownership could lead one to argue that this means of privatization is used to ensure that private owners do not fully control the bank. Considering the strong performance improvement after share-issue privatization in Australia, it also seems likely that such privatization is problematic in weak institutional environments, perhaps because it disperses ownership widely to poorly informed investors who have even less than the usual limited power of minority shareholders to resolve agency problems.

Fourth Hypothesis: Foreign Ownership Improves Performance

Foreign ownership is associated with greater performance improvement in our cases. In the Czech Republic, Mexico, and Poland the government prohibited or tacitly discouraged foreign ownership in the initial round of privatization. In none of these cases did the initial privatization produce performance benefits. Performance did improve after a subsequent round of privatization in which foreign ownership was permitted, although in all three cases the postprivatization time series is not long.

Again, we cannot ascribe poor performance solely to restrictions on foreign ownership. As we know, in Poland and the Czech Republic the governments also used share-issue privatization and retained relatively large shareholdings in these banks. One study does suggest strongly that foreign ownership produced a much more stable banking sector in these two countries, at least compared to their experiences just after their initial bank privatizations.[32] In addition, this study points to the positive postprivatization performance of banks in Hungary, the first country in the region to embrace foreign ownership.

Mexico's banks were initially privatized unsuccessfully to locals, renationalized after a systemic crisis, and then sold to outside investors, many of them foreign.[33]

30. Bonin, Hasan, and Wachtel (forthcoming b).
31. Otchere (forthcoming).
32. Bonin, Hasan, and Wachtel (forthcoming b).
33. Haber (forthcoming).

Mexico's first privatization is the only case in which the government relinquished all shareholding and sold to strategic investors yet produced no performance benefits. To the contrary, the banking system went into crisis shortly afterward. Foreign investors in the second Mexican privatization helped created a more stable and efficient banking sector, albeit one that has responded to the failure of Mexico's legal system to enforce banks' property rights by making few loans and charging high margins. The poor performance of Mexico's first privatization cannot be wholly attributed to the prohibition on foreign ownership; competition was also curbed. Mexico's initial privatization program may have been fundamentally flawed because of Mexico's political economy.[34]

Cross-country evidence from transitional economies also suggests that the type of buyer has an important effect on postprivatization performance. While privately owned banks proved unambiguously more efficient than government banks in a study of eleven transitional economies (Bulgaria, Czech Republic, Estonia, Croatia, Hungary, Latvia, Lithuania, Poland, Romania, Slovenia, Slovakia), foreign-owned banks outperformed other privately owned banks within their own countries.[35] Foreign bank entry has generated more competitive and efficient banking systems in these countries, and this is associated with higher gross domestic product growth as well. Not all foreign investors produce these benefits: Participation in bank ownership by international institutional investors such as the European Bank for Reconstruction and Development (EBRD) and the International Finance Corporation (IFC) is associated with higher returns on assets and more profits but not with greater cost efficiency than their counterparts, which may reflect the selection preference of these investors.

Fifth Hypothesis: Competition Improves Performance

The impact of competition on performance is ambiguous in the studies we are analyzing. In a study of Australia and another of nine countries, privatization announcements resulted in abnormally negative returns for rival banks, a sign of increased competition.[36] The cross-country results suggest that privatization has procompetitive effects even in instances in which the performance of the privatized banks was below market standards.

In the Australian case the procompetitive effects are not surprising, since the privatized bank was large and its performance improvements substantial. The announcement of the privatization in Australia had adverse effects on rivals' share prices, effects that were most pronounced after the announcement that the gov-

---

34. Haber (forthcoming).
35. Bonin, Hasan, and Wachtel (forthcoming a).
36. For Australia, see Otchere and Chan (2003); for the nine countries, see Otchere (forthcoming).

ernment would cede its entire shareholding in the bank. More surprising, rivals also exhibited negative abnormal returns in the cross-country analysis despite little evidence of performance improvement on the part of the privatized banks. These results may suggest that increased competition is not sufficient to improve the performance of banks with substantial government shareholdings or with widely dispersed or weak domestic owners. They may also support the financial literature that suggests that competition can be harmful if regulation and policy encourage risky behavior. Nevertheless, the experience of Mexico suggests that giving buyers an oligopoly has strongly negative effects and contributes to deterioration in bank performance—one of the few cases of a postprivatization decline. Competition may be a necessary but not a sufficient condition for performance gains in privatized banks.

Summary

The general conclusion that emerges from these results is that, when done correctly, bank privatization yields benefits in terms of profitability, portfolio quality, and operating efficiency. Given the multiple objectives faced by state-owned banks (for example, to extend credit to underserved market segments) and the inherently political nature of some their lending, these results might not be surprising. Indeed, political pressure makes it impossible for public banks to lend to underserved market segments at market interest rates that appear exorbitant.[37] The subsidies implicit in the rates that they do charge make it highly likely that even the best run public banks will eventually encounter difficulties in portfolio quality and, ultimately, profitability.

A relevant question, then, is how big are the costs associated with those subsidies? While the performance improvements implied by the coefficients from many of the econometric studies described above suggest that those costs could be large, the only attempt to directly estimate the fiscal costs of maintaining public ownership is for Argentina's provincial banks. Based on the loss rates uncovered in detailed preprivatization audits, one study finds that the cost of recapitalizing those banks was more than double the net costs associated with privatization (that is, the costs of removing nonperforming assets from the banks' balance sheets and recapitalizing the privatized entity, which were offset to a small extent by the prices paid by the private purchasers).[38] The estimated median saving for provinces that privatized were equal to about one-third of their total expenditures, which suggests that the gains associated with successful privatization are large.

37. See the chapter by James A. Hanson, this volume.
38. Clarke and Cull (1999).

Political Economy

The privatization literature summarized above documents how political incentives and institutions determine the design and outcomes of privatizations. For a sector often intimately connected with government finance, it comes as little surprise that political factors also played a decisive role in the nature and timing of the bank privatizations studied here—and in their eventual success or failure.

A World Bank study suggests that politicians usually privatize a firm when the political benefits of privatization (increased revenues for spending on constituents, elimination of a poorly performing state-owned enterprise that has become a political liability) outweigh the political costs (layoffs of constituents, price increases, an end to services or subsidies for favored groups).[39] The political economy of privatization is more complicated than this simple equation suggests, since the design is also affected by a country's political institutions—for example, electoral laws that determine politicians' time horizon and the strength of political parties, or constitutional provisions that determine the number of political actors who can veto the privatization policy, or the likelihood that the policy will be sustained through changes in leadership. Nevertheless, case studies of bank privatization do suggest certain regularities in the interplay between privatization and politics.

Detailed evidence on how political factors affect bank privatization comes from the hazard models estimated for Argentina.[40] The worst performing provincial banks in Argentina are more likely to be privatized than better performing provincial banks, something that was also true in Croatia and Nigeria.[41] Large, overstaffed banks in provinces with high levels of both unemployment and public sector employment are less likely to be privatized, which suggests that the strength of political opposition is also a key determinant of outcomes. Similar results were found for Brazil, whose government offered multiple privatization options, which varied in the extent to which state governments would relinquish control over their banks and the transformation process.[42] States would relinquish greater control when they were able to establish a development agency, which presumably would assume some of the mandate of the former state-owned bank and thus assuage political opposition. As in Argentina, fiscal concerns related to the quality of the bank also play a role in privatization outcomes. States that were

---

39. World Bank (1995).
40. Clarke and Cull (2002).
41. For Croatia, see Bonin, Hasan, and Wachtel (forthcoming a); for Nigeria, see Beck, Cull, and Jerome (forthcoming).
42. Beck, Crivelli, and Summerhill (forthcoming).

more dependent on federal transfers and whose banks were already under federal intervention relinquished greater control.[43] Those intervened banks tended to be among the most poorly performing banks in the system.

Despite the difficulties in assembling reliable cross-country data on the extent of privatization over a long time horizon, similar results were found for a sample of 101 countries over a twenty-year period.[44] In non-OECD countries, bank privatization is more likely the lower the quality of the nation's banking sector, the more fiscally conservative the government, and the more accountable the government. While not directly comparable to the results for Argentine provinces, one could argue that overstaffing and a high level of public employment are signs that a government is not responsible to the full electorate but only to a narrow set of favored constituents. There is also weak evidence that provinces with governors from the more fiscally conservative of Argentina's two major political parties (Partido Justicialista) were more likely to privatize than those with governors from the other major party (Unión Cívica Radical).

Political factors also affected the design of the privatization contract in Argentina: Provinces with high fiscal deficits were willing to accept layoffs and to guarantee a larger part of the privatized bank's portfolio in return for a higher price. Exogenous factors sometimes stimulated political reactions as well. In particular, the "tequila crisis" and the associated fiscal costs caused politicians to agree to protect fewer jobs and to retain a higher share of public banks' nonperforming assets in a residual entity.[45]

Since most banks effectively ceased operations during Argentina's latest crisis, it is not possible to test directly whether specific features in the privatization contract had adverse effects on bank performance, but there are suggestive similarities. For example, the privatized provincial banks improved profitability, profit efficiency, and portfolio quality, while showing no improvement in terms of cost efficiency or the ratio of operating costs to assets.[46] These results suggest that the contract provisions that protected workers and limited branch closures made it more difficult for the privatized banks to reduce their costs.

43. Clarke and Cull (forthcoming).
44. Boehmer, Nash, and Netter (forthcoming).
45. The "tequila crisis" of 1994–95 started in Mexico, when exchange rates and the banking system collapsed. The crisis then spread to other countries in Latin America. Because investors were concerned about the stability and sustainability of Argentina's currency board arrangement, Argentina was more seriously affected than other countries. As a result, Argentina "saw contractions of debt, outflows of capital, and rises in interest rates." See Calomiris (1999). Poorly performing banks, including the publicly owned provincial banks, lost substantial deposits as depositors withdrew funds. See Clarke and Cull (1999); Alston and Gallo (2002).
46. Berger and others (forthcoming).

Indirect evidence on the effects of timing, and in particular the costs of delay, comes from comparisons of transition countries. Early in the 1990s, Hungary moved decisively to privatize its banks and to permit greater de novo foreign entry. As noted, the strategy paid substantial dividends, providing the country with a strong, stable banking system long before its neighbors. However, speed in bank privatization is not sufficient to ensure success. The Czech government was quick to sell some of its ownership stakes in the four large banks that dominated the financial system, but as we have seen they also chose to retain a sizable and, in some cases, controlling, interest in these banks.[47] Performance improvements did not materialize, as the banks maintained their old links with their most influential former clients, who were often borrowing to channel funds into their private uses or to prop up unproductive firms. As noted above, it was not until a second round of bank privatization reduced the government's stake in the banks in the late 1990s that performance improved. In the Polish case, the authorities moved much more slowly than in the Czech Republic, but they avoided the near-crisis situation faced by the Czechs.

The Mexico case study shows most clearly the decisive effects that political factors can have on the success of bank privatization. Until 1997, Mexico's government was a one-party political system dominated by the PRI (Partido Revolucionario Institucional), with few constraints on the authority and discretion of the government. The lack of constraint had three important consequences: high expropriation risk, distortion of privatization policy to serve PRI's political needs, and weak mechanisms to enforce contractual rights. These three characteristics of Mexico's political economy led to fundamental flaws in the design of the privatization program.[48]

The risk of expropriation was real. PRI-controlled governments expropriated Mexico's banks twice in the twentieth century (in 1915–16 and in 1982) and also carried out de facto expropriations through drastic increases in the money supply or draconian regulation of interest rates. Potential buyers of privatized banks would not bid unless they were compensated for the risk of expropriation with the promise of high rates of return secured by protection from competition.

The second feature, the political distortion of privatization policy, became evident when President Carlos Salinas de Gortari (1988–94) decided to sell the nationalized banks and other state-owned enterprises. The government had strong political incentives to sell the banks for the highest price possible. Salinas faced a fiscal crisis fed by years of deficit spending and the Mexican government's

---

47. Bonin, Hasan, and Wachtel (forthcoming a); Cull, Matesova, and Shirley (2002).
48. Haber (forthcoming).

lack of administrative capacity to raise taxes effectively. At the same time, the future survival of the PRI required social spending programs to shore up political support in the face of rising political competition: Salinas's electoral victory had been won by the smallest margin in the history of the PRI.

Four features of the privatization program seem designed to maximize revenues from sales. First, the government did not break up Mexico's highly concentrated banking system but sold the banks as is, with 70 percent of assets controlled by four banks. Second, the banks were auctioned sequentially, which led to increased competition for banks in later rounds and pushed up the bid-to-book ratio in every round. Third, entry into the banking industry required permission of the secretary of the treasury, who could decline a charter for any reason, thereby raising the charter value of the privatized banks. Fourth, foreign banks were not allowed to bid, and the North American Free Trade Agreement (NAFTA) was structured so that only the smallest banks could be foreign owned. These four features of the privatization program signaled to bidders that they were buying the secure oligopoly they needed to compensate for the expropriation risk, contributing to much higher than expected prices for the banks. A less charitable interpretation is that the government was tacitly permitting the new owners to attract deposits that its owners could later divert to their own accounts through loans to insiders. On average, Mexico's banks sold for over 3.0 times their book value, compared to the 1.7–1.8 bid-to-book ratio typical in most less developed countries.

The new owners of the privatized banks proceeded to lend aggressively and to open new branches in order to quickly reap high returns. The total stock of lending doubled in real terms from 1990 to 1994. Many of these loans were poor choices, reflecting perhaps Mexico's lack of creditor information, while many others appear to have been loans to groups and individuals closely linked to bank owners. The proportion of nonperforming loans expanded rapidly, from 2 percent in 1990 to 9 percent in 1994 to 13 percent in 1995. Since Mexico's accounting standards grossly underestimated the size of nonperforming assets, the real numbers were probably much worse. At the same time, the banks were undercapitalized: The capital ratio was probably only 6.5 percent during this period, while operating costs stayed high, averaging about 7.5 percent per loan.

As the bad debt of the banks began to mount, the third characteristic of Mexico's political economy (the weakness of mechanisms to protect contractual rights) became important. Delays and obstructions in Mexico's legal system meant that banks could not repossess collateral on their bad loans. Relational loans to family and network members did not prove any easier to collect. In short, there were no checks on bad banking. Unlimited deposit insurance gave bankers little incentive to recreate the strong networks that bankers had once used to monitor each other's behavior. Instead, the prospect of a bailout motivated bankers to increase lending to family and friends, with the expectation of default.

Mexico's political economy had created a fragile banking system, poised for collapse. The devaluation in December 1994, which led the central bank to raise interest rates, exposed the unsustainable situation of the banks. As the banks faltered, the 100 percent deposit insurance system bailed out depositors, and the government took over insolvent banks. To recapitalize the banks, Mexico turned to foreign capital, removing all restrictions on foreign bank ownership in Mexico. The privatization to foreign banks in 1996 drove down operating costs (to 1.8 percent per loan), raised the rate of return on assets, and increased the capital-asset ratio to 11 percent. The government assumed all bad debts, and Mexico's banks now follow much more prudential policies. Since contracts are still difficult to enforce, banks make far fewer loans: Bank lending averages only 15 percent of Mexico's gross domestic product, compared to 150 percent in the United States, 200 percent in Japan, and 25 percent in Mexico in 1910.

The remaining case studies offer some indications of the importance of political-economic factors for bank privatization outcomes, although this is not the focus of those studies. For example, one study discusses the preponderance of former military officials and politicians who were—and are—owners of Nigerian banks.[49] It argues that the government's multiple exchange rate regime created arbitrage opportunities for financial institutions that had privileged access to foreign exchange, fostering a banking sector focused on rent seeking rather than on financial intermediation. These incentives continue to influence the behavior of the privatized banks. Another study describes the way the unstable macroeconomic situation made privatization infeasible in Bulgaria and Romania until the late 1990s.[50] By that time, the state banks had suffered such large losses that substantial recapitalization was necessary to make the banks attractive to investors, especially foreign investors.

Conclusions

The cases studies and the cross-country analyses strongly support the conclusion that privatization improves performance over continued state ownership, even the privatization of relatively poorly performing banks. However, several policies reduce the benefits:

49. Beck, Cull, and Jerome (forthcoming).
50. Bonin, Hasan, and Wachtel (forthcoming b).

—Continued state ownership, even of minority shares, harms the performance of privatized banks.

—In weak institutional environments, share offerings produce lower performance gains than direct sales to concentrated strategic investors.

—Prohibiting foreigners from participating in privatizations reduces the gains from both direct sales and share-issue privatization.

—Competition alone will not secure performance improvements in privatized banks, but oligopolistic banking is likely to lead to highly negative consequences for the banks and the financial system.

There is evidence that foreign banks tend to be highly prudent, which may result in little lending in weak regulatory environments. This is an appropriate response to the true hazards, but it may be politically problematic. The best solution to lack of credit in risky environments is not to sell banks to risk-loving owners, or to increase government subsidies or bailouts, or to extend World Bank loans for small borrowers, but rather to put in place safeguards against expropriation, protection of lenders' property rights, and creditor information. While some of these reforms may have to await a change in a country's political economy, others—such as creditor information—are amenable to short-term reform.

Privatization improves performance even in poor regulatory environments, as we have seen in Nigeria, although poor regulation reduces the gains. This suggests that it is better to privatize even with weak regulation rather than await reforms that may be a long time coming. Selling to foreigners may be especially important in a poor regulatory environment, since the regulation in their home country may curb their opportunism, as evidenced by their bias toward prudence. Foreign investors may also lobby more for regulatory improvements and legal reforms if they cannot take full advantage of regulatory or judicial lacunae. More research is needed to determine whether foreign-owned banks indeed behave less opportunistically and have a stronger preference for better regulation than domestically owned banks in weak regulatory environments.

The Mexico and Argentine cases also suggest some political economy lessons. Mexico's experience in particular illustrates that politicians who are motivated to maximize revenues design privatization programs that raise the risk of crisis, especially if prudential regulations are weak and there is deposit insurance. Seeking to maximize revenues from sales is shortsighted, since the cost may greatly outweigh the revenue gains in the medium term. Politicians with a short time horizon may not be disposed to heed this advice, but their preferences for revenues should not be encouraged by outside advisers, who are also sometimes focused on short-term public deficits rather than long-term efficiency gains. Making privatization politically palatable can be risky, as Argentina's provincial bank privatizations show.

The restrictions on bank closures and firings there appear to have reduced cost efficiency. In short, the less the political process dictates the specific features of the privatization transaction, the better.

Appendix: General Literature on Privatization

A large theoretical and empirical literature examines government ownership and privatization of state-owned enterprises.[51] Much of the rationale for government ownership in this literature comes from the theoretical view that government is composed of well-informed (even perfectly informed) agents, whose principal goal is to maximize social welfare. Under this assumption, government ownership reduces the cost of government intervention to correct market failures, including natural monopolies, and to reduce income inequality in addition to a host of other social goals.[52] Seen in this light, state ownership of banks could be justified as a way to raise capital for projects with high social returns but low private returns or as a way to provide finance to poorer borrowers that would be neglected by less well informed—or less-motivated—private bankers.

With the advent of public choice theory, this unrealistic assumption of a benevolent, all-knowing government was discredited. Public choice theory postulates that government actors may use state ownership to secure political office, accumulate power, or seek rents.[53] These actors may therefore have less reason to monitor enterprises than a profit-motivated private owner.[54] The theory further predicts that state actors are likely to act in self-interested ways in weak institutional settings, in which voters have little information and little capacity to require good performance: in other words, less developed countries.

Theories about why privatization might be beneficial to an economy are usually grounded in this public choice assumption that government consists of normal, fallible, and self-interested individuals. These theories fit with the empirical findings: that state-owned enterprises have been used in developing countries to finance politically motivated projects or to provide subsidized financing to favored groups; and that they open too many offices and hire too many employees.[55]

---

51. This literature is summarized in Shirley and Walsh (2003).
52. See Sappington and Stiglitz (1987); Millward and Parker (1983); Willner (1996).
53. Buchanan (1969); Niskanen (1971, 1975).
54. Alchian (1965).
55. See for example, Jones (1985); Donahue (1989); Kikeri, Nellis, and Shirley (1992); World Bank (1995).

We group the privatization literature around three main themes: competition, political intervention, and corporate governance.[56] The competition argument assumes that privatization improves the operation of the firm and allocation of resources if it expands competition. A private firm might face a more competitive market than the same firm under government ownership for several reasons.

First, self-interested politicians may use state-owned enterprises to pursue political goals, such as expanding the number of patronage jobs or providing subsidies to favored constituents.[57] Under these circumstances, state-owned enterprises cannot compete effectively with profit-maximizing firms and run deficits in competitive markets, deficits that have to be covered by subsidies from the government treasury or by government-guaranteed debt. Politicians and bureaucrats have a strong incentive to reduce the fiscal drain of such subsidies by giving state-owned enterprises monopolies, erecting barriers to entry or trade in the markets of state-owned enterprises, or preventing competition with state-owned enterprises in other ways, all with adverse effects on efficiency.[58]

Second, state-owned enterprises face less competition than private firms because a subsidized state-owned enterprise can undercut private rivals that have to make a profit to survive.[59] For example, a state-owned bank might have more branches, higher deposit rates, and lower lending rates than its rivals because its excess costs are covered by government subsidy. Instead of a competitive market improving its performance, the state-owned bank hampers market performance. There is supportive empirical evidence for the protection of such market power and subsidies.[60]

Even without changing market structure, privatization could improve efficiency if it hinders interventions by politicians or bureaucrats intent on using state-owned enterprises to further their political or personal goals. Political actors could also try to influence private firms to hire or subsidize their constituents, but this is harder to hide, and private owners have stronger incentives and capabilities than the managers of state-owned enterprises to oppose such interventions.[61] For example, the profit-oriented owners of a private bank, especially one that must answer to foreign owners, would be more strongly motivated to protect its

---

56. This paragraph draws on Shirley and Walsh (2003).
57. Shapiro and Willig (1990); Jones (1985); Vickers and Yarrow (1991).
58. Shleifer and Vishny (1994); Boycko, Shleifer, and Vishny (1996).
59. Sappington and Sidak (1999).
60. Jones (1985); Kikeri, Nellis, and Shirley (1992); World Bank (1995).
61. Shleifer and Vishny (1994); Galal (1991); Shirley and Nellis (1991); World Bank (1995).

prudential lending policies or cost-minimization rules from government intervention than would a state-owned bank. Privatization could also prevent the employees of state-owned banks and other interest groups from "capturing" the government body charged with monitoring the state enterprise or from bribing corrupt politicians to protect their interests.[62] Capture or corruption could also occur with private firms, but the assumption is that the direct ownership link, by making the government an employer as well as a regulator, increases the likelihood of capture and corruption. The argument that state-owned enterprises are more subject to intervention and will receive larger subsidies than private firms is substantiated by empirical observations.[63]

Third, corporate governance might be weaker in state-owned enterprises than in private firms because of agency problems. State-owned enterprises have multiple objectives and many principals who have no clear responsibility for monitoring.[64] Large private corporations can also have many small shareholders, information asymmetries between owners and managers, and problems defining goals and holding management accountable. Yet even private firms with highly diffuse ownership are better governed than state-owned enterprises. Since all citizens can be considered the owners of a state-owned enterprise, its ownership is more widely distributed than a private firm's ever could be, and since there is no way for any single owner to sell its shares, public owners monitor performance less than private owners do.[65] Without a market for ownership, information on firm performance is scarce and noncomparable.[66] Alternatively, government might be considered the sole, concentrated owner.[67] The government owner would then be free to pursue inefficient goals without the checking influence of small owners and without much motivation to monitor.[68] Another reason that state-owned banks might have poorer corporate governance is weak incentives for managers to perform efficiently: They do not face a market for their skills or a credible threat of losing their job for nonperformance, and bankruptcy, liquidation, and a hostile takeover are not credible threats for state-owned firms.[69]

62. Borcherding, Bush, and Spann (1977); Borcherding, Schneider, and Pommerehne (1982); Shleifer and Vishny (1994).

63. Shirley and Nellis (1991); World Bank (1995); Claessens and Peters (1997); Djankov (1999).

64. Alchian (1965).

65. Alchian (1965).

66. Vickers and Yarrow (1991); Lin, Cai, and Li (1998).

67. Yarrow (1986).

68. Vickers and Yarrow (1991); Boardman and Vining (1992).

69. Berglof and Roland (1998); Dewatripont and Maskin (1995); Schmidt (1996); Sheshinski and Lopez-Calva (2003); Vickers and Yarrow (1989, 1991).

Less competition, greater political intervention, and weaker corporate governance are strong theoretical arguments against state ownership, but it does not necessarily follow that privatization will cure these ills. The same government actors responsible for the poor performance of state-owned enterprises are responsible for the design and execution of the privatization program. Political objectives, poor information, and principal-agent problems can compromise the privatized firm in ways that keep it from performing as well as a de novo private enterprise.

Does this mean that a privatized firm will perform better, the same as, or worse than it would under state ownership? There are many critics of privatization on the grounds that privatized firms do not perfectly mimic private firms.[70] But this criticism is misguided if privatized firms still outperform state-owned firms. Some authors even argue that if the root cause of poor performance among state-owned enterprises is an institutional environment that hampers voters from holding politicians accountable, then private management will be as prone to error as the management of state-owned enterprises.[71] Others believe that underdeveloped capital markets, weak court systems, and inadequate procedures for bankruptcy or takeover will prevent privatized firms from performing efficiently, especially in developing countries in which these market and institutional failures are common.[72] Privatized firms in transitional economies will be less efficient if they are sold to their managers and workers, since this may prevent necessary restructuring and limit capital infusion.[73]

The empirical evidence suggests that, while privatized firms may not be identical to private firms, they are usually superior to state-owned enterprises.[74] The most important exceptions to this conclusion are the firms sold to incumbent managers and employees in the former Soviet Union, especially in Russia in 1992–93. When majority shareholdings are sold to outsiders, especially to foreigners, performance

70. See Stiglitz (1999a, 1999b); Cook and Kirkpatrick (1988, 1997); Caves (1990); Kay and Thompson (1986).

71. Stiglitz (1999a, 1999b).

72. Adam, Cavendish, and Mistry (1992); Caves (1990); Commander and Killick (1988); Cook and Kirkpatrick (1988, 1997); Stiglitz (1999a).

73. Earle, Estrin, and Leschenko (1995); Frydman, Hessel, and Rapaczynski (1998); Barberis and others (1996); Havrylyshyn and McGettigan (1999); Kane (1999); Dyck (2001); Claessens and Djankov (1999); Nellis (2000).

74. See the studies reviewed in Millward (1982); Millward and Parker (1983); Borcherding, Schneider, and Pommerehne (1982); Boardman and Vining (1989); D'Souza and Megginson (1999); Megginson and Netter (2002).

improves there as well.[75] Exceptions notwithstanding, the usual effect of privatization has been to improve efficiency.[76]

References

Abarbanell, Jeffrey S., and John P. Bonin. 1997. "Bank Privatization in Poland: The Case of Bank Slaski." *Journal of Comparative Economics* 25, no. 1: 31–61.

Adam, Christopher, William Cavendish, and Percy S. Mistry. 1992. *Adjusting Privatization: Case Studies.* London: James Currey.

Akerlof, George A., and Paul M. Romer. 1993. "Looting: The Economic Underworld of Bankruptcy for Profit." *BPEA,* no. 2: 1–60.

Alchian, Armen. 1965. "Some Economics of Property Rights." *Politico* 30, no. 4: 816–29.

Alston, Lee J., and Andrés Gallo. 2002. "The Political Economy of Bank Reform in Argentina under Convertibility." *Journal of Policy Reform* 5, no. 1: 1–16.

Baer, Werner, and Nader Nazmi. 2000. "Privatization and Restructuring of Banks in Brazil." *Quarterly Review of Economics and Finance* 40, no. 1: 3–24.

Barberis, Nicholas, and others. 1996. "How Does Privatization Work? Evidence from the Russian Shops." *Journal of Political Economy* 104, no. 4: 764–90.

Barth, James, Gerard Caprio Jr., and Ross Levine. 2001a. "Banking Systems around the Globe: Do Regulation and Ownership Affect Performance and Stability?" In *Prudential Supervision: What Works and What Doesn't,* edited by Frederic Mishkin, pp. 31–96. National Bureau of Economic Research Conference Report. University of Chicago Press.

———. 2001b. "Bank Regulation and Supervision: What Works Best?" Policy Research Working Paper 2725. Washington: World Bank.

Bauhmol-Weintraub, Daniela, and Marcio I. Nakane. Forthcoming. "Bank Privatization and Productivity: Evidence for Brazil." *Journal of Banking and Finance.*

Beck, Thorsten, Juan Miguel Crivelli, and William Summerhill. Forthcoming. "The Transformation of State Banks in Brazil." *Journal of Banking and Finance.*

Beck, Thorsten, Robert Cull, and Afeikhena T. Jerome. Forthcoming. "Bank Privatization and Performance: Empirical Evidence from Nigeria." *Journal of Banking and Finance.*

Beck, Thorsten, Asli Demirgüç-Kunt, and Ross Levine. 2003. "Bank Concentration and Crises." Paper presented at World Bank conference on bank concentration and competition, April 3-4, Washington.

Berger, Allen N., and others. Forthcoming. "Corporate Governance and Bank Performance: A Joint Analysis of the Static, Selection, and Dynamic Effects of Domestic, Foreign, and State Ownership." *Journal of Banking and Finance.*

Berglof, Erik, and Gerard Roland. 1998. "Soft Budget Constraints and Banking in Transition Economies." *Journal of Comparative Economics* 26, no. 1: pp. 18–40.

Berle, Adolf A., and Gardiner C. Means. 1932. *The Modern Corporation and Private Property.* New York: Macmillan.

Black, Bernard, Reinier Kraakman, and Anna Tarassova. 2000. "Russian Privatization and Corporate Governance: What Went Wrong?" *Stanford Law Review* 52, no. 6: 1751–808.

75. Bornstein (1994); Earle (1998); Earle and Estrin (1998); Black, Kraakman, and Tarassova (2000).
76. Megginson and Netter (2002).

Boardman, Anthony E., and Aidan R. Vining. 1989. "Ownership and Performance in Competitive Environments: A Comparison of the Performance of Private, Mixed, and State-Owned Enterprises." *Journal of Law and Economics* 32, no. 1: 1–33.

———. 1992. "Ownership versus Competition: Efficiency in Public Enterprise." *Public Choice* 73, no. 2: 205–39.

Boehmer, Ekkehart, Robert C. Nash, and Jeffry M. Netter. Forthcoming. "Bank Privatization in Developing and Developed Countries: Cross-Sectional Evidence on the Impact of Economic and Political Factors." *Journal of Banking and Finance.*

Bonaccorsi di Patti, Emilia, and Daniel Hardy. Forthcoming. "Bank Reform and Bank Efficiency in Pakistan." Paper presented at World Bank conference on bank privatization, November 20–21, Washington.

Bonin, John P., Iftekhar Hasan, and Paul Wachtel. Forthcoming a. "Bank Performance, Efficiency, and Ownership in Transition Economies." *Journal of Banking and Finance.*

———. Forthcoming b. "Bank Privatization and Performance: Evidence from Transition Countries." *Journal of Banking and Finance.*

Bonin, John, and Paul Wachtel. 2000. "Lessons from Bank Privatization in Central Europe." In *Bank Privatization: Conference Proceedings of a Policy Research Workshop,* edited by Harvey Rosenblum, pp. 35–51. Federal Reserve Bank of Dallas.

Borcherding, Thomas E., Winston C. Bush, and Robert M. Spann. 1977. "The Effects on Public Spending of the Divisibility of Public Outputs in Consumption, Bureaucratic Power, and the Size of the Tax-Sharing Group." In *Budgets and Bureaucrats: The Sources of Government Growth,* edited by Thomas E. Borcherding, pp. 211–28. Duke University Press.

Borcherding, Thomas E., Friedrich Schneider, and Werner Pommerehne. 1982. "Comparing the Efficiency of Private and Public Production." *Zeitschrift fur Nationalokonomie* 2 (Supplement): 127–56.

Bornstein, Morris. 1994. "Russia's Mass Privatization Program." *Communist Economies and Economic Transformation* 6, no. 4: 419–57.

Boycko, Maxim, Andrei Shleifer, and Robert Vishny. 1996. "A Theory of Privatization." *Economic Journal* 106, no. 435: 309–19.

Brock, Philip L. 2000. "Emerging from Crisis: Bank Privatization and Recapitalization in Chile." In *Bank Privatization: Conference Proceedings of a Policy Research Workshop,* edited by Harvey Rosenblum, pp. 97–118. Federal Reserve Bank of Dallas.

Buchanan, James M. 1969. *Cost and Choice: An Inquiry in Economic Theory.* Chicago: Markham.

Calomiris, Charles W. 1999. "Lessons from the Tequila Crisis for Successful Financial Liberalization." *Journal of Banking and Finance* 23, no. 10: 1457–61.

Caprio, Gerard, and Patrick Honohan. 2001. *Finance for Growth: Policy Choices in a Volatile World.* Oxford University Press.

Caprio, Gerard, and Maria Soledad Martinez Peria. 2002. "Avoiding Disaster: Policies to Reduce the Risk of Banking Crises." In *Monetary Policy and Exchange Rate Regimes: Options for the Middle East,* edited by Eliana Cardoso and Ahmed Galal, pp. 193–230. Cairo: Egyptian Center for Economic Studies.

Caves, Richard E. 1990. "Lessons from Privatization in Britain: State Enterprise Behavior, Public Choice, and Corporate Governance." In *Journal of Economic Behavior and Organization* 13, no. 2: 145–69.

Claessens, Stijn, and R. Kyle Peters Jr. 1997. "State Enterprise Performance and Soft Budget Constraints: The Case of Bulgaria." *Economics of Transition* 5, no. 2: 305–22.

Clarke, George R. G., and Robert Cull. 1999. "Why Privatize? The Case of Argentina's Public Provincial Banks." *World Development* 27, no. 5: 865–86.

———. 2002. "Political and Economic Determinants of the Likelihood of Privatizing Argentina Public Banks." *Journal of Law and Economics* 45, no. 1: 165–97.

———. Forthcoming. "Bank Privatization in Argentina: A Model of Political Constraints and Differential Outcomes." *Journal of Development Economics*.

Clarke, George R. G., Robert Cull, and Maria Soledad Martinez Peria. 2001. "Does Foreign Bank Penetration Reduce Access to Credit in Developing Counties? Evidence from Asking Borrowers." Policy Research Working Paper 2716. Washington: World Bank.

Clarke, George, and others. Forthcoming. "Bank Lending to Small Businesses in Latin America: Does Bank Origin Matter?" *Journal of Money, Credit, and Banking*.

Commander, Simon, and Tony Killick. 1988. "Privatization in Developing Countries: A Survey of the Issues." In *Privatization in Less Developed Countries,* edited by Paul Cook and Colin Kirkpatrick. New York: St. Martin's.

Cook, Paul, and Colin Kirkpatrick. 1988. *Privatization in Less Developed Countries.* New York: St. Martin's.

———. 1997. "Privatization and Public Enterprise Reform in Developing Countries: The World Bank's Bureaucrats in Business Report: Introduction and Overview." *Journal of International Development* 9, no. 6: 843–47.

Cull, Robert, Jana Matesova, and Mary Shirley. 2002. "Ownership Structure and the Temptation to Loot: Evidence from Privatized Firms in the Czech Republic." *Journal of Comparative Economics* 30: 1–24.

Dewatripont, M., and E. Maskin. 1995. "Credit and Efficiency in Centralized and Decentralized Economies." *Review of Economic Studies* 62, no. 4: 541–55.

Djankov, Simeon. 1999. "The Enterprise Isolation Program in Romania." *Journal of Comparative Economics* 27, no. 2: 281–93.

Djankov, Simeon, Jan Jindra, and Leora Klapper. Forthcoming. "Corporate Valuation and the Resolution of Bank Insolvency in East Asia." *Journal of Banking and Finance*.

Donahue, John D. 1989. *Privatization Decision: Public Ends and Private Means.* New York: Basic Books.

D'Souza, Juliet, and William L. Megginson. 1999. "The Financial and Operating Performance of Privatized Firms during the 1990s." *Journal of Finance* 54, no. 4: 1397–438.

D'Souza, Juliet, William L. Megginson, and Robert Nash. 2001. "Determinants of Performance Improvements in Privatized Firms: The Role of Restructuring and Corporate Governance." University of Oklahoma.

Dyck, Alexander. 2001. "Privatization and Corporate Governance: Principles, Evidence, and Future Challenges." *World Bank Research Observer* 16, no. 1: 59–84.

Earle, John. 1998. "Post-Privatization Ownership and Productivity in Russian Industrial Enterprises." Working Paper 127. Stockholm Institute of Transition Economics, Stockholm School of Economics.

Earle, John S., and Saul Estrin. 1998. "Privatization, Competition, and Budget Constraints: Disciplining Enterprises in Russia." Working Paper 128. Stockholm Institute of Transition Economics, Stockholm School of Economics.

Earle, John S., Saul Estrin, and Larisa L. Leschenko. 1995. "Are Russian Enterprises Restructuring?" University of London.

Fama, Eugene F., and Jensen, Michael C. 1983. "Separation of Ownership and Control." *Journal of Law and Economics* 26, no. 2: 301–25.

Frydman, Roman, Marek P. Hessel, and Andrzej Rapaczynski. 1998. *Why Ownership Matters. Politicization and Entrepreneurship in the Restructuring of Enterprises in Central Europe.* Research Report 98-14. C. V. Starr Center for Applied Economics, New York University.

Frydman, Roman, and others. 1997. "Private Ownership and Corporate Performance: Some Lessons from Transition Economies." Policy Research Working Paper 1830. Washington: World Bank.

Furubotn, Eirik, and Svetozar Pejovich. 1972. "Property Rights and Economic Theory: A Survey of Recent Literature." *Journal of Economic Literature* 10, no. 4: 1137–62.

Galal, Ahmed. 1991. *Public Enterprise Reform.* Discussion Paper 119. World Bank, Washington.

Greenwald, Bruce, and Joseph E. Stiglitz. 1986. "Externalities in Economies with Imperfect Information and Incomplete Markets." *Quarterly Journal of Economics* 101, no. 2: 229–64.

Haber, Stephen. Forthcoming. "Mexico's Experiments with Bank Privatization and Liberalization, 1991–2002." *Journal of Banking and Finance.*

Hart, Oliver D. 1983. "The Market Mechanism as an Incentive Scheme." *Bell Journal of Economics* 14, no. 2: 366–82.

Havrylyshyn, Oleh, and Donal McGettigan. 1999. "Privatization in Transition Countries: A Sampling of the Literature." Working Paper 99-6. Washington: International Monetary Fund.

Jensen, Michael C., and William H. Meckling. 1976. "Theory of the Firm: Managerial Behavior, Agency Costs, and Ownership Structure." *Journal of Financial Economics* 3, no. 4: 305–60.

Jones, Leroy P. 1985. "Public Enterprise for Whom? Perverse Distributional Consequences of Public Operational Decisions." *Economic Development and Cultural Change* 33, no. 2: 333–47.

Kane, Edward J. 1999. "The Limits of Stockholder Privatization." Boston College.

Kay, John A., and D. J. Thompson. 1986. "Privatisation: A Policy in Search of a Rationale." *Economic Journal* 96, no. 381: 18–32.

Kikeri, Sunita, John Nellis, and Mary M. Shirley. 1992. *Privatization: The Lessons from Experience.* Washington: World Bank.

La Porta, Rafael, Florencio López-de-Silanes, and Andrei Shleifer. 2002. "Government Ownership of Banks." *Journal of Finance* 57, no. 1: 265–301.

Lin, Justin Yifu, Fang Cai, and Zhou Li. 1998. "Competition, Policy Burdens, and State-Owned Enterprise Reform." *American Economic Review, Papers and Proceedings* 88, no. 2: 422–27.

Makler, Harry M. 2000. "Bank Transformation and Privatization in Brazil: Financial Federalism and Some Lessons about Bank Privatization." *Quarterly Review of Economics and Finance* 40, no. 1: 45–69.

Megginson, William L., and Jeffry M. Netter. 2002. "From State to Market: A Survey of Empirical Studies on Privatization." *Journal of Economic Literature* 39, no. 2: 321–89.

Meyendorff, Anna, and Edward A. Snyder. 1997. "Transactional Structures of Bank Privatizations in Central Europe and Russia." *Journal of Comparative Economics* 25, no. 1: 5–30.

Millward, R. 1982. "The Comparative Performance of Public and Private Ownership." In *The Mixed Economy,* edited by Lord E. Roll, pp. 58–93. New York: Macmillan.

Millward, R., and D. M. Parker. 1983. "Public and Private Enterprise: Comparative Behavior and Relative Efficiency." In *Public Sector Economics,* edited by R. Millward and others, pp. 199–274. London: Longman.

Nellis, John. 2000. "Time to Rethink Privatization in Transition Economies?" In *Privatization and Corporate Performance*, edited by David Parker, pp. 613–42. Cheltenham, U.K.: Elgar.

Ness, Walter L., Jr. 2000. "Reducing Government Bank Presence in the Brazilian Financial System: Why and How." *Quarterly Review of Economics and Finance* 40, no. 1: 71–84.

Niskanen, William A. 1971. *Bureaucracy and Representative Government.* Chicago: Aldine, Atherton.

———. 1975. "Bureaucrats and Politicians." *Journal of Law and Economics* 18, no. 3: 617–43.

Omran, Mohammed. 2003. "Privatization, State Ownership, and the Performance of Egyptian Banks." Paper presented at World Bank conference on bank privatization, November 20–21, Washington.

Otchere, Isaac. Forthcoming. "Do Privatized Banks in Middle- and Low-Income Countries Perform Better than Rival Banks? An Intra-Industry Analysis of Bank Privatization." *Journal of Banking and Finance.*

Otchere, Isaac, and Janus Chan. 2003. "The Intra-Industry Effects of Bank Privatization: A Clinical Analysis of the Privatization of the Commonwealth Bank of Australia." *Journal of Banking and Finance* 27, no. 5: 949–75.

Sappington, David E., and J. Gregory Sidak. 1999. "Incentives for Anticompetitive Behavior by Public Enterprises." Working paper. Joint American Enterprise Institute–Brookings Center for Regulatory Studies.

Sappington, David E., and Joseph E. Stiglitz. 1987. "Privatization, Information, and Incentives." *Journal of Policy Analysis and Management* 6, no. 4: 567–82.

Schmidt, Klaus M. 1996. "The Costs and Benefits of Privatization: An Incomplete Contracts Approach." *Journal of Law, Economics, and Organization* 12, no. 1: 1–24.

Shapiro, Carl, and Robert D. Willig. 1990. "Economic Rationales for Privatization in Industrial and Developing Countries." In *The Political Economy of Public Sector Reform and Privatization,* edited by Ezra Suleiman and John Waterbury, pp. 22–54. Boulder, Colo.: Westview.

Sheshinski, Eytan, and Luis Felipe Lopez-Calva. 2003. "Privatization and Its Benefits: Theory and Evidence." *CESinfo Economic Studies* 49, no. 3: 429–59.

Shirley, Mary M., and John Nellis. 1991. *Public Enterprise Reform: The Lessons of Experience.* Washington: World Bank.

Shirley, Mary M., and Patrick Walsh. 2003. "Public versus Private Ownership: The Current State of the Debate." Washington: Ronald Coase Institute.

Shleifer, Andrei, and Robert Vishny. 1994. "Politicians and Firms." *Quarterly Journal of Economics* 109, no. 4: 995–1025.

———. 1995. "A Survey of Corporate Governance." Discussion Paper 1741. Institute of Economic Research, Harvard University.

Shleifer, Andrei, and others. 1999. "Investor Protection: Origins, Consequences, and Reform." Working Paper 7428. Cambridge: National Bureau of Economic Research.

Stiglitz, Joseph E. 1993. "Some Theoretical Aspects of the Privatization: Applications to Eastern Europe." In *Privatization Processes in Eastern Europe,* edited by Mario Baldassarri, Luigi Paganetto, and Edmund S. Phelps, pp. 179–204. New York: St. Martin's.

———. 1999a. "Corporate Governance Failures in the Transition." Keynote address, annual World Bank conference on development economics, Europe. Washington.

————. 1999b. "Whither Reform?" Keynote address, annual World Bank conference on development economics. Washington.

Unal, Haluk, and Miguel Navarro. 1999. "Policy Paper: The Technical Process of Bank Privatization in Mexico." *Journal of Financial Services Research* 16, no. 1: 61–83.

Verbrugge, James, William L. Megginson, and Wanda L. Owens. 2000. "State Ownership and the Financial Performance of Privatized Banks: An Empirical Analysis." In *Bank Privatization: Conference Proceedings of a Policy Research Workshop,* edited by Harvey Rosenblum, pp. 1–34. Federal Reserve Bank of Dallas.

Vickers, John, and George Yarrow. 1989. *Privatization: An Economic Analysis.* MIT University Press.

————. 1991. "Economic Perspectives on Privatization." *Journal of Economic Perspectives* 5, no. 2: 111–32.

Weiss, Andrew, and Georgiy Nikitin. 1998. *Performance of Czech Companies by Ownership Structure.* Discussion Paper 85. Institute for Economic Development, Boston University.

Willig, Robert D. 1985. "Corporate Governance and the Product Market Structure." Princeton University.

Willner, Johan. 1996. "Social Objectives, Market Rule, and Public Policy." In *Competitiveness, Subsidiarity and Industrial Policy,* edited by Pat Devine, Yannis Katsoulacas, and Roger Sugden, pp. 12–41. New York: Routledge.

World Bank. 1995. *Bureaucrats in Business.* Policy Research Report. Oxford University Press.

Yarrow, George. 1986. "Privatization in Theory and Practice." *Economic Policy* 2 (April): 324–64.

FRED E. HUIBERS

14

Initial Public Offerings

SINCE THE EARLY 1980s, a growing number of state-owned enterprises have been privatized, with the total value of privatization transactions in the period 1982–2000 amounting to more than $1 trillion.[1] After privatizing industrial firms, governments increasingly began to dispose of companies from regulated industries such as telecommunications, utilities, and banks.

Bank privatization has been prevalent throughout the world. Of the 101 countries that conducted privatization transactions between 1982 and 2000, about half privatized state-owned banks. Overall, privatization of state-owned banks accounted for approximately 11 percent of the number and 10 percent of the value of transactions. Bank privatization has been much more frequent in developed than in emerging economies. Almost 86 percent of the Organization for Economic Cooperation and Development (OECD) countries that privatized enterprises also privatized banks. To date, only 41 percent of the non-OECD countries with an active privatization program have sold a state-owned bank. While bank privatization seems to be in the final phase in OECD countries, governments in emerging economies are only about halfway through the process.

In emerging economies, bank privatization did not gather momentum until the early 1990s. Increasingly, governments have changed their views on the strategic role of banking in relation to government dirigisme in economic development

1. Boehmer, Nash, and Netter (2003).

315

planning. To date, the value of state-owned bank privatization in emerging economies is close to $38 billion. Of the eighty non-OECD countries that have privatized enterprises, thirty-three have privatized 156 state-owned banks. For the average non-OECD country, 9 percent of the total transactions have consisted of bank privatizations, representing 11 percent of total dollar value.

In about 44 percent of the emerging economies, banks were privatized by means of a share offering (mostly initial as opposed to secondary offerings). This chapter examines the use and efficacy of initial public offerings as a strategy for bank privatization in emerging economies, outlining the relevance of bank privatization, describing the process, and analyzing the objectives of bank privatization in relation to the use of initial public offerings. Case studies from Mexico and Poland point out practical lessons.

The Relevance of Bank Privatization

Bank privatization in emerging economies merits attention for a number of reasons. For one, the volume of bank privatization in emerging economies is likely to be significant in the coming years. Developing country governments have only partially progressed with bank privatization. On average, about 30 percent of banking assets are held by state-owned banks in low- and lower-middle-income countries compared to about 10 percent in OECD countries. Consequently, state-owned banks still play an important role in the non-OECD banking sector. South Asian countries have the highest proportion of banking assets that are government controlled (60 percent), followed by the developing economies of Europe and Central Asia (more than 30 percent).[2] It is in these regions of the developing world that the economic effects of privatization are likely to be most pronounced.

Bank privatization plays a key role in economic development. An analysis of empirical studies on bank privatization shows that privatization improves performance over continued state ownership even in poor regulatory environments.[3] An investigation of bank privatizations that use public security offerings as the divestment mechanism concludes that profitability, operating efficiency, leverage, and noninterest revenue improve after privatization.[4] The positive efficiency effects of bank privatization, in turn, are of great importance in the economic development of emerging economies. State ownership negatively affects bank performance and

2. Barth, Caprio, and Levine (2001).
3. Clarke, Cull, and Shirley (2003).
4. Verbrugge, Megginson, and Owens (1999).

financial sector development.[5] Greater state ownership in 1970 was found to be associated with less financial development, slower growth, and lower productivity in 1995.[6]

However, bank privatization will deliver significant efficiency gains only if government relinquishes control and abstains from interfering in the affairs of the privatized bank. Banks in emerging economies have a strong, perverse incentive to fund former debtors—even though these state-owned enterprises are less efficient and more risky than private firms—because by doing so they have the potential to receive payment for previous debts.[7] This inevitably leads to lower productivity of investment and greater concentration of risk. It is worth examining the effectiveness of different methods of privatization for avoiding this suboptimal behavior.

A related issue is the fact that interest groups often strongly oppose bank privatization. Apart from the employees of state-owned banks, the beneficiaries of the perverse lending practices often try to obstruct bank privatization. In addition, some interest groups may be effectively subsidized by the allocation of state-owned bank funds. For this reason, initial public offerings may be an effective method of bank privatization because their use may blunt or even overcome the opposition of interest groups.

The Initial Public Offering Process

The first step for a government that has decided to privatize a bank by means of an initial public offering is to select a syndicate of investment banks. These banks provide advice, write investment research, and access investors for the government.

Investment banks are invited to participate in a so-called beauty contest to inform the government of their skills and assets that are of importance in selling the shares of the state-owned bank. Banks make presentations highlighting their knowledge of the state-owned bank and the strategic environment in which it operates. In addition, banks present their knowledge of the likely purchasers of the shares and the banks' relationship with these investors. The government selects a number of investment banks based on their ability to sell the shares.

Typically, the syndicate consists of one domestic bank and at least one international investment bank in the most senior role. The domestic bank sells shares to domestic retail investors and to employees of the state-owned bank. Its presence in

5. Barth, Caprio, and Levine (2001).
6. La Porta, López-de-Silanes, and Shleifer (2002).
7. Perotti (1993).

the syndicate is intended to appease groups that are skeptical of bank privatization and, more important, believe that the process will allow foreigners to benefit at the expense of the local public. The international investment bank brings extensive international experience with initial public offerings as well as international distributive power.

There is a clear hierarchy in the banking syndicate. The most senior banks are the book runner and global coordinator. In descending order of seniority, the next lower level is taken by the lead managers, followed by banks in a coleader role and banks in a comanagement role. The global coordinators—in consultation with the government—set a timetable and determine the scope and pace of the due diligence process. Due diligence consists of legal, fiscal, and financial reviews of the state-owned bank in order to collect the information needed to write an accurate and complete prospectus. This document is presented to investors when soliciting their orders for the shares.

The technique most frequently used to convert investor interest into actual orders is book building. At the start of book building, the investment banks and the selling shareholder agree on a price range and the number of shares they will offer investors. During so-called road shows, the management of the company makes presentations to investors in order to convince them to purchase shares. At this stage, investors are invited to subscribe to a number of shares with or without a price limit. The price limit should be within the range of the offer price. All orders of the syndicate banks are transmitted to the book runners, who—as the road shows progress—gradually get a view of the demand curve. At the end of book building, the orders of investors can no longer be adjusted and become definite. Immediately thereafter, the book runner and the selling shareholder determine the offer price; all investors who have submitted orders at a price below the offer price are allocated shares.

When the number of shares demanded exceeds the number of shares that can be allocated, the investors receive fewer shares than they requested. The rationing occurs according to three main criteria: the promptness with which investors submitted orders during book building, the consistency of their order, and the quality of their reputation. To obtain a reliable demand curve during book building, investment banks must persuade investors to reveal their price sensitivity at an early stage. Moreover, investors must be not only truthful but also consistent in the information they supply in order to allow the investment banks to make an informed decision on the stock price that investors will pay once the new shares start trading. In addition, investment banks have a strong interest in allocating shares to investors who are unlikely to sell these shares in the first few days of trading. This implies that investment banks will offer investors who have a reputation as long-term investors (that is, high-quality investors) proportionally more shares than other investors. After all, investment banks do not want to see the shares trade below the offer price once trading commences. Such a situation would create dissatisfied buyers and sellers and have a negative impact on the chances that the investment bank will be awarded new initial public offerings in the future.

Since investment banks have a strong interest in persuading investors to reveal their true demand preferences, they have to offer something in exchange for this valuable information. Besides a proportionally better allocation, they can offer a price incentive by intentionally underpricing the shares. A survey of empirical studies shows that, on average, the closing price of shares on the first day of trading is about 15 percent above the offering price.[8] Moreover, the underpricing is significantly greater for public sector offers (that is, privatization) than for those of the private sector. The phenomenon of underpricing is pervasive in stock markets around the world.

To maximize the chances that the share price will not fall below the offering price in the first weeks of trading, investment banks purchase shares in order to support the share price. This typically happens in the first month of trading. Investment banks use the so-called overallocation option (or "green shoe") as an important instrument for stabilizing prices in the aftermarket. This option, which is granted by the selling shareholders, allows the investment banks to issue up to 15 percent more shares than are communicated to investors. In practice, the banks overallocate (that is, allocate 115 percent of the number of shares) to investors. If banks do not need to stabilize prices in the aftermarket, they announce that they have exercised the overallocation option. If, however, they have to support the share price by purchasing shares in the market, they can do so without risking their own capital up to the amount of shares in the overallocation option. In this case, they announce that they have refrained from exercising the green shoe option. Thus the announcement concerning the exercise of the green shoe option contains useful information about the enthusiasm with which investors have been trading the newly listed shares.

The Objectives of Bank Privatization and the Use of Initial Public Offerings

Although the proportion of banking assets in state ownership has been falling, state-owned banks are still prominent in many emerging economies. The most important reason for the existence of state-owned banks is that governments,

8. Huibers (1994).

especially in emerging economies, regard them as an instrument for channeling funds to sectors and groups that are perceived to lack private capital due to low financial but high social returns. State influence is deemed necessary to keep banks from focusing exclusively on profits in their allocation of credit. The private sector is not trusted to balance social and economic goals.

There are two reasons that governments privatize state-owned banks. First, mounting empirical evidence shows that privately owned banks perform better than state-owned banks. Second, governments have come to appreciate the importance of a well-functioning banking sector for economic growth and development.[9]

In formulating the bank privatization process, governments have multiple (and often conflicting) objectives: increasing efficiency, developing a market-oriented industry, importing new capital and know-how, ensuring stakeholder support, developing the local stock market, building confidence in the privatization program, eliminating soft lending, maximizing proceeds, and stimulating wider ownership of shares. This section examines each of these objectives in turn and analyzes how the use of initial public offerings as a privatization strategy is likely to help governments achieve these objectives.

Increasing Efficiency

In theory, benevolent government officials could influence decisionmaking in the banking sector such that credit is allocated to the most productive use. Much research in the area of public choice theory, however, indicates that bureaucrats more often than not act in a self-interested manner. In practice, state-owned banks are effective tools of redistributive politics, since politicians use the firms to pursue noneconomic goals such as subsidizing favored constituents and expanding patronage employment.[10]

As a consequence, state-owned banks cannot compete effectively with profit-maximizing private sector banks, and they run losses in competitive markets—losses that have to be covered by subsidies from the government treasury or by government-guaranteed debt. Typically, state-owned banks suffer from excess staffing, an expensive and large branch network, and a lower return on equity and assets than their rivals. Moreover, stakeholders in state-owned banks often "capture" the government body charged with monitoring the bank by bribing corrupt politicians to protect their interests.[11]

---

9. La Porta, López-de-Silanes, and Shleifer (2002) offers the clearest empirical evidence supporting this relation.

10. Shleifer and Vishny (1994).

11. Shleifer and Vishny (1994).

Another reason that state-owned banks are less efficient is weak corporate governance. Monitoring by the owners is less effective. First, a severe free-rider problem occurs because all citizens are co-owners (the ultimate atomistic ownership structure). As citizens cannot effectively influence management of the state-owned bank and cannot vote with their feet (that is, sell their shareholding), there is less incentive and return from monitoring efforts. The government is the only agent that can realistically influence the performance of state-owned banks. But, as noted, government often has objectives that lead to economic inefficiencies.

In addition, the market for corporate control does not effectively discipline the managers of state-owned banks. In the private sector, bank managers who are not operating efficiently are replaced—either by current shareholders, through a hostile takeover, or through bankruptcy. Because the political costs of allowing a state-owned bank to go bankrupt outweigh the political costs of subsidization, governments rarely allow state-owned banks to fail. The comforting knowledge that the manager of a state-owned bank can rely on state funding does not provide the manager with a strong incentive to ensure an efficient use of resources. In sum, less competition, greater political intervention, and weaker corporate governance produce inefficiencies that are likely to be eliminated by privatization.

Empirical studies find evidence of improved bank efficiency as a result of privatization. A 1999 study of bank privatization through a public offer of securities on the stock market documents improvements in bank profitability, operating efficiency, leverage, and noninterest revenue after privatization.[12] However, the study also shows that substantial government ownership often remains after privatization and that the government's stake is completely eliminated at the initial public offering stage in only a few cases. The study suggests that continued significant government ownership of banks raises serious problems for establishing market-oriented governance and decisionmaking systems in the banks and that this, in turn, stands in the way of operational improvements. A 2002 study also offers empirical evidence that performance improves after privatization.[13]

Developing a Market-Oriented Banking Sector

Privatization programs during the past twenty years have significantly reduced the role of state-owned enterprises in the economic life of most countries.[14] Most of this reduction occurred in developing countries during the 1990s. The state-

12. Verbrugge, Megginson, and Owens (1999).
13. Megginson and Netter (2002).
14. Megginson and Netter (2002).

owned enterprises' share of global gross domestic product (GDP) declined from more than 10 percent in 1979 to less than 6 percent in 2004.

The theoretical arguments, based on public choice theory, that government intervention lowers welfare are backed by a number of empirical studies. In an analysis of bank privatization by means of initial public offerings in nine emerging economies, regression results indicate that the proportion of ownership retained by the government significantly explains the underperformance of the privatized banks.[15] Listed rival banks react negatively to the announcement of privatization (by initial public offering) of a bank, because market participants expect, on balance, that the privatization will create a more competitive environment. In addition, the negative reaction seen in the stock price of rival banks is more pronounced for tranches of seasoned equity offerings. Market participants seem to conclude that the competitive threat becomes more severe as government increasingly retreats from interfering in the affairs of the previously state-owned bank. Thus a stock market listing of a state-owned bank facilitates the adoption of market-oriented compensation plans that make management work better. There is also pressure from the product market. However, some concern exists as to the sophistication of investors and regulators regarding the level and effectiveness of monitoring in emerging stock markets. One way to ensure optimal monitoring is to consider a (dual) listing. An American depository receipt may be considered in these cases.

Bank performance in the Czech Republic and Poland did not improve in the first round of privatization because government retained a substantial stake. Only after the government surrendered control (often to a foreign strategic investor) did performance improve.[16]

Importing New Capital and Know-How

Empirical studies demonstrate that performance improves more with foreign ownership of privatized banks than with purely domestic ownership. In the Czech Republic, Mexico, and Poland the government prohibited or tacitly discouraged foreign ownership in the initial round of privatization. The initial privatization did not improve performance in any of these cases.[17] Performance did improve after a subsequent round of privatization in which a degree of foreign ownership was permitted. The postprivatization performance of banks in Hungary, the first country to embrace foreign ownership, was also positive.[18]

15. See Otchere (2003).
16. Clarke, Cull, and Shirley (2003).
17. Clarke, Cull, and Shirley (2003).
18. Bonin, Hasan, and Wachtel (2003).

Another hypothesis is that foreign ownership of industries considered of strategic significance (such as banking) is often politically unacceptable. If this is the case, initial public offerings probably will not be the chosen means of privatization for strategic industries. However, evidence does not support this hypothesis.[19]

An overview of empirical privatization studies concludes that foreign ownership is in fact associated with greater improvements in postprivatization performance than is purely domestic ownership.[20] An examination of the performance of banks in eleven emerging economies shows that majority foreign ownership is associated with improved bank performance.[21] In addition, bank privatization improves the financial performance (that is, the stock market performance) of banks, and the new, mainly foreign, owners incur costs to upgrade technology and to develop new business lines as well as to offer more fee-based services.

Ensuring the Support of Stakeholders

Politicians use state-owned banks to provide employment and funds for favored constituents. As bank privatization severely endangers the privileges of employees and other interest groups that have something to lose if the bank is sold, these stakeholders generally oppose privatization. In addition, the ruling government may want to minimize the chances that a subsequent administration will reverse bank privatization. This can be achieved by persuading the majority of voters to support privatization and oppose renationalization.

Initial public offerings provide an ideal strategy for ensuring that diverse stakeholders support bank privatization. The process provides multiple tools to discriminate among investors and to favor particular investor groups. Both preferential allocation and underpricing can be used to allow the targeted investor groups, such as employees of the state-owned bank and domestic individual investors, to realize good investment returns from the privatization.

In Poland trade unions have historically been very powerful. It can therefore be expected that the government will try to persuade employees of the state-owned bank to participate in the initial public offering. In Poland underpricing and preferential allocation have been used extensively, and government has allocated shares in a politically inspired manner.[22] To achieve political goals, governments divide issues into several tranches and give preference to employees and domestic retail investors by assigning a certain number of shares to each tranche. On average, 19.4 percent (median 18.7 percent) of the shares sold during the initial offer

19. Megginson and others (forthcoming).
20. Megginson and Netter (2002).
21. Bonin, Hasan, and Wachtel (2003).
22. Aussenegg (1999).

are sold to employees. This value is more than twice as high as the international evidence: In a sample of fifty-nine countries, the portion sold to employees averaged 8.5 percent (median 7.0 percent).[23] Former state employees in one sample received preferential allocations in 91 percent of offers.[24] On average, 7 percent of the shares of the state-owned bank in one initial public offering were allocated to employees.[25]

Developing the Local Stock Market

Typically, capital markets of emerging economies are underdeveloped. Few companies are listed on the stock markets, and trading volumes are relatively modest. The bond market is small or nonexistent. As the capital market develops, companies gain access to an alternative source of funds and are able to profit from a lower cost of capital. A deeper and more liquid capital market attracts foreign portfolio investment and allows emerging economies to benefit from this inflow of capital. This in turn stimulates the rate of economic growth in these countries.

Several studies note that privatization through public share offerings can jump-start stock market development and trigger gains in economic growth and efficiency.[26] Since bank privatizations tend to be large, these transactions stimulate the liquidity of a nation's stock market. This encourages more firms to go public and further stimulates growth in the capital market. Therefore, if governments use public sector initial public offerings to encourage stock market development, we expect state-owned bank privatizations to be more likely in nations with less developed equity markets. The use of initial public offerings to privatize, according to one study, is more likely in less developed capital markets.[27] However, the more developed the market, the easier it is to sell shares in the capital market. Alternatively, privatization of state-owned banks offers governments the opportunity to use initial public offerings to support development of the domestic capital market. The second effect dominates: The less developed the capital market, the more likely government will use initial public offerings as a method of privatization. This finding suggests that governments use initial public offerings as a means to develop the domestic capital market. Another study notes that countries that have launched large-scale public offering programs have experi-

23. Jones and others (1999).
24. Megginson and Netter (2002).
25. Otchere (2003).
26. McLindon (1996); Perotti and van Oijen (2001); Subrahmanyam and Titman (1999).
27. Megginson and others (forthcoming).

enced rapid growth in the capitalization and trading volume of the national stock market.[28]

Building Confidence in the Privatization Program

Populist governments tend to maximize proceeds by selling as many shares as possible while minimizing underpricing. After the initial public offering they are inclined to introduce legislation that earns votes but is detrimental to the newly privatized company—for example, by forcing utilities to lower tariffs. Obviously, this destroys any nascent confidence that investors have in the truthfulness of the privatization program. Conversely, governments ideologically committed to privatization and economic reform deliberately underprice shares and privatize in stages to signal their commitment to protecting the property rights of investors.[29] The risk sensitivity of this policy tends to be resolved over time.[30]

The greater the government's ability to credibly commit to the privatization policy and the protection of property rights, the greater the likelihood that a state-owned enterprise will be sold in an asset sale as opposed to an initial public offering.[31] Investors are more willing to make the substantial investment of purchasing a state-owned enterprise through an asset sale when the government can be trusted to proceed with its policy of privatization. After all, it is much easier to reverse the privatization in the case of an asset sale (when the former state-owned assets are owned by a few individuals) than in the case of an initial public offering (when investors number in the thousands). Since investors' perception of policy risk tends to be high in the early stages of privatization, governments have to resort to (heavily underpriced) public offerings rather than asset sales to make the first disposals.

In addition, the most profitable firms are more likely to be offered to stock market investors first, a strategy consistent with building popular support for the privatization program.[32] Early privatizations must be financially successful in order to build credibility for the government and to encourage investors to participate in subsequent privatizations. The average (and median) public sector initial public offering (and secondary public placing of shares) is about three times larger than that of a private transaction (that is, asset sales). The average state-owned enterprise privatized through an initial public offering is about seven times larger than one privatized through asset sales. On average, a much smaller portion

28. Megginson and Netter (2002).
29. Biais and Perotti (1997); Perotti (1995).
30. Huibers and Perotti (1999),
31. Megginson and others (forthcoming).
32. Megginson and others (forthcoming).

of a state-owned enterprise's capital is privatized through an initial public offering (35 percent) than through asset sales (74 percent). This is consistent with the confidence-building hypothesis that governments tend to privatize the largest, most profitable enterprises in a sequential manner by way of initial public offerings in order to signal that they are committed to the privatization program. The majority of state-owned banks (88 percent) are only partially privatized at the initial public offering stage.[33] On average, government retains a 49 percent stake after the offering.

Actively building confidence in the privatization program has clear benefits. An overview of empirical studies of the long-term performance of public sector initial public offerings concludes, "The market-adjusted return earned by international investors in share issue privatizations is economically and significantly positive. . . . These excess returns result from a gradual resolution of uncertainty on the part of investors regarding both the micro-economic success of privatization programs and the ability of governments to resist the temptation to expropriate shareholder wealth in privatized firms through direct intervention or through targeted regulation or taxation."[34]

Eliminating Soft Lending

A study that examines more than sixty bank privatizations through initial public offerings identifies only seven cases in which government ownership is eliminated altogether.[35] For those public offerings by emerging economies, the average government ownership afterward is 58 percent (median, 72 percent). This figure is substantially higher than in developed countries (47 and 52 percent, respectively).[36] Moreover, the government's stake tends to remain high even after secondary offerings have taken place. The average remaining stake is 20 percent (median, 5 percent) in developed economies but 49 percent (median, 57 percent) in emerging economies. The study suggests that, more often than not, governments in emerging economies are more interested in generating revenue than in surrendering their role.

If not fully privatized, banks continue to subsidize former debtors by granting them concessionary loans. There are strong, but perverse, incentives to continue funding former state-owned enterprises even though these enterprises are more risky than private firms. By doing so, banks gain the potential to receive payment of previously granted debt. There seems to be a natural tendency for governments

33. Otchere (2003).
34. Megginson and Netter (2002, p. 42).
35. Verbrugge, Megginson, and Owens (1999).
36. This finding is consistent with Perotti (1995).

in emerging economies to retain effective control of banks in order to lessen the shock of transition by propping up borrowers with easy credits. This "soft lending" plays a role in the long-run underperformance of stock prices and also leads to operational underperformance. Thus the government's continued participation undermines one of the goals of privatization: increased efficiency.

Maximizing Privatization Proceeds

There is evidence that, similar to private firms attempting to time the market with an initial public offering, governments are more likely to privatize using such offerings during a period of high valuations.[37] That is, the correlation between the level of the stock market and government use of initial public offerings and the relation between the size of the state-owned enterprise to be privatized and the use of initial public offerings are both positive.

Book building, the main technique applied to initial public offerings, offers multiple opportunities to maximize proceeds. Compared to a fixed-price or an auctioned public offering, investment banks require a lower fee because they run less risk of a failed issue. Auctions can be considered a subset of book building, wherein the issuer commits to certain price and allocation rules.[38] Book building allows issuers to be flexible on price and allocations and to have leeway to adjust pricing to ensure full subscription and allow certain groups of investors preferential allocation. In the book-building process, investment banks offer preferential allocations in exchange for a truthful revelation of the demand by investors. By obtaining a fairly exact demand curve, investment banks—together with the government—can choose the highest price that market participants are willing to pay.

Stimulating Wider Ownership of Shares

Widening ownership to promote an equity culture is an explicit goal of many privatization programs.[39] The initial public offerings of state banks play an important role due to their relatively large size and their ability to use preferential pricing (discounts to retail) and allocation (clawbacks and special tranches).[40] The use of public sector initial public offerings has led to rapid growth in individual ownership of shares in many countries.[41] The broad ownership of shares thus created

---

37. Megginson and others (forthcoming); see also Loughran, Ritter, and Rydqvist (1994).
38. Sherman (2002).
39. Megginson and others (forthcoming).
40. The term *clawback* describes the decision of government to allocate more shares to individual investors (at the expense of institutional investors) in response to higher than expected demand from them.
41. See McLindon (1996); Megginson and Boutchkova (2000); Subrahmanyam and Titman (1999).

binds the government to continuing its privatization stance and to avoiding policy shifts that could be harmful to the new shareholders.[42] Such widespread ownership of shares has been called an insurance policy against a subsequent return to nationalization.[43] A government would incur a substantial political cost if it renationalized a privatized firm at the expense of citizen shareholders. Asset sales do not create the same element of irreversibility, because asset sales involve a small number of private investors. These private investors (particularly wealthy individuals) in fact are attractive targets for renationalization. Thus the use of initial public offerings as a privatization strategy signals a government's commitment to respect the private ownership of assets, and this may be necessary to convince investors of the robustness of economic reform.

Underpricing is a tool to entice individual investors (who typically have not been active investors in the stock market) to participate in public sector initial public offerings. In order to convince median-income voters to buy enough shares so that their political preferences are similar to those of the government, underpricing is necessary in most cases. The more income inequality in the population, the poorer the median-income voters and the greater the underpricing (to persuade these voters to buy shares). Because a reversal of the privatization program will decrease the value of privatized firms, median-income voters will support the privatization efforts of the government and likely support the government in elections.[44] On average, public sector initial public offerings are more underpriced than those of the private sector.[45] Governments' desire to widen share ownership significantly explains this underpricing differential.[46]

However, governments need to avoid creating an atomistic shareholder structure, because free-rider problems cause ineffective corporate governance. This in turn allows incumbent managers to stay in power. Majority ownership by outside investors (investors who are not employees) is associated with a significantly greater improvement in performance than any form of insider control because

42. Perotti and Guney (1993).

43. Menyah, Paudyal, and Inyangete (1990).

44. Jones and others (1999) examine a sample of fifty-nine countries and 630 privatization initial public offerings and conclude that underpricing increases with a country's income inequality.

45. Huibers (1994) finds that, on average, public sector initial public offerings in Singapore and the United Kingdom were underpriced compared with private sector offerings by 22 and 29 percentage points, respectively. Ljungqvist, Jenkinson, and Wilhelm (2000) examine a sample of 2,051 initial public offerings (including 185 public sector offerings) and find that public sector offerings are significantly more underpriced (by about 9 percentage points) than are those in the private sector. Huibers (1994) provides evidence that government's desire to widen share ownership significantly explains this underpricing differential.

46. Huibers (1994).

restructuring is more likely to take place.[47] Performance improves more when new managers are brought in to run a firm after it is privatized than when the original managers are retained. An example of a failed insider privatization is the transfer of twelve natural resource firms to a small group of oligarchs at very low prices, which precipitated widespread insider expropriation.[48]

Case Studies: The Polish and Mexican Bank Privatization

The Mexican and Polish governments have implemented radically different bank privatization programs, which offer valuable lessons for policymakers.

The Mexican Bank Privatization Program

The Mexican banking system has experienced multiple cycles of expropriation and privatization. In 1916 President Venustiano Carranza expropriated the banks to finance his military effort during the Mexican Revolution. Five years later, these banks reverted to private ownership after the government no longer required war funding. In the 1970s the Mexican government spent far more than it could raise through the country's inadequate taxation system. These deficits were financed by expanding the money supply, by borrowing from foreign banks, and by directing the banking system to lend to unprofitable state-owned firms (soft borrowing). By the summer of 1982 this strategy had become unsustainable, as Mexico entered a period of hyperinflation and the government was unable to service outstanding foreign debt. President López Portillo defaulted on the debt, allowed the exchange rate to collapse, and converted dollar-denominated accounts into pesos. He blamed the banks for the crisis and subsequently expropriated the banking system.

The crisis substantially weakened the power base of the ruling Institutional Revolutionary Party. The population experienced falling standards of living in the years after the crisis. The subsequent administrations of Miguel de la Madrid and Carlos Salinas felt that they could not afford to cut spending or raise taxes for political reasons. At the same time, the Mexican government did not have access to meaningful amounts of credit to fund the looming budget deficit. In the absence of other options, the sale of government-owned enterprises was the main source of funding for the budget deficit. The most valuable assets that could be privatized were those of the state-owned banks.

47. Megginson and Netter (2002).
48. Black, Kraakman, and Tarassova (2000).

In this setting, the Mexican government devised a bank privatization program that was geared to maximizing revenues. The privatization plan was announced on October 25, 1991.[49] To receive the highest price possible for its banking assets, the government organized an auction process, focusing exclusively on maximizing proceeds at the expense of making the banking sector more efficient and market oriented. First, the government clearly communicated that the winners of the bidding process would be selected solely on the basis of price rather than a mix of price and quality of the management team. Second, it was made clear that the government would not allow (foreign) entrants into the banking system, which would have improved the attractiveness of the existing banking franchise, which had oligopoly characteristics. Third, the government did not indicate the valuation (methodology) that would be applied to the banking assets. Finally, it did not restate financial reports according to international accounting standards, which would have shown that the Mexican banks were much less profitable than they appeared.

As a result, the Mexican banks were sold to domestic investors at an excessively high price. On average, investors in Mexico paid more than three times the (inflated) book value, whereas investors in comparable emerging economies do not pay more than two times the book value of state-owned banks. Enthusiastic domestic investors, who more often than not lacked experience and capital reserves, believed that they had purchased a protected position in a stable, oligopolistic industry. The assumption that they would easily recoup their investment turned out to be overly optimistic. Once the government sold off all banking assets, it started to grant charters to additional banks in order to raise further revenues. Banks scrambled for market share in order to protect revenues and massively expanded lending, especially to homeowners. While GDP grew at only 3 percent a year from 1991 to 1994, bank lending increased at an annual rate of 24 percent. In the same period, reported nonperforming loans more than doubled. The actual situation was much worse because Mexico's departure from internationally accepted accounting standards meant that the value of nonperforming loans was understated by a factor of two. The lax local accounting standards also allowed the banks to overstate capital reserves. Instead of the reported average capital ratio of 8 percent, the ratio of capital to assets was actually closer to 5 percent.

---

49. The government had introduced certificates of ordinary participation (*certificados de aportación patrimonial*) representing an average of less than 20 percent of the equity of state-owned banks on the Mexican Stock Exchange. Given that the government was still firmly in control, these banks were not considered to be privatized at the time.

In addition, Mexico installed an unlimited deposit insurance system, which created serious moral hazard problems. A curious phenomenon accompanying the Mexican banking operations was that those in control of lending decisions made large loans to themselves. Clearly, these insiders had strong incentives to misrepresent the true state of affairs and keep the bank afloat as long as it was of use to them. Even if there had been no tequila crisis in 1994–95, the undercapitalized and inefficient banking system would have collapsed.

In 1996 the government lifted all restrictions on foreign bank ownership in an effort to attract the capital and expertise required for recovery of the banking system. In response to the demand of foreign banks, Mexican banks started reporting according to internationally accepted accounting standards. While only 7 percent of banking assets were controlled by foreign banks in 1996, this percentage grew steadily to 14 percent (1997) and then to 48 percent (2000); it is currently 66 percent.

The combination of foreign bank entry and the introduction of new accounting standards dramatically reduced the level of nonperforming loans from 11 percent in 1997 to around 4 percent in 2003. In addition, the (cost) efficiency of the Mexican banking system improved markedly.

The Polish Bank Privatization Program

Poland took the first step in preparing for bank privatization by passing two pieces of legislation—the National Bank of Poland Act and the Banking Act—in 1989. These acts created a two-tier banking structure: One tier consisted of nine state-owned regional commercial banks; the other tier consisted of specialized banks (for example, Bank Handlowy, BGZ, PEKAO, and PKO BP). In 1992, after prompting from the G-7 donor countries, the Polish government announced a timetable for privatizing the nine regional commercial banks sequentially over a three-year period: Bank Depozytowo-Kredytowy (BDK), Bank Gdanski (BG), Bank Przemyslowo-Handlowy (BPH), Bank Slaski w Katowicach (BSK), Bank Zachodni (BZ), Pomorski Bank Krewdytowy (PBKS), Powszechny Bank Gospardarczy (PBG), Powszechny Bank Kredytowy (PBK), and Wielkopolski Bank Kredytowy (WBK).[50] The Ministry of Finance had communicated its intention to retain a 30 percent interest; 15 percent of the shares would be allocated preferentially to bank employees, while domestic investors would be able to purchase 30 percent of the shares. This left 25 percent of the shares on offer to foreign investors, who would be allowed to tender for the remaining equity, which was to be privatized through an initial public offering.

50. Specialized banks were to be privatized after 1996.

Two banks were selected to kick off the privatization program: WBK and BSK. These banks were widely regarded as the strongest of the nine banks in terms of financial position and management capability. The desire to minimize the impact of possible shortcomings motivated the treasury to start with WBK, the smaller of the two banks.

Before launching the initial public offering in March 1993, the Polish government tried to attract a foreign bank to invest $12.6 million for a 28.5 percent stake in WBK. As no banks were willing to act as a strategic investor in the bank, the European Bank for Reconstruction and Development finally purchased the new issue at a price of PLZ 115,000 per share.[51] This price was used as the offering price, with preset tranches for employees (15.0 percent), small investors (20.0 percent), and institutional investors (7.2 percent). The initial public offering was fully subscribed in early May, and when trading started on June 22 the share price increased to PLZ 350,000. The threefold increase in the share price led to some criticism of intentional underpricing. The treasury, however, referred to the 260 percent increase in the local stock market index between March and June 1993, pointing out that it was unlikely that the shares had been massively underpriced since no foreign investor had been willing to purchase a stake in WBK at the offer price.

Nevertheless, in pricing the shares of the next offering—BSK—the government wanted to avoid the criticism that it had set the price too low but, at the same time, was very much aware that it had failed to attract a foreign strategic investor in the previous privatization. In an attempt to reconcile these conflicting pricing objectives, the Polish government decided to organize a tender offer for the 45 percent equity stake reserved for institutional and strategic investors.

The government set a minimum offer price of PLZ 230,000, at which BSK valuation was equal to its book value. This was a premium valuation compared to that of WBK, which had a ratio of offer price to book value of 75 percent. The smallest allowable bid in the institutional investor tranche was PLZ 42.55 billion ($2.1 million), and no single investor was allowed to purchase more than a 25.9 percent stake. As the minimum tender size was a hurdle for Polish institutions, the offer was structured to allow foreign investors to bid exclusively for a minority stake.

BSK was one of Poland's larger commercial banks, with forty-four branches and six branch offices (predominantly in Silesia). At the time, BSK was a regional

---

51. In the four years following this transaction, Allied Irish Bank became majority owner by purchasing 60 percent of the equity of WBK.

bank with a 4.2 percent share of total banking assets in Poland. Although BSK was considered an attractive bank, the tender was canceled in October 1993 due to lack of institutional investor interest.

The Polish government decided to press on with the small-investor tranche and offered the shares at PLZ 500,000 on November 22, 1993. At that price, BSK was valued at twice the book value. Employees of BSK were allowed to subscribe to the shares at PLZ 250,000. Not only were they allowed to purchase shares at half price, but a special tranche of 10 percent of the shares also was reserved for them. The share offering was heavily oversubscribed. While allocations were being administered, the Polish government announced on December 15 that it had reached an agreement with Internationale Nederlanden Group (ING), the banking and insurance group of the Netherlands. ING was willing to purchase a 25.9 percent stake of BSK for PLZ 1.2 trillion ($60 million) at the share offering price. As the treasury decided to hold a 33 percent stake, the remaining 31 percent ended up in the hands of institutional investors.

When trading commenced in January 1994, the stock price shot up to PLZ 6.5 million, leading to strong criticism that the shares had been heavily underpriced. In the first days of trading about half of newly issued shares typically change ownership. In the case of BSK, less than 0.5 percent of the new shares were traded on the first day at the Warsaw Stock Exchange. While employees were able to sell shares, the general public could only watch the spectacular increase in share price because their shares had not been properly administered yet. This was seen as one privilege too many for the employees and caused dissatisfaction among the hundreds of thousands of individuals who had purchased BSK shares.

Another heavily criticized element of the privatization of BSK was that the negotiations with ING had been conducted privately. Although an investigation into the fairness of these negotiations did not find any evidence that they were tainted, the public outcry ultimately led to the resignation of the Polish finance minister and the president of BSK's executive board.

The Polish government had multiple, often conflicting, objectives for the bank privatization program. The rest of this section evaluates the extent to which the government was successful in achieving its targets.

INCREASING EFFICIENCY. The main criterion for judging the success of a bank privatization is the extent to which performance improves after privatization. This improvement can be observed by measuring returns (return on equity, return on assets), the extent to which the banking sector can effectively compete with foreign banks, the level of product innovation, and the quality of management information systems.

Table 14-1. *Indicators of Profitability, Asset Quality, and Capitalization, Poland, 1993–2001*
Percent

Indicator	1993	1994	1995	1996	1997	1998	1999	2000	2001
Return on equity	−0.48	0.11	1.91	2.24	1.82	0.67	0.94	1.10	1.15
Return on assets	−6.56	6.10	37.57	35.17	24.96	7.67	12.10	13.99	n.a.
Nonperforming loans as percent of total loans	31.00	28.50	20.90	13.20	10.50	10.90	13.70	15.30	n.a.
Ratio of equity to total assets	4.22	5.00	5.17	6.39	7.24	7.05	7.06	7.12	7.22

Source: Poloucek (2003).
n.a. Not available.

Poland's privatization improved the effectiveness of the banking sector and strengthened its stability.[52] Specifically, indicators of profitability (return on equity and return on assets), asset quality (nonperforming loans as a percentage of total loans), and capitalization (equity to total assets) improved after privatization in Poland (see table 14-1).

Improvement in the operating performance of BSK was particularly pronounced. Better credit assessment and monitoring, personnel training, and the introduction of new financial products contributed to both higher profitability and a stronger financial position for the bank.[53]

DEVELOPING A MARKET-ORIENTED BANKING SECTOR. It is of critical importance for the government to reduce its influence over the privatized bank. Otherwise, noneconomic objectives are likely to reduce the speed and lower the depth of the restructuring required to improve the performance of the banking sector. Regression results of bank privatization by initial public offering in nine emerging economies, including Poland, indicate that the proportion of ownership retained by the government significantly explains the underperformance of privatized banks.[54]

52. Poloucek (2003).
53. Abarbanell and Bonin (1997) describe BSK's development after privatization. In addition, D'Souza and Megginson (1999) examine the operating performance of privatized firms and find stronger efficiency gains for firms in developing countries, firms in regulated industries, firms that restructured operations after privatization, and firms in countries providing greater amounts of shareholder protection.
54. Otchere (2003).

Specifically, in the case of BSK the government retained a 33 percent stake. This made the government the largest shareholder, as ING was limited to a 25.9 percent stake. In practice, the Polish government interfered in the day-to-day management of the bank. A clear example is the decision of the Ministry of Finance to increase the dividend payout against the wishes of BSK's management. Another example is persistent overstaffing during the period in which the state held onto its minority equity stake. While the management of BSK publicly stated that staff could be cut 50 percent, government representatives at BSK blocked such reductions. Only after two and a half years did the government effectively retreat, allowing ING to obtain a majority position in BSK.

ELIMINATING SOFT LENDING. At the time of the initial public offering, BSK was a regional bank with strong ties to the underperforming, state-owned, heavy industry in Silesia. Since the government retained influence and actively interfered, it is unlikely that BSK halted soft lending practices. Only after the initial public offering did stricter enforcement of bad loan regulation start to have an impact on BSK's soft lending practices.[55]

IMPORTING NEW CAPITAL AND KNOW-HOW. In the period 1989–93 the Polish government had a liberal licensing policy, with low equity requirements. In this period, sixty-one new private domestic banks were established that were small and often owned by the state or municipalities. Also during this period eleven foreign banks started operating in Poland, among them Citibank of the United States and Creditanstalt of Austria. The number of commercial banks grew from 17 to 104, and their share of deposits increased from 1 percent to 20 percent.

However, the liberal licensing policy led to an accumulation of bad loans caused by a lack of know-how and proper credit monitoring. Nonperforming loans stood at 31 percent of the loan book at the end of 1993. The central bank had to step in and recapitalize an important part of the banking sector. In reaction to this, the central bank increased liquidity and solvency requirements, set stricter risk management standards, and installed more rigorous reporting procedures for the banks. In addition, it forced foreign banks to clean up the balance sheet of a specific domestic bank in order to obtain a license. In the period 1993–97, fourteen foreign banks were granted banking licenses.

As a consequence of the new licensing policy, a number of foreign banks that had set up branch networks in Poland began merging their networks with local banks. Examples are ING with Bank Slaski, Citibank Poland with Bank Handlowy, Bank Austria Creditanstalt with Powszechny Bank Kredytowy, and

---

55. Mondshean and Opiela (1997) offer a good overview of such enforcement.

HypoVereinsbank Polska with Bank Przemyslowo-Handlowy. These combined banks saw significant improvements in market share and operational efficiency.

In the case of BSK, ING contributed to an improvement in credit assessment, credit monitoring, and workout procedures. As a consequence, the dominance of corporate lending to the traditional industries in the region of Silesia was gradually reduced, and nonperforming loans as a percentage of total loans fell from 50 percent in 1992 to 23 percent in 1995. BSK ventured outside Silesia and started lending to industries with better growth prospects. In addition, there was a continuous drive to upgrade the average skill level of bank personnel by intensifying training and recruitment efforts. During the first two and half years, when ING was the second largest shareholder after the Polish government, it would often encounter resistance when it tried to make personnel changes too rapidly. Only after July 1996 did this resistance subside. Finally, ING stimulated the adoption of new information technology, contributed required capital to expand both in retail and corporate banking, and introduced new products in the field of asset management, employee benefits, and insurance. One study of the influence of ING on the operations of BSK concludes, "There is no substitute for a properly incentivized, highly knowledgeable financial investor in initiating and carrying through fundamental change in a privatized entity."[56]

DEVELOPING THE LOCAL STOCK MARKET. The Warsaw Stock Exchange was founded in 1817 but was closed during World War II and the following decades of communism. It reopened on April 16, 1991, as a joint stock company with brokerage firms, the main banks, and the treasury as its shareholders. At reopening, five firms were listed (the privatized firms Exbud, Kable, Krosno, Prochnik, and Tonsil). At the end of 1991 twelve companies were quoted on the Warsaw Stock Exchange, joined by an additional six in 1992 and nine in 1993. The number of new listings accelerated during the bull market that ended abruptly in March 1994, when thirty-three companies went public. Between April 1991 and the end of 1998, 187 firms became public, with a listing on the Warsaw Stock Exchange. Four firms were delisted (three merged and one became private). Table 14-2 illustrates the massive growth in market capitalization and trading value (also relative to GDP) of the Warsaw Stock Exchange.

Due to the growth in the number of brokers and analysts, road show activity, and the number of trading sessions a week, the price efficiency of the Warsaw Stock Exchange improved dramatically in 1993–94, when bank privatization started to gain momentum.[57] Of the firms that went public, fifty-one were pub-

56. Abarbanell and Bonin (1997, p. 31).
57. Trading sessions were initially held on a weekly basis and then gradually increased in frequency until conventional daily trading was established in October 1994.

Table 14-2. *Price Efficiency of the Warsaw Stock Exchange, 1991–96*

Indicator	1991	1992	1993	1994	1995	1996
Market capitalization						
Millions of dollars	144	222	2,706	3,057	4,564	8,390
As percent of GDP	0.2	0.3	3.2	3.5	3.9	7.9
Trading value						
Millions of dollars	28	167	2,170	5,134	2,770	5,538
As percent of GDP	0.001	0.2	2.6	5.5	2.4	5.2
Turnover ratio (ratio of trading to market capitalization)	0.19	0.75	0.80	1.68	0.61	0.66
Warsaw Stock Exchange index (year end)	919	1,040	12,439	7,473	7,586	14,343
Percent change in local currency	. . .	+13	+1,095	–40	+2	+89
Percent change in dollars	. . .	–21	+779	–47	0	+63

Source: European Bank for Reconstruction and Development; Business Central Europe; *Polish Securities Commission.*

lic sector initial public offerings. These privatizations represented 85.5 percent of total proceeds from such share offerings. The mean gross proceeds were more than eleven times higher for public sector initial public offerings (PLN 264.67 million) than for private sector initial public offerings. Clearly, public sector initial public offerings, including that of BSK (with a market capitalization at the time of its public offering of $240 million), played a key role in developing the Warsaw Stock Exchange.

BUILDING CONFIDENCE IN THE PRIVATIZATION PROGRAM. In 1992 the Polish government announced its intention to privatize the nine regional banks one by one over a period of four years. Next, it decided to privatize the strongest banks, such as WBK and BSK, first. The sequential nature of the program as well as the intention to attract (small) investors by offering shares at relatively low prices were in line with predictions.[58]

The privatization decisions of the Polish government are evidence it was committed to privatization and economic reform.[59] Compared to private sector initial public offerings, public sector offerings were sold at lower prices (lower price-to-earnings ratios and higher underpricing). This was true especially during the first part of the privatization process. The mean underpricing for public sector initial

58. Perotti (1995); Biais and Perotti (1997).
59. Aussenegg (1999).

public offerings was 62 percent, or 40 percentage points higher than that of private sector public offerings.[60] This underpricing decreased over time, declining from 191.0 percent (1993–94) to 46.8 percent over the next two years and to 13.8 percent in the period 1997–98.[61] Again, this was in line with the confidence-building hypothesis that a government needs to offer investors greater underpricing in the first phase of the privatization program, when uncertainty about the robustness and sustainability of economic reform is the highest. Over time, the Polish government's decisions convinced investors that it would remain committed to reform.

Regression results indicate that the underpricing of public sector initial public offerings is significantly and positively related to firm size (there is no significant relation in private sector initial public offerings).[62] This contradicts the traditional explanations for underpricing and supports the hypothesis that the Polish government sold larger and relatively solid enterprises first and at low issue prices in order to build confidence in the privatization program.[63]

Also, the long-run performance of Polish public sector initial public offerings is in line with the market. This neutral long-run performance is different from the underperformance that private sector share offerings (including those issued on the Warsaw Stock Exchange) exhibit in the long run.[64] The long-run performance of public sector initial public offerings is consistent with the government wanting to ensure a positive experience for (small) investors so that they would keep participating in the privatization program.[65]

MAXIMIZING PRIVATIZATION PROCEEDS. There is evidence that public sector shares were offered at a substantial discount both in terms of lower price-to-earnings ratios and in terms of underpricing.[66] This indicates that the Polish government was more interested in building confidence for the privatization program than in opportunistically maximizing proceeds for the treasury. In addition, there are no indications that the government tried to time the initial public offerings of state-owned banks. The banks were privatized in a sequential manner, and the rate at which banks were offered to stock market investors was more a function of circumstances (such as the time it took to find strategic investors) than the level of the Warsaw

---

60. Jones and others (1999) examine international evidence and find average underpricing of 34.1 percent for public sector initial public offerings.

61. Aussenegg (1999).

62. Aussenegg (1999).

63. For the traditional explanations for underpricing, see Rock (1986).

64. See Loughran, Ritter, and Rydqvist (1994).

65. Aussenegg (1999).

66. Aussenegg (1999).

Stock Exchange index. Moreover, these strategic investors were invited to tender shares before the initial public offering took place. Again, this is not consistent with a government trying to maximize demand tension in the book.

STIMULATING WIDER OWNERSHIP OF SHARES AND ENSURING THE SUPPORT OF STAKEHOLDERS. The privatization of WBK offered individual investors their first experience with the initial public offering of a state-owned bank. They fully subscribed to the small-investor tranche of 20 percent of the issue and, more important, experienced a threefold increase from the issue price to the price on the Warsaw Stock Exchange.

In setting the issue price of BSK, the government was aware of the criticism it had received on the pricing of WBK shares. The price was set so that the equity of BSK was at book value, which was a premium of 25 percent compared to the valuation chosen for the equity offering of WBK. Nevertheless, when trading commenced, the stock price increased more than thirteenfold from the issue price.

More than 800,000 individual investors participated in the initial public offering of BSK. Although these investors were required to subscribe to at least ten shares, this minimum dropped to three shares because demand far exceeded supply.[67] Due to administrative problems, however, these investors were not able to trade their shares. The BSK privatization caused public discontent with the government's execution of the initial public offering.

Due to the shareholder structure, the corporate governance of BSK was ineffective. The widespread ownership of BSK shares, combined with the dualistic ownership structure in which the state held 33 percent of the shares and ING was limited to slightly below 26 percent, created two captains for one ship. This allowed the incumbent management to retain much power and to play one party against the other. Numerous examples illustrate that when incumbent management is allowed to stay in place after privatization, performance does not improve or even declines. The reason for this disappointing performance is that the managers in control of the banks in the era before privatization are unlikely to change their behavior. Especially in transition economies such as Poland, bank managers are not used to applying management techniques that lead to optimal economic results. Management lacks the incentives and training to maximize profits. Economic performance of the banking sector often even declines when these managers remain in place if—due to a diffuse shareholding structure—no dominant shareholder replaces the government. Typically, the corporate governance system

67. The minimum subscription size for these investors was 10 shares; the maximum was fixed at 5,000 shares.

of emerging economies is too weak to discipline management. When incumbent managers are left unchecked, they often make self-serving decisions, to the detriment of the bank's performance.

In the case of BSK, shareholders replaced all but one member of the supervisory board at the general meeting in March 1994. In turn, the supervisory board replaced all but one member of the management board. However, the remaining Ministry of Finance appointee was named president of a team of three, which was responsible for the day-to-day management of BSK. While the majority of incumbent management was replaced in a matter of months after the conclusion of BSK's initial public offering in January 1994, the Ministry of Finance ensured that it would be able to influence the management policy of BSK. Again, the Polish government's decisions were steps in the right direction. However, at the time of the share offering, the government was unwilling to complete the required trajectory to achieve the privatization objectives.

In July 1996 ING gained a majority interest (54 percent) in BSK by purchasing all but 5 percent of the state's stake. The privatization of BSK to a majority foreign owner and the creation of a clearly independent governance structure took two and a half years from the time of the initial public offering.

Lessons Learned from the Mexican and Polish Experience

The Mexican bank privatization was fundamentally flawed in that the government focused solely on maximizing revenue. The government selected inexperienced bidders, who overpaid on the basis of overly optimistic expectations. Moreover, the government set the scene for an unsustainable credit boom, which ended with the collapse of the banking system. The resulting bailout cost taxpayers more than $100 billion, about 16 percent of Mexican GDP.

The main faults of the bank privatization program could have been avoided if the Mexican government had used initial public offerings as the disposal strategy. First, the use of initial public offerings would have required the restructuring of banks considered too weak to survive in their current form. Second, international investors would have demanded realistic valuations based on financial reports compiled in line with internationally accepted accounting standards. Third, initial public offerings would have involved the participation of foreign banks, which would have brought the capital and expertise required to become internationally competitive. Fourth, initial public offerings would have penalized the government for altering institutional arrangements immediately after disposing of banking assets and would have required the government to build confidence by sequentially selling stakes in the state-owned banks. Public markets effectively block governments from opportunistically changing the rules midgame, as happened in the failed Mexican bank privatization program.

While the Polish privatization program was far from perfect, it compares favorably with that of Mexico. It achieved a number of objectives in due course and avoided an all-out collapse of the banking system. However, multiple, often conflicting, objectives, in combination with changing political priorities, led to suboptimal results and delayed the process. Stimulating wider ownership of shares, developing the local stock market, and building confidence in the bank privatization program were at least as important as improving the efficiency of the banking sector. These three objectives conflicted with the goal of restructuring the banking sector as a dispersed shareholder structure and combined with an underdeveloped corporate governance system unlikely to discipline (incumbent) bank management into making the painful but needed restructuring decisions. The sequential manner in which state-owned banks were privatized—in order to build confidence with investors—had a negative impact on the pace of banking reform.

Also, too much of the banks' equity remained in the hands of the treasury. This made improvements in corporate governance difficult, as there was much room for politicizing nominations for the board of directors. The government's interference in management decisions at the privatized banks slowed the pace of reform. Only after a significant period of time did the Polish government allow a foreign strategic investor to obtain a majority stake. This important decision removed an obstacle to restructuring the privatized banks, allowing foreign banks to inject needed capital, expertise, and technology. Ultimately, initial public offerings proved to be a productive strategy for privatizing banks in Poland.

Conclusions

Bank privatization has been prevalent throughout the world and is gathering momentum in the developing economies as a means of fostering economic development. However, governments pursue privatization for various reasons, including increasing efficiency, developing a market-oriented industry, importing new capital and know-how, ensuring stakeholder support, developing the local stock market, building confidence in the privatization program, eliminating soft lending, maximizing proceeds, and stimulating wider ownership of shares.

Some privatization programs (as in Mexico) fail because the government focuses too narrowly on the desire to maximize proceeds while ignoring other important goals, such as the need to improve efficiency. Poland, in contrast, pursued conflicting objectives, which led to suboptimal results and slow progress. As a starting point for privatization, governments should recognize that a competitive banking sector is a critical ingredient of economic development and pursue privatization with the primary goal of fostering a more efficient and market-oriented banking sector. This means reducing the influence of the state on credit allocation decisions and allowing the participation of international investors.

Some methods of privatization are more effective than others. Initial public offerings, in particular, tend to minimize suboptimal behavior and eliminate inefficiencies, while achieving the other goals, such as overcoming the opposition of interest groups. The value of initial public offerings as a way to privatize state-owned banks are as follows:

—They require reliable numbers and realistic valuations of banks' assets.

—They may require the restructuring of the bank.

—They allow foreign banks to purchase a significant stake, attracting much-needed capital and expertise.

—They block governments from opportunistically changing the rules midgame.

References

Abarbanell, Jeffrey S., and John P. Bonin. 1997. "Bank Privatization in Poland: The Case of Bank Slaski." *Journal of Comparative Economics* 25, no. 1: 31–61.

Aussenegg, Wolfgang. 1999. "Going Public in Poland: Case-by-Case Privatizations, Mass Privatization, and Private Sector Initial Public Offerings." Working Paper. Vienna University of Technology.

Barth, James, Gerard Caprio Jr., and Ross Levine. 2001. "Banking Systems around the Globe: Do Regulation and Ownership Affect Performance and Stability?" In *Prudential Supervision: What Works and What Doesn't*, edited by Frederic Mishkin. National Bureau of Economic Research Conference Report. University of Chicago Press.

Biais, Bruno, and Enrico Perotti. 1997. "Machiavellian Underpricing." Working Paper. Université des Sciences Sociales de Toulouse, University of Amsterdam, and Centre for Economic Policy Research, December.

Black, Bernard, Reinier Kraakman, and Anna Tarassova. 2000. "Russian Privatization and Corporate Governance: What Went Wrong?" *Stanford Law Review* 52: 1731–808.

Boehmer, Ekkehart, Robert C. Nash, and Jeffrey M. Netter. 2003. "Bank Privatization in Developing and Developed Countries: Cross-Sectional Evidence on the Impact of Economic and Political Factors." Paper presented at the World Bank conference on bank privatization, Washington, November 20–21.

Bonin, John P., Iftekhar Hasan, and Paul Wachtel. 2003. "Bank Privatization and Performance: Evidence from Transition Countries." Paper presented at the World Bank conference on bank privatization, Washington, November 20–21.

Clarke, George, Robert Cull, and Mary Shirley. 2003. "Empirical Studies of Bank Privatization: An Overview." Paper presented at the World Bank conference on bank privatization, Washington, November 20–21.

D'Souza, Juliet, and William L. Megginson. 1999. "The Financial and Operating Performance of Privatized Firms during the 1990s." *Journal of Finance* 54, no. 4: 1397–438.

Huibers, Fred E. 1994. *The Pricing of Public Sector and Private Sector IPOs: Theory and Evidence.* Delft: Eburon.

Huibers, Fred E., and Enrico C. Perotti. 1999. "The Performance of Privatization Stocks in Emerging Markets: The Role of Political Risk." *Advances in Financial Economics* 4: 1–27.

Jones, Steven, and others. 1999. "Share Issue Privatizations as Financial Means to Political and Economic Ends." *Journal of Financial Economics* 53, no. 2: 217–53.

La Porta, Rafael, Florencio López-de-Silanes, and Andrei Shleifer. 2002. "Government Ownership of Banks." *Journal of Finance* 57, no. 1: 265–301.

Ljungqvist, Alexander, Tim Jenkinson, and William Wilhelm. 2000. "Has the Introduction of Book Building Increased the Efficiency of International IPOs?" Working Paper. Stern School of Business, New York University.

Loughran, Tim, Jay Ritter, and Kristian Rydqvist. 1994. "Initial Public Offerings: International Insights." *Pacific-Basin Financial Journal* 2, no. 2–3: 165–99.

McLindon, Michael P. 1996. *Privatization and Capital Market Development: Strategies to Promote Economic Growth.* Westport, Conn.: Praeger.

Megginson, William, and Maria Boutchkova. 2000. "The Impact of Privatization on Capital Market Development and Individual Ownership." *Financial Management* 29: 31–76.

Megginson, William L., and Jeffrey M. Netter. 2002. "From State to Market: A Survey of Empirical Studies on Privatization." *Journal of Economic Literature* 39, no. 2: 321–89.

Megginson, William, and others. Forthcoming. "The Choice of Private versus Public Market: Evidence from Privatizations." *Journal of Finance* 59 (December).

Menyah, Kojo, Krishna N. Paudyal, and Charles G. Inyangete. 1990. "The Pricing of Initial Offerings of Privatised Companies on the London Stock Exchange." *Accounting and Business Research* 21, no. 81: 50–56.

Mondshean, Thomas, and Timothy Opiela. 1997. "Banking Reform in a Transition Economy: The Case of Poland." *Federal Reserve Bank of Chicago Economic Perspectives* (March–April): 16–32.

Otchere, Isaac. 2003. "Do Privatized Banks in Middle- and Low-Income Countries Perform Better than Rival Banks? An Intra-Industry Analysis of Bank Privatization." Paper presented at the World Bank conference on bank privatization, Washington, November 20–21.

Perotti, Enrico. 1993. "Bank Lending in Transition Economies." *Journal of Banking and Finance* 17: 1021–32.

———. 1995. "Credible Privatization." *American Economic Review* 85, no. 4: 847–59.

Perotti, Enrico C., and S. E. Guney. 1993. "The Structure of Privatization Plans." *Financial Management* 22: 84–98.

Perotti, Enrico, and Pieter van Oijen. 2001. "Privatization, Stock Market Development, and Political Risk." *Journal of International Money and Finance* 49: 403–52.

Poloucek, Stanislav. 2003. "Privatization and Banking Sector Efficiency." In *Reforming the Financial Sector in Central European Countries,* edited by Stanislav Poloucek, pp. 1–30. Basingstoke: Palgrave Macmillan.

Rock, Kevin. 1986. "Why New Issues Are Underpriced." *Journal of Financial Economics* 15, no. 1–2: 187–212.

Sherman, Ann. 2002. "Global Trends in IPO Methods: Book Building versus Auctions." Working Paper. University of Notre Dame.

Shleifer, Andrei, and Robert Vishny. 1994. "Politicians and Firms." *Quarterly Journal of Economics* 109, no. 4: 995–1025.

Subrahmanyam, Avanidhar, and Sheridan Titman. 1999. "The Going-Public Decision and the Development of Financial Markets." *Journal of Finance* 54, no. 3: 1045–82.

Verbrugge, James, William L. Megginson, and Wanda L. Owens. 1999. "State Ownership and the Financial Performance of Privatized Banks: An Empirical Analysis." In *Bank Privatization: Conference Proceedings of a Policy Research Workshop,* edited by Harvey Rosenblum, pp. 1–34. Federal Reserve Bank of Dallas.

DAVID M. BINNS
RONALD J. GILBERT

15

Employee Stock Ownership Plans

INTERNATIONAL COMPETITIVE FORCES are accelerating the movement to-ward globalization of financial markets. As a result of lowered barriers to communications and information technology, political borders for financial services often include a much larger territory than do market areas for most goods and services. The rapid development of international financial markets has therefore increased the importance of restructuring financial institutions in developing countries to better facilitate their ability to provide the financial services that are key to supporting economic development.

Trade, the efficient use of resources, savings, and risk taking are the cornerstones of a growing economy; the biggest difference between rich and poor countries is the efficiency with which they use their resources. Finance is the key to investment and hence to economic growth, so the financial system's contribution to growth lies precisely in its ability to increase that efficiency. Governments in developing countries have therefore been obliged to restructure and privatize underperforming or insolvent financial institutions to ensure their ability to compete effectively in the increasingly international financial markets.

This process of restructuring and privatization of financial institutions provides governments with an opportunity to rethink and reshape their financial systems to support the development of a more robust and balanced financial structure, which in turn will help improve the ability of the domestic financial systems to contribute to growth. The process of restructuring and privatization is nevertheless an inherently political process. Governments must be sensitive to the need to balance the necessary process of restructuring with an eye to both preserving domestic financial stability and ensuring the opportunity of domestic investors to participate in the financial restructuring process.

As the rate of reform and privatization increases around the world, privatization programs are increasingly incorporating an element of employee ownership. The purpose of employee participation is to encourage greater support for these initiatives and to ensure that ownership of the enterprises will be shared broadly by its workers and citizens at large, not just by domestic and foreign investors. Even a relatively small employee ownership component in a restructured enterprise can play a key role in the reform and privatization process. Employee stock ownership plans can help create a constituency for the reform process, broaden participation in the ownership of capital assets, help raise capital for the financial institution, and recruit and retain key employees.

There is extensive international experience with the use of employee ownership plans in the context of reform and privatization programs in both the developed world and emerging market economies. Over the past fifteen years, well over twenty countries have incorporated some form of employee ownership in privatized enterprises and, in many cases, have adopted specific legislative and fiscal policies to facilitate the acquisition of share ownership by employees. While these plans have historically played a limited role in the context of reforming or privatizing state-owned financial institutions as compared to other corporate entities, the potential advantages that properly structured employee ownership transactions offer for financial sector reform merit consideration.[1] Over a thousand financial institutions in the United States (banks, insurance companies, holding and investment companies, investment banking firms, and thrift institutions) have successfully implemented such plans. Most employee stock ownership plans in financial institutions hold a minority stake in the company, though in a few cases the plans acquire a majority ownership position (see appendix 15A on regulatory guidelines).

In the developing world the experience of financial institutions with employee ownership plans, though limited, nevertheless suggests that such plans can play an important role in the restructuring and privatization of the financial sector. Properly structured, these plans offer the potential to facilitate the privatization of financial institutions and to help broaden participation in capital formation associated with economic development efforts. Countries as diverse as Argentina, Bolivia, Chile, China, Egypt, France, Hungary, Jamaica, Pakistan, Poland, Russia,

---

1. These plans are commonly referred to as employee stock ownership plans, or ESOPs.

Slovenia, South Korea, the United States, and the United Kingdom have made employee ownership and broad-based ownership a key element of their privatization and economic development strategies.

The Varieties of Employee Ownership

Specific techniques for utilizing employee ownership vary widely from country to country, and the use of employee ownership in international privatization efforts is subject to different social, legal, and economic conditions. Indeed, the flexibility of the concept is one of the key attributes of employee ownership. In its simplest terms, however, employee ownership seeks to create incentive reward systems predicated on widespread ownership of productive capital.

One of the main attractions of employee ownership is its broad appeal in terms of both macroeconomic policy and corporate reorganization. Policymakers implement employee ownership strategies for a variety of reasons, ranging from distributing private ownership broadly throughout the economy, enhancing enterprise performance by giving workers an economic stake in its financial success, improving labor-management relations, and promoting notions of economic and social justice. Establishing widespread capital ownership is seen as a means of strengthening the constituency for free enterprise by giving large numbers of employees a direct financial stake in the performance of private corporations.

It is important to emphasize in this context that employee ownership does not necessarily mean ownership exclusively by employees. Particularly in the context of the privatization of state-owned enterprises, "mixed" privatizations—involving outside investors (both individual and institutional), foreign companies, and employees—are likely to predominate. The state may retain some ownership rights, as well. In most cases, employee ownership is limited to a minority stake in the enterprise to avoid the problem of management entrenchment and insider control, which may be antithetical to the introduction of market reforms.[2]

Nor does employee ownership mean that day-to-day control, or overall management, or decisionmaking will be in the hands of a large group of employees. Just as in traditional corporations, boards of directors and management will continue to be responsible for developing long-range business plans, subject to the oversight and ultimate control of the company's shareholders. Properly structured

---

2. The experience of the Russian privatization program is illustrative in this context. Immediately following the first round of privatizations of medium-size and large enterprises, employees and managers owned an average of two-thirds of the enterprises' stock. In the absence of shareholder rights and securities law standards, however, most of that ownership was eventually acquired by an elite minority within the enterprise or by well-financed outsiders.

employee ownership plans can nevertheless ensure that employees have influence through voting rights, access to information, and representation in formal corporate governance structures.

Obviously, employee share ownership will be optimized in an environment that clearly defines private property rights, securities laws, shareholder rights (including voting and information disclosure), and the mechanisms for shareholders to sell their shares. The development of efficient domestic capital markets—which can be enhanced through state-sponsored efforts to promote broad-based participation in share ownership through citizen participation in privatization transactions—is particularly helpful in the context of employee ownership. Efficient capital markets provide privatized enterprises with a means to access much needed long-term capital to fund their growth. In addition, they strengthen employee stock ownership plans because they provide liquidity for the shares acquired by employees. Without such a liquidity mechanism, provisions must be made by the company or the employee plan itself to repurchase employees' shares. In cyclical downturns or in times of difficulties for the company, this repurchase liability can create additional cash demands, which might depress share values.

Attracting strategic investors who will provide capital, know-how, and potential openings for new markets to the privatized enterprise is another essential element of an overall privatization strategy. In that regard, the integration of employee ownership plans in restructured enterprises can be perceived as a positive development by investors.

The vast majority of successful employee stock ownership plans have been tied to some aspect of credit availability. It is in this context that financial institutions are in a unique position. Not only can these plans play a strategic role in the reform or privatization of the financial institution itself, but financial institutions can also provide credit for employee ownership programs in private sector companies or in other state-owned enterprises slated for privatization.

There is considerable empirical evidence, especially from the United States and the United Kingdom, of the beneficial effect that employee ownership can have on corporate performance.[3] The research indicates that companies that combine significant levels of employee ownership with participatory management techniques show productivity improvements compared to their non–employee-owned competitors.

---

3. See www.beysterinstitute.org; www.esopservices.com/research. For a comprehensive review of the evidence of the impact of employee ownership on corporate performance, see National Center for Employee Ownership (2002) (www.proshare.org/research/eso.asp).

Practical Considerations

Technically, in an employee stock ownership plan a trust is established for the exclusive benefit of employee participants, and the employees beneficially own the stock held in trust for them.[4] The essence of the trust vehicle is that there is some restriction on rights and benefits, compared to the rights enjoyed by individuals who own stock directly in their own name as minority shareholders. Along with these restrictions may come certain benefits, such as greater regulatory protections, corporate tax deductions, and the ability to use the stock ownership plan as a technique of corporate finance. The trust structure also helps to ensure a stable base of long-term employee holdings. In countries that do not have the proper legal structure for trust law, one approach has been to establish employee associations or other special-purpose vehicles (parallel to the trust structure) to hold shares on behalf of employees.

It is not uncommon for these trusts to acquire shares as a result of a contribution from the sponsoring corporation as an employee benefit. Such a nonleveraged employee stock ownership plan does not require the use of debt and is simply a means whereby the company chooses to share stock with employees as a long-term benefit or retirement award. The shares contributed to the trust are allocated to individual employee accounts according to a preestablished formula and are held in the trust for a specified period of time. As noted below, this approach can also be used to facilitate capital formation in banks and bank holding companies.

The fundamental principle underlying leveraged employee stock ownership plans is that it allows employees to access capital credit—backed by the sponsoring corporation's guarantee—to acquire an ownership stake. In addition, trust-based models aggregate ownership so that employees as a group can obtain efficiencies of scale in acquiring their shares. In the leveraged plan, the financial institution, in accepting its own stock as collateral for credit offered to employees, is providing an equity incentive on a low-risk basis. To the extent that the credit cannot be repaid, the financial institution recovers the shares that are pledged as collateral. Except for transaction costs and the administrative cost, there is no other loss to the financial institution, even in the event of a default. This should allow banks to be significantly more aggressive in extending credit to the leveraged plan.

---

4. In international practice, an employee stock ownership plan commonly can be any of a broad range of employee ownership vehicles, including direct purchases, stock options, and others. For purposes of this discussion, we use the term in its more narrow perspective to describe a trust-based or association vehicle with specific legal attributes.

The financing to acquire the stock for a leveraged plan can come from the financial institution itself, from the selling government, from an outside buyer, from a third-party lender, or from a combination of these sources. The package might include work-rule changes negotiated with employee groups or access to employee pension assets. The debt of these leveraged plans is typically repaid with contributions (sometimes tax deductible) made to the plan from the sponsoring corporation, based on future revenues. The plan then transfers those funds to the bank and releases an equivalent number of shares from collateral for allocation to individual employee accounts. Dividends on stock owned by a leveraged plan can also provide self-financing, to the extent that these dividends are sufficient to repay the principal and interest necessary to liquidate the acquisition debt.

There are four steps in a standard leveraged employee stock ownership plan:

—A loan is made to the employee stock ownership plan (backed by a company guarantee) to allow the plan to purchase company stock.[5]

—The plan uses those borrowed funds to purchase stock in the company and holds those shares in the plan on behalf of participating employees.

—The company guarantees the lender that the company will make regular payments out of future company earnings to enable it to service the debt. The company cash is contributed to the plan, which then forwards the funds to the lending institution.

—As the loan is repaid, a proportional amount of stock (based on a formula in the plan) is released from the collateral account and allocated to the individual accounts of participating employees in the plan.

For both the selling shareholder (the government) and the purchaser (the employees of state-owned financial institutions) it is exceedingly important to establish initial and ongoing standards for determining the fair market value of the shares. This is typically done by retaining the services of an independent appraisal firm to conduct an arm's-length appraisal of the financial institution and provide an opinion as to the appropriate enterprise value. Such an analysis will include a comprehensive assessment of the earnings and cash flow and market position of the financial institution, including comparisons with comparable institutions.[6]

5. The more common practice is for the lender to make a loan to the company, which then reloans the money to the employee stock plan on substantially similar terms. This "back-to-back loan" procedure simplifies the loan documentation between the company and the lender without respect to the plan itself. In repaying the loan, the company debt and the plan debt are typically amortized on the same schedule, although the amortization schedule can differ.

6. For a detailed discussion of the process of valuing shares in the context of employee ownership transactions, see ESOP Association, "Valuing ESOP Shares" (www.esopassociation.org).

There are several key issues to consider when valuing a financial institution. The first issue is the quality of the financial institution's earning assets, such as types of loans to businesses and consumers and investments in money market instruments, bonds, and notes. A close examination of the way loan portfolios are underwritten, priced, collateralized, diversified, monitored, and reserved for is also necessary. Tied to this examination of asset quality is the adequacy and soundness of the financial institution's capital structure. Due to the fact that financial institutions operate with a high degree of financial leverage, lenders must have adequate reserves and capital bases to absorb loan losses.

The second issue is the financial institution's asset-liability management practice and policy. It is necessary to evaluate whether the institution is properly matching or hedging its loans with a deposit structure that will generate a net interest margin sufficient to produce returns on equity that will attract and retain investor support. (In the United States, banking institutions typically generate a 15–20 percent return on equity, with 1.25–1.75 percent return on assets.) Improper asset-liability management practices caused many U.S. savings and loan institutions and banks to suffer in the late 1970s and early 1980s, when interest costs for funding assets (such as fixed-rate home mortgages) exceeded the rates being earned by the institutions.[7]

A third issue is the financial institution's management of noninterest, or overhead, expenses, which are largely related to personnel and the operation of the facilities. The development of noninterest sources of income (cash management, asset management, trust banking, investment banking, and merger and acquisitions advisory services) has become increasingly important for many financial institutions, to reduce dependency on making money purely through net interest margins generated by loans and deposits. Understanding a financial institution's earnings capabilities with respect to noninterest income-generating services has thus become an essential part of assessing an institution's earning capacity.

Creating New Capital

In addition to the benefits cited above, employee stock ownership plans offer other advantages to financial institutions. Prominent among these are the creation of pools of capital, often on a tax-advantaged basis, and the use of employee stock plans to facilitate a restructuring of the bank's ownership, including privatization. This section describes the benefits of employee stock ownership plans in countries in which a tax deduction is available for contributions made to the plans.

---

7. Personal communication from Gregory W. Feldmann, executive vice president, FNB corporation.

The principle upon which an employee stock ownership plan can be used to create capital is based on the fact that the plan is itself a form of an employee retirement trust. As such, contributions to the plan can be tax deductible for the sponsoring institution, as is the case with all tax-qualified retirement plans. In the case of an employee stock ownership plan, the contribution can be in the form of newly issued shares from the institution itself. This noncash contribution generates a year-end tax deduction based on the current value of the shares contributed to the plan by the institution. In addition, employee purchases of shares also generate new capital. The multiyear contribution stream generated by such transactions can result in substantial benefits to the institution.

The benefit of tax deductions is even more important for financial institutions, which leverage deposits to make loans and investments to produce income. The following illustrates the impact of employee stock ownership plan contributions in helping a bank meet its return-on-assets and return-on-equity goals. The key profit goal of a bank is, of course, to enhance the spread between the rates paid to depositors and the interest rate the bank earns on loans. For purposes of the following example, assume that a reasonable return on assets is 1.25 percent. Assume furthermore a tax rate of 42 percent.

After establishing the employee stock ownership trust, the sponsoring banking institution contributes to the trust $100,000 worth of newly issued shares from the bank's authorized share capital. Based on a tax rate of 42 percent, the $100,000 stock contribution generates a tax deduction of $42,000, which increases the bank's retained earnings by a like amount (table 15-1).

Assuming a bank's normal operating leverage of approximately fourteen times its capital base, this additional capital may allow the bank to generate earning assets (that is, loans) of $588,000. Assuming a 1.25 percent return on assets, the $630,000 ($42,000 + $588,000) of additional loans can generate an end-of-year after-tax profit of $7,875. That profit could be similarly leveraged to produce additional earning assets, further expanding the bank's ability to generate profits. Table 15-1 provides a simple example of how a retail bank could maximize its capital from tax-deductible contributions to an employee stock ownership plan by attracting new deposits. If the bank were to contribute $100,000 worth of company shares to the plan every year, and if it were able to successfully leverage the contributions as per the example above, it could generate $797,000 in after-tax profits over ten years, based on a 1.25 percent return on assets. Contributions to the plan of newly issued stock must, of course, be tempered by the bank's ability to grow effectively so that the shareholder dilution resulting from newly issued shares would be compensated for through accelerated growth in the value of the bank's shares.

Table 15-1. *Growth over Ten Years, Annual $100,000 Contribution by Employee Stock Option Plan*
Dollars

Year	Plan deposit	Retained earnings	New capital from profit	Total new capital	Leveraged assets	After-tax return on assets of 1.25 percent
1	100,000	42,000	0	42,000	630,000	7,875
2	100,000	42,000	7,875	91,875	1,378,125	17,226
3	100,000	42,000	17,226	151,101	2,266,523	28,331
4	100,000	42,000	28,331	221,433	3,321,496	41,518
5	100,000	42,000	41,518	304,951	4,574,277	57,178
6	100,000	42,000	57,178	404,130	6,061,954	75,774
7	100,000	42,000	75,774	521,904	7,828,570	97,857
8	100,000	42.000	97,857	661,761	9,926,427	124,080
9	100,000	42,000	124,080	827,842	2,417,632	155,220
10	100,000	42,000	155,220	1,025,062	15,375,938	192,199
Total	1,000,000	420,000	605,059	. . .	. . .	797,258

Source: Price (1997).

Creating a Market

Whether in the context of privatizing state-owned banks or of restructuring the ownership of private financial institutions, employee stock ownership plans offer a practical means for transferring stock to employees. This can be accomplished through direct company contributions of stock as in the example above, by employee purchases of shares, or by leveraged acquisition of stock, with the loan repaid out of future bank profits. Each of these scenarios can, and often is, facilitated by tax incentives (see appendix 15B, at the end of this chapter, for a list of typical tax incentives).

There are also a number of practical issues unique to financial institutions that require special approaches to such transactions. For example, in some jurisdictions banks cannot purchase their own shares. In those cases, the plan or a bank holding company can facilitate the transaction. If the plan acquires its shares on credit, the resulting debt reduces the amount of capital available to the bank by an equivalent amount. However, if the loan is not guaranteed by the bank itself but by a bank holding company, capital requirements may not be reduced. In addition, regulatory requirements typically limit the amount of debt that financial institutions may carry. In the United States, financial regulators also must approve change of control of bank ownership, with reporting requirements for employment stock ownership plans acquiring more than 10, 25, or 50 percent of a bank's share capital.

Impediments

Over twenty years of experience with implementation of employee stock ownership plans demonstrates that one or more circumstances can substantially reduce the probability that a plan can facilitate the restructuring or the privatization of state-owned financial institutions. The following outlines the most commonly encountered impediments to effective utilization of these plans.

—Distressed situations: Over the past twenty years, approximately 2–3 percent of employee stock ownership plans formed in the United States have been as a result of distressed situations, in which employee groups bought the company as a means of preventing either a total shutdown or large-scale layoffs. While there are some success stories with such buyouts, there have also been a number of failures. Employee ownership will not turn bad managers into good managers, nor will it change negative market conditions into positive ones. Perhaps the most visible failure was United Airlines, which declared bankruptcy in 2002. The airline was more than 50 percent owned by an employee stock ownership plan established under distressed conditions. Significant cuts in pay and benefits were agreed to by most employees (the Flight Attendants Union declined to participate in the stock ownership plan). Most observers agree that the unique problems faced by the airline industry were the primary cause of United's bankruptcy (several other major U.S. airlines also declared bankruptcy), and clearly United Airlines could not be "saved" merely by being employee owned.

—Lack of credit availability: Without access to capital credit, normally provided by the state, the employee ownership plan would typically be unable to acquire any significant block of stock. Even in developed economies, rank-and-file employees rarely have the financial resources to purchase shares. If the plan cannot borrow funds, or if it borrows on unfavorable terms, its effect on restructuring or privatization will be nominal at best.

—Ideological opposition: Even in countries with a long history of successful employee ownership plans, government officials still may not understand what these plans are and how they work. This is even more so the case in developing countries. In the early 1990s in Poland, key officials in the privatization ministry labeled the employee stock ownership plan a "communist" approach and strongly opposed it. This opposition was partially overcome, and Poland now has more of these plans per capita (approximately a thousand) than any country other than the United States. However, because of such opposition, these plans were limited to small and midsize companies in Poland, so their full potential impact in the privatization process was never realized.

—Inexperienced management: Employee ownership is no substitute for experienced professional management. While research overwhelmingly demonstrates that companies with employee stock ownership plans outperform companies without them, a strong management team and an experienced board of directors is still essential for long-term success.

—Lack of public markets: Access to public stock markets is not a requirement for implementation of an employee stock ownership plan. In fact, the substantial majority of these plans in the United States, including many financial institutions, are in privately held companies. However, if a company remains without a publicly traded market, then the requirement to pay plan participants for the value of their stock upon death, disability, retirement, or termination of service—or after some specified minimum number of years of employment—can become a significant financial burden to the company. This so-called repurchase liability competes for capital needed for business expansion. In the early years of a privatized or restructured employee-owned company, the lack of a publicly traded market is not a major issue. The longer the plan is in existence, the greater this problem can be.

—Lack of outside investors: Lack of outside investors is not in itself an impediment to a successful employee ownership plan. However, in many instances the capital from outside investors is key to initial capitalization and to enabling a financial institution to effectively function and grow. Experience shows that if there are no initial investors outside the employee plan, it will be important to attract investors once the financial institution begins operations.

—Cutthroat competition: If after a company becomes privatized through employee stock ownership, competitors offer below-market prices, lure away talented management with lucrative compensation packages, or block potential customers, then the probability of a successful transition is dramatically lowered.

—Competition from management: Key management personnel may desire to obtain significant equity in the privatized or restructured company. While research demonstrates that management ownership combined with broad-based employee ownership provides the most effective model for enhanced performance, management buyers may view the employee plan as their competition and wish to minimize or eliminate it over time. If the privatized company is initially structured with broad-based employee ownership but there are inadequate safeguards in place, then management may seize the opportunity to buy stock from employees at what can prove to be a very low or unfair price; in a relatively short time, stock ownership may be concentrated in the hands of a small number of managers or investors.

—Lack of legal and regulatory protections: In the absence of established legal and regulatory standards governing the operation of employee stock ownership plans, as well as protections for minority shareholder rights in a given jurisdiction, such protections must be incorporated into the plan's documents. The experience of the Russian privatization program is illustrative in this respect. Immediately following the initial phase of privatization in the 1990s, employees owned, on average, approximately two-thirds of the shares in the majority of medium-size and large Russian companies. But without sufficient securities laws and protections for the rights of minority shareholders, these shares were consolidated into the hands of managers and investors in a relatively short period of time, providing employees with little of the intended benefits of broad-based stock ownership.

Case Studies

The following six case studies illustrate how employee stock ownership plans can facilitate the restructuring or privatization of financial institutions. The three cases in developing countries provide differing perspectives on the role of employee stock ownership plans in privatization and wealth creation. The two case studies of community banks in the United States illustrate the benefits of employee stock ownership plans from a perspective of capital formation, ownership transition, and employee benefits.

Royal Bank of Trinidad and Tobago

Royal Bank of Trinidad and Tobago (RBTT) was established in 1971, when the Royal Bank of Canada (RBC) decided to divest itself of its bank holdings in Trinidad and Tobago.[8] Though not the result of privatization in the formal sense, RBTT was nevertheless created as a result of a divestiture that was similar in many respects to what would have occurred if the bank had been sold by the government.

As part of the buyout of RBC, the employee pension fund was frozen and the plan's excess assets (funds left after purchasing annuities for participating employees) were transferred to a newly created employee stock ownership plan in 1976. The plan became a major equity investor in the new RBTT by purchasing a block of stock at the offering price of $1.55 a share. All full-time RBTT employees

8. Personal communication from Hubert Alleyne, executive officer (retired), Royal Bank of Trinidad and Tobago.

were assigned individual accounts in the plan, and RBTT stock acquired with the pension assets was allocated on a pro rata basis to these accounts based on each employee's assets in the frozen pension plan. Employees were also given an opportunity to purchase additional RBTT shares for their accounts, using their own funds. As a result, the plan became the bank's largest single shareholder, and it has remained one of the largest shareholders up to the present time. Employee ownership of RBTT has been as high as 20 percent of total shares outstanding, the legal limit for a single shareholder under Trinidad and Tobago law without triggering a requirement to bid for the whole company.

The plan is administered by RBTT's trust company. Three trustees have the fiduciary responsibility to ensure that the plan's assets are managed in the best interests of the employees. Two of the trustees are appointed by RBTT management; one trustee is elected by employees every five years. Under the laws of Trinidad and Tobago, trustees are required to act in unanimity on all official activities, including the voting of the plan's stock.

RBTT employees are eligible to receive year-end bonuses, subject to the bank's earning net profits. Bonuses over the years have typically amounted to an average 8 percent of annual pay. Employees are legally required to invest 40 percent of their net bonus into the plan but may invest the entire bonus. Any money invested into the plan is exempt from taxation. (RBTT permits employees to access the value of their accounts for current liquidity by taking out loans backed by their shares.) When no additional shares are available (as when the plan held the legal limit of 20 percent of RBTT's shares), employees were able to invest their bonus payments into phantom shares or options that provided equivalent value to actual RBTT shares.

RBTT also pays an annual dividend to all shareholders of record. Over the years the average value of share dividends has been about 6 percent of per share value. Dividends on ESOP shares are also exempt from taxation.

Employees must stay with RBTT for at least five years to become fully vested in the shares in their accounts. When they leave the bank they are required to sell their shares back to the plan at the current market value. Employees receive a lump-sum distribution in cash for the entire value of their account. Those employees leaving the bank before attaining qualified retirement age are taxed at an average of 15 percent (which is lower than the standard tax rate). Employees who attain retirement age (sixty or sixty-five years, depending on their position in the bank) receive their distribution tax-free.

RBTT stock has performed quite well over the years. The employee stock ownership plan bought stock in 1976 at $1.55 a share. In 2004 each share was $45. As a result, many employees have received handsome distributions, which have enabled them to enjoy a secure retirement. A typical employee leaving before retirement with at least five years with the bank could qualify for a distribution two or three times his or her annual salary.

Phelps County Bank

Phelps County Bank (PCB), a state-chartered commercial bank in Rolla, Missouri (United States), offers an example of the benefits that employee stock ownership plans offer to financial institutions in terms of both facilitating ownership transition and enhancing the bank's competitive position.[9]

PCB was primarily owned by a one-bank holding company, Phelps County Bancshares (Bancshares), the stock of which was owned by one individual. The employee stock ownership plan at PCB was established in 1980, when the plan purchased 5 percent of the bank's outstanding shares. The sale was financed by the selling shareholder, who took back a note to be paid over four years. The selling shareholder was able to obtain a market price for a minority interest in the company, and the bank was able to use the stock in the employee plan as a benefit for employees, who would thereby acquire an ownership interest in the long-term growth of the bank. In 1984 the plan acquired an additional 8 percent stake, this time financed by a loan from another bank and guaranteed by Bancshares.

PCB's continued growth and stock price appreciation was facilitated by a general increase in the market value of community banks due to consolidation in the U.S. banking industry in the 1980s. The bank's management began to increasingly believe that the employee stock ownership plan provided PCB with a strategic competitive edge by cultivating an ownership culture in which employees benefited financially from the company's success. This led to a decision to pursue a strategy whereby planned transfer of ownership from the primary owner to the plan would help PCB maintain its independence and reinforce its competitive advantage in attracting qualified personnel.

In 1988 the plan increased its ownership to 35 percent with another debt-financed share acquisition. Under U.S. banking regulations, a plan's acquisition of more than a 25 percent stake triggered change of control provisions, which required PCB to register with the Federal Reserve Bank. As before, PCB's Bancshares holding company guaranteed the loan, which meant that the guarantee was recorded as a contingent liability on Bancshares' balance sheet and subtracted from equity in determining debt-to-equity ratios for meeting Federal Reserve requirements. Because the loan was guaranteed by the holding company and not the bank itself, the loan amount was not considered as a deduction from bank capital.

9. Brent (1997).

In 1990 PCB's management agreed with Bancshares' majority owner on a strategy to have the plan buy out the remainder of the shares in the holding company. As a first step, the plan acquired a majority ownership stake in PCB by purchasing another block of stock from Bancshares' owner. That purchase, which again required regulatory approval by the Federal Reserve, increased the employee ownership to 68 percent and resulted in PCB having a debt-to-equity ratio of 2.94 to 1. In 1993 the remaining stock was offered to the plan at a discounted price. The consummation of that transaction resulted in the plan becoming the sole owner of Bancshares.

PCB's president, Emma Lou Brett, is convinced that the employee stock ownership plan has made PCB a stronger institution.

> As we have seen two of our [independent bank] competitors sell more than once during the past ten years, our employee ownership has put us in a good position to gain new deposits and loans from customers who still want to bank with a local bank. We use our employee ownership in all our marketing, including business cards and messages on our phone system. Our stock has increased in value over 900 percent since we purchased our first stock in 1980. We have had no turnover in officer staff in ten years and very little turnover in other staff. This has allowed us to get excellent returns on the dollars invested in training and education. It is also a pleasant surprise for new customers to find knowledgeable and empowered bankers to handle their financial needs in an employee-owned bank. . . . Even though we have faced some serious regulatory concerns, we do not hesitate to recommend employee ownership to other banks. We think it is an excellent way for a community bank to retain its independence. We have a great deal of pride in our bank. We feel that we have proven to our community, our directors, and the regulators that employee ownership of a community bank can produce a winning formula. We have outgrown all of our competitors, and each employee-owner is building wealth for his or her future.

Virginia Community Bankshares

The experience of Virginia Community Bankshares (VCB) illustrates how an employee stock ownership plan can provide a valuable retirement benefit for employees of a successful community bank in a rural area.[10]

10. Personal communication from A. Pierce Stone, chairman, Virginia Community Bank, immediate past chairman, Independent Community Bankers of America.

VCB started business in 1976 in Louisa, Virginia (United States), and operated for seven years without a retirement plan for its employees. This is fairly typical for start-up banks, which often make little if any profit for the first five years. It generally takes that long to establish a book of business that is profitable. The bank's board of directors reviewed various types of retirement and profit-sharing plans and concluded that an employee stock ownership plan offered the most benefits both for the bank and for the employees. Not only would the plan provide bank employees with a long-term ownership stake in the bank, but it also offered a tax-advantaged vehicle to provide new capital for the bank and create a source of liquidity for the bank's common stock. VCB subsequently established its plan in 1983.

VCB funded the plan with annual contributions of newly issued stock. As noted above, this not only provided VCB employees with a valuable long-term ownership benefit but also served to enhance the bank's capital formation. In one instance, VCB had a serious need for new capital at the bank level to support rapid growth, and this was accomplished with ease and no expense to the bank by contributing additional stock to the employee plan. While such a strategy is potentially problematic for bank shareholders, it has not been a problem to date for VCB, as the value of VCB stock has grown at a rapid pace, and the bank has continued to increase its dividends annually.

The value of VCB stock has grown at an average of 16 percent a year for the past eighteen years and has never declined in value in twenty-eight years. VCB stock, which sold for $10 a share in 1976, in 2004 had an adjusted value of $310 a share. Dividends have been paid annually and have increased for the past twenty years. Though the stock is not traded on an established stock market, the company's stock is widely held by approximately 350 shareholders.[11] Demand for the stock is strong, but there are few willing sellers given its excellent performance and the regular dividend.

Today the VCB employee plan owns 19 percent of the bank. The board of directors and the management believe that employee ownership has helped the bank attract excellent employees, who stay for the long term. Employees who have retired to date have been very pleased with the value passed on to them after a fairly short period of participation in the plan. As of 2002 the average account balance of plan participants was more than 180 percent of their annual wages. The overall value of the plan, including cash assets, is approximately $4.5 million, which is held in trust for the benefit of VCB's seventy-two employees.

11. In a typical employee stock ownership plan, the shares are held in a trust fund on behalf of employees. As a result, the plan counts as only one shareholder since the shareholder of record is the trustee. The employees are considered beneficiaries of the trust rather than shareholders of record.

National Commercial Bank of Jamaica

The employee stock ownership plan established by National Commercial Bank of Jamaica (NCB) played an important role in the transition of the bank from a 100 percent state-owned financial institution to full private ownership.

The Jamaican government nationalized NCB in 1977. At that time, NCB had the second-largest banking operation on the island, with total assets of more that $236 million. Since 1978 NCB has had a strong record of growth and profitability. In 1985 a holding company, NCB Group Limited, was incorporated to reorganize NCB and its subsidiaries. In 1986 National Investment Bank of Jamaica (NIBJ), a government-owned company, acquired the entire issued share capital of NCB Group.

NIBJ subsequently offered for sale 51 percent of NCB's share capital, including 30,600,000 ordinary shares of $1.00 each in NCB Group, of which 26,683,560 were offered to the public at $2.95 a share and the remainder (13 percent) was made available to the trustees of the NCB Employee Share Scheme. The company was listed on the Jamaica Stock Exchange in December 1986. In 1991 NIBJ sold a further 6,000,000 ordinary shares of $1.00 each to the trustees of the Employee Share Scheme.

The initial employee shares were sold in stages, with different payment arrangements and share restrictions associated with each stage. In the first stage, 13 percent of the shares were reserved for employees via a "step" approach, comprising four categories of employee preference shares: grant shares, matching shares (one for one), shares purchased at a discount, and shares purchased at full price. The overall first-round ceiling was 2,070 shares per person. This 13 percent block of shares was held in a trust, with the purchase from the government financed with a loan from NCB to be repaid out of future employee earnings, either in cash or in installments, over a two-year period. Ninety-eight percent of eligible employees participated.

Shares unsold after the first round were offered again in a second round, at less preferential rates and with a ceiling of 50,000 shares per person. Payment arrangements were similar to the first round. Employees' access to the shares depended on payment terms. Grant shares were not tradable for two years, matching and discount shares were tradable only to other employees via internal trading within the trust, and full-price, "priority," shares were freely tradable.

In 1992 NIBJ sold the remaining 39 percent of NCB to Jamaica M&N Investments Limited. In 1996 NCB merged with Mutual Security Bank Jamaica Limited, thus becoming a dominant force in the financial sector. In 2002 AIC Limited, Canada's largest privately held mutual fund company (whose majority owner is Jamaican-Canadian), acquired just over 75 percent of NCB's shares.

Allied Bank of Pakistan Limited

The employee stock ownership plan of the Allied Bank of Pakistan Limited (ABL) offers another creative example of facilitating the privatization of a state-owned financial institution.[12] Unfortunately, it also offers a cautionary tale of problems that can result from a lack of regulatory oversight of bank operations.

ABL is the fifth largest bank in Pakistan in terms of assets, deposits, and loans, with a network of 825 branches and 7,082 employees. In 1991 the government of Pakistan approved the partial privatization of ABL, which took place via an employee stock ownership plan that combined employee wage concessions, stock purchases, and corporate financing and provided employees with management control of the bank. The Allied Bank Management Group (AMG), led by the bank president and representing the employees of ABL, purchased 26 percent of ABL's shares at a price of Rs 70 a share, leading to the transfer of management. The purchases were funded through two pay increases (of 25 percent and 20 percent), paid out of increased bank earnings (profits increased 268 percent in the year following sale of the first tranche to employees); and through a 10 percent dividend on those shares. Also, under Pakistani law, banks may grant employees interest-free loans based on their salary level.

The pay hikes, therefore, qualified Allied Bank employees for larger loans with which to acquire shares. Although characterized as an employee purchase, this purchase of shares was substantially financed via increased company profits, first paid out as employee salaries and then paid over to the seller (the government). In the first year following privatization, employment at the bank increased from 7,200 to approximately 8,000. Under the sale agreement, AMG had an option to acquire a further 25 percent of the share capital at the same price within one year of the first sale. The second transaction was concluded in August 1993, resulting in AMG owning 51 percent of ABL.

Unfortunately, the evidence suggests that over time the ABL employees' group had been infiltrated by some unscrupulous parties. In 2001 Pakistan's Privatization Commission subsequently attempted to sell the Government of Pakistan's remaining 49 percent equity stake in ABL. However, the Privatization Commission was unable to sell the Pakistani government's stake in ABL because of the problems being faced by the bank, including the existence of huge *benami* accounts (accounts hiding illicit transactions). Due to the poor performance of ABL no annual report was published in 2000, 2001, and 2002. By June 2003 the

12. Gates and Saghir (1995); Privatization Commission (2001); Ihtasham ul Haque, "Two Banks in Run to Buy 51 pc ABL Shares" (www.dawn.com/2004/02/12/ebr4.htm [February 11, 2004]).

deposit base of the bank amounted to Rs 105 billion and total assets to Rs 114 billion. The paid-up capital was Rs 1 billion, and its equity account had a deficit of Rs 3.969 billion. The capital adequacy ratio was a negative 14 percent.

The privatization of the remaining 51 percent of ABL has been taken away from the Privatization Commission and handed over to the Central Bank of Pakistan. Under section 47 of the Banking and Companies Ordinance, the central bank is empowered to dispose of any mismanaged bank or arrange its merger with any other bank. In August 2004 a 51 percent majority stake in ABL was sold to an investor group for Rs 14.2 billion, subject to an agreement with the State Bank of Pakistan.

K-REP Bank of Kenya

K-REP was established in 1984 as a USAID-sponsored project with the objective of supporting nongovernmental organizations engaged in small and microenterprise lending through grants, technical assistance, and training.[13] K-REP operated as a cooperative for approximately ten years before making the decision to transform itself into a licensed commercial bank. As part of that commercialization effort, K-REP attracted equity financing from the International Finance Corporation (IFC), the African Development Bank (AfDB), and several private investors. At the time of the transformation, K-REP had a staff of 120, of which approximately 80 were field staff.

As part of the transformation, the ownership distribution also included a 10 percent stake for an employee stock ownership plan, which was financed with a grant from the World Bank's Consultative Group to Assist the Poor (CGAP). The Kwa Multipurpose Cooperative Society, a credit and savings cooperative representing K-REP staff, was used to purchase the plan's shares and to assign the initial ownership rights to members. Staff members who had been employed by K-REP for three years or more were eligible to participate in the plan. Participation was voluntary.

Half of the shares were allocated based on a point system incorporating the employees' positions within the bank and their tenure with K-REP. K-REP initially allocated 50,000 shares to staff, with the balance allocated as annual bonuses over five years. In addition, one free share was granted for every share purchased by an employee. The share purchases were supported through a loan scheme from K-REP. In case of payment default, all shares would be forfeited. In addition, if an employee left K-REP before completing five years, the employee forfeited rights to the "free" shares. Shares can be sold at times and dates specified by Kwa,

---

13. Campion and White (2001); Bohstedt, Kalyango, and Musana (2001).

though in case of death or permanent disability shares can be cashed out immediately. The employee plan has no representation on the K-REP board.

To the extent that employees' own funds are used to purchase shares, the element of risk in employee ownership plans can be significant in transforming microfinance institutions. There is usually a great deal of pressure to participate in the program, yet there is no proven stream of earnings to aid employees in making informed decisions, as the plan is typically launched in conjunction with the opening of the newly formed bank. Transforming microfinance institutions, therefore, need to be aware of this element of risk when launching an employee ownership plan to ensure a balance between individual risk and salary stability.

Employee Stock Ownership Plans in Korea

Over 25 percent of Korean financial institutions (banks, life and fire insurance companies, securities firms) have employee stock ownership plans (see table 15-2). The Korean Securities Finance Corporation (KSFC) is the largest administrator of such plans in Korea. Based on the twenty-four plans that the corporation administers, it has compiled the following advantages of such plans:

Advantages for employees are the following:

—They do not pay tax on the difference between the market price and the purchase price for stock acquired through the plan..

—They may deduct from their taxable income the contributions they make to the plan to purchase additional shares.

—Contributions of stock by the employer or major stockholders to the plan and subsequently allocated to the individual accounts of plan participants are nontaxable within the tax law limits.

—Dividend income on stocks is nontaxable up to 18 million won if the specific requirements in the tax law are satisfied.

—Income arising from the withdrawal of stock is subject to separate taxation at a lower rate if the participants have owned the stock more than three years.

—Deemed interest (benefits participants may have by receiving money without consideration or by borrowing money at a low interest rate from the employer to acquire stocks) may be exempt from tax.

Advantages for employers are the following:

—Contributions to the plan, compensation paid through the plan in the disposal of surplus funds, and expenses to support plan operations are deductible expenses.

—Deemed interest on the employer's loan to the plan are not included in gross income in tax treatment.

Type of firm	Participation ratio	Percent of average ownership
Securities (15 firms)	45.46	0.83
Life or fire insurance (4 firms)	80.55	6.45
Banks (5 firms)	76.11	0.73

Facilitating the Formation of Employee Stock Ownership Plans

Absent government support for employee ownership reforms, the viability of employee ownership as a significant factor in reform and privatization transactions will be limited. Employees lack the financial resources, the experience in negotiating the complexities of financial transactions, and the support of legal structures intended to promote the acquisition of capital assets for a broad range of workers.

Thus government policy must be supportive of employee ownership of privatized financial institutions and be consistent in regard to the principle of plan participation in privatization transactions. However, government policy needs to be flexible enough to encourage creative strategies for the design and implementation of these plans. Financial institutions are unique among institutions desiring to restructure or privatize due to their ability to, directly or indirectly, create the credit needed to form an employee stock ownership plan. These strategies will vary considerably among scenarios.

For example, the design of an employee stock ownership plan will be influenced by the timing of any initial public offering of stock. If the public offering is likely soon after implementation of the plan, a smaller set-aside for the plan may be justified based on the potential for significant share appreciation. In conjunction with an initial public offering, two other factors influence the size of the set-aside: the structure of the plan's trust (whether the trustee can sell shares on the market and thereby create liquidity for purchasing employee shares) and the structure of management share incentives (one set of incentives targeted at achieving the initial public offering and another in conjunction with the initial public offering and financed from the proceeds of that sale of stock).

If an initial public offering is not contemplated in the foreseeable future, the design of the employee stock ownership plan will need to take that into account in terms of the valuation of the shares and provisions for their sale by employees. Providing liquidity for employee shares is particularly important, since the plan's trust or the sponsoring corporation must eventually finance the repurchase of employees' shares.

The involvement of a strategic investor in the privatization scheme could also influence the structure of the employee stock plan. For example, the strategic investor may offer employees of the restructured company options on shares in the parent company or may finance additional shares in the restructured company on the condition of reaching employment agreements with a union or other organization representing the employees. One could imagine a competitive bidding scenario in which a strategic investor would agree to finance the acquisition of shares for the employee stock ownership plan in order to improve the competitiveness of its bid for the company; or the strategic investor might work with organized labor's financial advisers to structure a mutually financed bid to acquire a larger stake for the employee stock ownership plan.[14] Such innovative approaches will obviously be subject to a case-by-case analysis, but if the government were to build incentives into the rules (as proposed below), giving strategic investors credit in the bid selection process for enhancements to the state-owned enterprise's employee stock ownership plan, there may well be a number of innovative approaches proposed for structuring the plan.

In situations in which additional structural reform is required to prepare a financial institution for privatization, it may be appropriate to allow an employee stock ownership plan to buy stock at a nominal value. The design of the plan in such a scenario would need to incorporate longer-term expectations for providing employees with an opportunity to sell their shares. In cases in which the government does not intend to sell shares to outside investors, the plan could provide employees with an incentive to improve enterprise performance. Such a plan could use actual shares or share options or could create synthetic equity (phantom shares or share appreciation rights). In either case, the plan would be subject to the same rules (in regard to valuation standards and provisions for employee liquidity) as those proposed for plans in restructured enterprises that are not yet publicly listed.

Transactions in which the government contemplates a sale of its entire (or virtually all of its) ownership stake could be structured to allow for a pretransaction sale of a minority interest to an employee stock ownership plan to enable employees to benefit from a potential premium share price upon sale of the enterprise

---

14. There is ample international experience in which organized labor has entered into a financing arrangement to acquire a larger stake in employee stock ownership plans, often in conjunction with negotiated work rule changes.

(subject to deferred sale terms to require them to stay with the privatized company for a minimum period of time). In situations in which it may be preferable to facilitate a divestiture of a noncore asset (for example, a small division that provides printing or transportation or training services tangential to the financial institution's primary operations) that is not likely to attract strategic investors, it may be justifiable to permit management buyouts. Under these limited circumstances, government could provide management with an opportunity to acquire larger-than-normal equity stakes in exchange for ensuring that a broad-based employee stock ownership plan could also acquire a comparatively large ownership stake.

One of the most efficient ways of structuring privatization operations in developing countries is to divide the share for sale into several tranches. Each tranche is then sold to targeted investors in separate transactions. Hence a public tender can be used to sell a substantial block of shares to a strategic investor, a share flotation can be used to sell shares to the general public, and a private placement or negotiated sale can be used to sell shares to employees. In that context, it may be appropriate to consider simultaneous flotation of shares on the stock exchange so as to develop immediate liquidity for the shares. Creating a ready market for the shares in this way can support share value and enhance the attractiveness of the investment for strategic partners.

Conclusions

The use of employee stock ownership plans in restructuring state-owned financial institutions can be considered from several perspectives. The plans can be seen simply as a means of providing employees with an opportunity to receive a benefit from their companies in the form of company shares contributed to their plan accounts or purchased on some subsidized basis. But these plans are more than this: They are also tax-qualified employee benefit plans and vehicles for managing share capital, suggesting that carefully designed plans can facilitate capital formation that financial institutions can leverage to enhance their earning potential. In other words, these plans can be seen as a technique of corporate finance, which can be easily integrated with fiscal strategies to broaden the ownership of productive capital. The plans' financing technique, once used to restructure the financial institutions themselves, can be incorporated as a service that these institutions can provide to other corporate entities, both public and private.

Employee stock ownership plans are often the best vehicle for broad participation in the ownership of productive property. The shared risks and rewards of ownership hold the promise for not only broad-based capital appreciation but also enhanced labor-management relations resulting from a shared commitment to a common enterprise. In the context of reform or privatization of state-owned assets, the plans can help governments combine economic, political, and social goals by providing citizens with an opportunity to benefit from needed economic restructuring efforts.

As the data from Trinidad and Tobago, the United States, Jamaica, Pakistan, Kenya, and Korea amply demonstrate, employee stock ownership plans can benefit governments, financial institutions, and employees. They can also fail, suggesting the necessity of appropriate regulatory guidelines and management checks and balances. Nothing in the concept of employee stock ownership plans is antithetical to an economic reform agenda, and indeed the concept has much to offer in terms of enhancing efforts to restructure and privatize financial institutions.

Appendix 15A: Regulatory Guidelines, Employee Stock Ownership Plans

Guidelines for the operation of employee stock ownership plans help ensure they will achieve their intended goal of promoting broad-based employee participation in ownership and also encourage the use of such plans in private companies.

—Trust. Shares must be held in a trust or similar arrangement established to hold employee shares, share equivalents, or share options.

—Eligibility. All full-time employees who have worked at the enterprise for a minimum period of time, such as one year, must be eligible to receive offers of shares.

—Allocation of shares. The allocation of shares must be determined according to a written formula in the trust document. The formula could provide for any combination of the following: equal allocation for all eligible employees; allocation based on a percentage of annual salary or a combination of salary and years of service or similar formula; allocation based on the discretion of company management or plan trustees according to an assessment of individual employee performance, subject to antidiscrimination standards.

—Vesting of shares. Shares may be subject to vesting schedules to defer the time in which employees obtain full rights to the shares allocated to them. One example is five-year vesting in equal annual percentages, so that an employee would be 20 percent vested after one year, 40 percent after two years, and so on.

—Valuation of shares. Companies whose shares are not listed on an established stock exchange must have their shares valued by an independent valuator at least annually. The valuator must be independent of the company to ensure an arm's-length analysis.

—Record-keeping, communications, and disclosure. The compliance officer must maintain accurate records of plan transactions and the status of individual employee accounts and provide employees with timely information about their assets in the trust.

—Sale of shares. The trust document must clearly state the means by which employees may sell their shares. Upon termination of employment, employees must have the right to transact for all vested shares. Upon termination of employment, shares will be deemed to have been sold.

Appendix 15B: An Overview of Incentives

The following incentives for the establishment of employee stock ownership plans have been adopted in different countries. The various incentives illustrate the flexibility and range of choices available to policymakers in crafting an employee ownership strategy.

Incentives for Companies

—Tax deductions for contributions to the employee stock ownership plan, including contributions to repay the plan's debt.

—Use of profits to buy shares for employees.

—Tax deductions for matching contributions to the employee trust to purchase shares.

—Tax deduction on dividends used to repay debt on the acquisition of employee shares or paid in cash to employees based on their shareholdings.

—Tax deferral or tax reduction on the value of stock distributed to plan participants.

—Lower tax rates for meeting or exceeding minimum ownership levels by employees.

—Corporate tax reduction based on percentage of company owned by employees.

Incentives for Employees

—Tax deferral on voluntary savings (and interest earned) held in trust to purchase shares.

—Tax deferral on shares held in trust (or subject to restrictions) until distributed.

—Tax exemption on dividends paid on shares held in trust.

—Discounts on stock purchased under an approved employee share scheme.

—Deferred income on pretax basis to purchase shares.

—Exemption of shareholdings from social security taxes.

—Lower tax rates on distributions of employee shares held in trust for longer periods of time (typically three to six years).

—Tax credit up to 25 percent of salary for share purchases or investments in employee venture capital companies.

—Permission to purchase shares at asset valuation or book value before competitive bidding by strategic investors.

—Tax deduction for voluntary employee contributions used to repay plan's debt.

Incentives for Shareholders

—Extension of taxes on an estate that sells stock to an employee stock ownership plan.

—Deferral of capital gains taxes for stock sold to an employee trust and reinvested in domestic securities.

Credit Support for Companies

—Tax deduction for companies that make loans available to employees to purchase shares.

—Reduced taxes for financial institutions on interest income from loans to employee stock ownership plans or other employee trusts.

—Reduced corporate income tax for lenders that commit a minimum percentage of their loan portfolio to employee ownership plans loans.

—Long-term leases on the company for employee-owned companies, with a 20 percent down payment.

Credit Support for Employees

—Extended repayment terms for employee loans.

—Use of government pensions or severance pay as collateral for loans to acquire shares.

—Subsidized interest rates for loans to employees to buy shares.

References

Bohstedt, Andrea, David Kalyango, and Fiona Musana. 2001. "The Formalization Experience of K-Rep Bank: Some Lessons to Learn." Financial Systems Development Project 5. Kampala: Bank of Uganda–German Technical Cooperation.

Brent, Emma Lou. 1997. "Regulatory Issues for ESOPs in Closely Held Banks: The PCB Experience." *Journal of Employee Ownership Law and Finance* 9, no. 4: pp. 71–79.

Campion, Anita, and Victoria White. 2001. "NGO Transformation." Microenterprise Best Practices Project. Washington: U.S. Agency for International Development, June.

Gates, Jeffrey R., and Jamal Saghir. 1995. "Employee Stock Ownership Plans: Objectives, Design Options, and International Experience." CFS Discussion Paper 112. Washington: World Bank.

National Center for Employee Ownership. 2002. *Employee Ownership and Corporate Performance*. Special issue of *Journal of Employee Ownership Law and Finance* (Winter).

Price, David. 1997. "ESOPs: The Banker's Advantage." *Journal of Employee Ownership Law and Finance* 9, no. 4: table.

Privatization Commission. 2001. "Sale of the Government of Pakistan's 49% Equity Stake to the General Public." Investor brief, October 30. Government of Pakistan.

Contributors

David M. Binns
Beyster Institute

Gerard Caprio
World Bank

George R. G. Clarke
World Bank

Robert Cull
World Bank

Jonathan L. Fiechter
International Monetary Fund

Manal Fouad
International Monetary Fund

Ronald J. Gilbert
ESOP Services

James A. Hanson
World Bank

Richard Hemming
International Monetary Fund

Fred E. Huibers
ING Barings

Ishrat Husain
State Bank of Pakistan

Barry Jackson
Development Bank of Southern Africa

Louis Kasekende
World Bank

Marie Kirsten
Development Bank of Southern Africa

Paul H. Kupiec
Federal Deposit Insurance Corporation

Nicholas R. Lardy
Institute for International Economics

Robert E. Litan
Ewing Marion Kauffman Foundation
   and Brookings Institution

Davide Lombardo
International Monetary Fund

Moraka Makhura
Development Bank of Southern Africa

Wojciech Maliszewski
International Monetary Fund

David Marston
International Monetary Fund

Lewis Musasike
Development Bank of Southern Africa

Aditya Narain
International Monetary Fund

Urjit R. Patel
Infrastructure Development Finance
   Company, India

Michael Pomerleano
World Bank

Pak Rudjito
Bank Rakyat Indonesia

Mary Shirley
Ronald Coase Institute

Djauhari Sitorus
World Bank

P. S. Srinivas
World Bank

Ted Stilwell
Development Bank of Southern Africa

Hendrawan Tranggana
Bank Rakyat Indonesia

Index